SCULPTURE BOOKS FROM CRESCENT MOON PUBLISHING

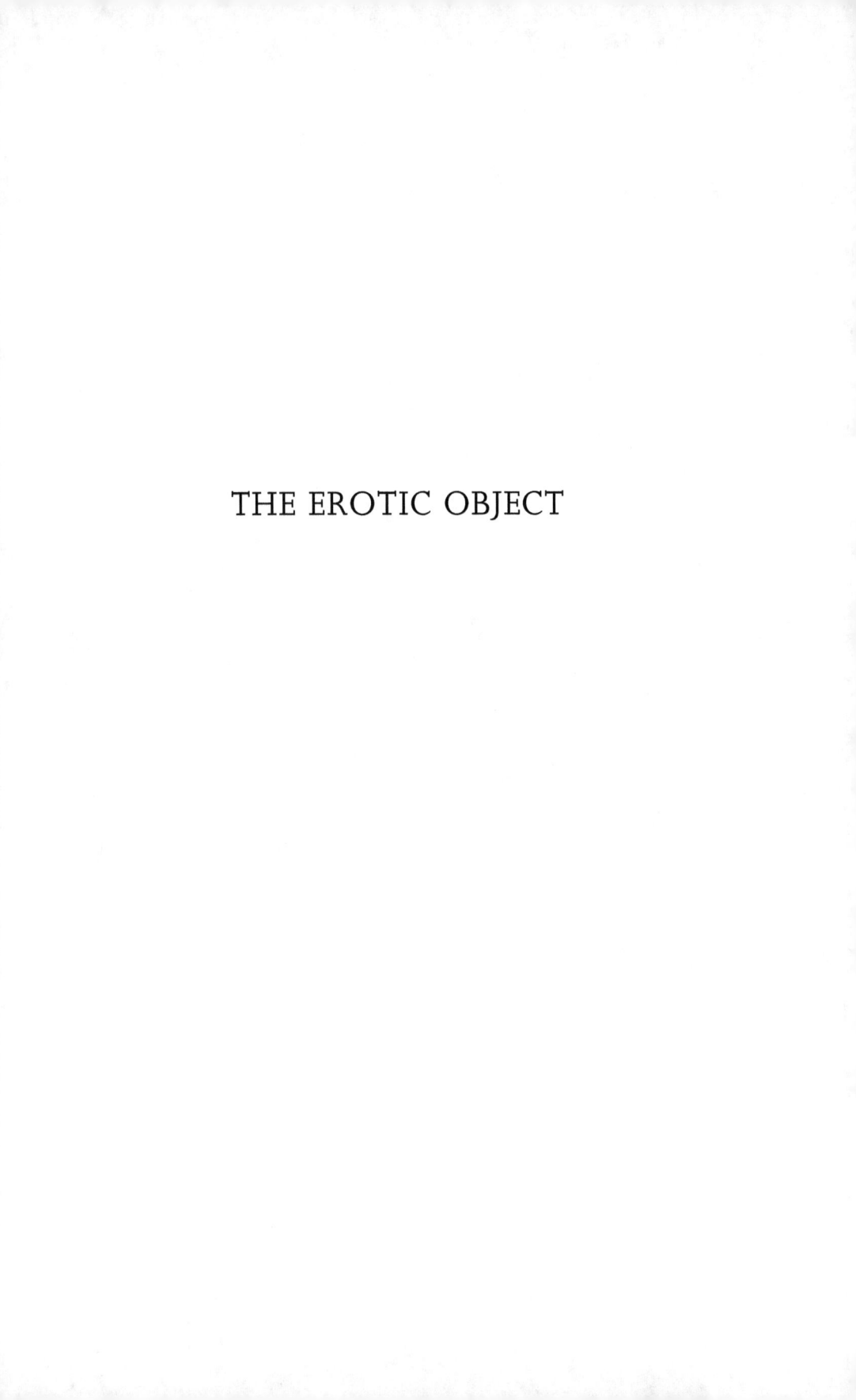

THE EROTIC OBJECT

Susan Quinnell

The
Erotic Object

Sexuality In Sculpture
From Prehistory To the Present Day

CRESCENT MOON

Crescent Moon Publishing
P.O. Box 1312,
Maidstone, Kent
ME14 5XU, Great Britain
www.crmoon.com

First published 1994. Fifth edition 2012.
© Susan Quinnell, 1994, 2012.

Printed and bound in the U.S.A.
Set in Gill Sans 10 on 12pt.
Designed by Radiance Graphics.

British Library Cataloguing in Publication data

Quinnell, Susan
The Erotic Object: Sexuality in Sculpture
from Prehistory to the Present Day. — 4th ed. — (Sculptors Series)
1. Erotic sculpture 2. Erotic sculpture — History
I. Title
731.8'28

ISBN-13 9781861714084 (Pbk)

ISBN-13 9781861714091 (Hbk)

Contents

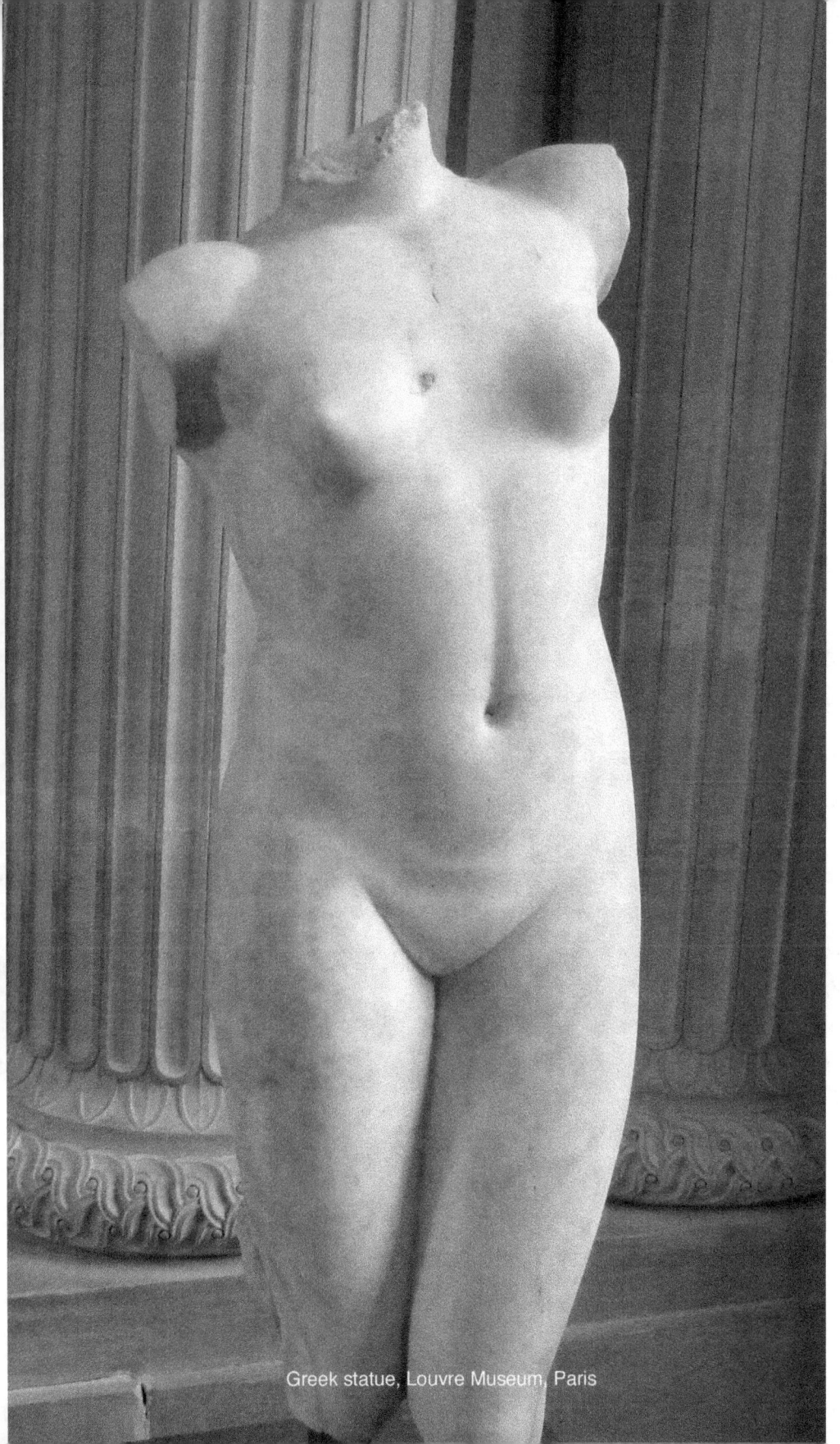

Greek statue, Louvre Museum, Paris

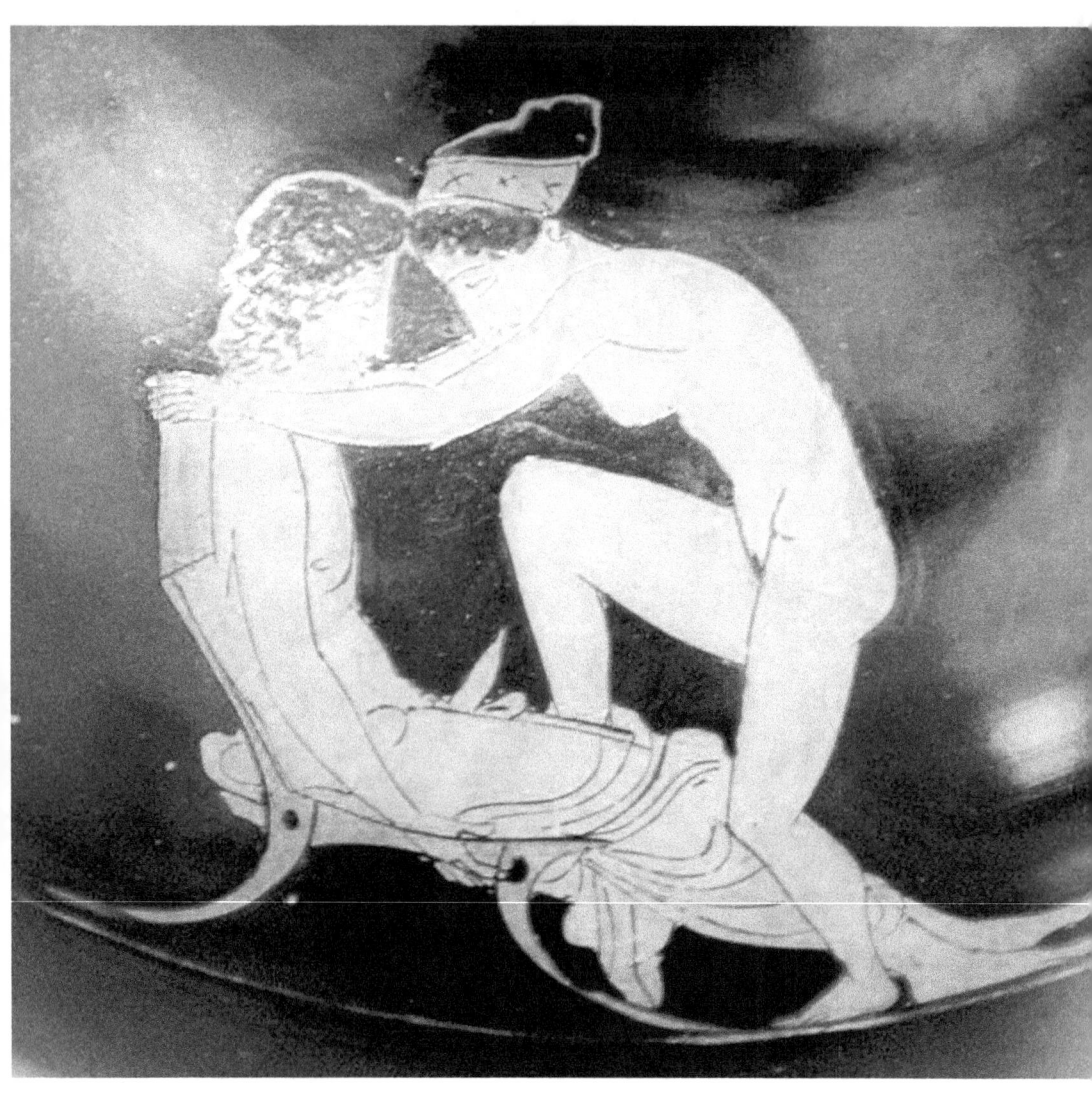

Shuvalov Painter, Ancient Greek, Berlin

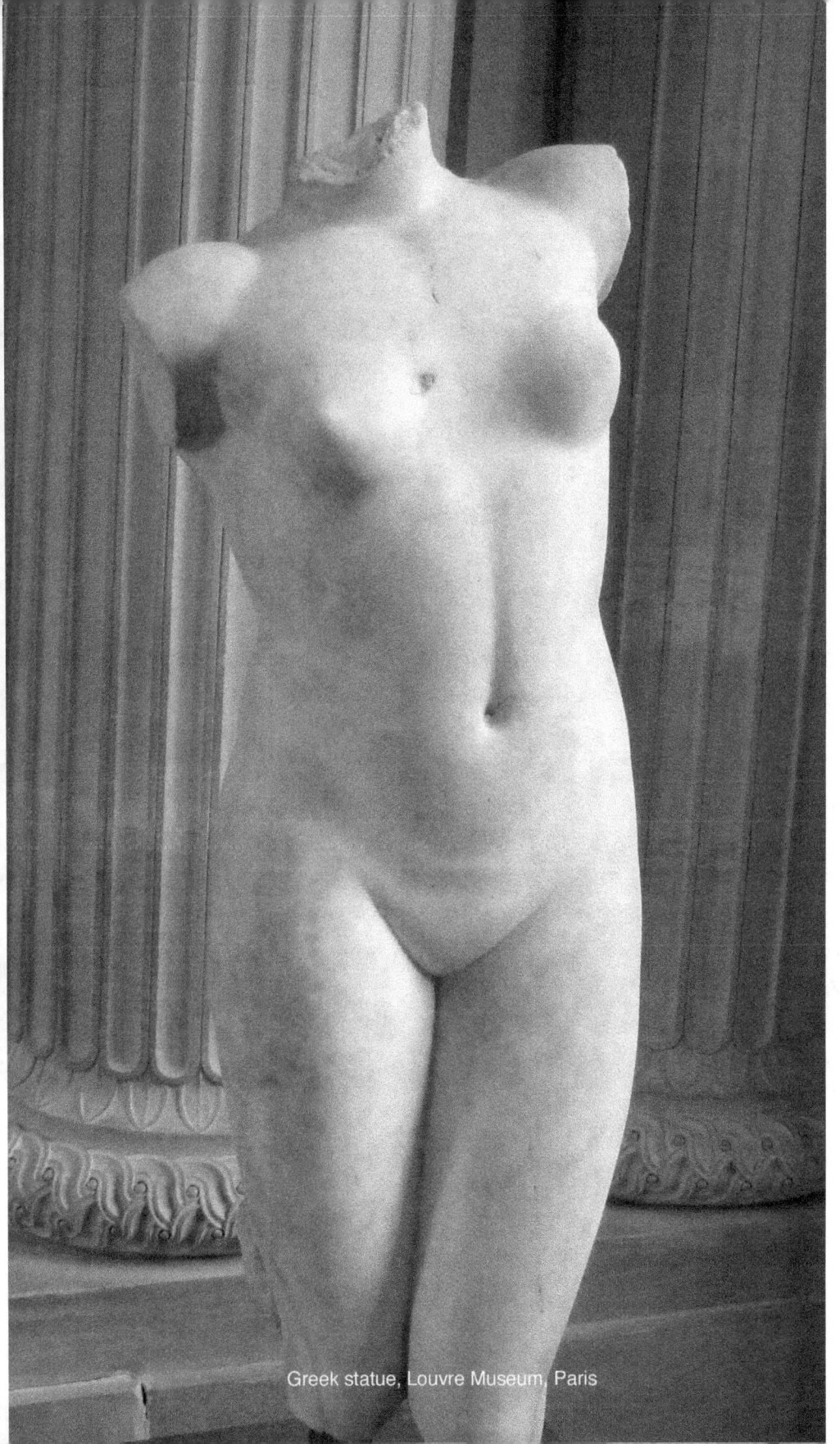

Greek statue, Louvre Museum, Paris

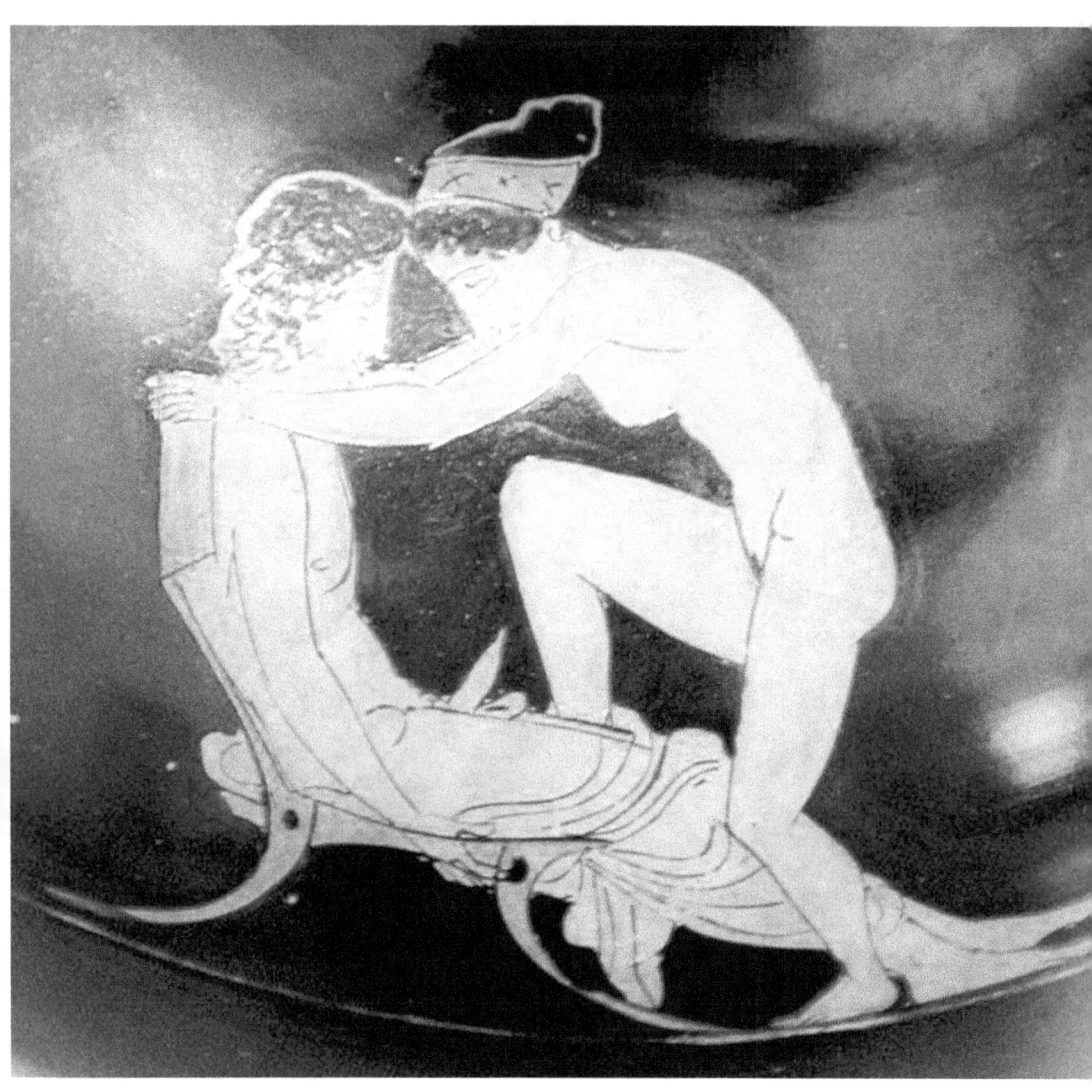

Shuvalov Painter, Ancient Greek, Berlin

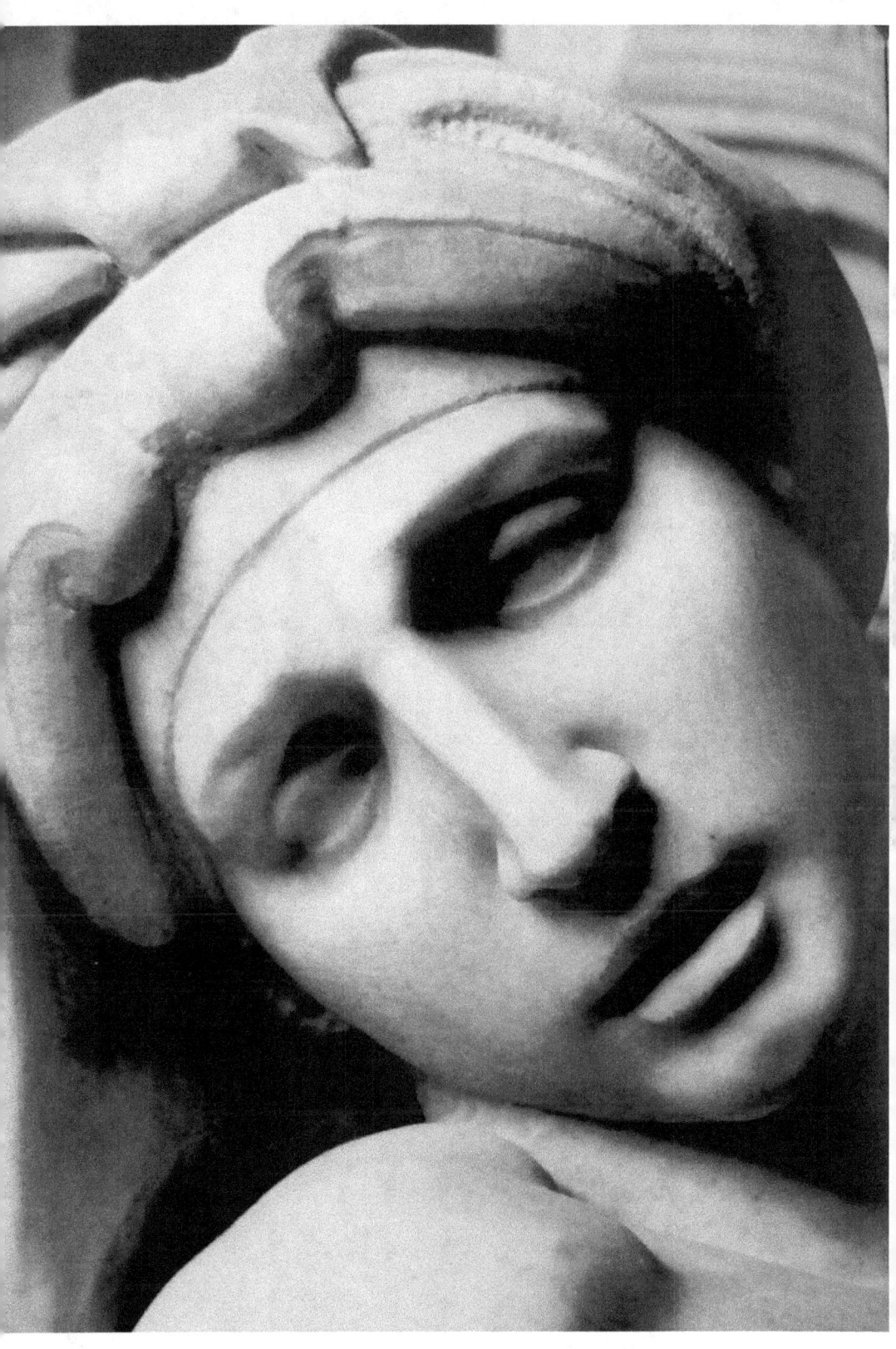

Michelangelo, Dawn, detail, Medici Chapel, Florence

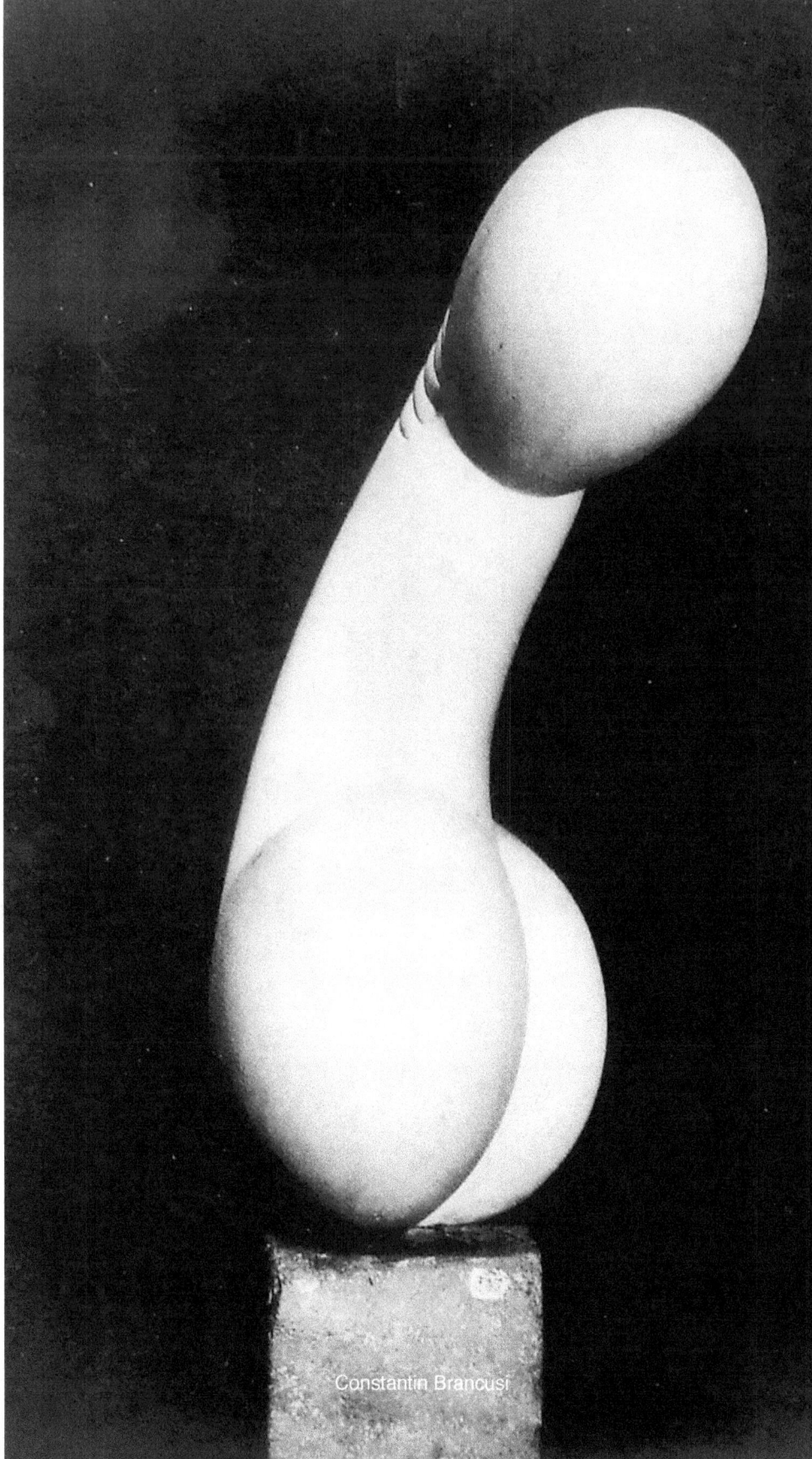

Constantin Brancusi

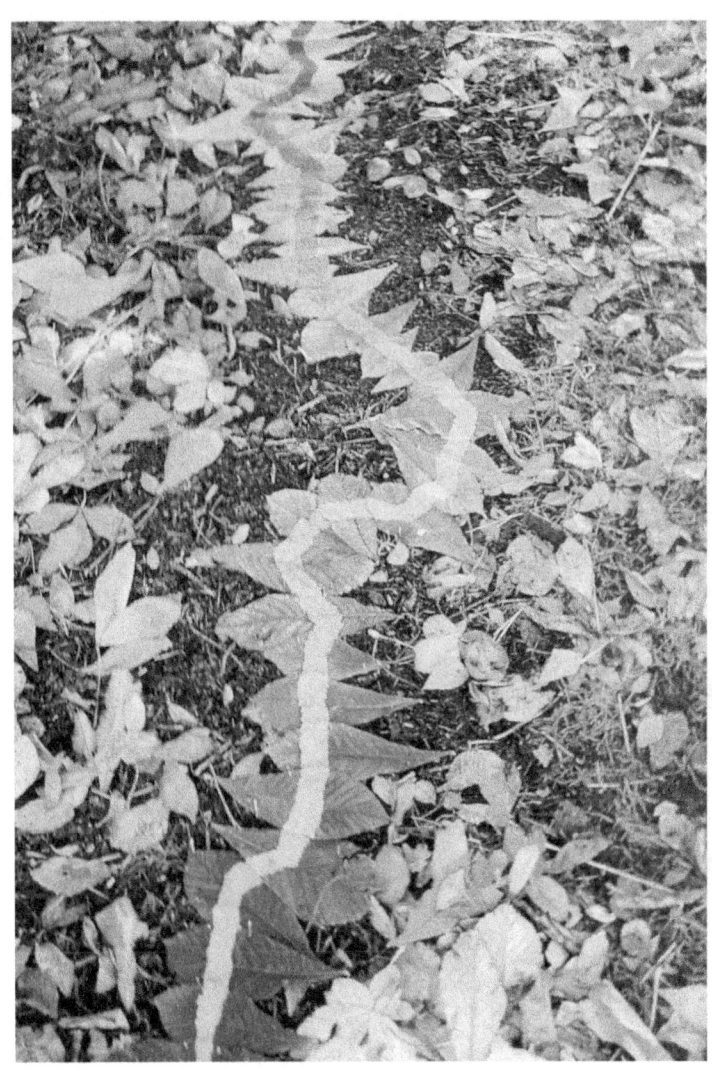

Andy Goldsworthy, Leaves On Leaves, 1987

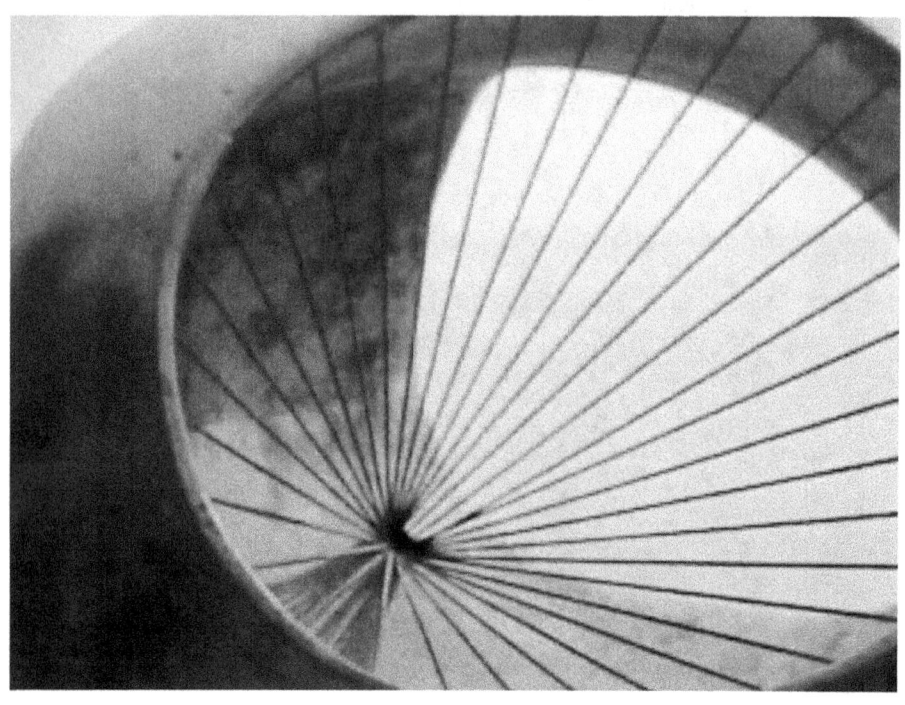

Barbara Hepworth, Sculpture with Colour and String, 1939-61

1

Do Not Touch the Sculpture!

Sculpture is a three dimensional projection of primitive feeling: touch, texture, scale, hardness and warmth, evocation and compulsion to move, live and love.

Barbara Hepworth[1]

Sculpture, of its nature, is object, in the world, in a way in which painting, music, poetry are not.

William Tucker[2]

1 B. Hepworth: quoted in A.M. Hammacher, 1968, 99
2 W. Tucker: *The Language of Sculpture*, 107

THE SENSUALITY OF SURFACES

Sculpture is the ultimate erotic art object, the final fetish in a long line of fetishes stretching back to antiquity, from today to 100,000 years ago. So many sculptures are softly rounded objects, reminiscent of the breasts, belly and hips of the (primordial) mother, reassuringly contoured, like the inside of the womb (remember that?), as if the sculpted object recreated the maternal realm (or a memory of it), and the primal objects of art, such as the placenta and the womb.

Sculpture (and art) is in its very nature supremely erotic. On so many levels. Start with the obvious ones: it has a sublime sense of surface, texture, caresses, an embrace. Sculptures, such as Michelangelo Buonarroti's *Dying Slave* or his statue of *Dawn* in the Medici tombs in Florence,[3] *beg* to be touched. The *Dying Slaves* are among most erotic works in the history of sculpture

Spectators approach sculptures erotically, as if they were fetish objects to be gently stroked (sculptures for the blind). Some sculptures in public places reveal the touch of many hands: they are worn away. Statues of naked women are

3 Michelangelo Buonarroti: *Dawn*, 1524-5, Lorenzo Medici tomb, New Sacristy of S. Lorenzo, Florence

rubbed away around the vulva and breasts. Children automatically reach out to touch sculptures in museums: sculpture has a pre-œdipal, prelapsarian magnetism. Some sculptures in museums these days have glass or perspex cases built around them, thereby flatly denying the spectator the pleasure of interacting directly with the sculpture (of being in the same space as the sculpture, which's one of the primary joys of visiting a museum or gallery in the first place. You don't have that 'thereness' from looking at art in books). Sculptures are very definitely presences, objects that are really 'there', in that space. They have 'thereness', as Rainer Maria Rilke put it, an *innigkeit* or 'thingness'.

Regardless of what sculpture depicts, it can be seen as erotic. The surfaces, materials and forms are sensuous: wood, glass, marble, granite, clay, china, and bronze. Touching is pure pleasure. It is a pleasure that is, perhaps, pre-institutional, pre-industrial, pre-political. Touching cuts through socio-cultural constructs, such as art, ideology, education or war, and goes back to a primæval form of being (touch is the first sense to develop in the foetus). At the same time, touching re-activates a sense of the past, both personal and societal. As the

British poet John Keats said, '[t]ouch has a memory'.4

Sculpture activates this fundamental relation with things. Sculpture renews contact with simple but utterly crucial experiences such as touch, sight, smell.

The sensuality of surfaces, of textures, of brushwork, of the artist's sense of touch, is crucial to the 'greatness' of art, as Lynda Nead wrote:

> the artist's subjectivity that is registered by the brushwork and surface is sexualized. Art criticism writes sex into descriptions of paint, surface and forms (58)

The American artist Frank Stella wrote (in *Working Space*) of the space a painting creates, and how this space can envelop the viewer, sensually:

> An effective painting should present its space in such a way as to include both viewer and maker each with his own space intact. It is not that this experience should be literal; it is simply that the sense of space projected by the painting should seem expansive: expansive enough to include the viewing and

4 John Keats, quoted in W. Jackson Bate: "Keats' Style: Evolution toward Qualities of Permanent Value", in C.D. Thorpe, ed: *The Major English Romantic Poets: A Symposium in Reappraisal*, Southern Illinois University Press, 1957

the creation of that space.
(9)

Other artists have spoken
of the loving nature of the
painting canvas itself, the beauty
of the art object. Maurice Denis
wrote:

> The emotion – bitter or
> sweet, "literary" as the
> painters say – emerges from
> the canvas itself, a plane
> surface covered with
> colours.[5]

RAINER MARIA RILKE ON SCULPTURE

It is this palpable sense of touch
in sculpture that the German
poet Rainer Maria Rilke (1875-
1926) described in his famous
poem 'Archaic Torso of Apollo'
(1908), perhaps the finest poem
on the haptic sense (and one of
the finest poems about sculpture). Rilke worked with one of
great erotic modern sculptors,
the flamboyant, angst-ridden and
womanising Auguste Rodin.
Rilke's poem lucidly evokes the
animal, sexual nature of statues.
The poet is standing in the
Luxemborg Gardens in the city
of modern art, Paris. The Rilke-
poet gets to the heart of the
matter of the relation between
sculpture and living things swiftly
and lucidly:

> We cannot know his
> legendary head
> with eyes, like ripening
> fruit. And yet his torso is
> still suffused with brilliant
> form inside,
> like a lamp, in which his
> gaze, now turned to low,
>
> gleams in all its power.
> Otherwise the curved
> breast could not dazzle you
> so, nor could
> a smile run through the
> placid hips and thighs
> to that dark centre where
> procreation flared.
>
> Otherwise this stone would

5 M. Denis: "Definitions of neo-
traditionism", 1890, in *Theories:
1890-1910*, Rouart et Watelin,
Paris 1920, 5f

                  seem defaced
beneath the translucent
cascade of the shoulders
and would not glisten like a
           wild beast's fur:

would not, from all the
           borders of itself,
burst like a star: for here
           there is no place
that does not see you. You
must change your life.[6]

In Rainer Maria Rilke's sinuous 'Archaic Torso of Apollo' sonnet the statue comes alive like an animal, and the stone becomes fur. This is an alarming, arresting transformation, and one that occurs often in modern and contemporary sculpture – think of the felt in Dorothea Tanning's sculptures, or the fur in Meret Oppenheim's *Object* or wood in Louise Bourgeois' works.[7] Bourgeois explores the relations between form and eroticism, volume and psychology, shape and nature.[8] Her forms are nearly always dealing with eroticism – her *Nature Study* (1984), for instance, feature the bulbous volumes which are her trademark, echoing buttocks, heads, hands, breasts, clitorises, vulvas, knees, tongues, all the parts of the eroticized body.[9]

The works of contemporary sculptors such as Alice Aycock, Eva Hesse and Alison Wilding are distinctly erotic. Wilding's *Hemlock III* (1986) and *Blueblack* (1984) are wooden dishes containing hemlock, lead, lime and beeswax, hinting at alchemical transmutations.[10] The dish with its dangerous substances is a kind of womb, a crucible or vessel – a motif or experience that appears in much of contemporary sculpture, from Judy Chicago's *Dinner*

---

6 In *The Selected Poetry of Rainer Maria Rilke*, 61.
7 Louise Bourgeois: *One and Others*, 1955, painted wood, 18 x 20 x 17in, Whitney Museum of American Art, New York.

8 See D. Wye: *Louise Bourgeois*, MOMA, New York 1982, C. Baldwin: "Louise Bourgeois: An Iconography of Abstraction", *Art in America*, April, 1975; C. Robbins: "Louise Bourgeois: Primordial Environments", *Arts Magazine*, June, 1976; P. Gardner: "The Discreet Charm of Louise Bourgeois", *Art News*, Feb, 1980, 80-86; R. Storr: *Louise Bourgeois*, Galerie Maeght Lelong, Zurich, 1985.
9 Louise Bourgeois: *Nature Study*, 1984, bronze, 30 x 19 x 15in, Serpentine Gallery, London.
10 Alison Wilding: *Hemlock III*, 1986, lime, hemlock, lead, beeswax, pigment, Karsten Schubert; *Blueblack*, 1984, lime & elm woods, wax, lead, 36 x 28 x 49cm, collection: the artist.

Table (1979) to the womb interiors of Louise Bourgeoise and others (in the 1970s, some feminists dubbed it 'cunt art').

D.H. LAWRENCE ON TOUCH

The British author D.H. Lawrence (1885-1930) wrote extensively on the importance of touch. In short stories such as *You Touched Me* and *The Blind Man,* Lawrence explored the mystery of the direct touch. It was all to do with Lawrence's cult of a new relation with the body, which must be physical, he said.[11] In *Lady Chatterley's Lover,* Tommy Dukes yearns for touch: "'[g]ive me the democracy of touch, the resurrection of the body!'" he exclaims (78). Lawrence's model for this new sense of touch was Mary Magdalene touching the resurrected Christ,[12] that *touch me/ touch me not* tension (*noli me tangere*), explored in many Renaissance paintings – most famously, perhaps, by Titian.[13] Lawrence's sense of touch is soft, holy, of softly flowing blood.[14] This poem is typical:

11 D.H. Lawrence, *John Thomas and Lady Jane,* Penguin, London, 1973, 265

12 D.H. Lawrence, *The First Lady Chatterley,* Penguin, London, 1973, 85

13 Titian, *Noli me tangere,* c. 1510, 109 x 91cm, National Gallery, London.

14 D.H. Lawrence, *Pansies,* in *The Complete Poems,* ed. V. de Sola Pinto & W. Roberts, Heinemann, London, 1972, 468, 471.

Touch comes when the
    white mind sleeps
and only then.
Touch comes slowly, if ever;
    it seeps
slowly up in the blood of
    men and women.

Soft slow sympathy
of the blood in me, of the
    blood in here
rises and flushes insidiously
over the conscious
    personality
of each of us, and covers us
with a soft one warmth,
    and a generous
kindled togetherness, so we
    go
into each other as tides
    flow
under a moon they do not
    know.

Personalities exist apart;
and personal intimacy has
    no heart.
Touch is of the blood
uncontaminated, the
    unmental flood.

When again in us
the soft blood softly flows
    together
towards touch, then this
    delirious
day of the mental welter
    and belter
will be passing away, we
    shall cease to fuss.[15]

The sense of touch is not crucial to all sculpture, but without it sculpture loses some of its *frisson*, its visceral effect. Painters too explore the eroticism of touch, the tactile element in paintings. Rebecca Purdun painted (as thousands have done) with her fingers. Her billowy, smeared canvases resound with the vibrancy of the touch of the human hand, the eloquence of the pure gesture.[16] She wrote:

> The more you get physically into the paint, you lose, you forget yourself. You become the paint, you become the form, you become the structure.[17]

---

15 D.H. Lawrence: *The Complete Poems.*

16 R. Purdum: *In Threes,* 1985, oil on canvas, 210.2 x 204.5cm.
17 R. Purdun, in C. Jolles: *Rebecca Purdun: Abstract Painting,* Jack Tilton Gallery, catalogue, 1986.

TOUCH AND POWER

At the same time, however, touching is an exercise of power, as the U.S. feminist Andrea Dworkin asserted in *Intercourse*:

> Anyone whose legal status is that she exists to be touched, intimately, inside the boundaries of her own body, is controlled, made use of: a captive inside a legally constructed cage. (196)

Sigmund Freud too recognized the power relation exercised in the mere act of touching in *Totem and Taboo*:

> Touching is the first step towards obtaining any sort of control over, or attempting to make use of, a person or object.[18]

The eroticism of sculpture is everywhere affirmed in high art itself, and in high art cultural criticism. Of course, a lot of this has to do with the eroticism of the nude human form, something that thousands of sculptors have explored and exploited. Renaissance sculptors – Luca della Robbia, Lorenzo Ghiberti, Andrea del

Verrocchio, Pietro Lombardo – systematically exaggerated the sexuality of the body. Donatello's famous *David* (1440-42), for instance, is a highly camp boy, an icon of stylized homoeroticism.[19] Similar eroticization occurs in Verrocchio's *David* (c. 1475), Benvenuto Cellini's *Perseus* (1554), Giovanni da Bologna's *Mercury* (1564).[20] This Renaissance eroticization of the human form finds its apotheosis in, of course, the art of Michelangelo, – the *Dawn*, the *David*, the early and late *Pietàs*, and of course the most voluptuous of all figurative statues, the *Dying Slaves*.

The heroic homoeroticism of Michelangelo Buonarroti's sculpture continues throughout post-Renaissance sculpture. In, for instance, the bombast and masculine power of Gianlorenzo Bernini's *David* (1623-24) and Antonio Canova's *Hercules and Lichas* (1812-15)[21] And there is a gay subtext in that most sinister of all forms of

18 S. Freud: *Toten and Taboo and Other Works*, tr. J. Strachey & A. Freud, *Standard Works*, vol. 13, Hogarth Press, London, 1955, 33-34.

19 Donatello: *David*, c. 1440-42, bronze, Museo Nazionale, Florence
20 Benvenuto Cellini: *Perseus with the Head of Medusa*, 1554, bronze, Loggia dei Lanzi, Florence; Giovanni da Bologna: *Mercury*, 1564, Museo Nazionale, Florence; Andrea del Verrocchio: *David*, c. 1475, bronze, Museo Nazionale, Florence
21 Antonio Canova: *Hercules and Lichas*, 1812-15, marble, 138in high, Gallery of Modern Art, Rome; Gianlorenzo Bernini: *David*, 1623-24, marble, Galleria Borghese, Rome.

sculpture, modern fascist art: in, for instance, Josef Thorak's *Comradeship* (1937), two monumental male nudes with the bodies of he-men, supermen, Nietzschean *Übermensch*, clasping each other by the hand. The statues were commissioned by the Nazi government. Fascist sculpture typically presents an ascetic, aggressive but banal stance, where eroticism is suppressed but never completely erased, as so much of fascist art depicts naked people. See, for the apotheosis of violence and banality, Ferruccio Vecchi's statue of Benito Mussolini of the late 1930s.[22]

DISFIGUREMENT

The eroticism of celebrated statues of the ancient and Classical world, such as the *Venus de'Milo*,[23] has been seen by some feminists as another manifestation of patriarchal culture's dismemberment of the female form. So many statues of the ancient world are headless or armless. For feminists, this fragmentation of the female body (could it be wear and tear after two thousand years?), echoes that of pornography, where women's bodies are cut up, sometimes literally (as in S/M and the porn of amputees). Any number of (mainly male) artists have depicted armless and/ or legless and/ or headless women (Gustave Courbet in his infamous painting of a torso of a woman, entitled *The Origin of the World,* Eric Gill's sculpted reliefs, Bill Brandt's nude photographs, Edvard Munch in his 'cruel' *Madonna,* and so on.)[24] This second wave feminist view is a rather literal interpretation of ancient world statuary – one could probably find just as many statues of men or boys who're legless, armless or penisless.

23 *Venus de Milo,* 2nd or 1st centuries B.C., Parian marble, Louvre, Paris.
24 See Bill Brandt: *Nude: London 1977,* Estate of Bill Brandt; Eric Gill: *Life study of a woman,* 1927, pencil, Victoria & Albert Museum, London; and see G. Saunders, 75f.

22 Ferruccio Vecchi: *The Empire,* 1939-40.

Other sexist depictions of people (i.e. women by men) in modern sculpture include Alberto Giacometti's *Spoon Woman* (1926), a view of woman as Earth Mother, a totemic figure;[25] Gaston Lachaise's *Standing Woman* (1912-27), one of those smooth, curvy Goddess types, also favoured by Aristide Maillol;[26] Hans Bellmer's Surrealist bizarre *Dolls*, where the slit of a vulva is where the head would be (and vice versa), and set amidst exaggerated, bulbous forms;[27] Henri Gaudier-Brzeska's *Red Stone Dancer* (1914), though it attempts a new way of depicting gesture and posture in space, is still sexist;[28] Elie Nadelman's *Dancer* (c. 1918), like Paul Manship's *Dancer and Gazelles* (1916), and Edgar Degas' *Dancer*

sculptures, is also sexist;[29] and Ernest Kirchner's *Standing Nude* (1908-12) is erotica masquerading as art, but then, many of his depictions of women are erotica.[30]

25 Alberto Giacometti: *Spoon Woman*, 1926, bronze, 57.2in high, Kunsthaus, Zurich.
26 Gaston Lachaise: *Standing Woman*, 1912-27, bronze, 70in high, Whitney Museum of American Art, New York.
27 Hans Bellmer: *La Poupée*, 1936, painted bronze, 16.8in high, Musée National d'Art Moderne, Paris.
28 Henri Gaudier-Brzeska: *Red Stone Dancer*, 1914, waxed stone, 33.5in high, Tate Gallery, London.

29 Elie Nadelman: *Dancer*, c. 1918, painted wood, 28.5in high, Robert Isaacson Gallery, New York; Paul Manship: *Dancer and Gazelles*, 1916, bronze, 32.2in high, Smithsonian Institute, Washington, DC; Edgar Degas: *Dancer Putting On Her Stocking*, bronze, 17in high, Metropolitan Museum of Art, New York.
30 Ernest Kirchner: *Standing Nude*, 1908-12, wood, painted yellow, 35.5in, Stedelijk Museum, Amsterdam.

ARCHITECTURE AND SCULPTURE

Rarely is architecture thought of as erotic, or with the same urge towards eroticization that occurs in other arts. Paintings and sculptures, or dancing and music (rock 'n' roll, blues, soul, ballet, opera), have long been regarded as having an erotic component. But sexy buildings? Not so much. Yet spaces (if not architecture) are clearly erotic; they affect the whole body, and all six senses: one *feels* a space as much as sees it, one experience spaces sensually. How about a beach, a swimming pool, a nightclub, a luxurious garden? When we're talking about architecture and its function as providing spaces to live, entertain or play in, we are also dealing with an erotic element. The playfulness, the humour and the sensuality of some architecture makes its erotic components obvious to all.

When Lawrence Durrell, D.H. Lawrence and painters such as Claude Lorrain or J.M.W. Turner speak of the *genius loci* or 'spirit of place', they may be referring to the erotic sensuality of a landscape. People might not say 'I felt aroused being in the Notre Dame in Paris', or 'I was so turned on by the Marin County Civic Center', but why not? Maybe buildings possess erotic dimensions too? Why not see a particular place or space as erotic, just as one might view Francisco de Goya's painting of a voluptuous nude woman, *Maja,* or Jean Baptiste Carpeaux's statue *The Dance* or Giuseppe Verdi's opera *Falstaff* as erotic?

This leads on to what one defines as a 'sculpture'. Buildings may be sculptures: certainly what is stuck on to buildings – statues, ornaments, decoration – are usually thought of as sculptures. But what about pillars, or arches, or balustrades, or doorways, are these sculptures? Any object, it seems, can be seen as a sculpture, and any object can be viewed as erotic. If someone thinks a door is erotic, then that door is erotic. Every object in a domestic interior can be seen as erotic. (Pornography has things that appear again and again, standard erotic or fetishized objects: telephones, chains, clothes, lipstick, cameras, mirrors, wine, etc. In porn, anything can be eroticized. And porn is often merely an exaggeration of what art does). Many critics would not regard an ordinary spoon as a sculpture, though it could be an erotic object in its own right. Certainly spoons will have been used in sex acts, as has just about every object that exists in the domestic, day-to-day sphere.

Any object can be an 'erotic object', whether in fantasy or actuality. This broad definition of the 'erotic object' does not accurately define a sculpture, however. Mass produced items, such as a saucepan, are not regarded by art historians as 'sculptures'. They are products of design, of function, of economy, which have their own æsthetics. In the 1970s and 1980s in the West, 'design' became a category of art with its own æsthetics, discourse, structures. Design museums and magazines sprang up to reflect the commodification of advanced capitalism.

But design (consumer design, industrial design, car design) does not have as high a status in art criticism as true high art, as the products of genius *auteurs* such as Pablo Picasso, Édouard Manet, Titian, Michelangelo Buonarroti or Rembrandt van Rijn. So design objects are not 'high sculpture' objects: the saucepan ain't as exalted as the marble statue.

WHAT IS SCULPTURE?

The definition of 'sculpture', then, in the art historical sense, is some highly refined and æstheticized object, an object made to be looked at, free-standing perhaps, an object of veneration and contemplation, a one-off, sculpted by one artist, often with a 'high' or 'serious' theme or content (war, heroism, divinity, state power, commemoration, etc). Not all erotic objects, then, are sculptures, but all sculptures can be seen as erotic. Since Jasper Johns and Robert Rauschenberg and Pop Art, though, *any* object can be included in a high art sculpture. Paintings can have everyday objects attached to them, and still remain high art objects. Since Rauschenberg's famous *Monogram* (1955-59), with its combination of flat, painted objects and 3-D objects, the relation between reality and illusion, between painting and sculpture, between objects and their representation, has become ambiguous. Rauschenberg said that 'a picture is more like the real world when it's made out of the real world'. Since the art of Rauschenberg (some would say since Kurt Schwitters and Marcel Duchamp, some would go back further), painting and sculpture are not two parallel but distinct forms of representation. Rather, they are a continuum, and with the rise of kinetic sculpture, light sculpture, installation sculpture and Conceptual sculpture, they flow into dance, theatre, movement and performance art.

SCULPTURE AND CENSORSHIP

Sculptures in themselves are sometimes 'controversial', though few sculptors have been as controversial as, say Andres Serrano, or Robert Mapplethorpe, two American photographers, or the filmmakers Jean-Luc Godard, Mel Gibson and Martin Scorsese, whose movies about Christ kicked up a good deal of anger.[31]

Sculptures have rarely been this blasphemous, although Auguste Rodin's *Christ and Magdalene* depicts the 'holy whore' of the Christian religion making love to Christ on the Cross (sculptor Eric Gill also illustrated this theme). Andres Serrano's photograph *Piss Christ* used bodily fluids to shape and sculpt a traditional theme of art,

31 Jean-Luc Godard's film *Hail Mary* (1985) created enormous controversy when it depicted the Blessed Virgin as a high school gas station attendant. There were bomb threats, 5,000 protesters reciting the rosary to cinema queues, and the 'film bears the distinction of being the first ever condemned by a pope (Pope John Paul II), and being the first instance in 400 years that a pope directly intervened in the suppression of a work of art' (Steven Dubin, 93). And see J. Strong: "*Hail Mary* leaves council offended, box office booming", *Chicago Tribune*, 17 Apl, 1986; W. Smith: "Ecumenical crowd of protesters pans *Hail Mary*", *Chicago Tribune*, 5 Apl, 1986.

namely the fusion of sex and the sacred, eroticism and Christianity.[32] Serrano said that he wanted to be 'descriptive or literal' in his use of bodily fluids.[33] Artistic transgressions of the Christian religion upset people immensely, it seems. In 1984 a sculpture of a crucified woman, *Christa*, was taken out of a church in New York because it was 'theologically and historically indefensible'.[34] A crucified *woman*, now there's a blasphemous image to irritate people.

The feminist artist Judy Chicago's *The Dinner Party* (1975-79) was reviled by critics because it focused on the vulva, as a motif and icon of femininity and empowerment. Art critic Robert Hughes spoke disdainfully of 'Chicago's relentless concentration on the pudenda'.[35] It's OK for male artists to paint the female genitals over and over (Pablo Picasso, Titian, Correggio, Gustav Klimt, Willem de Kooning or Egon Schiele), but not for female artists. For Hilton Kramer, Chicago's *The Dinner Party* was 'vulgar',[36] while Robert K. Dornan called it 'ceramic 3-D pornography'.[37]

32 Andres Serrano: *Piss Christ*, 1987, Cibachrome photograph, Stux Gallery, New York.
33 A. Serrano, quoted in S. Dubin, 98; See M. Brenson: "Andres Serrano: Provocation and Spirituality", *New York Times*, 8 Dec, 1989, C1, 28.
34 K.A. Briggs: "Cathedral Removing Statue of Crucified Woman", *New York Times*, 28 Apl, 1984.
35 R. Hughes: "An Obsessive Feminist Pantheon", *Time*, 15 Dec, 1980, 85-86.
36 H. Kramer: "Art: Judy Chicago's *Dinner Party*, Comes to Brooklyn Museum", *New York Times*, 17 Oct, 1980. And see C. Rickey: "Judy Chicago, *The Dinner Party*, The Brooklyn Museum", *Artforum*, Jan, 1981; R. Pedersen: "The Bitter Taste of *The Dinner Party*", *Los Angeles Times*, 5 Nov, 1990; J.R. Barras: "UDC's $1.6 million 'Dinner': Feminist artwork causes some indigestion", *The Washington Times*, 18 July 1990; C. O'Neil: "House cuts D.C. Funding over Judy Chicago display", *Outweek*, 15 Aug, 1990.
37 *Congressional Record*, 101st Session, vol. 136, no. 98, 26 July 1990.

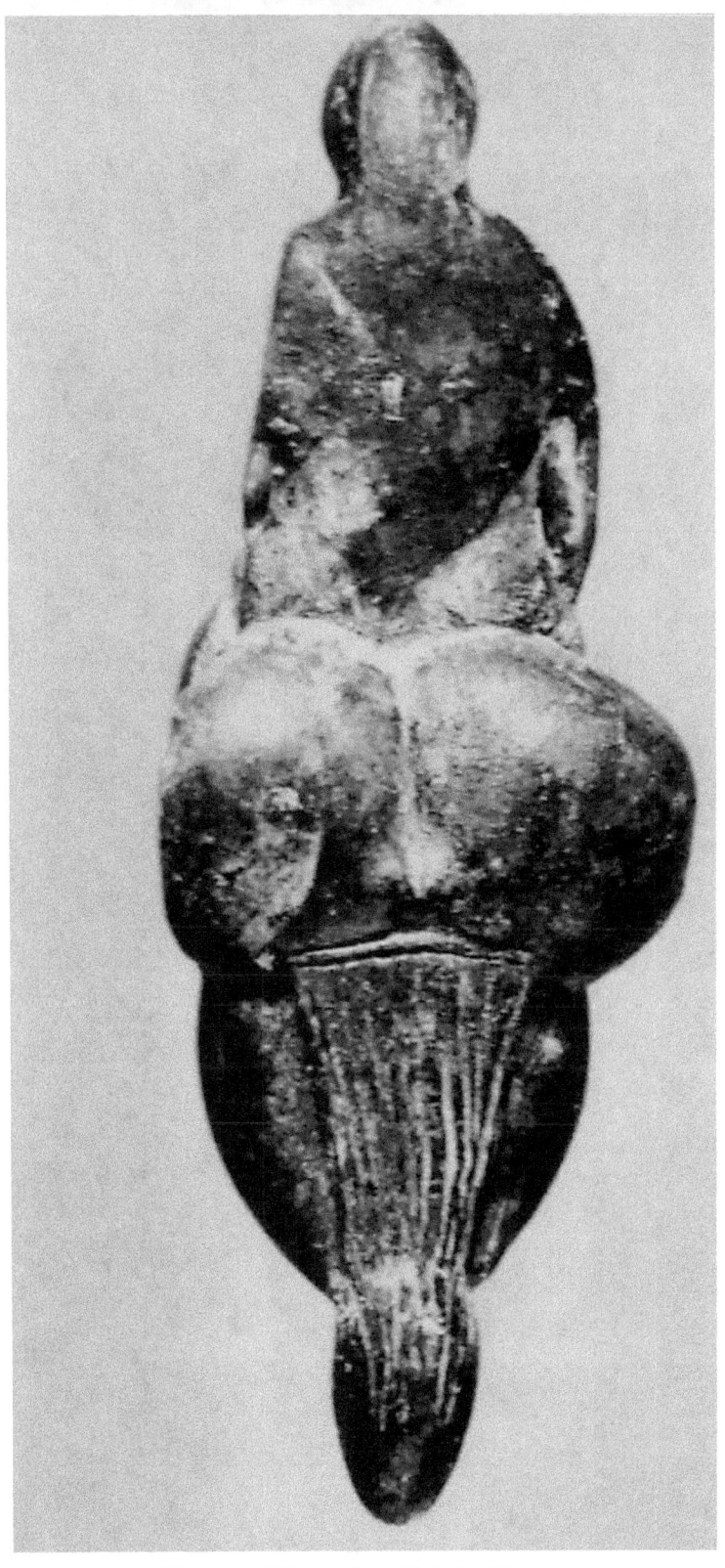

Venus of Willendorf, prehistoric, Vienna

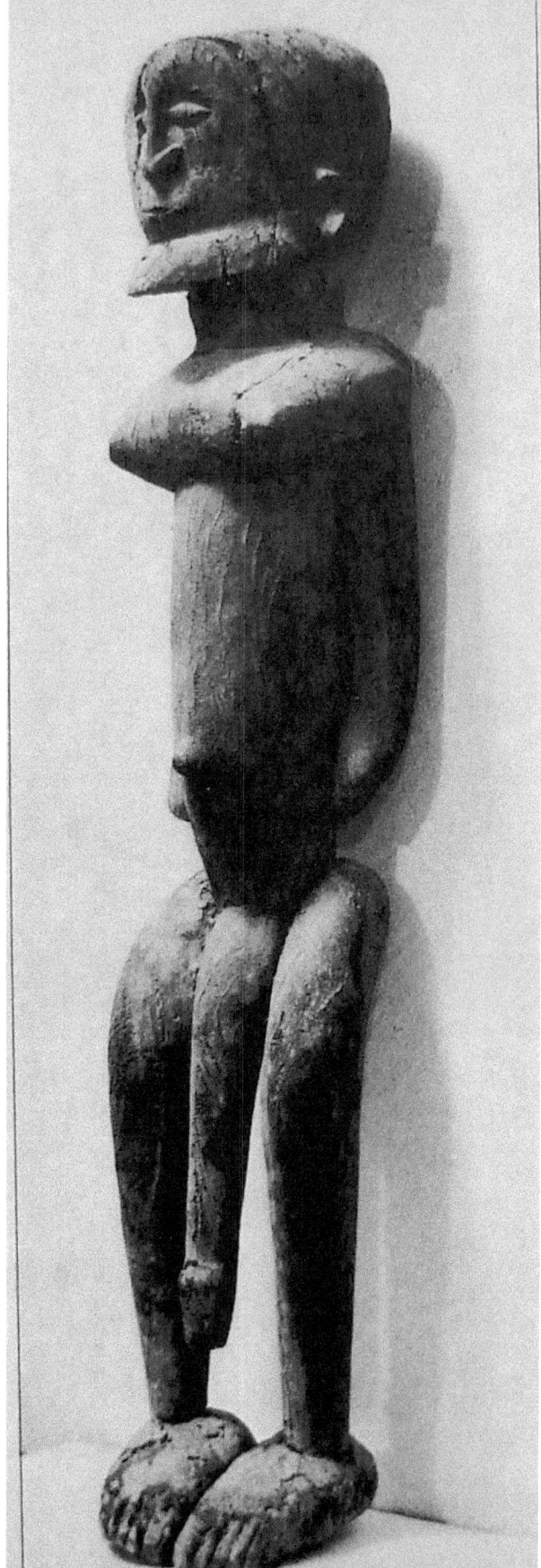

Wood figure, Ivory
Coast

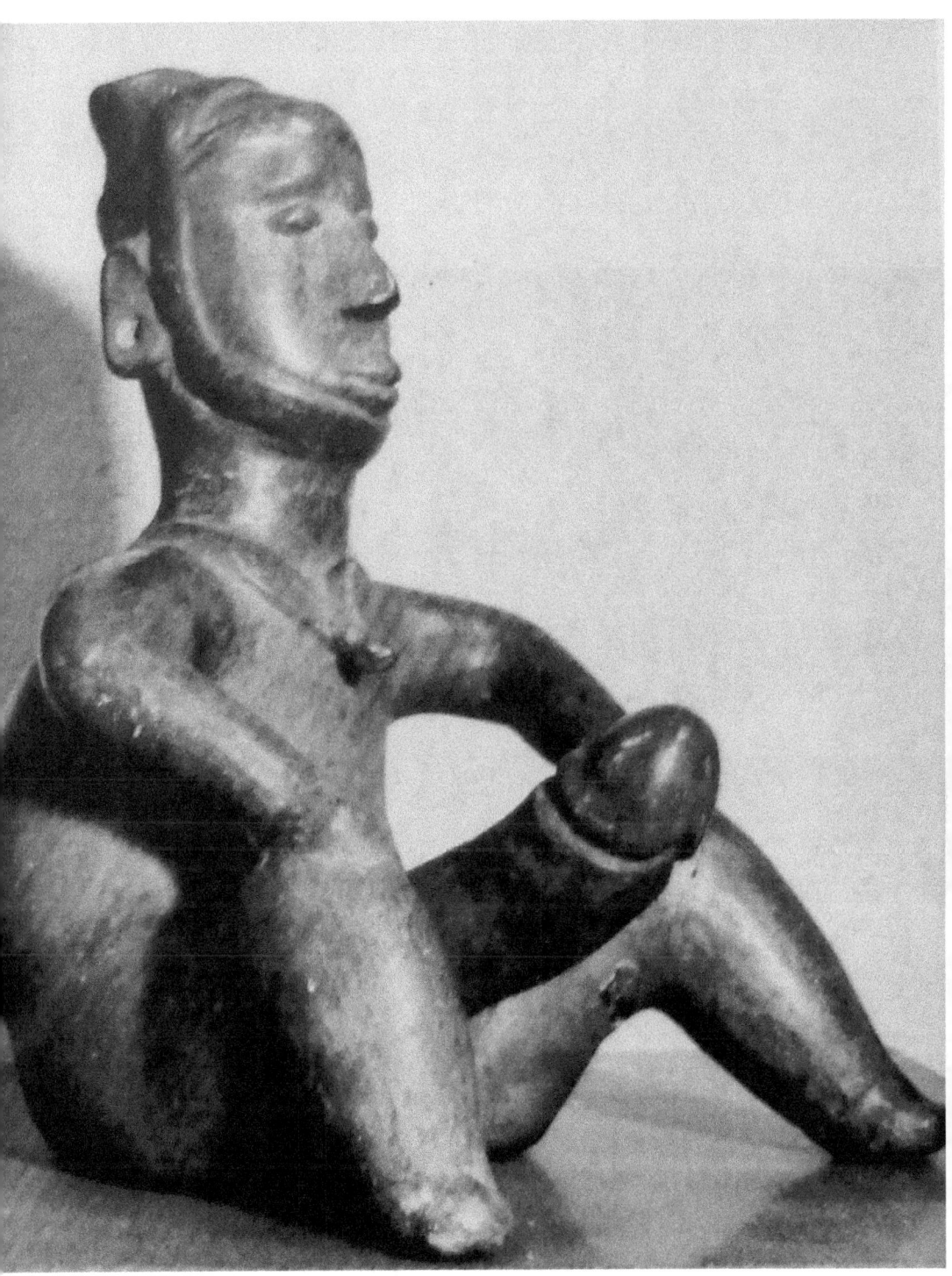

Terra cotta figure, 3rd century BC. Mexico

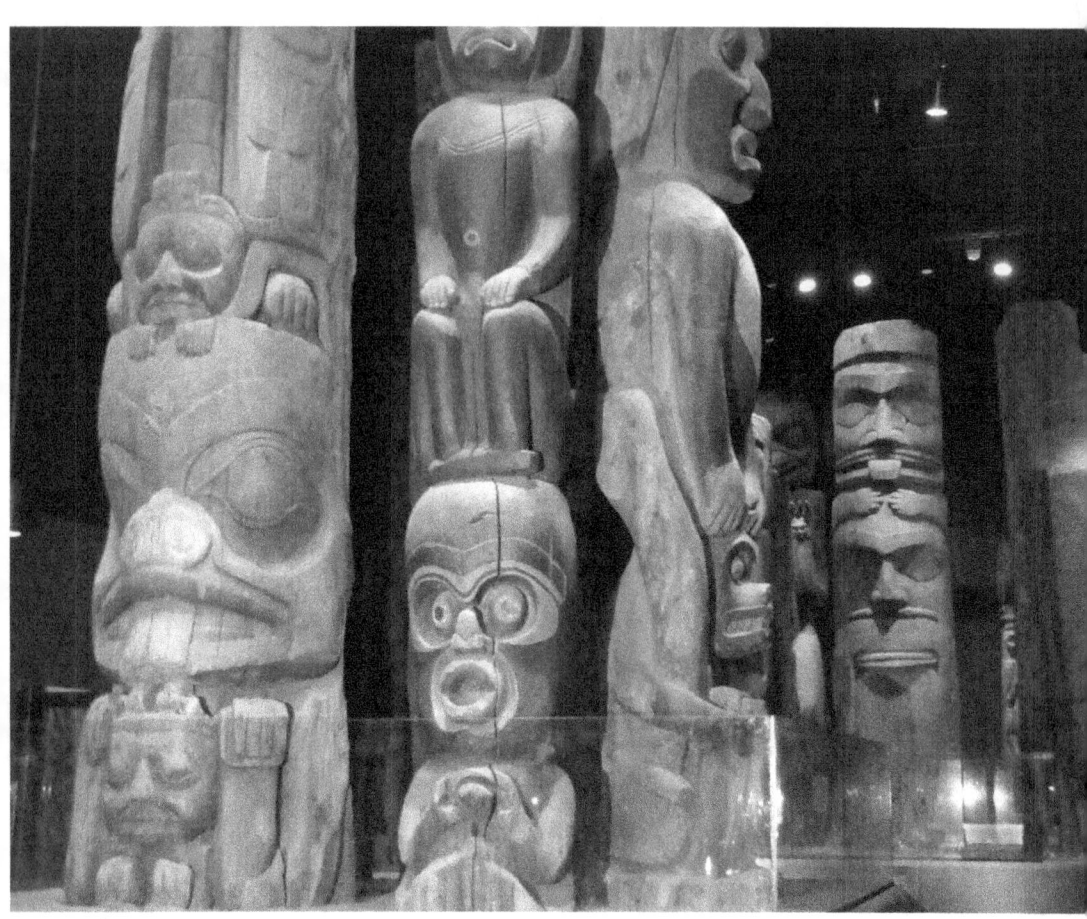

Ethnographic art, Art Institute, Chicago

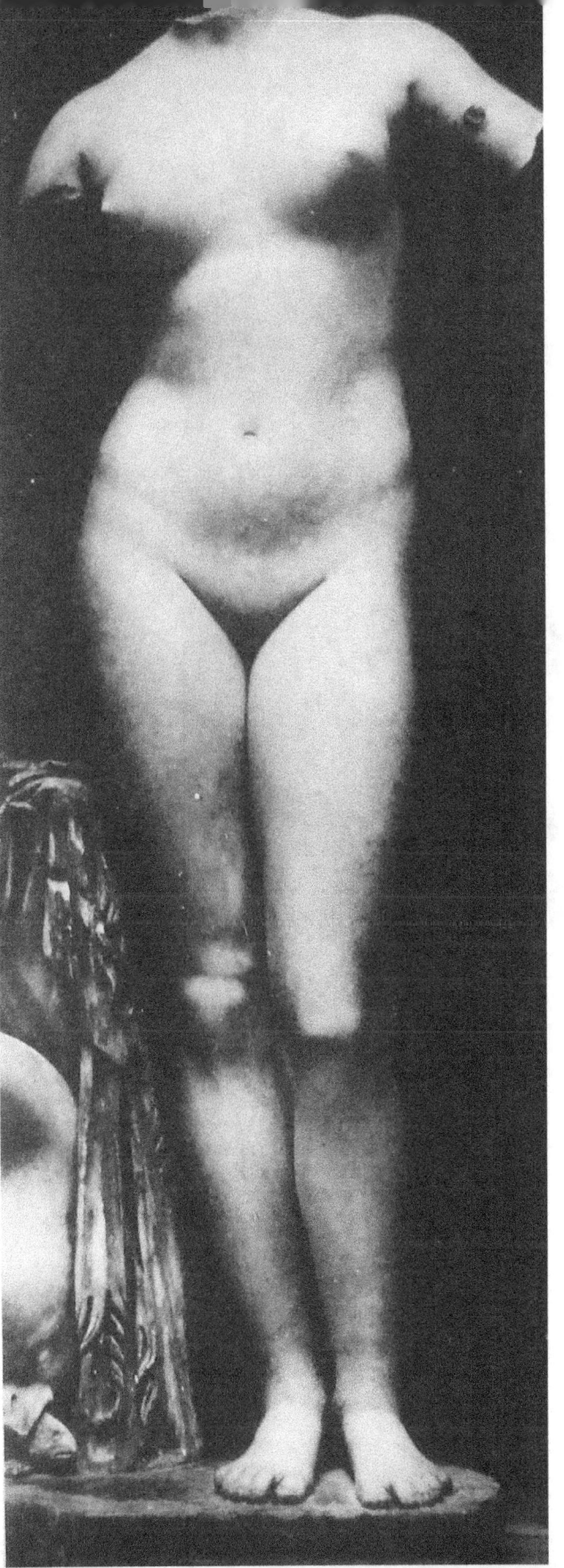

Aphrodite of Cyrene

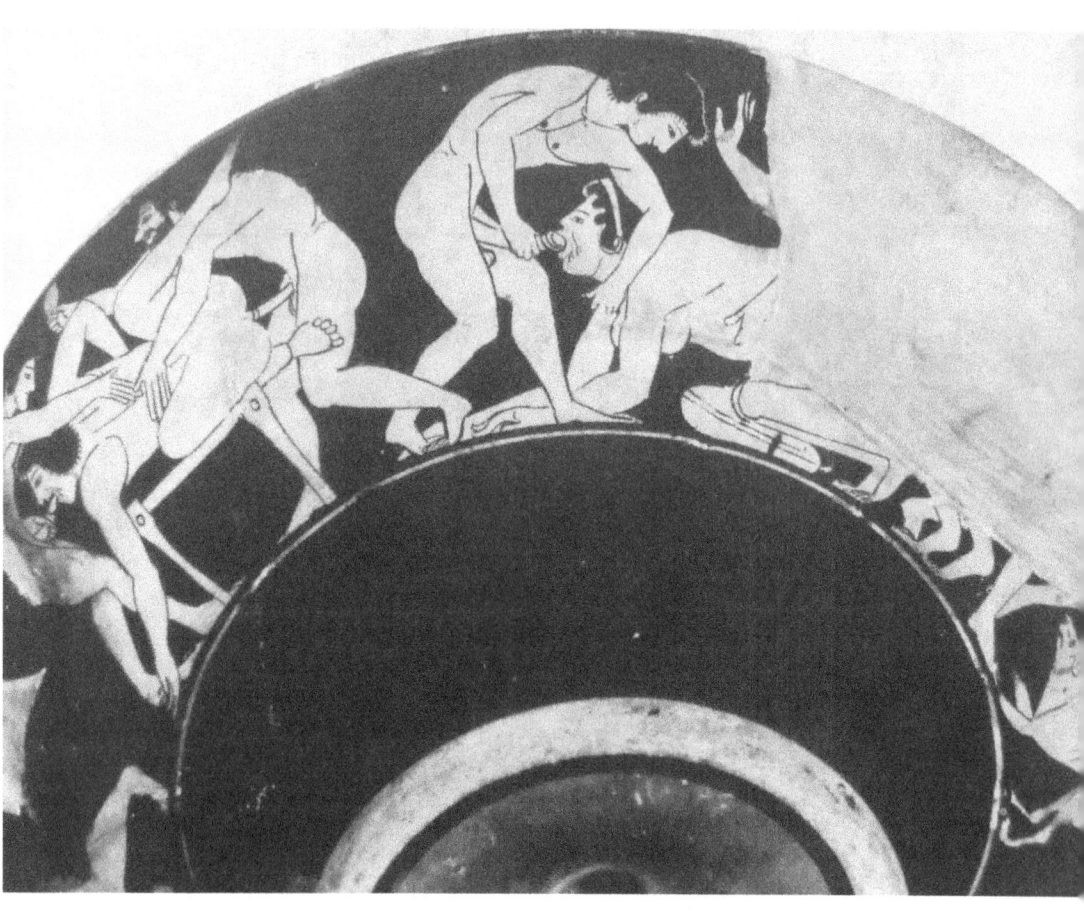

Greek Cup, Attic, attributed to Skythes

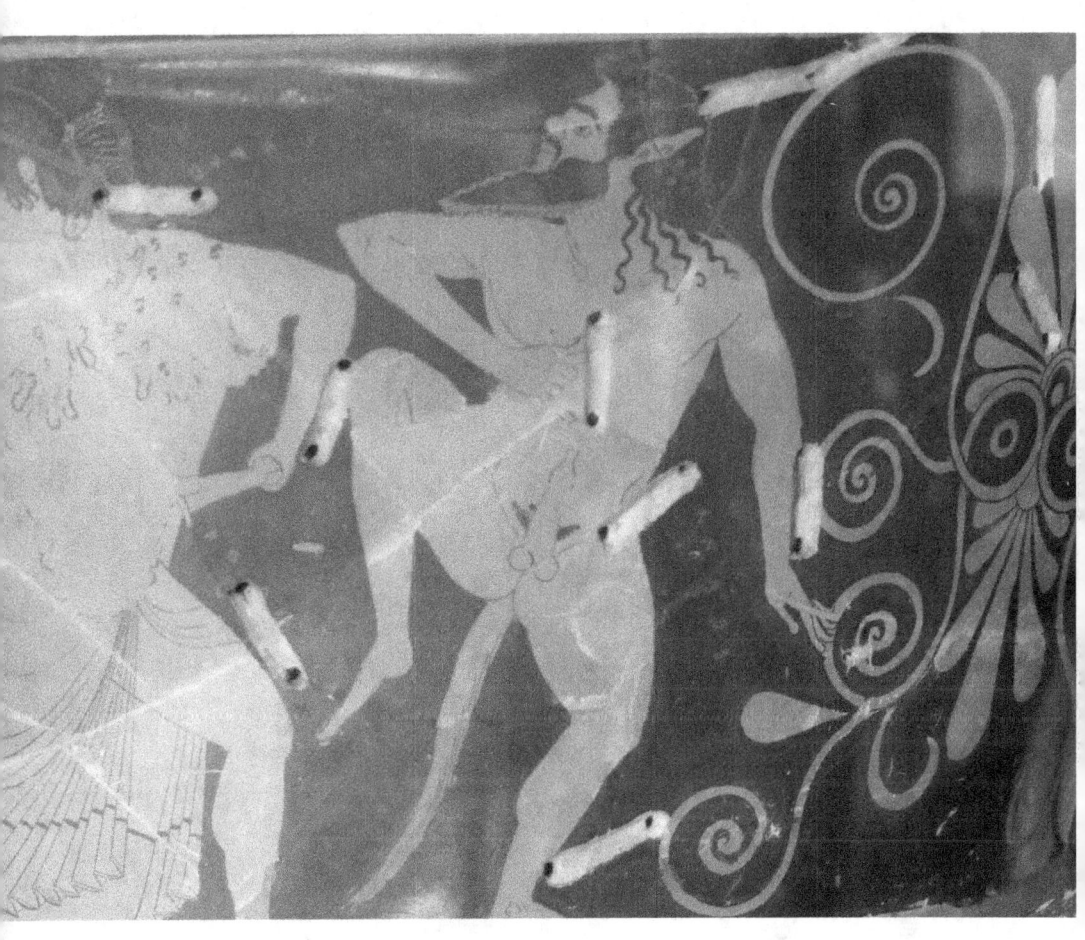

Greek Vase, 5th century, Louvre Museum, Paris

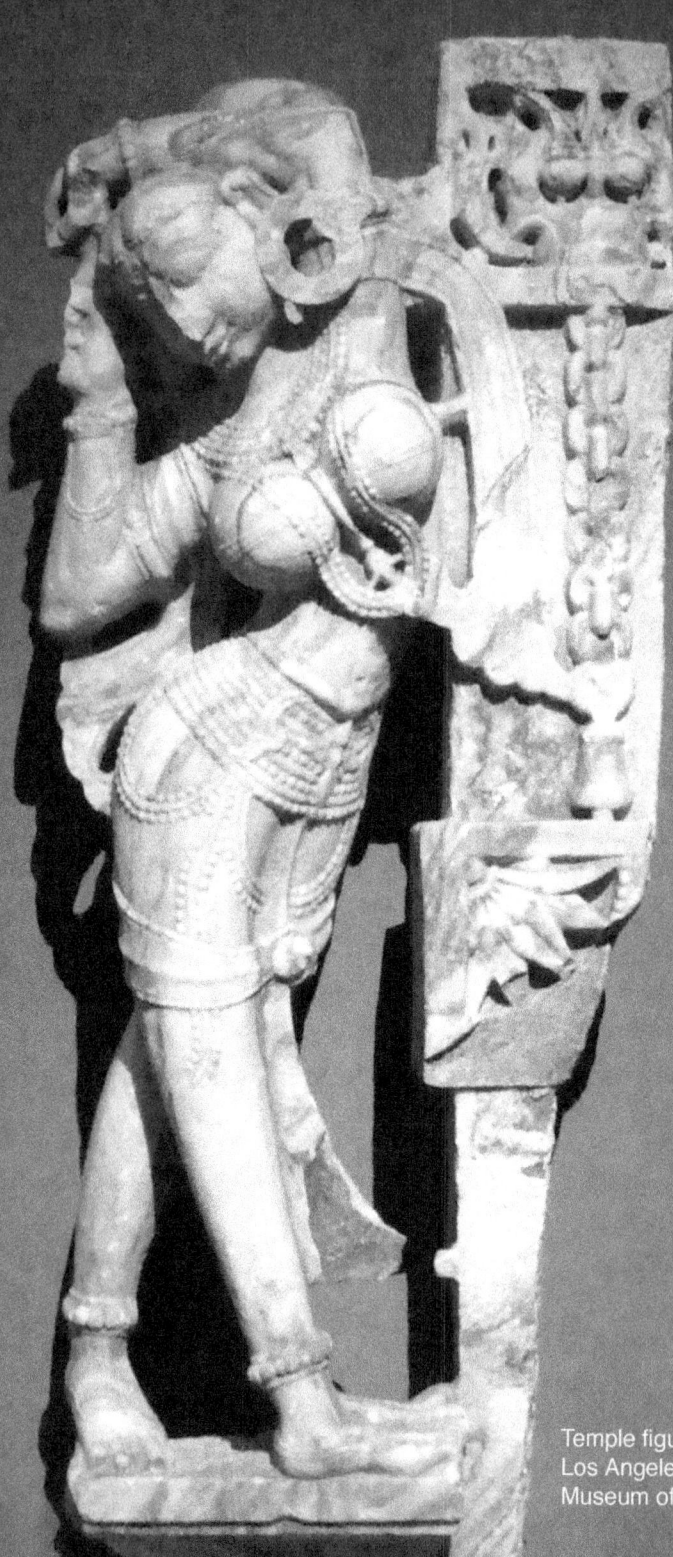

Temple figure, Indian,
Los Angeles County
Museum of Art

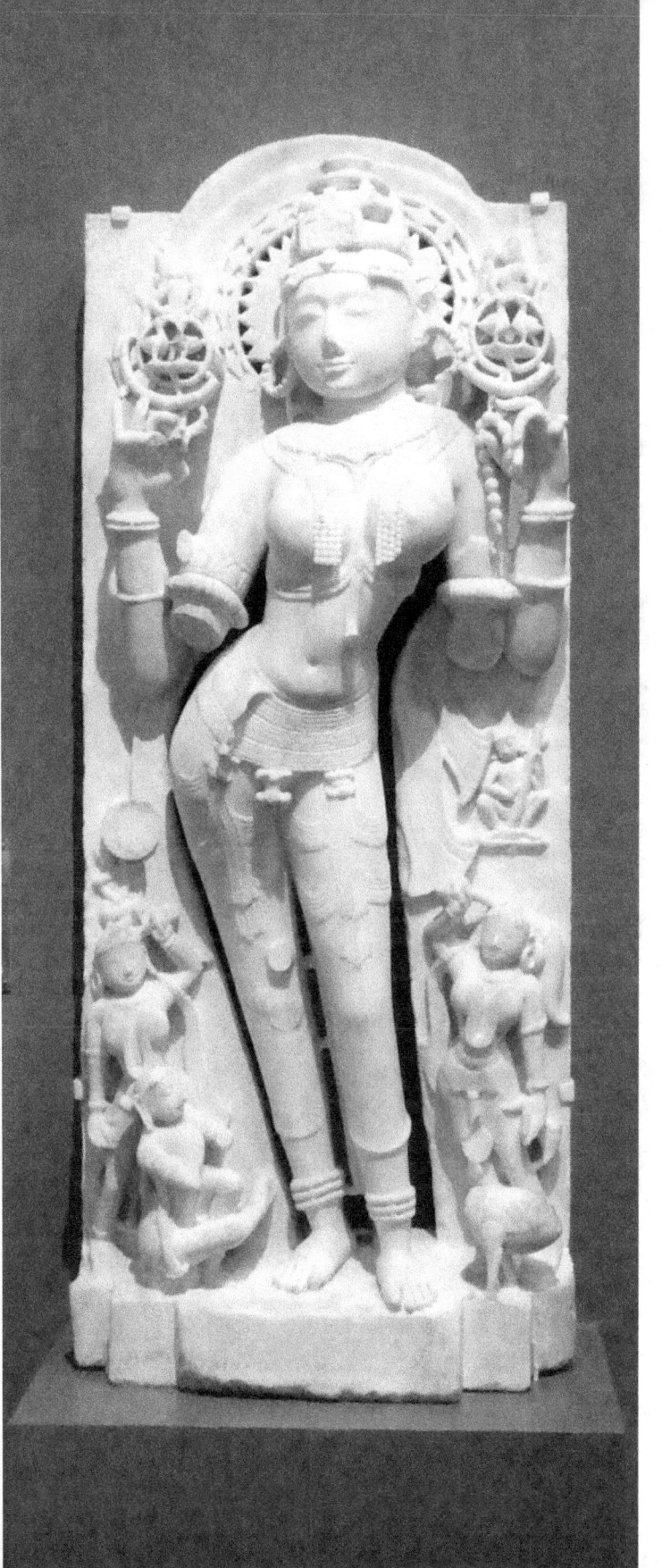

Indian temple figure,
Norton Simon Museum,
Pasadena, CA

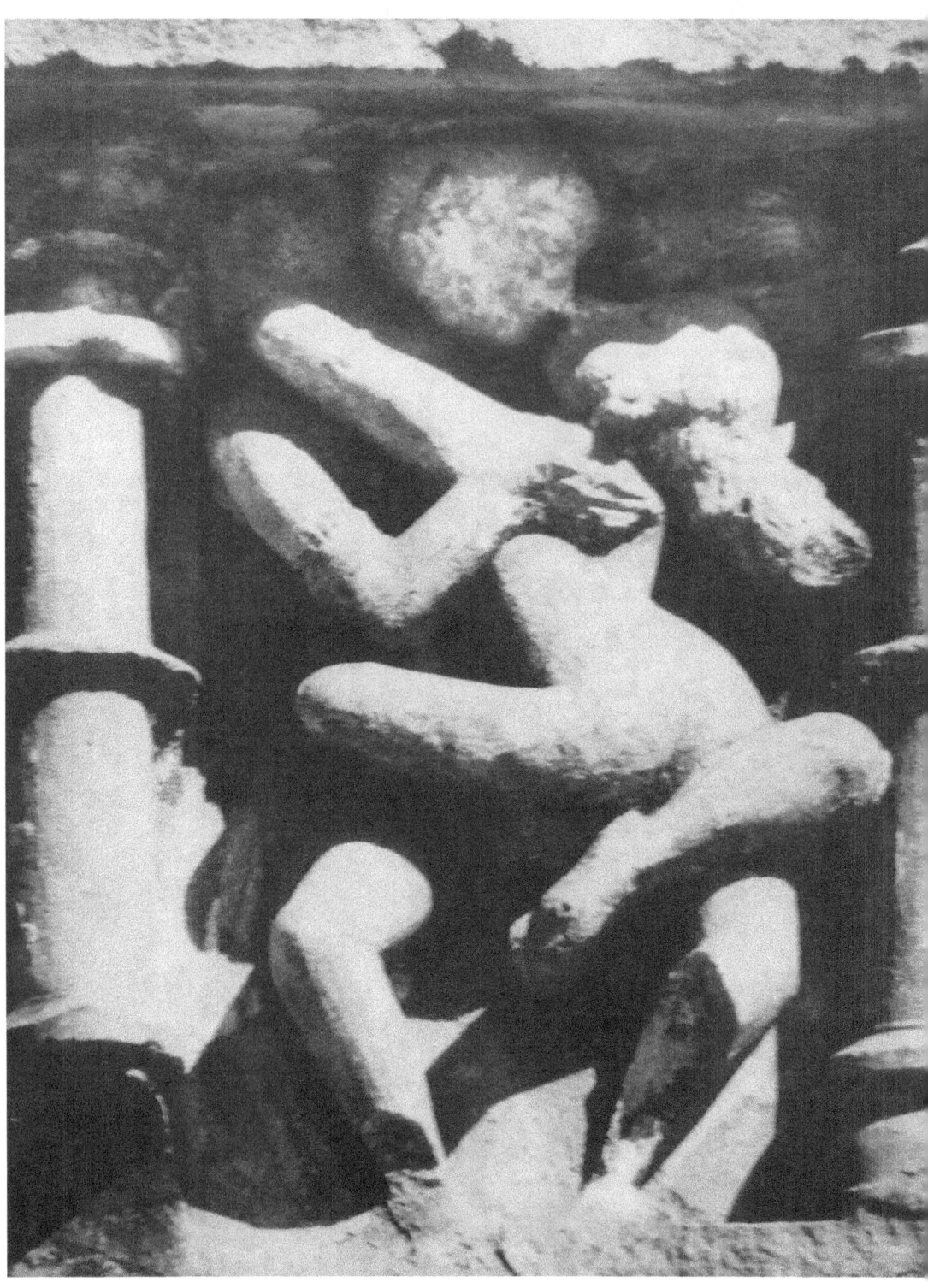

Khajuraho temple, 9th-11th century, North India

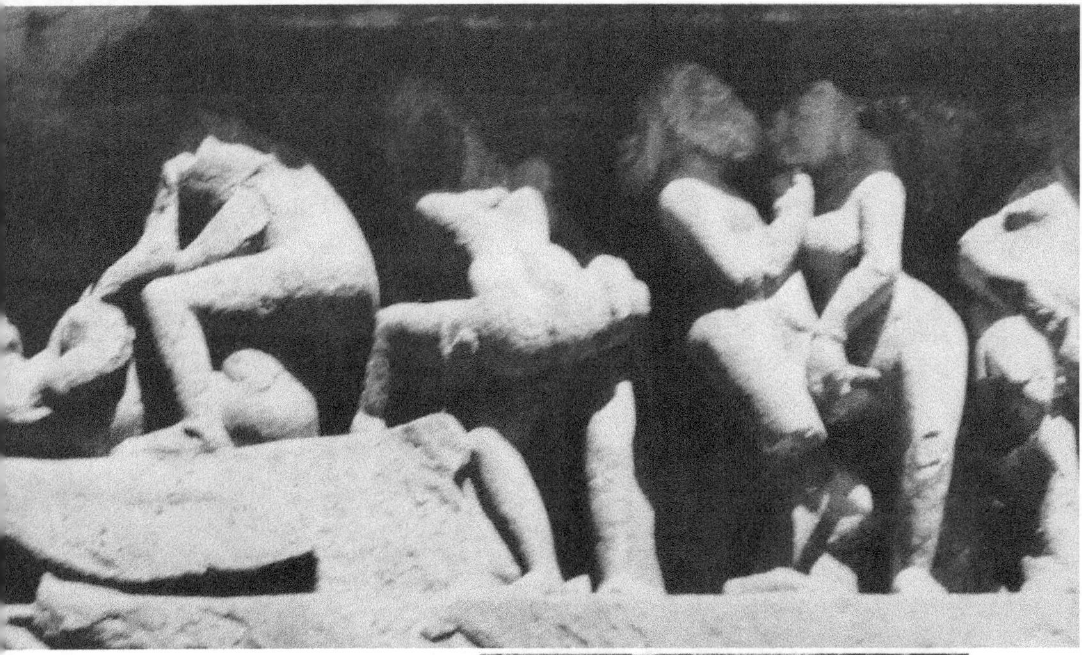

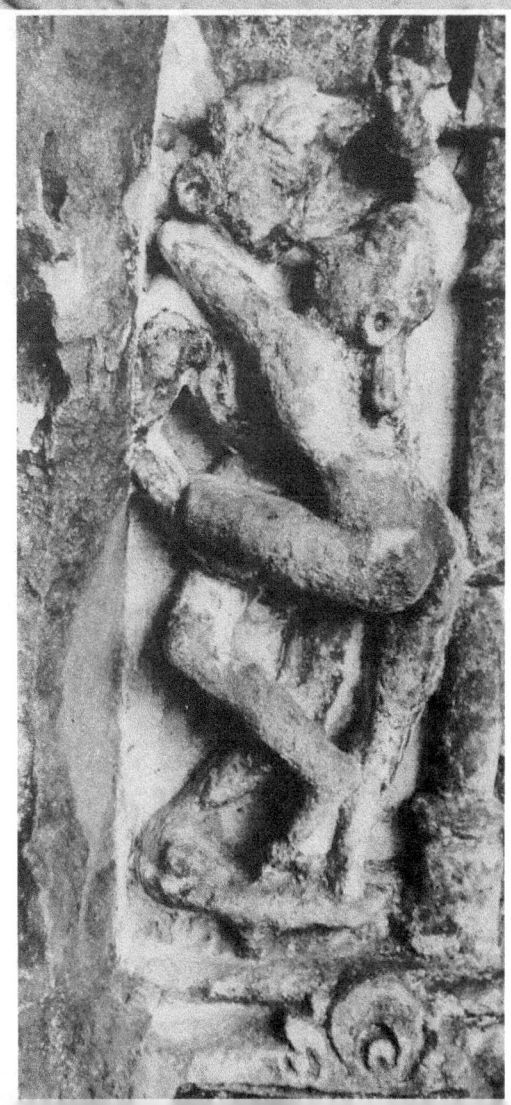

Khajuraho temple, 9-11 century, Northern India, right.

Temple, 11th century, Mount Abu area, Northern India

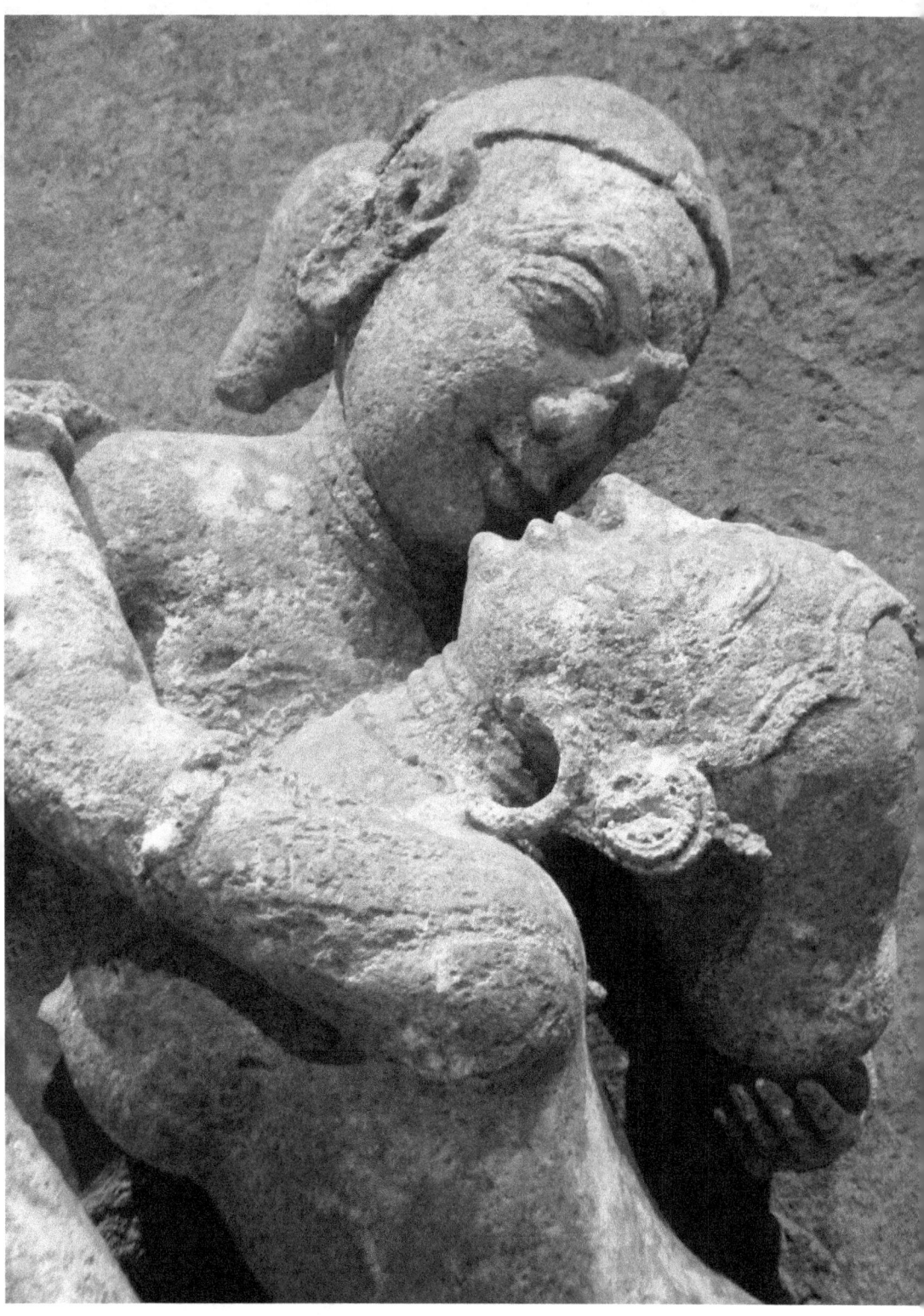

Temple figures, Indian, Norton Simon Museum, Pasadena, CA

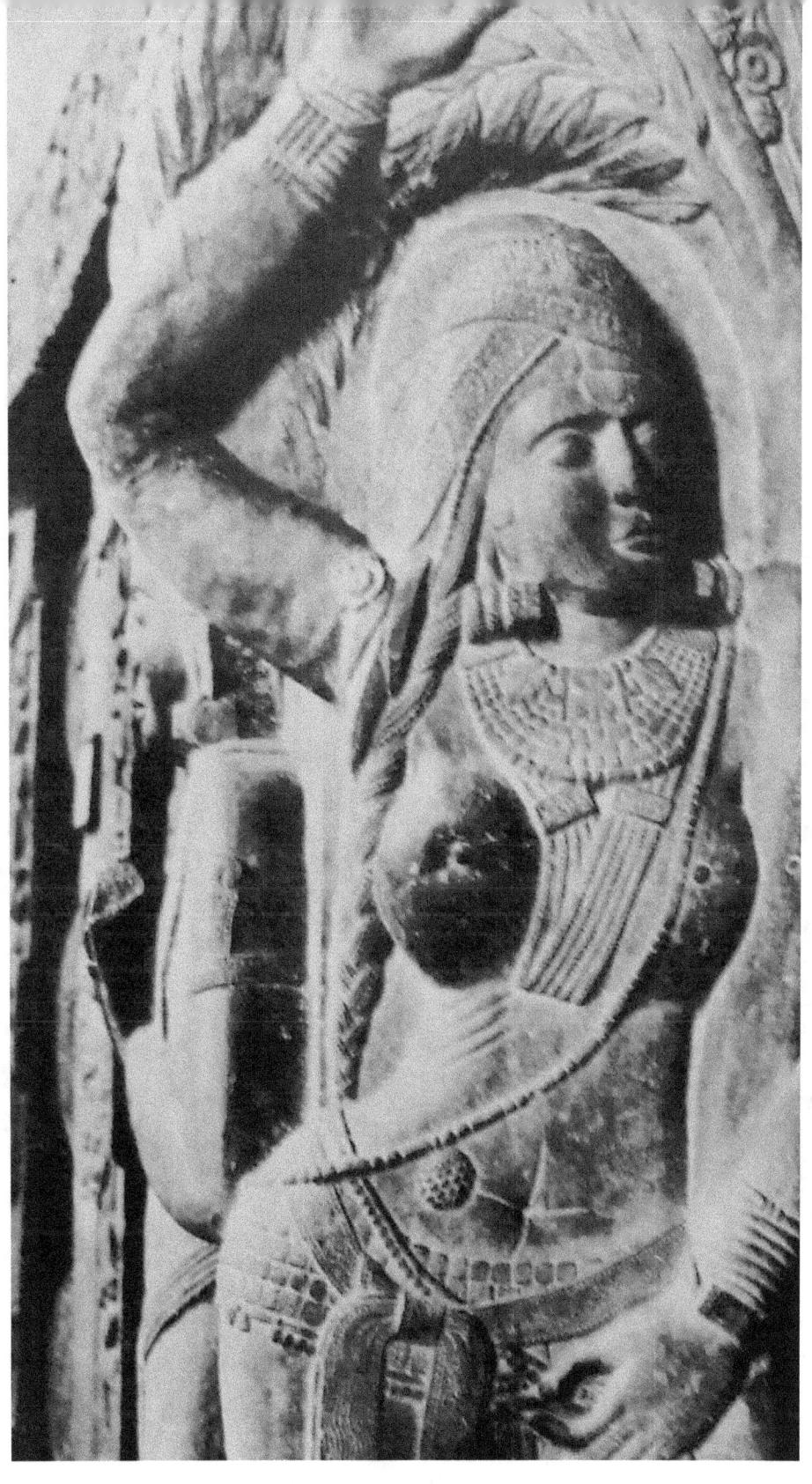

Yakshi figure, Indian Museum, Caluctta

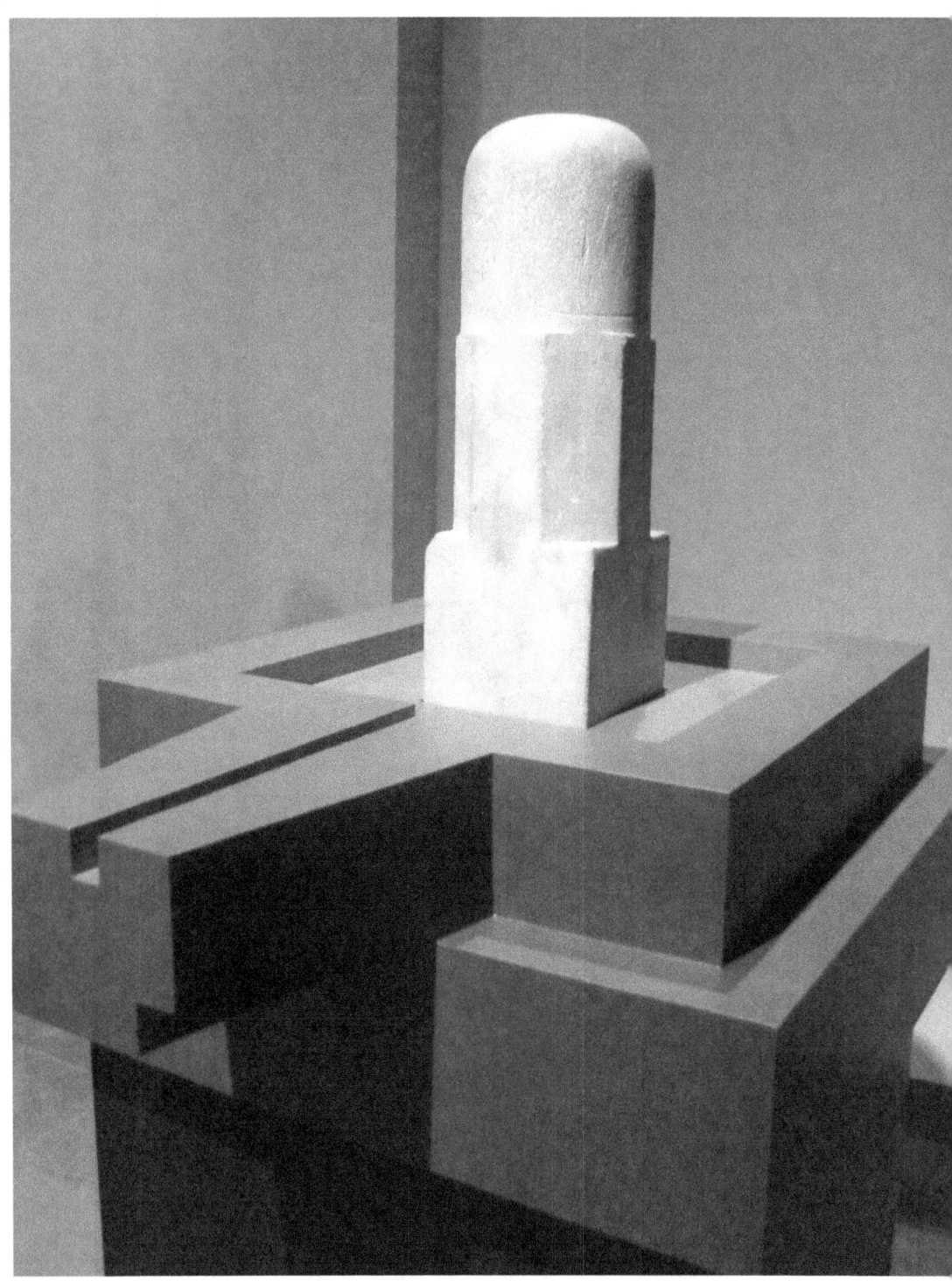

Lingam and Yoni, Cambodian, Norton Simon Museum, Pasadena, CA

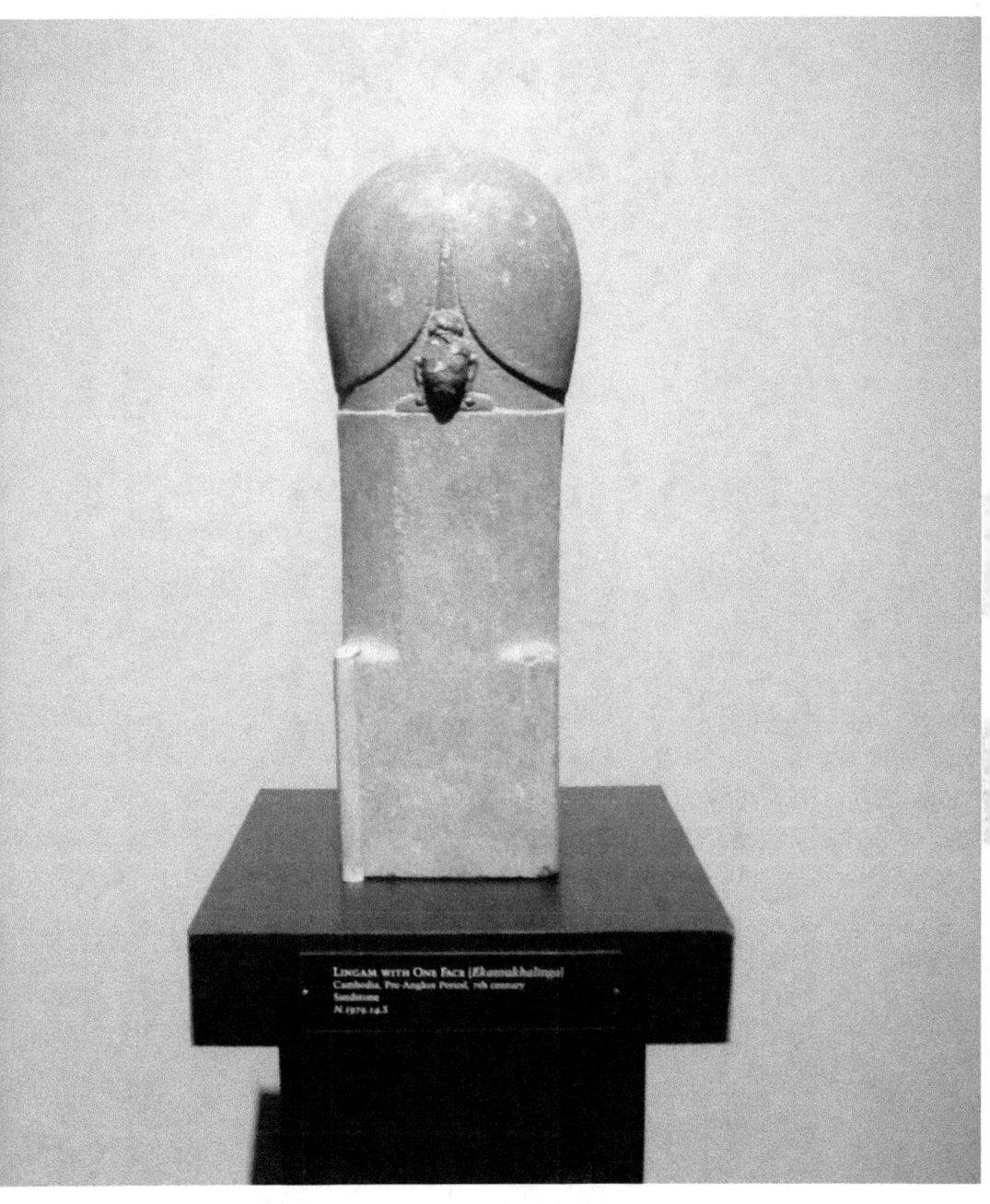

Lingam, Cambodia, 7th Century,
Norton Simon Museum, Pasadena, CA

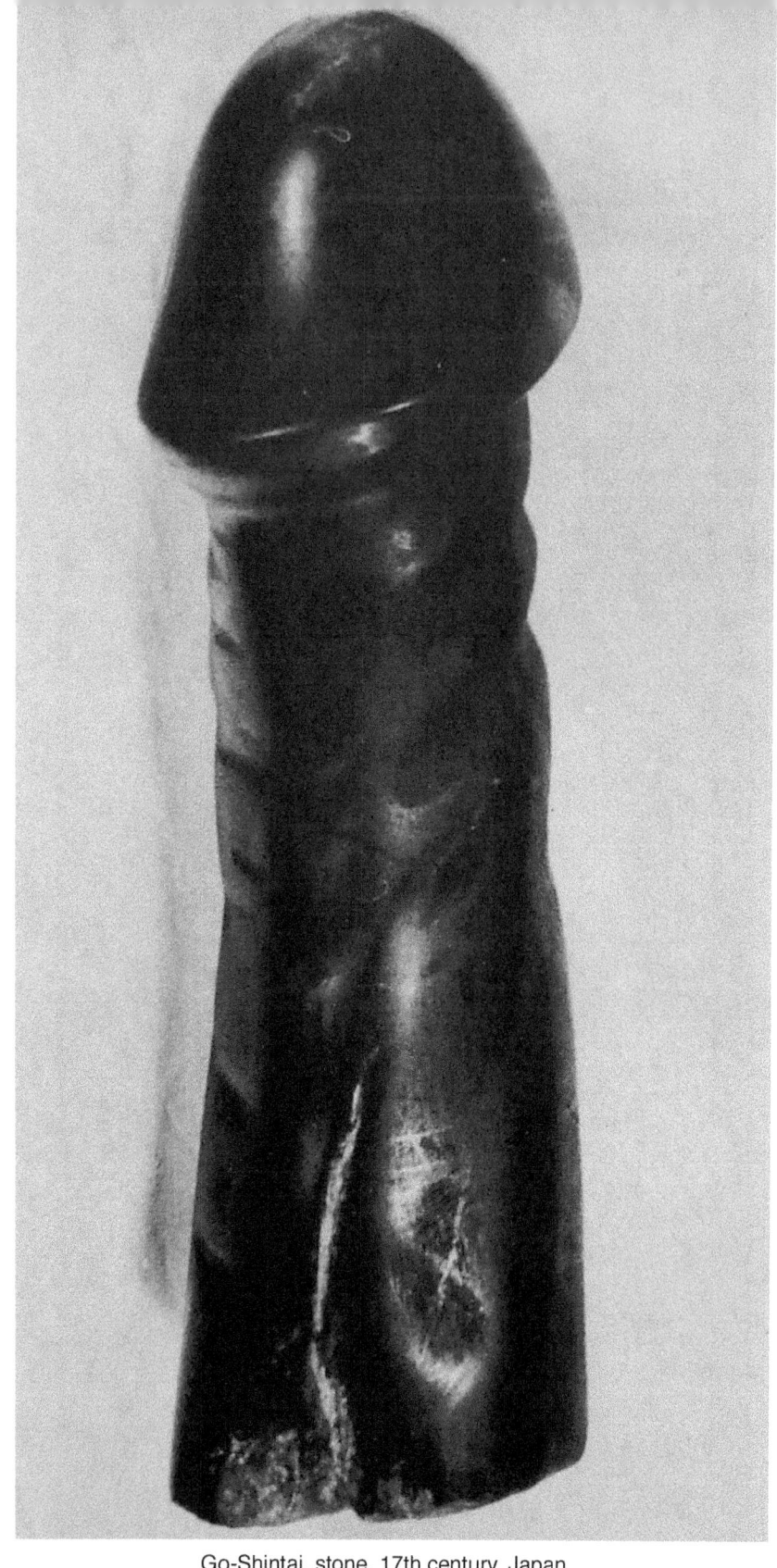

Go-Shintai, stone, 17th century, Japan

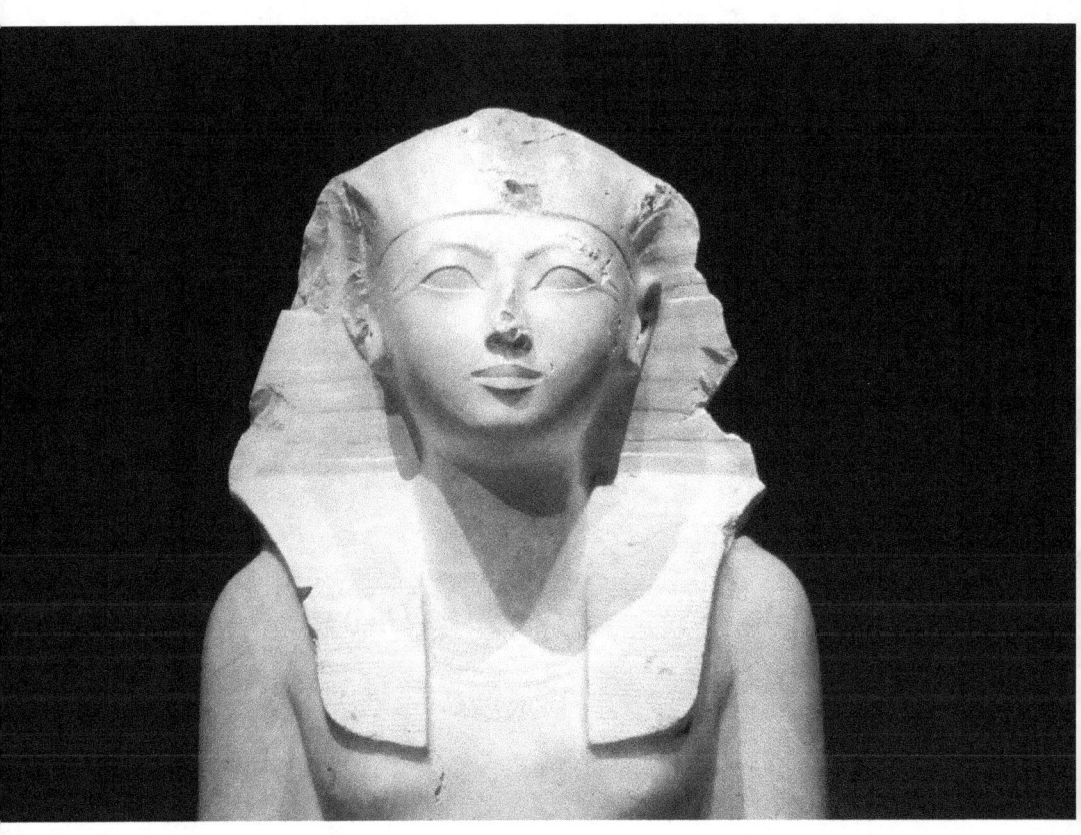

Ancient Egyptian sculpture, Metropolitan Museum of Art, New York

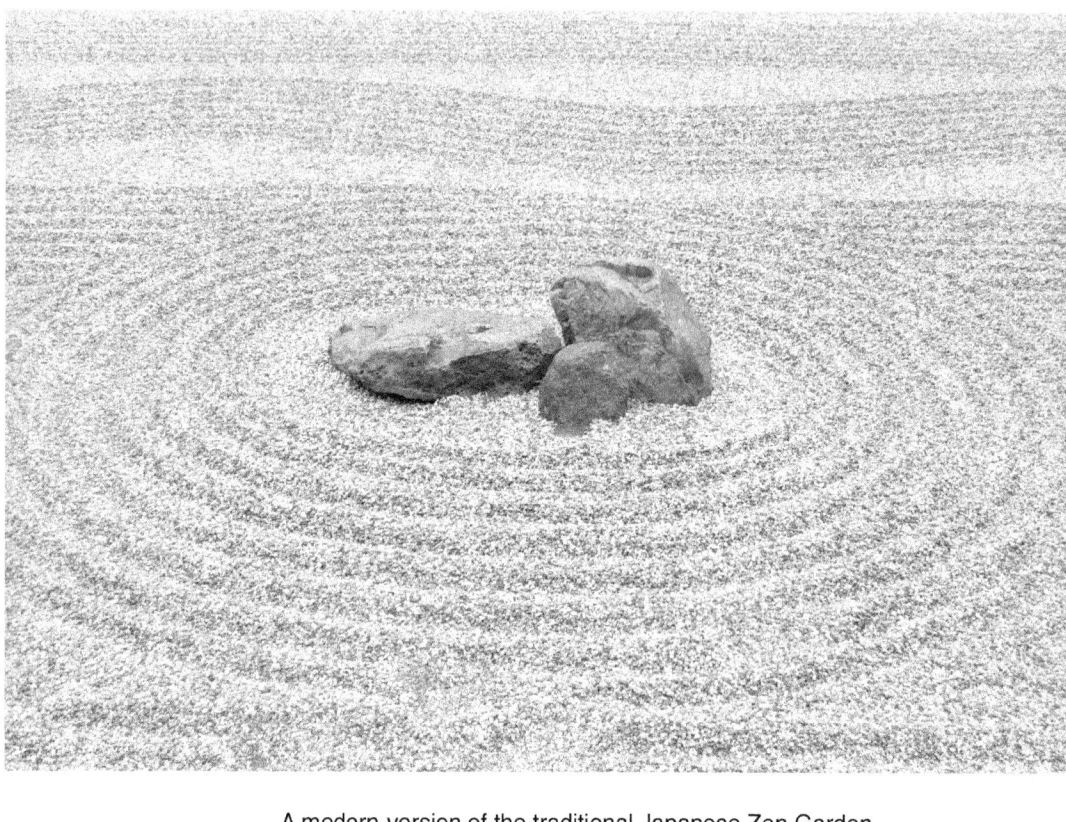

A modern version of the traditional Japanese Zen Garden,
in Pasadena, California

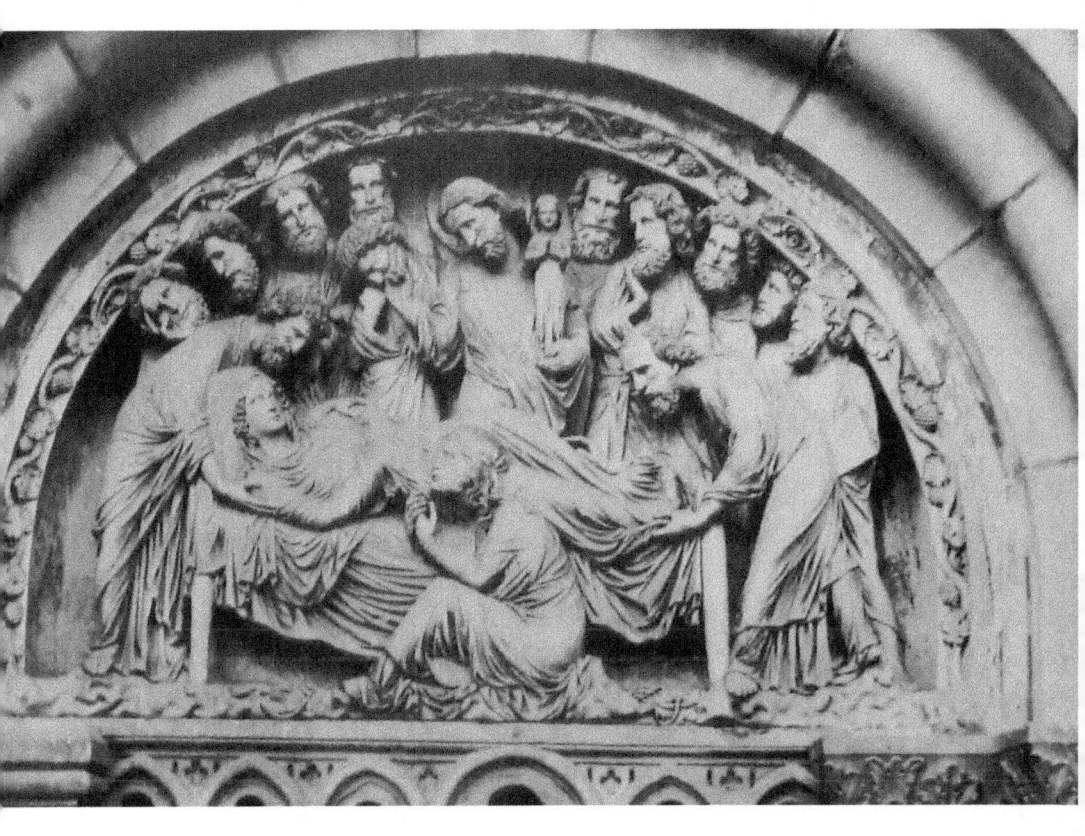

Death of the Virgin, 1230, Strasbourg Cathedral

2

Sexuality and Prehistoric Sculpture

"STONE VENUSES"

It would be possible to argue
that prehistoric art is patriarchal
and masculine in nature, with its
images of hunting and killing
animals, its emphasis on death
and survival (masculine, Existential themes, from Charles
Darwin to Jean-Paul Sartre), and
the harshness of its environment. In fact, there is a mass of
feminine mystery and imagery in
prehistoric art, not least in the
several statues or figurines of
nameless Goddesses, known as
"Stone Venuses", which have
been found.1 These are some of
the earliest examples of sculptures (the most famous is the
Venus of Willendorf). Modern
artist Louise Bourgeois has
produced sculptures that are
very much like the "Stone
Venuses": her *Stake Woman* is a
rounded, headless, armless
volume, with two prominent
'breasts' and the overall shape of
a vessel.2

There is a widespread
acceptance of Goddess worship
as being older than God worship. The Goddess, writes
Robert Graves in *The Greek
Myths*, is 'immortal, changeless,

1 *Venus of Willendorf*, Austria,
limestone, palæolithic (end of
Gravettian); *Venus of Kostenki*,
Moravia, mammoth ivory, palæolithic (Gravittian)
2 Louise Bourgeois: *Stake Woman*,
c. 1970, pink marble, 11.4cm high,
private collection

and omnipotent'.[3] In the beginning, it seems, was the Mother, not the Father. As Robert Briffault noted in The Mothers: '[t]he All-Mother is older than the All-Father'.[4] Some commentators extend Goddess religion back beyond the cults of Classical and ancient Goddesses – back beyond Isis, Ishtar, Aphrodite, and Diana – to prehistoric times. Of course, no one can say for certain that prehistoric people believed this or that. We do not have any writing or explicit records of that sort from the prehistoric period. We have artifacts and buildings. These are largely to do with death – all those tombs and graves filed with objects, the bones smeared with red ochre (perhaps alluding to the (menstrual) blood of life), and so on. Thus, anthropologists conclude that death was a major factor in prehistoric religion, for death was a primal certainty, inescapable, always there, always having to be dealt with.[5] Much of prehistoric sculpture is associated with death.

A host of writers and thinkers have suggested that the 'eternal feminine', the Earth Mother, the Mistress of All, the plenum, the mater, the Lady of Wild Things, the Magna Mater, Matrix, Ma-Gog, Great Round, Primum Mobile, the Tellus Mater, was the Goddess, a female deity who presided over all life and death.[6]

There is a widely held belief that in prehistoric times the mysteries of life – birth, growth, love and death – were bound up with the feminine. The Goddess is thus the manifestation of a relation with the world, the expression of a 'mystic solidarity' with the earth, with agriculture, with animals, with survival. Any number of commentators have noted the connections between women, wombs, fertility, growth, agri-culture, sexuality, death, and religion. Mircea Eliade voices the typical view in A History of Religious Ideas:

> The sacrality of sexual life, and first of all of feminine sexuality, becomes insepar-able from the miraculous enigma of creation. Parthenogenesis, the hieros gamos, and the ritual orgy express, on different planes,

3 Robert Graves: The Greek Myths, I, Penguin 1948, 13
4 R. Briffault: The Mothers: A Study of the Origins of Sentiments and Institutions, Allen & Unwin 1927, III, 180
5 See Weston La Barre: The Ghost Dance.
6 See Marija Gimbutas, Monica Sjoo, Shirley Nicholson, Ean Begg, Robert Graves, Elinor Gadon, Merlin Stone, Esther Harding, Peter Redgrove, Marina Warner, Barbara Walker, J.G. Frazer, Erich Neu-mann, Joseph Campbell, Geoffrey Ashe, Robert Briffault and Bach-ofen, who have all written about the Goddess

the religious character of sexuality. A complex symbolism, anthropo-cosmic in structure, associates woman and sexuality with the lunar rhythms, with the earth (assimilated to the womb), and with what must be called the "mystery of vegetation."[7]

Prehistoric sculpture can be read as dealing with 'feminine' issues, issues which feminists have brought to the forefront of the feminist debate: notions of sexuality, the body, identity, spirituality and art. The first works of sculpture were anonymous, made by artists often for a ritual or religious purpose: the circular shapes of Avebury or Stonehenge in Britain, for instance: these have to do with the ancient symbolism of the circle, with time, seasons, cycles, infinity, the 'great round' of life: this is the Goddess, as eco-feminists and spiritual/ poetic feminists tell us. The circle becomes a womb, if you want, the circular space in which the mysteries of life are experienced, or ritualized. The circle is 'female', a feminized construct.

You can see the Goddess or the 'eternal feminine' in the "Stone Venuses", and, later, in the Neolithic stones or menhirs, the standing stones, some of which had Goddesses carved onto them.[8] You can see the feminine element in the long uterine passages and entrances to tombs, so that the poetic connection of womb = tomb has an ancient dimension, as well as occurring in Western poetry, for instance ('from womb to tomb', 'from the cradle to the grave', as the clichés go). Thus, in prehistoric burials, the bones, covered in red ochre, are put back into the 'womb' of the earth, and bodies lie in the foetal position.

---

7 Mircea Eliade: *A History of Religious Ideas*, 40-1

8 Menhir statue of a woman, sandstone, St-Sernin, France. Neolithic, c. 2000 B.C., Musée des Antiquités

PREHISTORIC SEXUALITY

Female eroticism plays a large part in prehistoric art. Women, in the stone and bone figurines, are mothers, and birth and motherhood are exalted. Hence some archaeologists and feminists think women were at the centre of prehistoric life in some places. Women, some people reckon, held positions of power: they controlled 'trade' in sexual pleasure, for instance; they could withhold pleasure, and thus, with their knowledge of the menstrual cycle, they could exert power over men.[9] Eventually, men took over most forms of trade, until, as French feminist Luce Irigaray writes in Ce sex qui n'en est pas un:

> The trade that organizes patriarchal societies takes place exclusively among men. Women, signs, goods, currency, all pass from one man to another.[10]

Mary Jane Sherfey has written this in "A Theory on Female Sexuality" of the controversial matter of sexual politics in the prehistoric era:

There are many indications from the prehistory studies in the Near East that it took perhaps five thousand years or longer for the subjugation of women to take place. A data from the 12,000 to 8,000 B.C. period indicate that pre-civilized woman enjoyed full sexual freedom and was often totally incapable of controlling her sexual drive. Therefore, I propose that one of the reasons for the long delay between the earliest development of agriculture (c. 12,000 B.C.) and the rise of urban life and the beginning of recorded knowledge (c. 8,000-5,000 B.C.) was the ungovernable cyclic sexual drive of women. Not until these drives were gradually brought under control by rigidly enforced social codes could family life become the stabilizing and creative crucible from which modern civilized man could emerge.[11]

Whatever the conflicting views on prehistoric sexuality are, it is always seen as hetero-sexual, fiercely heterosexual, and this is expressed in pre-historic sculpture. It is never homosexual nor lesbian. It is the *representations* of sexuality that are heterosexual. In other words, what we know about

9 See Chris Knight: *Blood Relations*, Yale University Press 1991; Peter Redgrove: *The Black Goddess*; Penelope Shuttle & Peter Redgrove: *The Wise Wound*.
10 Luce Irigaray: *Ce sexe qui n'en pas un*, Minuit 1977, in E. Marks, 107.

11 Mary Sherfey: "A Theory on Female Sexuality", in S. Cox, ed: *Female Psychology: The Emerging Self*, Science Research Associates, Chicago 1976

prehistoric sexuality comes from depictions of certain kinds of sexuality. And we know that sculptures often have little to do with emotional or psychological or even physical realities.

The views on prehistory, then, say more about the people who are propounding the views than about prehistory itself. Views on prehistoric eroticism say more about the psychologists, anthropologists, biologists, historians and thinkers who make those views, than about prehistoric eroticism itself. Thus, ecological, pagan and spiritual feminists have reclaimed prehistoric art as 'feminine' or Goddess art. These reclamations clearly indicate the political agendas of feminists.

PHALLIC CULT

While it's nice to think of those early sculptures, the "Stone Venuses", as proof of the religious significance of women in the palæolithic era (c. 30,000-10,000 B.C.), they are stereotypes too. Stereotypes of 'woman' as divine nurturer and carer, a stereotype of 'woman' as 'mother' which still today is very prevalent. Prehistoric representations, then, objectifies people sexually, sometimes reducing them to genitals, as art has done throughout its 40,000/ 100,000/ 2 million year history. There are a lot of genitals in prehistoric art, as in Neolithic art. There are the usual phalluses and wombs, men dressed in animal skins, with the phallic horns or antlers on their head, men as ithyphallic hunters or shamans.

As the French feminist Julia Kristeva says, the art object is the original fetish object, and for so long that fetish has been the phallus. Phallic cults are found everywhere, in all times of history, in one form or another. Sculpture plays a large part in phallic rituals. During the ancient Roman honeymoon, for instance, the bride was expected to sit on the erect phallus of a statue of the god Tutinus, before going to the marriage bed.[12]

One thing is certain: art was, originally, religious. It had a religious function, it was often made for religion, or by religion, or within religion. Modern commentators sexualize pre-history, so that everything connotes sexuality in one way or another. So that, according to the modern view, people in ancient times were rutting away madly, emulating and far surpassing the animals they hunted in terms of sexual appetite. The modern view promotes, in fact, the male idea of paradise: when not eating or hunting (hunting being a synonym for men's violent 'games', such as war), people were tupping like mad things. This is a patriarchal paradise, a Golden Age when only a bearskin stood between people and pleasure. By the same token, we sexualize the prehistoric era when we emphasize erotic sculptures, leaving out other sculptures – cooking utensils, for instance, or charms, or vernacular architecture.

Art critics and historians look back fondly to erotic primitive art, for there was a time, it is felt, when sexuality was freely expressed in art, without the hang-ups and anxieties of the modern era.

Clearly, art critics, sociologists, historians and psychologists look back at prehistoric and primitive art nostalgically, in their search for a 'sexually liberated' space, to use the 1960s term. Depictions of sex abound, or seem to, in prehistoric and ancient art. A 2000 B.C. terra-cotta relief from Babylonia shows two people making love from behind; a Libyan demon tups to a woman, in a 5000 B.C. engraving; someone sucks someone else's penis on a ceramic vessel from 500 A.D. Peru.[13]

In prehistoric art, sexuality is associated with religion; sexuality is religious, and the religious dimension has an erotic element in it. Notions of fertility, magic, sexuality, agriculture and so on are entwined. The obviousness of such statements needs to be remembered constantly, especially since our modern era is so unmagical. J. G. Frazer prudishly writes in *The Golden Bough,* one of the key works on mythology in the modern era:

---

12 See Julius Evola, 174; A. De Marchi: *Il Culto Privato in Roma Antica*, Milan 1896

---

13 *Terracotta relief depicting copulation from behind*, Meso-potamia, Babylonian period, c. 2000 B.C.; *Semi-human sexual demon*, rock engraving, Ti-n-Lalan, Libyan Fezzan, c. 5000 B.C., Fabrizio Mori, Rome; *Ceramic Vessel*, Mochica Culture, Peru, c. 500 A.D., Institute for Sex Research, Indiana University

ruder races in other parts
of the world have con-
sciously employed the
intercourse of the sexes as
a means to ensure the
fruitfulness of the earth.14

---

14 J.G. Frazer: *The Golden Bough*,
136

3

Ancient and Oriental Sculpture: Greece, Rome, India, China

GREECE

Greek culture is everywhere celebrated as the foundation of Western culture. So much of ancient Greek culture – the arts, politics, philosophy, writing, structures and ideas – is found throughout Western culture. Greek art remains the highpoint of Western art. You name it, the ancient Greeks did it – and much better than just about every artist or society that followed them. Poetry, sculpture, architecture, philosophy, political systems, erotic art – the ancient Greeks were brilliant at everything, it seems. The great leap in art made by the ancient Greeks from what had gone on before (a rugged prehistory and Bronze Age), seems much larger than the development of the Renaissance compared to mediæval art, or the emergence of abstract art at the beginning of the 20th century. What the ancient Greeks did overshadows the Renaissance, and modern art. Greek art is truly 'beautiful', to use the most apposite of all Platonic terms. Look at Greek sculpture, from the female figures of Auxerre to the wonderful *Victory of Samothrace*, a powerful deity striding confidently through space, her wings magnificently outstretched, her clothes flowing around in the breeze. No wonder tourists flock around this statue in the Louvre, Museum in Paris, for it proclaims the total authority and magic of sculpture (as well as its mystery – the *Victory of Samothrace* can be interpreted any way you like).15

Here, in ancient Greek art, we find the birth of modern æsthetics, modern notions of beauty, of ideal form and of the stature of high art. In ancient Greek art, we find the amalgamation of art and philosophy – that great art must be produced from a great philosophy – which has remained with high art ever since.

When you look at Greek mythology you see a wild celebration of the central mysteries or experiences of life; birth, growth, love, sex, death, violence, desire, loss, departure, etc. For, despite its exaltation of Goddesses – Athene, Hera, Aphrodite, Diana, Artemis, Kore, Persephone – Greek culture is supremely masculinist and patriarchal. Zeus, for instance, is astonishing in his wildly phallic, wildly sexual exploits. He seems to have taken every Goddess in Greek mythology. He thunders about the sky, raging like the most macho instinct gone wild. He slept with Mnemosyne over nine nights and she later gave birth to nine daughters, the Muses; he raped Demeter in the form of a bull, and she bore Kore; he married Hera; he 'pursued' (raped) Electra, Taygete, Callisto (in the form of Artemis), Aegina, Antiope, Niobe, Mera, Leto, Danaë, Semele, Europa, Leda, Hesione, Elara, Naerea, Protgenia, Thalia, and many others. Zeus had everybody, it seems. He appeared to Semele in all his thunderous majesty, but the sight killed her. Nevertheless, he took the child in her womb, put it in his thigh, and later it became Dionysus, the wild god of wine. Some Greek sculpture loudly proclaims the strident phallic force that Zeus embodies, but there is much also that speaks of harmony and repose – the *Lapith Woman*, for instance, on the temple of Zeus at Olympia, or the bronze statue of a youth, the *Kouros from Piraeus*.16

There are many other phallic gods in Greek mythology – Pan, for instance, often depicted in statues as an

15 *Female Figure*, from Auxerre, c. 625B.C., limestone, daedalic style, Louvre, Paris; *Victory of Samothrace*, c. 200 B.C., marble, Louvre, Paris

16 *Kouros from Piraeus*, c. 520 B.C., bronze, National Museum, Athens; *Lapith Woman*, c. 460 B.C., marble, west pediment of the temple of Zeus at Olympia, Museum, Olympia

ithyphallic raper, or Dionysus, the god of the wild cult of the mænads, as sculpted by Scopas.[17] These gods are the beings that transgress boundaries, that bring wildness back into the world. The deities are personifications of human feelings, on one level, and what is clear is that Greek mythology and art is a manifestation of mainly male or masculine emotions. And if feminine feelings are represented, they are usually male views of female emotions. For although we do not know who most of the sculptors and artists of ancient Greece (or Rome, or Sumer, or Egypt) were, they were probably mainly male. Even if women artists contributed, the results are still patriarchal. For this is the problem, always the problem: that, whoever the author is, most art is patriarchal. Because the codes, structures, contexts and representations are biased towards the masculinist or patriarchal viewpoint.

Generally, Greek mythology follows the usual heterosexual pattern of masculine power and male submission, but with a few exceptions, such as Goddesses like Hera, Artemis, Athene and Diana, who were not always to be taken by any god that lusted after them.

There are some powerful representations of women in Greek sculpture: of Athene as a warrior, with shield and spear, of Leto striding through the world carrying two children, of Persephone returning to her mother, the Corn Goddess Demeter, of Artemis setting the hounds on Actaeon. These are powerful images of women, set within patriarchal discourse, certainly, but at least they're not maids, drudges and bimbos.[18]

The representations of the Olympians are some of the highpoints of Greek art: Zeus, Poseidon, Hestia, Artemis, Athene, Apollo, Ares, Hera, Demeter, Aphrodite and Hermes. The statues and friezes of the Greek deities show them to be very confident beings, and often *smiling*. Many of the statues, of Artemis, Athene, and others, are smiling, often softly, secretly, to themselves, much as so many Oriental statues

---

17 Scopas: *Dancing Mænad*, 4th century B.C.

18 *Artemis and Actæon*, metope from Temple E, Selinus, National Museum, Palermo; *Demeter and Persephone*, 5th century B.C., Mansell Collection; *Athene*, from the temple of Aegina, Munich Museum; *Leto with Apollo and Artemis*, c. 600 B.C., limestone; *Athena and Alkyoneus*, from the Altar of Zeus from Pergamon, marble relief, Hellenistic, c. 180 B.C., State Museums, Berlin

smile.[19] The softly smiling sculptures, such as the *Mænad with Goat*, a Græco-Roman relief (late 5th century), the headless *Nike Untying Her Sandal* (c. 410 B.C.) and the delicious *Aphrodite of Knidos* (c. 350 B.C.), are pure mystery. The artist is lost to time, but the sculptures live on.[20] The polychromed marble statue of the Goddess Kore in the Acropolis Museum in Athens is an exquisite example of archaic Greek sculpture. Made two thousand years before Michelangelo Buonarroti's *Moses*, the *Kore* statue has that mysterious Orential smile, the smile that Leonardo da Vinci captured in his *Mona Lisa* and *The Virgin and Child with St Anne*. Few other Western artists apart from Leonardo have created these soft, enigmatic smiles. They seem to belong to the East, to points East of Greece. Here, Kore is the benevolent deity of fertility, and her smile connotes the total authority of a divine personage. The sculpture itself is rich in detail, from the plaited hair hanging down around her shoulders, to the folds of her clothes, always a challenge to the sculptor. Rare among Greek sculpture in museums, the *Kore* statue retains some of its original colours: it reminds us that Greek sculpture was painted with colours. Our view of Greek sculpture is of objects worn with age, bits broken off them (arms, noses, penises, breasts), and whitened. As Germain Bazin wrote:

> Writers on Greek art have evaded this matter of polychrome architecture and sculpture – as though Greek art were somehow tainted by the sin of realism (symbolized by the story of the *Aphrodite of Knidosi*, whose original colours were so lifelike, it is said, that she provoked an indecent assault)...[21]

When one meets polychrome sculpture these days, it can seem out of place. Eric Gill, for instance, coloured in parts of his stone sculptures, leaving the rest untouched.

---

19 *Artemis*, Greek, Pompeii, Mansell Collection; *Artemis Bendis*, relief sculpture, 4th century B.C., Mansell Collection; *Marine Aphrodite*, late 1st century B.C., British Museum;
20 After Praxiteles: *Aphrodite of Knidos*, c. 350 B.C., marble, Roman copy of a lost Greek piece, Vatican Museum, Rome; *Mænad with Goat*, late 5th century B.C., marble, Roman copy of a lost Greek work, Palazzo dei Conservatori, Rome; *Nike Untying Her Sandal*, c. 410 B.C., Classical Greek, Akropolis Museum, Rome; *Kore*, c. 530-520 B.C., from the Athens Acropolis, marble, polychromed Greek, Acropolis Museum, Rome

21 Germain Bazin: *World Sculpture*, 51

When Gill dabs a little red on lips or black on eyes of a statue, it seems unexpected, so used are we to viewing stone and marble sculpture unadorned by colour. The paint sits oddly on the surface of marble and stone. The polychrome wooden statues of the Virgin Mary in Polish churches can seem overpainted too, after the austerity of Greek sculpture. However, it would be odd indeed to visit a show by Frank Stella or Tony Cragg and not see any colour, as if all their works were weathered Greek sculptures, devoid of colour. We may imagine all Greek sculpture as being basically white or grey (made of marble or stone). But we would not perhaps enjoy Titian or Henri Matisse if they were colourless. True, some modern century artists have explored predominantly white in their work – Agnes Martin and Robert Ryman, for instance. It is crucial, then, to remember that Greek architecture and sculpture was colourful.

As Michel Foucault notes in *The Uses of Pleasure*, Greek notions of sexuality identity and activity were different those of the modern Western world. Sex was more of a continuum, without the boundaries between normality and 'deviant' behaviour that are found everywhere in the West.[22] Greek sexuality is regarded as healthy and open, even though it was shaped by economy, class, status, place, gender, power and culture, as much as modern concepts of sexuality. The depictions on vases are famous: people being tupped from behind while they suck someone's penis, a woman carrying a giant phallus, a man balancing a wine jar on his shaft, etc. It's Orgies 'R' Us.[23]

Greek art is perhaps at its loveliest, tenderest and most lyrical in decorated vases and cups. You can wander around the amazing collections of Greek vases in the Louvre in Paris or the Metropolitan Museum of Art in Gotham or the British Museum in London for many hours: the red and black vases are a window into a whole world. You see an entire society laid out in elaborate lines and intricate details, not forgetting a delightful sense of humour.

---

22 'The Greeks did not see love for one's own sex and love for the other sex as opposites, as two exclusive choices, two radically different types of behaviour.' (Michel Foucault: *The Uses of Pleasure*, 187).
23 *Orgy Scene*, Attic cup, Greece, attr. to Skythes, Louvre, Paris; *Naked Woman Carrying Giant Phallus*, Attic vase, Greece, Painter of Pan, Staatliche Museen, Berlin; *Revelling Seleni*, Attic vase, Greece, British Museum

Ancient Greek vase and cup art seems a world away from the heavy, death-obsessed stone and pillar art and architecture of the ancient world.

ROME

Ancient Greek and Roman art is described as a permissive, open sexual zone, a period in history when any kind of debauchery was permitted. It wasn't like that, but the legends persist. 'Debauchery' is the right word for modern views of Roman excesses, the orgies of Emperors such as Nero, Caligula and Tiberius. It was the world of the phallus, we are led to believe by art critics and historians, a world in which phalluses were everywhere. On vases, in carved stone, in reliefs, on amulets, in mosaics. The Romans had phallic shrines; an erect penis set in a miniature temple, like a god in a temple (to be propitiated and blessed). The Romans had phallic figures: penises with legs, the glans of the penis as someone's head, and so on.[24] The Roman world, even more than the Greek, was the supremely phallic/ ithyphallic era in history. The Roman warriors, the battle, the legions, the massive, monumental architecture, the erotic poetry, all of Roman culture is patriarchal and phallic.

Anything went, it seems, in art. There are statues of the

24 *Roman Phallic Amulets*, Pompeii, Italy, 1st century A.D., British Museum; *Roman Phallic Shrine*, Pompeii, Italy, 1st century A.D., Naples Museum

goat-god Pan making love with a goat, of copulation in brothels in frescoes.[25] It certainly was a bawdy era, a priapic age. Or it was an era in which erotic art flourished in some areas (but that is true of any era: there probably *hasn't* been a time when people *haven't* made erotic art of some kind or another, since the origins of art-making, back in the mists of time, tens of thousands of years ago).

Or, more correctly, it was an epoch in which erotic art was displayed in public to a degree that doesn't occur in the 21st century of the West (though there is plenty more erotic art around in modern times, millions more express-ions of erotica than the anything in the ancient world – but it exists in niches and enclaves, like areas of the internet, video production, books and maga-zines, DVDs, photographs, and clubs).

---

25 Joseph Nollekens: *Pan and the Goat*, 1760s, terracotta, British Museum; *Brothel Scene*, Pompeii, Italy, 1st century A.D., Naples Museum

INDIA AND CHINA

Hindu, Tantric, Taoist and Chinese erotic art is founded in a religion quite different in some key areas from Western religion. There is less guilt, sin, body-hating and suppression in Indian and Chinese erotic art than in Judaeo-Christianity and Islam. The cosmic energy of life has a sexual dimension which is gloriously celebrated. Indian and Chinese erotic art may be just as sexist and misogynist and patriarchal as Western erotic art, but it is also freer, more exuberant, more joyous.

In Oriental erotic art, sexuality is a cosmic energy, an essential part of an authentic religious worldview. Indian and Chinese erotica is still thoroughly sexist, though. As with witches' covens and Western magic, erotic energy manifests itself in men and women, in heterosexual components, and the symbols of the *lingam* and *yoni* are, yet again, the penis and vagina.

Maithuna are the figures of lovemaking couples found on Indian temples (most famously at Khajuraho), though, again, it is nearly always men and women that are depicted writhing together. Lesbian and gay and other forms of sex are rarely depicted. There are renditions of lesbian and gay sex acts, in the Moghul Indian erotic manuals, for instance, and in the Turkish Khamas poems.26

The figures on the temples of Khajuraho or in Rajasthan, they're having a great time. They make love and they *smile*. Sex is portrayed as fun – and the carvings on the Indian temples show lovemaking as intimate, sensual pleasure, unblemished by death-consciousness or sin or guilt.27

The carvings on the temples of India, such as Khajuraho temple, are among the most celebrated examples of erotic art from the history of art, and rightly so. The images of a woman climbing up a man's body, thighs spread, with him deep inside her, and the two of them kissing, are rapturous and totally unforgettable. These stone couplings are among art's most ecstatic images – and the effect is greatly enhanced by the frieze format, by collecting so many figures into the same space. And all of them are making love, or standing there exuding infinite desire.

Some Eastern erotic art is based in sex magic, which is a broad term covering many ways of controlling of sexual energy, involving yoga, meditation, ritual, mantras and yantras. Typical is the conservation of orgasmic energy, where the man does not ejaculate. As Philip Rawson puts it in *The Erotic Art of the East*, '[t]o every Oriental mind, mere orgasm is never the goal of love'.28 Oriental sex magic is, as in Western sex mysticism, a male-made construct, built around masculinist notions of sexuality. The emphasis on not ejaculating is but one indication of the male-favoured slant of sex magic. The vulva or *yoni* is glorified: there are images of *yonis* everywhere in India – in Hyderabad, as a woman lying back with her legs spread wide open, in holy water containers, in coco-de-mer shells split open to serve as a *yoni* image, etc.29

Although the vulva is revered – there is a sculpture showing a man worshipping the *yoni* of the Yogini as Goddess30 – the phallus is the essential component in sex magic. The

26 *Lesbian scene*, 17th century, Koka Shastra, Bibliotheque Nationale, Paris; *Homosexual scene*, Khamsa poems, Ata'î, Turkey, 19th century, Museum of Turkish and Islamic Art, Istanbul
27 Couple from the heaven bands of a temple, Rajasthan, 13th century, sandstone, 11in high; naked ascetic coupling with a Yogini, from Laksmana temple at Khajuraho

28 P. Rawson: *The Erotic Art of the East*, 29.
29 Coco-de-mer, South India, 19th century, 17in high; Icon, 11th century, Hyderabad, stone, from a temple; Holy water container, Bengal, 18th century, copper, 12in long
30 A Madura, South India, 17th century

central image – of the *yoni* and *lingam* – requires the fire, the creative spirit of the male phallic element to set the cosmic, divine energies alight. In Tantrism, the female creative aspect is exalted, either depicted as the *yoni*, or a Goddess, as Philip Rawson explains in *The Art of Tantra*:

> Hindu Tantra proclaims everything, the crimes and miseries as well as the joys, to be the active play of a female creative principle, the Goddess of many forms, sexually penetrated by an invisible, indescribable, seminal male. In ultimate fact He has generated Her for his own enjoyment.[31]

Philip Rawson's last sentence gives the game away: the god creates the Goddess for his own pleasure. The man has his mistress – this is a common set-up, found in so many stories of men who 'keep' women for sex. Everything, it seems, reverts back to the male. Tantric and Taoist sex magic, which aims for multi-orgasmic sex for both partners, reverts back in the end to the man. The male becomes the measure for everything, as in human-(man)-centred Renaissance philosophy, which is the basis of Western philosophy.

In Indian religion there is the figure of the *yakshi*, found on many temples. The *yakshi* figure is supremely sexual, with her enlarged breasts, rounded hips and seductive poses, her body slunk to one side, 'alluring', as art critics would have it. Indeed, the *yakshi* statue on a pillar of the court of the Emperor Kanishka, of the 2nd century A.D. has dark patches on the breasts and between the legs, where people have stroked the statue.[32]

In Indian culture there is a flipside to the phallic *shiva-shakti, yoni-lingam* scenario of mystical lovemaking, and that is the Great Goddess Kali, probably the wildest Goddess in history, in East or West, North or South. The Goddess Kali stands, not sits, on the corpse of the god Shiva. She looms over his erect phallus, brandishing in her many arms a sword to behead/ castrate Shiva. As she makes love to him, she kills him. She is the phallic, Devouring, Terrible Mother.[33] It's easy to see the Goddess Kali in her

31 P. Rawson: *The Art of Tantra*, 11

32 *Pillar with a yakshi*, 2nd century A.D., Kushan period, red sandstone, Bhutesar, Mathura, Indian Museum, Calcutta
33 *Goddess Kali*, Orissa, 19th century, gouache on cloth, 15 x 13in, collection: Ajit Mookerjee, New Delhi; *Icon of the Terrible Goddess Seated in Intercourse on the Corpse of Siva*, Rajasthan, 18th century, brass, 5in high, collection: Ajit Mookerjee

'terrible' aspect as yet another example of male projection of male fear of women, of women as creators and destroyers, as mothers or whores, birthers or murderers.

In Hindu depictions of eroticism, such as that of the Goddess Kali when she is in her devouring or deathly aspect, male fear of women reaches a peak. Kali is a Black Goddess who dances on top of men; she copulates with them and slays them at the same time. Statues of Kali show her sucking the life or essence (sperm or *soma*) out of the male, while she brandishes a sword, fire, skulls and snakes in her many arms.[34] Kali is the 'dark one', the Queen of Blood, who presides over extraordinary blood sacrifices. She is the ultimate manifestation of the 'monstrous feminine', the Freudian 'Terrible Mother', the castrating, devouring, corpse-eating Goddess.[35]

Kali is the manifestation of excessive anxiety about sexuality and relations with women amongst patriarchal religions. What Western religionists did in the Judæo-Christian era was to suppress what Robert Briffault in *The Mothers* calls 'the chthonic aspects of the Queen of Heaven' (III, 183), all of that wild sexuality, producing the Devil, notions of 'sin', 'guilt' and 'evil', witches, and any other scapegoats they could muster.

34 *Kali the Devourer*, copper casting, northern India, modern, Victoria & Albert Museum, London
35 See Heinrich Zimmer: "The Indian World Mother", in *The Mystic Vision, Eranos* Yearbooks, 6, Bollingen Series XXX, 1968

4

Mediæval and Renaissance Sculpture

MEDIÆVAL SEXUALITY

Representations of sexuality in the prehistoric and ancient worlds conform to (largely heterosexual and patriarchal) stereotypes. Women are depicted as mothers (there are countless images of women suckling babies), sometimes as warriors or angry wraiths (Artemis, Athena, Kali), some-times offering their breasts, sometimes as passive virgins (Diana, Mary), or intercessors, or as sexual beings, either voraciously devouring men and beheading/ castrating them, or coupling with them in ecstatic/ spiritual union (Kali, Ishtar, Isis).

Rare it is to find a depiction of eroticism that stands outside the accepted hetero-patriarchal culture of the ancient worlds. One such non-orthodox image of eroticism is found in the sculpted relief of Lilith, four thousand years old, where the Goddess is the 'Lady of Beasts', the Queen of 'wild things', of nature in its unreigned state. Here, Lilith is the denied and suppressed aspect of patriarchal religion, the 'first wife' of Adam, the 'first man'; she is the negative dimension of sexuality, the opposite of motherhood, nurturance and passivity, the opposite of the woman who stays in the home, who rules the domestic side of things. Lilith usurps that masculinist notion of women being 'in their proper place', beside the hearth. Lilith is a Gorgon or Medusa figure, one of the originals of the later witch figure.[36] Lilith throws her sexuality flagrantly into the face of the patriarchal establishment, as Mary Magdalene does later in Christianity. During the Christian era, female wildness and eroticism was suppressed in the West, and focused onto one woman, the Magdalene. Statues of the Renaissance era depict her as a bedraggled, repentant sinner.[37]

MADONNA AND CHILD

In Western art, we find the *Madonna and Child* everywhere; but deeper, perhaps, are the (rarer) images of the primal matriarchal trinity, of child, mother and grandmother. In Catholic art, this means St Anne, the Virgin and Jesus. Leonardo da Vinci painted the trio of holy figures,[38] and there was a cult of St Anne in the Netherlands.[39] Masaccio's image is probably the best known in Renaissance art.[40] But an artwork in Western art that shows just how much patriarchal religion still regards 'Woman' or the 'eternal feminine' or the Goddess as central and crucial to life are those sculptures of the seated Virgin which open up to reveal

38 Spatially, Leonardo da Vinci creates very deep space, deep shadows, sculptural forms, dark tones and glowing lights. His art is 'deep', you might say: artistically, psychologically, emotionally and spiritually. His attempts at sculpture, however, were not as successful as his paintings or drawings. For years he dreamt of his cast horse, planning its manufacture in detail, but the project was never realized, as with so many of Leonardo's other ideas.
39 See Leon Dresen-Coenders, ed: *Saints and She-Devils: Images of Women in the 15th and 16th Centuries*, Rubicon Press 1987; Margaret Whinney: *Early Flemish Painters*, Faber 1968; Jeremy Robinson: *Glorification*, 45f
40 Masaccio: *Madonna and Child with St Anne*, c. 1423, panel, 175 x 103cm, Uffizi, Florence

36 *Lilith*, terracotta relief, Sumer, Larsa dynasty, c. 2000 B.C., Museum Antiker Klein-kunst, Munich
37 Gregor Erhart: *St Mary Magdalene*, early 16th century, polychromed wood, Louvre, Paris

the Christian figures inside: God, crucified Christ and several saints.[41] Here, the Madonna envelops not only all of humanity, as in the *Madonna della Misericordia* paintings, where the Virgin shelters everyone under her cloak,[42] but also all the protagonists of Christian religion. All the mysteries of religion, including the Creator Himself, God, are contained within the body of the Madonna. Here, Mary is the Mother not only of Christ but of God, the Mother behind everything. She is also the church, the very building of the church. You enter her body when you enter a church. The cathedrals of the mediæval era were called 'Notre Dame', Our Lady, and they are explicitly wombs of the Goddess (inside they are hot and dark, and blood mysteries, such as the Mass or Eucharist, occur there, as in wombs. The entrances to cathedrals, those Gothic arches, can be seen as evoking vulvas. The entrances to churches are often narrow slits, shaped like vaginas. The ribbed shapes

41 "*Vierge Ouvrante*", 15th century, painted wood, France, Musée de Cluny, Paris; *Virgin*, c. 14th century, wood covered with linen, gesso and gilt, Germany, Metropolitan Museum of Art, New York
42 See Piero della Francesca: *Madonna della Misericordia*, centre of a polyptych, c. 1460?, 134 x 91cm, Town Hall, Sansepulcro, Italy

around the pointed doorways echo the labia.

The Christian view, then, echoes that of antiquity and prehistory; that, behind everything that male gods may create, is the Goddess. She is the primordial darkness of the universe behind everything, or, in ecological terms, she is the primal sea out of which life grew. These notions are found everywhere, in one form or another, in most ancient societies. 'Woman', the 'eternal feminine', the Goddess is exalted, but again, always in patriarchal terms (that is, the Goddess is always interpreted in patriarchal terms, then as now, always represented within a patriarchal context, and always comes down to us today via patriarchal culture). The Goddess is sexualized still, even in motherhood. As psychologists note, the mother-child relation is the first sexual relation in one's life, and the feminist Andrea Dworkin has brought attention to a 'pornography of pregnancy'. It seems, then, that even in the seemingly positive exaltation of 'women' in mothering, there is sexism, and porn. That, even in the glorification of 'women' as Goddesses, as very space and time itself, as the universe behind God, Jesus, Zeus, etc, there is sexism, stereotyping and patriarchal control at work.

Much of mediæval sculpture pivots around the deep sexism in the mythology of the Fall, for it is the woman who picks the apple and offers it to Adam. From the beginning, in the Judæo-Christian tradition, it is the woman who makes men 'fall'. In some depictions, the sexism is doubled, by having the serpent shown as a snake-woman – the torso of a woman, the legs, like those of a mer-maid, as in Michelangelo Buon-arroti's *Temptation and Expulsion*.[43] The symbol of the half-woman half-fish, still in use today,[44] is another manifestation of patriarchal people's pro-jection of their sexual fears onto women, so that what lies 'below the waist' is feared and objectified as something slimy and fishlike, something dark, from the depths of the unconscious, which is the sea. The mermaid appears sculpted on mediæval churches, some of the mermaids expose their genitals, like the *sheila-na-gig* figure, which again fuses sacred and profane, spiritual and sexual,

desire and fear.[45] The mermaid appears in much of Victorian art, as an image of men's ambivalent views of female sexuality – in E. M. Hale's *Mermaid's Rock* (1894), for instance, or John William Waterhouse's Pre-Raphaelite *A Mermaid* (1901).[46] 'Art is never chaste', said Pablo Picasso, 'if it's chaste it isn't art'.[47]

43 Michelangelo: *Temptation and Expulsion*, 1508-12, fresco, Sistine Chapel, Vatican, Rome
44 See the depiction of the Mary Magdalene in the wilderness sequence of the 1988 Universal film *The Last Temptation of Christ*, 1988, USA

45 See Anthony Weir & James Jerman: *Images of Lust: Sexual Carvings on Mediæval Churches*, B. T. Batsford, 1986, 48ff
46 John William Waterhouse: *A Mermaid*, 1901, 38.5 x 36.3in, Royal Academy of Arts, London; Edward Matthew Hale: *Mermaid's Rock*, 1894, 48 x 78in, City Art Gallery, Leeds
47 P. Picasso, in Dore Ashton, 1972, 15

VENUS AND VIRGIN

The common subject of the Renaissance nude in art was Venus. As the Goddess of Love in mediæval and courtly love poetry, Venus, with her phallic assistant, Cupid, as the cherub armed with bow and arrow, presided over erotic experiences. The poetry of the troubadours, *Minnesängers* and minstrels was distinctly erotic and physical, despite its insistence on manners, etiquette and morals. The aim of courtly love poetry was to get into the bed of the beloved woman, basically. Venus was called upon to aid the lover in this pursuit of the Holy Grail, the mystic cauldron of Woman, her womb. Venus is both Holy Whore and chaste Mistress of Love. She is Love personified. In the Louvre Museum in Paris there's a birth plate (c. 1400), which shows the Goddess Venus hovering over a Tuscan Garden of Love attended by two angels (it's a plate, not a sculpture, but it's definitely an erotic object). Below are six 'famous warriors'. All of them are staring intently at the genitals of the floating Goddess.[48] The lines of sight are marked on the painted salver. The Goddess is depicted in a mandorla, just like the Virgin Mary in *Assumption* images. The centre of the picture is Venus' vulva.[49]

Man is the active one, the doer, the toucher; woman is passive, the acted upon, the touched: see, for instance, Piero di Cosimo's *A Mythological Subject,* where a Pan-figure, a satyr, touches a sleeping woman, who is naked, of course (and in sculpture, too: see Antonio Canova's *Cupid and Venus*).[50]

In the modern era, Eric Gill put the eroticism back into the crucified Christ by drawing his penis, and by drawing attention to the penis, by enlarging it, in many woodcuts and sculptures.[51] Gill's Christs are distinctly eroticized, as for Gill religion and sex were part of the same mystery.

---

48 See Paul Watson: *The Garden of Love in Tuscan Art of the Early Renaissance*, Associated University Press 1979, 17, 23

49 *The Triumph of Venus*, anonymous, birth plate, School of Verona (?), c. 1400, Louvre, Paris
50 Antonio Canova; *Cupid and Venus*, marble, Villa Carlota, Lake Como; Piero di Cosimo: *A Mythological Subject*, panel, 65 x 183cm, National Gallery, London
51 Eric Gill: *Crucifix with Crown of Thorns*, 1922, print, Victoria & Albert Museum

MICHELANGELO BUONARROTI

Michelangelo Buonarroti (1475-1564) is the king of Renaissance sculpture, and of Western sculpture since Classic Greek times. In Michelangelo's art, you sense the urge to out-do everyone else, to be the best. Thus, he looked down on the use of bronze in sculpture as unworthy, because it was too easy to carve the clay and wax models (too easy for him maybe! Pretty darn impossible for the rest of us mere mortals). Only direct carving into stone, it seems, was good enough for him, as for Eric Gill.

Michelangelo Buonarroti dazzles in the range of his expression, in his imagination, in his skill, in his conceptions, from the Sistine Chapel ceiling to the great building projects. The architectural creations by Michelangelo are at the heart of Italian Renaissance state power: the Medici Chapel, the extraordinary Tomb of Lorenzo de' Medici, St Peter's, the cool interior of the Laurenziana Library in Florence, the Capitoline Hill and Palace. In every area Michelangelo seems to excel; it's as if there was nothing that Michelangelo couldn't do. His architecture is distinctive and idiosyncratic. For Linda Murray (in *The High Renaissance*), Michelangelo's technique was to view architecture as sculpture:

> Basically, Michelangelo's architecture is sculpture, in that he models the units as if they were free-standing statues, and the elements as if they≈were the limbs and features of a figure. He concentrates on movement, on a sense of tension and vitality, and every element no matter how small contributes to the enrichment of the surface, and to the contrasts of void and solid, light and shadow. He is endlessly inventive, in planning, in his detail, and in his sense of proportion, and the freedom with which he created a whole vocabulary of new architectural forms was of vital consequence not only to his contemporaries and successors, but also well into the Baroque. (123)

Michelangelo Buonarroti treats buildings as erotic objects in their own right. His architectural creations are very much human-scale, monumental but always related to the human body. The body, especially the male form, is at the heart of Michelangelo's work. His large, muscley bodies seem masculine, in the traditional sense. They are powerful, well-fed bodies, with all the muscles and bones clearly drawn. Michelangelo's bodies are aware of themselves as flesh-and-blood, as organic forms well used to walking, fighting, sleeping, running, bodies that celebrate the active life, much as ancient Greeks celebrated the mobile body in their athletic games.

There is undeniably a deep sensual enjoyment of the male form in the art of Michelangelo Buonarroti – in his *Ignudi* in the Sistine Chapel,[52] for instance, while his *Dying Slaves* are among most voluptuous images of eroticism combined with death in Western art.[53] Michelangelo's slave dies utterly voluptuously, his arms pulled up to expose his body. It is a pose designed to emphasize the eroticism of the nude male form: Michelangelo's *Dying Slave* as an image would be quite at home in gay erotica (indeed, with *David*, it *is* the primary gay male icon). Michelangelo's figures are confident in their nudity and their sexuality. They do not disguise the erotic attraction of their bodies. The huge *David* is at ease with his nakedness and sexuality. Michelangelo's sculptures are full of the spirit of life which is expressed with an assurance of touch and modelling that is in

itself erotic (as well as utterly extraordinary in terms of skill and accomplishment). Michelangelo's sculptures assert their eroticism, whatever the subject, from the superb *Dawn* and *Dusk* of the Medici tomb, to the late *Pietà*.[54]

Michelangelo Buonarroti's figures add angst-ridden and 'modern' tensions – of self, identity, passion and Existential awareness – to the basically life-affirming gestures of ancient Greek sculpture. Michelangelo takes the anonymous, often indifferent eroticism of Greek statues and turns it into something 'modern' or Renaissance, something decidedly individual and subjective. The anguish of (some of) Michelangelo's figures is that of a great artist striving to achieve the Holy Grail or Philosopher's Stone of sculpture, the perfect form, that Neoplatonic impossibility. 'Beautiful' as they are ('beauty' is precisely the right term for Renaissance's Neoplatonic notions of perfection), Michelangelo's statues are often not final, finished forms. They are fluid, aching for the touch of completion which nobody can give them (who would dare to 'finish' a Michelangelo work? Of

52 Michelangelo Buonarroti: *Ignudi*, 1508-10, fresco, Sistine Chapel, Vatican, Rome
53 Michelangelo Buonarroti: *Dying Slave*, 1513, marble, 229cm high, Louvre, Paris

54 Michelangelo Buonarroti: *Tomb of Lorenzo de' Medici*, h. 173, Medici Chapel, Florence; *Pietà*, late 1550s, marble, 226cm high, Florence Cathedral

course, some people in the
modern era have dared).
Besides Michelangelo, other
Renaissance sculptors' works
seem indistinct, weak,
dispassionate or inconsequential
– Lucia della Robbia, Benvenuto
Cellini, Baccio Bandinelli, Giovanni da Bologna, Bartolommeo
Ammanati and Donatello. In
Michelangelo's art, eroticism is
passionately – sometimes
desperately – asserted.

5

Sculpture in the Modern Era

AUGUSTE RODIN AND ARISTIDE MAILLOL

There are a number of great modern artists who are unrestrained in their exaltation of women, a glorification which emerges in their sculptures. Auguste Rodin (1840-1917) is the typical example in the modern era. Of the *Venus de'Medici* Rodin wrote:

> Notice all the voluptuous curvings of the hip...And now, here, the adorable dimples along the loins...It is truly flesh...You would think it moulded by caresses! (in R. Goldwater, 325)

Here, Auguste Rodin speaks of sculpture as the ultimate love object or fetish, fashioned by caresses. Like Pygmalion in ancient times, who made love to the statue he created, Rodin was the classic womaniser artist, who made love to his models physically as well as psychologically and æsthetically. As with Egon Schiele and Eric Gill, his models became his mistresses (such as Camille Claudelm herself a sculptor). Like many artists, Rodin produced erotica for private consumption.

But an enthusiastic eroticism infuses everything Auguste Rodin created. Sculpture such as *The Metamorphoses of Ovid* is typical – it depicts two lovers embracing.[55] The sculpture *Christ and the Magdalene* is more controversial, for it depicts Mary Magdalene sexually embracing the crucified Christ.[56] The image is blasphemous, fusing sex and religion in age-old fashion. This eroticization of Mary Magdalene occurs also in the work of Félicien Rops and Eric Gill. Rodin was an important influence on Gustav Klimt.[57]

In Auguste Rodin's art, figures writhe out of rough marble, and, as their bodies emerge, they are made blissfully smooth, verily 'caressed' into existence, to use Rodin's phrase in his description of the *Venus de'Milo*. 1905's *The Oceanides* is typical, with its use of the chunk of rough stone, as in Michelangelo Buonarroti, which's left unfinished.[58] Rodin's emphasis on the softly rounded limbs, polished smooth in the marble, is not disguised. Like Aristide Maillol and Pierre Renoir, Rodin recreated his love of female limbs time after time.[59]

Love infuses every gesture Aristide Maillol (1861-1944) makes. There are no blemishes, no irregularities, no awkward poses in Maillol's city of women. Each figure is gently curved, softly sculpted. It seems as if male artists have loved creating rounded forms in women since time immemorial – large-hipped women appear not only throughout Western art (in the art of Peter Paul Rubens, Titian, Rembrandt van Rijn, and Henri Matisse), but also in prehistoric imagery, in the faceless "Stone Venuses". These 'large' women are less like potential lovers than mothers. They seem to conform to the Freudian and

55 A. Rodin: *The Metamorphoses of Ovid*, plaster, height 13in
56 A. Rodin: *Christ and the Magdalene*, 1894
57 Gustav Klimt drew women reclining, legs drawn up, masturbating, their hands moving dreamily over their vulvas and clitorises as they look at the viewer. They have titles such as *Reclining Woman*, or *Seated Woman, with Open Legs* (*Reclining Woman*, 1912-8, pencil, 37 x 56cm, Grapische Sammlung Albertina, Vienna). Rodin was the precursor of Klimt's masturbating nudes: Klimt had seen Rodin's erotic drawings, and they inspired him (A. Rodin: *Reclining Female Nude*, c. 1900, pencil, 12.2 x 8in, Musée Rodin, Paris). As with the images of pornography, these are anonymous women, any women, with faces but no names, no characters (G. Klimt: *Seated Woman, with Open Legs*, 1916/7, pencil, 57 x 38cm; *Recumbent Semi-Nude*, 1914/5, blue crayon, 37 x 56cm, Historical Museum, Vienna). These are orgasmic images, celebrating female orgasm.

58 A. Rodin: *The Oceanides*, 1905, Musée Rodin, Paris
59 A visit to the Rodin Museum in Paris is highly recommended. Apart from housing a very fine collection of Rodin's work, it is also a lovely building (and garden) to visit, right in the heart of the City of Light.

Lacanian emphasis on the mother as the male's first lover. The ample women in the art of Pablo Picasso, Henri Matisse, Auguste Rodin and Aristide Maillol are motherly, so clearly the mother figure of psychoanalysis, and the Goddess of ancient mythology.

HENRI MATISSE

For Henri Matisse (1869-1954), art is a celebration of life. No other of the great modern artists is as joyful as Matisse, except perhaps Paul Klee. Matisse exudes joy, throughout the different phases of his art, from paintings such as *The Joy of Living*,[60] which is a modernist pastoral scene, with people dancing, kissing, playing music, to the late cut-outs, which are really joyful, really exuberant.[61]

Henri Matisse's art is erotic in the sense that being out in the open air is erotic. His art is erotic in the sense that swimming can be erotic, or dancing, or playing music. Simple pleasures. You might see Matisse's joyful art as religious as well as erotic. That joy, seen in Existential terms, is both religious and erotic. As Matisse wrote: '[a]ll art worthy of the name is religious. Be it a creation of lines and colours; if it is not religious it does not exist.'[62]

For Henri Matisse, the site of this religious view is the human figure, and in male art that means the female figure.

60 H. Matisse: *The Joy of Living*, 1905-6, oil, 175 x 240cm, Barnes Foundation, Merion, Pennsylvania
61 Matisse: *Nude with Flowing Hair*, 1952, paper cut-out, 108 x 80cm, private collection, Paris
62 H. Matisse, 1951, in Jack D. Flam: *Matisse on Art*, E.P. Dutton, New York 1978, 140

Matisse writes:

> What interests me most is neither still life nor land-scape but the human figure. It is that which best permits me express my almost religious awe towards life.[63]

Henri Matisse pinpoints the role of the (female) figure in much of art: it is the site of religious feelings, as something to worship. Clearly, this worshipping of the (female) figure is sexist. It defines the dualities and paradoxes of art: consisting of the male artist, the female model; the male gaze, the passive female; the male man-pulator, the female victim.

PABLO PICASSO

Aristide Maillol, Auguste Rodin, Jules Pascin and Henri Matisse are relatively unambiguous in their adoration of the female form. Their art is partly an expression of male lust, and it admits its own lust. In Pablo Picasso's (1881-1973) art, sexual acts can be tender, as some commentators have noted,[64] but more typically they are brutal, and, in the late drawings, desperate. Picasso's treatment of women is often savage: there is as much loathing as there is love in many of his depictions of women in his sculptures.[65] In Picasso's erotic art, we find the age-old connections that men make between sex and death, between women and sex and death, as Janet Hobhouse observes.

> The output and intensity of Picasso's late work have often been attributed to the artist's notorious fear of death. If so, the image he contacted again and again as a source of energy and safety from mortal threat was emphatically female and sexual. The erotic con-tent is unlike anything else in his art, in its insistence,

---

63 H. Matisse: "Notes of a Painter", in J. Flam, 38

64 Robert Rosenblum: "Picasso and the Anatomy of Eroticism", 338
65 P. Picasso: *Woman in Garden*, 1929-30, bronze, 210cm high, Picasso Collection; *Woman's Head*, 1931, iron painted white, 10cm high, Picasso Collection

urgency and power. All reference to himself and his work is made in terms of the female, who seem to be endowed with the properties of creativity and immortality. (133)

For Pablo Picasso, then, as for Egon Schiele, Gustave Moreau, Leonardo da Vinci, Auguste Rodin and any number of artists, women are the site, the vehicle, the vessel or the space where sexuality, death, being, desire and fear meet and merge.

HANS BELLMER

One of the most bizarre modern artists, and one of the most violent, is the Surrealist Hans Bellmer (1902-75). His *Doll* is a deeply disturbing sculpture of the female body. The artist delighted in wrenching the *Doll* into all sorts of impossible contortions. In *The Doll*, Bellmer wrote a veritable summary of the erotic pleasure of the artist and viewer, the consumer who sucks up lasciviously the object:

> To adjust the joints to each other, coax the limbs, head and torso into winsome poses, then run the eye and hand over these softly dipping vales, relish the pleasure of the shapely curves, give them a pretty turn or with blood-rousing gusto wrench them out of shape.[66]

Hans Bellmer's *Doll* is the ultimate sex object, the ultimate fetish, a precursor of the blow-up doll of sex toys. Bellmer speaks of penetrating through layers until some core or womb is reached (a classic expression of modern Existential philosophy – seeking truth as penetration). His drawings and photographs are full of fingers or penises being thrust into orifices, into mouths, vaginas,

66 H. Bellmer: *The Doll*, 1934, in Picon, 153

anuses. Bellmer is obsessed with penetration. He drew penises entering vaginas many times.[67] Bellmer's art is the ultimate Surrealist transformative act, as vulvas turn into penises, and buttocks become the glans of the penis. Bellmer's drawings depict a continuous orgy, utterly pornographic, a feast of penetration and pleasure.[68] Faces are often left out: Bellmer's drawings create a frenzy of limbs and torsos, sometimes just buttocks and groins. 'All my work is erotic – it always has been', said Bellmer.[69] He is distinctly a part of that European intellectual tradition stemming from the Marquis de Sade and Charles Baudelaire. In Bellmer's philosophy, the Sadeian ethic of sex = death is exploited in endless variations. As Geza Roheim wrote, '[d]eath is coitus and coitus is death'.[70] This psychotic view, so mistaken, is central to much of modern, intellectual, bohemian art, from de Sade to Jasper Johns. Bellmer's art, and that of Surrealist artists such as René Magritte, Salvador Dali, Max Ernst, André Breton, Paul Éluard and Pablo Picasso, subscribes to this view of sex = death.

Hans Bellmer depicts nothing but the sex act. He is unusual in this. Other artists produced erotic art as part of their whole art: Eric Gill, David Hockney, Félicien Rops, and J.M.W. Turner, but Bellmer focuses entirely on genitals and sex. Very few artists have been so determined in their depiction of eroticism. It permeates every aspect of Bellmer's art. And it is a pornographic art. Bellmer's art, like the major erotic text of Surrealist and modern European art, Bataille's *The Story of the Eye*, is pornography masquerading as erotic or high art.

---

67 See H. Bellmer's *A Sade*, etchings, 1961
68 H. Bellmer: *A Woman From the Back*, coloured pencils, 30 x 37cm, private collection; *Traite de la Morale*, 1968, etching, collection: the artist, Paris
69 Quoted in Peter Webb, 369
70 G. Roheim: *Animism, Magic and the Divine King*, quoted in P. Webb

6

Eric Gill

Eric Gill (1882-1940) is one of the major erotic artists of the modern era. For him, eroticism was a vital part of life, and should be openly displayed in art. He moved from nudes to Madonna and Childs easily and simply: sex and religion were part of the same mystery for him. Gill built eroticism into most of his depictions of people. He continually drew attention to a figure's genitals. He was obsessed, for instance, by pubic hair. He was also fascinated by the penis, particularly his own.

Despite being open about sexuality, Eric Gill did keep some of his art secret. There are private drawings in the collections of the Victoria and Albert Museum and the British Museum in London, which depict, for instance, some seventy drawings of penises. The drawings are careful anatomical studies, complete with measurements. Some of the phallic drawings show Gill masturbating, or on a bed, or in a mirror. Sometimes the drawings of penises enter the critically acceptable arena, as in the prints entitled The 'Most Precious Ornament'.[71] Gill was meticulous in his recording of sexual activities. His private writings reveal a secret code for

71 E. Gill: The 'Most Precious Ornament', 1937, print, Victoria & Albert Museum

'acts' such as anal intercourse. He also 'experimented' with dogs, incest and group sex.[72] So many male artists have drawn, painted or sculpted their penises: Jasper Johns, Egon Schiele, Eric Gill, Pablo Picasso, Hans Bellmer, Robert Rauschenberg, Salvador Dali, and Tom of Finland.

In Eric Gill's art we find all the usual tensions of Western art: the relation between women and fertility, agriculture, nature and nurture; the constant eroticization of people, the reduction to sexual identities; the idea that sex can instigate a social and spiritual renewal or revolution.

Eric Gill's sense of sexuality is distinctly heterosexual, as with other campaigners for sexual liberty, such as D.H. Lawrence. It is useful to look at Gill, because Gill's views on sexuality have many affinities with other modern artists and thinkers, such as Wilhelm Reich, Georges Bataille, André Breton, Salvador Dali, Egon Schiele, Gustav Klimt, Hans Bellmer, Henri Matisse, Pablo Picasso, Gustave Moreau and Félicien Rops.

Like Bertie Lawrence, Gill exalted women and the idea of 'woman'; like Lawrence, Gill secretly admired the male form: in both Gill and Lawrence's

work there is an emphasis on the phallus, the symbolic erect phallus, which meant religious rebirth, as Lawrence evoked it in *The Escaped Cock,* a novella of the 'phallic' man, the new Adam. Lawrence's testament of erotic revolution, *Lady Chatterley's Lover*, was admired by Gill, and Gill illustrated it, depicting Mellors and Connie making love, kneeling in grass.[73]

Like Lorenzo, Eric Gill believed in the holiness of sex and the holiness of art. Sex, art and religion were a continuum for Gill, as for Lawrence and others, such as Gustav Klimt, Michelangelo Buonarroti, Salvador Dali and Pablo Picasso.

In most of his religious-erotic images, Eric Gill is wildly phallic and heterosexual. The woman is definitely 'passive' and the male is 'active'. The woman, as Earth, 'receives', while the man does the deed. The woman 'gives' herself, gives of herself, in Eric Gill's art, as in his series of erotic prints illustrating the most sensual poem in the *Bible*, the *Song of Songs*, where the woman offers her breasts to the man.[74] According to Marina Warner (in *Alone of All Her Sex*), the *Song of Songs* is immensely erotic: '[t]here has never been a

72 See Fiona MacCarthy, 1989

73 Eric Gill: *Lady C*, 1931, print, 2nd state, Victoria & Albert Museum
74 E. Gill: *Ibi Dabo Tibi*, 1925, Victoria & Albert Museum

more intense communication of the experience of desire' (126). The *Cantia Canticarum* allows for depictions of unbridled sensuality. The nuptial imagery allows for artists to be as sensual as they dare in a religious setting. Gill's merging of eroticism with Catholicism operates within the mystical tradition of Catholicism, as espoused by mystics such as St Bernard, Jan van Ruysbroeck, St Theresa and St John of the Cross. It is a wild and ecstatic mysticism which describes religious bliss in very sensual terms.

Eric Gill's art reveals the same power relations as depicted in high art, low art, porno, advertizing, TV and the media: male power is dominant, and sex revolves around the phallus. There is no clitoris, for instance, in Gill's art. Similarly, D.H. Lawrence condemned those 'cocksure' women who took control and employed 'clitoral sex', as he portrayed it in his 1920s novel *The Plumed Serpent*.

What's limiting about Eric Gill's art, as with the work of Pablo Picasso, Hans Bellmer, or Egon Schiele, is that it continually emphasizes the genitals, leaving so much out – sociopolitical considerations, for example, or issues of race, class, economy, homosexuality,

etc. Gill's sculptures bear this out: his acrobats, for example, are women holding their legs wide open, exposing their vulvas.[75]

Indeed, the very reason that Eric Gill turned to sculpture, so he says, was sexual: his wife was pregnant with their third daughter, Joanna, and because of the 'enforced abstinence', i. e., he couldn't have sex during her pregnancy, he turned to stone carving.

> ...as I couldn't have all I wanted in one way I determined to see what I could do about it in another – I fashioned a woman of stone. Up to that time, I had never made what is called an "erotic" drawing of any sort and least of all in so laborious a medium as stone. And so, just as on the first occasion when with immense planning and scheming, I touched my lover's lovely body, I insisted on seeing her completely (no peeping between the uncut pages, so to say), so my first erotic drawing was not on the back of an envelope but a week or so's work on a decent piece of hard stone. I say this seems praiseworthy, and so it is... no one would guess the fervours which conditioned its making. But there it was; it was a carving of a

75 E. Gill: *Splits II*, 1923, bath stone with added colour, Harry Ransom Humanities Research Center, University of Texas, Austin

naked young woman and if I hadn't very much wanted a naked young woman, I don't think I should ever have done it. Lord, how exciting! – and not merely touching and seeing but actually making her. I was responsible for her very existence and her every form straight from my heart. A new world opened before me. My Lord!... A new alphabet – the word was made flesh. (158-9)

Eric Gill tells this story in his Autobiography quite flatly, as if there is nothing wrong with it. Feminists such as Andrea Dworkin or Benoite Groult, though, would hack him to pieces for this. He couldn't have sex, poor thing, so he turned to sculpture!

Some of Eric Gill's finest works are sculptures: in *Divine Lovers* he produced an image of two people clasping each other in an embrace of complete closeness. There is no space between the lovers: Constantin Brancusi had done the same thing in his *Kiss* sculptures, which flattened the two bodies so they could be merged together completely. Brancusi recognized the anatomical problem, saying that kissing upright is difficult, because of the nose. His lovers are noseless: they simply kiss, eternally joined together,

veritably an expression in stone of the Platonic concept of two-as-one, of twin souls joined as one.[76]

The relief sculpture *Ecstasy* (Tate Gallery) was originally entitled *Fucking* by Eric Gill. It was carved in 1911, and shows two people making love standing up, the man's knees bent, his arms around her head, the woman's legs either side of his, her arms clasping him tightly. The sculpture has a number of details in the limbs – the muscles of the man's legs – but is an idealized portrayal.

Another relief sculpture, entitled *Lovers Relief* (1921, Texas) is also called *'Fucking'*, and is related to *Ecstasy*. Here, the two standing figures are all entwined limbs, the woman with her left leg raised high, which the man grips under his right arm, his left arm wrapped around her back, their heads pressed together. The genitals are prominent here – the penis and balls especially.[77]

The sculpture *Lovers* is particularly similar to the carvings on Indian temples (the *maithuna* figures, famously at

76 Constantin Brancusi: *The Kiss*, 1907-8, stone, 11in high, Museum of Art, Craiova, Romania; see also Eric Shanes: *Brancusi*, 19f
77 In another 1921 *Lovers Relief*, a stone-incised relief, the woman clings to a standing man, thighs clasping his torso, her buttocks spread to reveal his genitals.

Khajuraho, which Eric Gill
admired). The man is on top,
the woman is underneath,
accepting everything.[78]

By far the most common
subject in Eric Gill's sculpture,
however, was religious (and
Christian): the nudes, acrobats,
contortionists and divine lovers
tupping may receive more
attention in art criticism, but the
religious and Catholic sculptures
are more numerous: there are
Depositions, St Sebastians,
Annunciations, Crucifixions, Holy
Faces, Mary Magdalenes, angels,
crucifixes, memorials,
headstones, altarpieces, many
Madonna and Childs, and of
course the Stations of the Cross
series.

---

78 Except in rare instance, such as
the sculpted relief Votes for
Women, which Fiona MacCarthy
describes, oddly, as 'both very pure
and very shocking' (1989, 104).

7

Constantin Brancusi

ESSENCE

Constantin Brancusi (1976-1957) is one of the most erotic of all sculptors. His sculpture is more erotic than that of Gianlorenzo Bernini, Antonio Canova, Donatello, Louise Bourgeois and Judy Chicago. For some other commentators, Brancusi is the key sculptor of the modern period – not Auguste Rodin, Henry Moore, Pablo Picasso, Barbara Hepworth or others.[79] Brancusi is diametrically opposed, æsthetically, to Rodin, and quite different from Naum Gabo; his art has some affinities with Henri Gaudier-Brzeska – it is interesting to compare Gaudier-Brzeska's heavy, gaunt *Standing Birds* with Brancusi's slim *Birds in Space* series.[80]

[79] Friedrich Teja Bach: *Brancusi*, Du Mont, Cologne 1987; Barbu Brezianu: *Brancusi: A Retrospective Exhibition*, Muzeul de Arta R.S.R, Bucharest, 1970; Petry Comarnescu, Mircea Eliade & Constantin Noica: *Brancusi, Introduction Témoignages*, Arted, Paris 1982; Sidney Geist, 1983, also *Brancusi: The Sculpture and Drawings*, Harry N. Abrams, New York 1975; Pontus Hulten, Natalia Dumitresco & Alexandre Istrati: *Brancusi*, Harry N. Abrams, New York 1987; David N. Lewis, 1974; W. Tucker, 1974.

[80] H. Gaudier-Brzeska: *Standing Birds*, 1914, Museum of Modern Art, New York; Brancusi: *Bird in Space*, or *Yellow Bird*, 1923-4, yellow marble, 45.8in high, base; one marble, one oak and two limestone sections, 57.2in high, Philadelphia Museum of Art

Constantin Brancusi's eroticism stems from his superb forms, which are delicious in their form, shape, texture and feel. Brancusi develops all of the erotic formal aspects of sculpture to their extreme. He reduces organic, natural forms to 'essences'. Yet he maintained that his sculpture was not abstract. Wassily Kandinsky said that abstraction = realism,[81] and this is true of Brancusi, who vigorously stressed the realism of his works:

> They are imbeciles who call my work abstract; that which they call abstract is the most realist, because what is real is not the exterior form but the idea, the essence of things.[82]

It is a quest for things, for things-in-themselves, as modern Existential philosophers such as Jean-Paul Sartre and Martin Heidegger put it, the 'thingness' of Rainer Maria Rilke. The 'things' are organic forms, not abstract ideas or abstruse conceptualizations. As Henry Moore wrote, a 'sculptor is a person obsessed with the form and shape of things...the shape

of anything and everything.'[83]

Though Constantin Brancusi denies the urge towards abstraction, he founds his sculpture on the abstractions of Platonism. It is Plato's ideal philosophy that influences much of Brancusi's sculpture. Plato's notion of Ideal Forms and essences excited Brancusi. Reducing his art further and further, Brancusi aimed to get as close as possible to the 'essence of the thing'. It is a process of Neoplatonic purification, as Dorothy Adlow noted when she visited his studio in 1925:

> Brancusi has purified his sculpture of every attracting feature. He has swept out of his plan every motive that might distract him or the observer from what he considers the central idea...He has tried to make of his sculpture a working philosophy. He calls it the philosophy of Plato.[84]

There is a parallel to this æsthetic purification in poets and novelists. French writers, such as Stendhal, Gustave Flaubert, André Gide and Samuel Beckett spoke of wanting to clear away all the garbage that gets in the way of purity of expression. Beckett,

81 Wassily Kandinsky: "On the Problem of Form", Der Blaue Reiter, R. Piper, Munich 1912, and in H. Chipp, 162
82 C. Brancusi, in "Propos de Brancusi", Prisme des Arts, Paris, no. 12, May 1957, 6

83 In Philip James & Henry Moore: Henry Moore on Sculpture, Viking Press, New York 1971, 60
84 Dorothy Adlow, 1927, 37f

for instance, steadily pared away his language, moving from the relatively conventional novel forms of books such as *Mercier and Camier* through the reduced vocabulary and syntax of *The Trilogy* to the severely reduced poesie of *Company* and *Still*. For some artists, nothing must get in the way of expression of the idea or emotion. As Dorothy Adlow wrote in 1927:

> It is the *idea* that should be related, that is all. Everything else is superfluous... Brancusi is not satisfied with the things of the moment, he looks out for what is true of all time.

Henry Moore, who admired Constantin Brancusi, like so many other major modern artists (Amedeo Modigliani, Frank Stella, Donald Judd, Carl Andre, Barbara Hepworth and Andy Goldsworthy), wrote of Brancusi's search for pure, organic form:

> Since the Gothic, European sculpture has become overgrown with moss, weeds — all sorts of surface excrescences which completely concealed shape. It has been Brancusi's special mission to get rid of this overgrowth, and to make us once more shape-conscious. To do this he has had to concentrate on very simple direct shapes, to keep his sculpture, as it were, one-cylindered, to refine and polish a single shape to a degree almost too precious. Brancusi's work, apart from its individual value, has been of historical import-ance in the development of contemporary sculpture.[85]

Simplicity, as Constantin Brancusi and many artists have said, was the key: but it is a mystical simplicity, that arises out of the sculpture's materials:

> Simplicitly is not an object-ive in art, but one achieves simplicity despite oneself by entering into the real sense of things.[86]

For Mircea Eliade, a fellow Romanian, Constantin Brancusi's talent was one of 'interioriz-ation', a mythic descent simul-taneously into himself, into his personal and national past, and into mythic forms. Eliade writes in an important 1967 essay on Brancusi:

> Brancusi's encounters with the creations of the Paris-ian avant-garde and those of the archaic world (Africa) triggered a process

---

85 Henry Moore: "The Sculptor Speaks", *The Listener*, XVIII, 18 August 1937, 449
86 C. Brancusi: "Résponses de Brancusi; Aphorismes; Histoire de brigands", *This Quarter*, I, no. I, Paris 1925

of "interiorization," a journey back toward a world that was both secret and unforgettable because it was simultaneously that of childhood and that of the imagination...he set himself to "interiorizing," as it were, his own vital experience. So that he succeeded in rediscovering the "presence-in-the-world" specific to archaic man...thanks to the process of "interiorization"... and the anamnesis that followed it, Brancusi succeeded in "seeing the world" in the same way as the creators of prehistoric, ethnic, or folk-art master-pieces. He rediscovered, in a way, the presence-in-the-world that enabled those anonymous artists to create their own plastic universe within a space that had nothing whatever to do with, for example, the space of classical Greek art.[87]

The endpoint of Constantin Brancusi's quest for the 'essence of things' was a mystical sculpture. Although he declined to talk in religious terms of his art, it is distinctly mystical. Some of Brancusi's statements admit to a mystical solidarity with materials and sculptures:

> I am no longer of this world. I am far from myself, I am no longer a part of my own person. I am within the essence of things them-selves.[88]

87 Mircea Eliade: "Brancusi and Mythology", in *Témoignages sur Brancusi*, by Peru Comarnesco, Mircea Eliade and Ionel Jianou, Arted, Paris, 1967, and in M. Eliade: *Ordeal By Labyrinth: Conversations with Claude-Henri Rocquet*, tr. Derek Coltman, University of Chicago Press, Chicago 1984, 195-6

88 Quoted in David Lewis, 1937, 43.

RILKE, RODIN AND SCULPTURE

The German poet Rainer Maria Rilke (1875-1926), who worked with Auguste Rodin, widely regarded as the 'father' of modern sculpture, wrote illuminatingly of surfaces and essences. Of the transformation of his art in his *Neue Gedichte*, which was a breakthrough, Rilke wrote that 'it had to arrive at the essence.'[89] And in a fragment of his greatest work, the *Duino Elegies*, Rilke writes of 'the infinite thereness of statues', a thought that many artists, from Michelangelo Buonarroti to Constantin Brancusi, or philosophers from Plotinus to Friedrich Nietzsche would agree with.[90]

Rainer Maria Rilke's notion of 'Kunst-Ding' or innerness or thingness, also called *innigkeit*, has much in common with Constantin Brancusi's notion of 'the essence of things'. The poet's task, Rilke said, was to capture the 'thingness' of an object, without ornamentation or rhetoric, rather in the manner that Paul Cézanne did with his still life paintings. Brancusi's aim is also that of Rilke.

Rainer Maria Rilke's spatial mysticism is a poetic, lingual equivalent of Constantin Brancusi's sense of a spatial, Platonic essence. For Rilke, expressing a sense of space meant the poem could expand the Within outwards, towards the what Rilke called "Open": Brancusi too speaks of mystical openness, though he calls it 'infinity'. Brancusi's 'endless column' series explores a Rilkean 'openness'. In poems such as 'The Panther', 'Archaic Torso of Apollo' and 'Blue Hydrangea', Rilke tried to present things as they really were.

Rainer Maria Rilke's quest for mystical innerness and Constantin Brancusi's goal of mythic interiorization have affinities with Martin Heidegger's notion of being and presence, with Joyce's idea of the æsthetic 'epiphany' of authentic art, with Lawrence Durrell's poetic concept of the heraldic 'sigil' or signature of a thing, and with *sammadassana* of Zen Buddhism. D.T. Suzuki writes of Zen philosophy thus:

> Seeing is experiencing, seeing things in their states of suchness (*tathata*) or is-ness. Buddha's whole philosophy comes from this "seeing", this

89 R. Rilke, letter to 'une amie', 3, February 1923, quoted in R. Rilke, 1987, 299
90 R. Rilke, quoted in ib., 215

experiencing.[91]

Constantin Brancusi speaks of a similar mystical 'seeing', where the viewer of his sculptures sees not simply beautiful surfaces, but essences. He writes:

> What is real is not the external form, but the essence of things. Starting from this truth it is impossible for anyone to express anything luscious and real by imitating its exterior surface.[92]

Constantin Brancusi starts with the essence, and ends up with his severely reduced but open forms – the birds, heads, fish, eggs, lovers and columns.

Searching for the essence, Constantin Brancusi nevertheless bases his art on natural forms, on elemental forms. The material that makes the sculpture itself helps in the quest for the essence of things. The final form of the sculpture is, Brancusi believes, somehow buried in the material, whether it is stone, marble, wood or bronze. Brancusi has a *participation mystique* with his sculpture's materials, much as primitive or prehistoric societies had a *participation mystique* with nature and the Earth. Each material has its own feel, tensions, problems. Somehow, the material 'renders up' the final form. 'Each material has its own life,' Brancusi says.[93] The 'essence' must be brought out by the artist, as Brancusi asserts:

> The natural element in sculpture means allegorical thinking, symbol, sacred-ness or the search for essences hidden in the material and not the photographic reproduction of external appearances.[94]

Constantin Brancusi's sculptures bear out how successful he was in pursuing the Holy Grail of Platonic purity and mystical essence. His career was one whole quest for the essence of form. 'Everything I do is a seeking after form,' he said in 1949.[95]

When we look at his works, they seem to be so *right*, so spot on in their depiction of their subject. Thus, those

91 D.T. Suzuki: *The Basics of Buddhist Philosophy*, Allen & Unwin 1957, quoted in Richard Woods, ed, *Understanding Mystic-ism*, Athlone Press 1980, 126
92 Quoted in *Brancusi,* catalogue, Brummer Gallery, New York 1926
93 C. Brancusi, quoted in Dorothy Dudley: "Brancusi", *Dial*, 82, February 1927, 124
94 C. Brancusi, in Petre Pandrea: "The Laws of Craiova", *Portraits and Controversies*, Bucharest, Romania 1946, vol. I, 120
95 Quoted in Russell Warren Howe: "The Man Who Doesn't Like Michelangelo", *Apollo*, 49, May 1949, 124

sculptures based on fishes, birds, heads, cocks, seals, capture the 'essence' of their subject so brilliantly.[96] Barbara Hepworth, one of many sculptors who found Brancusi an inspiration, wrote of her 1932 visit to Brancusi's Paris studio:

In Brancusi's studio I encountered the miraculous feeling of eternity mixed with beloved stone and stone dust... The simplicity and dignity of the artist; the inspiration of the dedicated workshop with great millstones used as bases for classical forms; inches of accumulated dust and chips on the floor; the whole great studio filled with soaring forms and still, quiet forms, all in a state of perfection in purpose and loving execution, whether they were in marble, brass or wood – all this filled me with a sense of humility hitherto unknown to me.[97]

96 C. Brancusi: *Fish*, 1932, white marble, 5.3 x 16.8 x 1.1in, base, a mirror, diameter 17in, on oak, 24in high, Philadelphia Museum of Art; *Fish*, 1924, polished bronze, 5 x 16.5 x 1.8in, base, a polished steel disk, diameter 19.6in, Museum of Fine Arts, Boston; *The Cock*, 1935, polished bronze, 40.8in high, base of stone & wood sections, 76.1in, Brancusi studio, Musée National d'Art Moderne, Paris; *Golden Bird*, 1919, polished bronze, 38in high, base of stone and wood, 48.1in, Arts Club of Chicago; *The Seal*, 1943, blue-grey marble, 43.8in high, Musée National d'Art, Paris; *Head of a Woman*, 1910-c. 1925, white marble, 11.2in, private collection

97 Barbara Hepworth: *Barbara Hepworth, Carvings and Drawings*, Lund Humphries 1952

FISH

Constantin Brancusi's *Fish,* in marble or bronze, are a series of gorgeous objects, with their sleek bodies. They are supremely erotic sculptures, not least because they aim to be the mystic essence of animals that swim in the sea. There's an erotic dimension to fish, as many artists have long known, symbolic of the fecund oceans, the ocean being, quite literally, the womb of life on Earth. Brancusi in his *Fish* sculptures aimed to capture what it was that was special about fish. He said:

> When you see a fish, you do not think of its scales, do you? You think of its speed, its floating, flashing body seen through water...I've tried to express just that...I want just the flash of its spirit.[98]

The *Fish* sculptures are often set on mirrors, perhaps to hint at water (or the other realm they inhabit). The circular mirrors, like all circular forms in the art of Constantin Brancusi, hint at cosmic dimensions, representing the Great Round of existence, the cosmos itself, and those spherical forms from which all life comes: the circular ocean, cells, wombs, hearts,

planets. The 1926 *Fish* sculpture is set on an elaborate base.[99] The importance of the base upon which sculpture rests is crucial for Brancusi. His bases are very distinctive, setting him instantly apart from all other sculptors (this's brought home especially when you see a group of Brancusi works in one space). The Brancusi base is and is not part of the sculpture. William Tucker writes of the Brancusi base in *The Language of Sculpture:*

> The base is at once physical, in terms of support; visual, in terms of presenting the object at proper level; and symbolic, in terms of the objects' relation with the world. The bases are not works of art, but are as worth consideration as many works of art in view of the way they perform an exact ancillary function. Most of Brancusi's sculpture is modest in size, physically unobtrusive. Yet its presence is enormous even from a considerable distance, and where surrounded by the work of other artists. The Brancusi is marked off by its carved and constructed base as being not only different from other things in general, but as being different from all other sculpture, *a completely new order of*

98 C. Brancusi, in Malvina Hoffman, 1939, 52

99 C. Brancusi: *Fish*, 1926, polish bronze, 5in, private collection

object. (57)

William Tucker is absolutely right here, noting how Constantin Brancusi's forms leap out at you, how they make their presence felt immediately when surrounded by all manner of other works (visit a gallery or museum, and you see this distinctiveness straight away, even with the stiff competition of Pablo Picasso, Max Ernst, Auguste Rodin and Alberto Giacometti). Brancusi's art is, as Tucker writes, 'the antithesis of Rodin's – private, silent, withdrawn, morally neutral' (131). Despite being 'private, silent, withdrawn, morally neutral', Brancusi's sculptures have immense authority and presence. As Tucker argues, it is precisely this intimacy ('interiority', as Mircea Eliade calls it) that makes Brancusi's works so powerful (131-2).

There are inherent paradoxes in Constantin Brancusi's æsthetics. For example, Platonism emphasizes the 'idea' or 'essence'. Yet these 'essences' or 'ideas' must be manifested in flesh-and-blood bodies and organic forms. Platonism could not reconcile these two things – spirit and flesh – successfully, and neither could Christianity, even after two thousand years of hacking away at the problem. For, while Brancusi emphasizes 'essence', what we see in his sculptures are highly polished, highly worked surfaces, an emphasis on beautiful surfaces, on smoothness and sleekness. Brancusi's sculptures, like those of the Minimal artists Donald Judd or Ronald Bladen or Carl Andre, are smooth and slick. Roughness, where it appears, as in Brancusi's stone bases and pedestals, is similarly worked and carved, integrated stylishly into the design. Even as they exalt idealism and 'essence', then, Brancusi's sculptures are caught up in all kinds of problems to do with expression, manifestation, formalism, material and intention.

MASCULINE/ FEMININE

There is, for instance, an intrinsic sexism (or genderism, or gender duality) in Constantin Brancusi's treatment of male and female, masculine and feminine forms. His *Torso of a Young Woman III* is, typically, a softly rounded volume, like a vase, recalling the eternal and mythical association of women with vessels, of women as something to be filled.[100] Brancusi's *Torso of a Young Woman* is supremely stereotypical, sexist (from a second wave feminist point-of-view).

The male *Torso*, on the other hand, is, as you might expect, phallically upright. Indeed, it looks like a phallus.[101] Interestingly, however, Brancusi claimed that '[n]ude men in sculpture are not as beautiful as toads.'[102] Further sexism occurs in Brancusi's *Adam and Eve*, where people are reduced to genitals, once again. So Eve is a mouth and vagina, and Adam is a phallus and testicles.[103]

Constantin Brancusi's sculptures of women turn out to be as sexist as any portraits of depictions of the female (nude) body by artists such as Henri Matisse, Peter Paul Rubens, Jean Dominique Ingres, Pablo Picasso, etc. Brancusi's *Madame Pogany* and *Princess X* are the usual rounded, 'feminine' forms, while works such as *The White Negress* and *Blond Negress* stray too close to racism.[104]

When Constantin Brancusi exhibited the curved bronze *Princess X* in 1920, Pablo Picasso – or was it Henri Matisse – said: 'Voici, le phallus!' Indeed, *Princess X* does look phallic.[105] But the art object, sculpted, painted or otherwise is a kind of displaced phallus, a fetish object turned into 'high' culture. The

100 C. Brancusi: *Torso of a Young Woman III*, 1925, onyx, 10.4in, Musée National d'Art Moderne, Paris
101 C. Brancusi :*Torso of a Young Man*, after 1924, bronze, 18.4 x 12 x 6.7in, Cleveland Museum of Art
102 C. Brancusi, quoted in *This Quarter*, op.cit.

103 C. Brancusi: *Adam and Eve*, 1916-21, chestnut and oak, 89in high, base of limestone, 5.2in, Guggenheim, New York
104 Brancusi: *Madame Pogany III*, 1939, white marble, 17.8in high, Philadelphia Museum of Art;*Princess X*, 1916, polished bronze, 23 x 16.5 x 9in high, base of stone, 7.2in high, Philadelphia Museum of Art; *The White Negress*, 1923, white marble, 19in high, base of marble, 6.4in high, Philadelphia Museum of Art; *Blond Negress II*, 1933, polished bronze, 15.8in high, base of marble and limestone and two wood sections, 55.5in high, MOMA, New York
105 It is featured on the cover of a survey of erotic art (see Peter Webb's book).

art object is that item made to provide pleasure. Most of sculpture is designed and crafted as a 'beautiful' object, to use that key word of Platonic philosophy. Sculptures are 'The Beautiful'. Sculptures are 'beauty' concretized, eroticism made into bronze, marble and stone. The history of sculpture is the history of anal/ oral/ genital touches of pleasure, self-reflexive gestures where artists touch objects physically and, later, viewers drink them up visually, forbidden by the ropes of museums and guards to actually touch the sculpture itself. The sculpted object is indeed the erotic object *par excellence* in art. It is the phallus endlessly caressed by the eyes, in Lacanian, scopic, scopophillic, voyeuristic pleasure. As Julia Kristeva says, 'isn't art the fetish *par excellence*, one that badly camouflages its archeology?'[106]

WORLD EGG

Constantin Brancusi produced a number of sculptures that are pure phalluses, seen from one, religious, viewpoint. In Hindu culture, there is a holy object called Savayambhu, meaning the 'self-originated', a phallic emblem of cosmic energy. They are egg-shaped stones which are worshipped in Indian religion. They are the cosmic phallus, the *lingam*, and are associated with the World Egg or Cosmic Egg.[107] The Eggs of Brahman or Svayambhu *lingams* are phallic energy associated with cosmic/ religious solidified into stone. Typically seven inches long, these Hindu phallic stones are very much like the human penis. Indeed, as Philip Ransom notes in *The Art of Tantra*, the cosmic egg-stones have 'surface-divisions' that imitate those 'on the actual male penis'.[108]

Constantin Brancusi's own 'cosmic eggs' are given a clearly mytho-religious dimension, apparent not only in their supremely beautiful and erotic forms, but also in their titles: *Beginning of the World, The First*

---

106 J. Kristeva: *Revolution in Poetic Language*, tr. Margaret Walker, in *The Kristeva Reader*, 115

107 See P. Ransom: *The Art of Tantra*, 193-7.
108 In ib., 194; *Egg of Brahman*, Benares, age unknown, stone, 7in high; *Egg of Brahman*, Benares, age unknown, stone, 7 in high

Cry, The Newborn.[109] Sculptures such as *The First Cry* and *The Newborn* connect human birth with the birth of the cosmos, in a mythic, sensual volume. For the egg shape is obvious, as, like *The Kiss*, it looks towards a fundamental sense of life, where life begins, in the biology of cells and eggs. Indeed, Brancusi painted a version of his *The Kiss* on a real egg.[110] The lovers embracing on the egg pulls together any number of erotic and cosmic dimensions, from the egg-shape of genitals (womb, clitoris, testes, glans) to the Platonic two-in-oneness symbolized by two yokes in one egg, to the womb of the universe, the cells at the heart of organic life.

MAGICAL FLIGHT

Constantin Brancusi's most famous sculpture is probably the *Birds in Space* series.

> Much like certain mechanical objects, Brancusi's *Bird in Space* is polished to a mirrorlike smoothness. The high polish, although applied painstakingly by the artist, actually denies any handcrafted quality to this sculpture. In fact, this work was the object of lengthy litigation with U.S. Customs officials, who, perceiving similarities to airplane propellers, claimed that it was a manufactured object rather than art,

writes Peter Selz in *Art In Our Times*.[111] The many – 28 or so – *Birds in Space* sculptures are the manifestations of an artistic, spiritual quest for the essence of flight.[112] 'All my life I've been looking for one thing, the essence of flight...What a marvellous thing flight is',

---

109 C. Brancusi: *Beginning of the World*, c. 1920, marble, 7,2 x 10.25 x 6.5in, polished metal disc, 19.75in, diam., base: stone, 22.5in high, Dallas Museum of Art; *The First Cry*, 1917, polished bronze, 6.75 x 10.2in, Art Gallery of Ontario; *The Newborn*, 1915, white marble, 6 x 8.5in, Philadelphia Museum of Art
110 Brancusi: *The Kiss*, date unknown, paint on an egg, the Lydia & Harry L. Winston Collection

111 P. Selz: *Art in Our Times*, 272
112 C. Brancusi: *Bird in Space*, 1941, polished bronze, 76.2in high, Musée National d'Art Moderne, Paris; *Bird in Space*, 1925, white marble, 71in high, base: stone and wood sections, 64.5in high, National Gallery of Art, Washington DC; *Bird in Space*, 1931-6, black marble, 76.2in high, base: marble and sandstone sections, 53.25in high, Australian National Gallery, Canberra

Brancusi said.[113] Each *Bird in Space* is a slender, upright form, a mythic striving for the sky, for ascension, for space. Ionel Jianou said in *Brancusi* that the sculptor has succeeded in

> transforming his amorphous material into an ellipse with translucent surface, of a purity so dazzling that it irradiates the light around it and embodies, in its irresistible upward impulse, the very essence of flight.[114]

Constantin Brancusi's success of embodying the essence of flight in sculpture is all the more startling, Mircea Eliade says, because he used 'the very archetype of *heaviness*, that ultimate form of "matter" – stone.'[115]

The *Birds in Space* are shamanic sculptures, echoing so clearly the spiritual flight of the shaman, which is the central act of shamanism. The shaman travels to other worlds by drumming her/ himself up into a magical, ecstatic state, and by climbing up the 'World Tree', which is the *axis mundi*.[116] The Cosmic Tree or Column or mountain is the connection between the three realms of Heaven, Earth and Hell. Brancusi's *Birds in Space* are shamanic artworks, emblems of transcendence, the yearning for a 'magical flight' to other worlds, other states, other modes of being. They are sculptures of ecstasy, formed from the ecstasy of the shaman who rises up, spiritually, into the sky.

Archaic shamans dress in feathers, like birds, to emulate and take on the magic of birds, while souls are everywhere in religion associated with birds, and the soul was thought of as covered in feathers. As Mircea Eliade explains in *Shamanism*:

> Birds are psychopomps. Becoming a bird oneself or being accompanied by a bird indicates the capacity, while still alive, to undertake the ecstatic journey to the sky and the beyond.[117]

Constantin Brancusi's *Birds in Space* sculptures dispense with feathers and, typically for Brancusi, go for the essence of flight, symbolized and actualized by that slender, curving shape.

113 C. Brancusi, in Carola Giedin-Welcker: *Constantin Brancusi*, George Braziller, New York 1959, 220; see Sidney Geist, 1970, 74-82; Athena Tacha Spear: *Brancusi's Birds*, New York University Press, New York 1969
114 Ionel Jianou: *Brancusi*, Tudor Publishing, New York 1963
115 Eliade: *Ordeal*, op.cit., 201

116 Mircea Eliade: *Shamanism*: 1972, 143; M. Eliade: *Myths. Dreams and Mysteries*, 100f
117 M. Eliade: *Shamanism*, op.cit., 98

The *Birds in Space* sculptures are a stretching-up to the infinite. Brancusi spoke of a desire to extend the surfaces of his sculptures to infinity:

> In bad form...the surfaces and planes all come to an end. They finished themselves within the mass. I think the true form ought to suggest infinity. The surfaces ought to look as though they went on forever, as though they proceeded out from the mass into some perfect and complete existence.[118]

The *Birds in Space* pieces aim to be infinity-reaching sculpture, works that arch out into the 'open', into the 'beyond'. Mircea Eliade wrote in *Ordeal By Labyrinth*:

> ...it is not the ascension to heaven of the archaic and primitive cosmologies that obsesses Brancusi but the sensation of flight out into infinite space. He calls his column "endless" not only because such a column could never reach a structural conclusion but above all because it hurls itself out into space that must always remain without limits, since it is based on the ecstatic experience of absolute freedom. It is the same in

which his *Birds* fly. Brancusi has discarded everything from the old symbolism of the sky pillar except its central element: ascension as a transcendence of the human condition. But he successfully revealed to his contemporaries that what concerned him was an ecstatic ascension stripped of all mysticism.[119]

The endpoint of Constantin Brancusi's search was his *Endless Column*, a monumental structure at Tîrgu-Jiu,[120] which Brancusi called 'a stairway to heaven'.[121] The column, variously entitled *Column of Endless Remembrance, Infinite Column, The Column of Endless Memory, The Column of Endless Gratitude,* soars into space, literally and metaphorically, mythically and spiritually. Sidney Geist writes in *Brancusi: A Study of the Sculpture*:

> Marvellous is the fact that the elements of the *Column* do not diminish in size as they mount. The persistence of size and of shape, the

118 C. Brancusi, in Adeline L. Atwater: "A Recluse of Modern Art", *New York Herald Tribune Magazine*, 12 January 1930, 12

119 M. Eliade: *Ordeal*, op.cit., 199
120 C. Brancusi: *Endless Column*, 1937-8, cast iron, 96.2 ft x 35.4 x 35.4in, Tirgu-Jiu, Romania; Stefan Georgescu-Gorjan: "The Genesis of the 'Column Without End', *Revue roumaine d'histoire de l'art*, Bucharest, no. 2, 1964, 279-93
121 C. Brancusi, quoted in Barbu Brezianu: *Brancusi in Romania*, Editura Academiei R.S.R., Bucharest, Romantia, 1976, 134

constancy of the repetition, causes the *Column* to remain near to the mind as it moves off from the eye. We have here a poetry of the actual, without illusion or compensation, without tapering or entasis.[122]

Endless Column is, like the *Birds in Space* sculptures, a monument of magical, shamanic flight, a sculpture of pure ascension, which is pure desire. You don't need to have any time for Sigmund Freud to see the phallic aspects of such towers, totem poles, minarets and columns (or flying). Brancusi's *Endless Column* and *Birds in Space* sculptures can be seen in Freudian, genital terms as phallic erections.

The shaman's dance, trance and magical journey have erotic, phallic components. The shaman climbs up the World Tree, itself another phallic symbol, a manifestation of phallic power. Further, dreaming, which is the key state of shamanism, for the shaman is the one who can dream magically, is associated with phallic energy and arousal in both men and women, as Sigmund Freud noted: during REM sleep erections occur (what men refer to as their 'morning glory', a penis rising like the sun rising). All these things are caught up in Constantin Brancusi's sculptures

122 S. Geist, 1968, 124-5

of flight: shamanism, Cosmic Trees, phallic columns, erections, patriarchal power, religious/ mythic rebirth. Other forms of ithyphallic ascensions might include technology and machines, or even, at the heart of Western religion, Christ's Resurrection. This was a *bodily* resurrection from the tomb, as theologians have always stressed. And all of the body includes the penis, as D.H. Lawrence noted: for Lawrence, Christ rose in the flesh, meaning complete with phallus, ready for sex.

Not a few sculptors since Constantin Brancusi's egg-shaped 'heads' and *Beginning of the World* have created rounded, 'abstract' forms, such as Henri Matisse with his bulbous sculpture *Le Tiaré*; Jean Arp who produced a number of forms based on rounded, organic forms, including yet another one of those headless, armless female torsos found in so much of patriarchal art; and Barbara Hepworth, Henry Moore and Louise Bourgeois (cited above).[123] The upward-thrusting, semi-organic shape of Brancusi's

123 Jean Arp: *Torse de Femme*, 1953, 31in, Wallraf Richartz Museum, Cologne; *Human Concretion*, 1934, marble, Musée Nationale d'Art Moderne, Paris; Matisse: *Le Tiaré*, 1930, bronze, Ahrenberg Collection, Sweden; Jean Lipchitz: *Song of Songs*, 1945-8, bronze, 23.8 x 38in, private collection

Princess X occurs in the follower of Anthony Caro, William Tucker's work. His hand-modelled volumes curve up into space, sculptural equivalents of Samuel Beckett's 'little body upright'.[124] Tucker moved from tight, quasi-Minimal works in the 1960s to the looser, organic forms of the 1980s.[125]

KISSES IN STONE

Constantin Brancusi's most erotic sculpture was one of his early pieces, which turned up in several forms: *The Kiss*.[126] Unlike Auguste Rodin's *tour-de-force* depiction of erotic passion, *The Kiss*,[127] Brancusi's *The Kiss* is a 'primitive', non-naturalistic square block of stone, very far indeed from the art of Michelangelo Buonarroti, Gianlorenzo Bernini or Rodin. For Brancusi *The Kiss* was his 'road to Damascus', a key work.[128]

Much of Auguste Rodin's art pivots around eroticism. Rodin produced drawings of women masturbating, which influenced Gustav Klimt's images of masturbating women.[129] Rodin's *Oceanides*, like his *Gates of Hell*, depicts lovers entwining in a series of fluid lines and sensuous forms.[130] Rodin's depictions of *The Kiss* centre

124 William Tucker: *Gymnast III*, 1984-5, plaster, 90 x 60 x 33in, David McKee Gallery, New York; *Okeanos*, 1987-88, bronze, 12.6 x 9.7 x 6.6 ft, David McKee Gallery, New York
125 See Martin Kunz *et al*: *Starlit Waters: British Sculpture: An International Art, 1968-1988*, Tate Gallery, Liverpool 1988; Michael Newman: "New Sculpture in Britain", *Art in America*, 70, 8, September 1982

126 C. Brancusi: *The Kiss*, 1907-8, stone, 11in high, Museum of Art, Craiova, Romania; *The Kiss II*, c. 1908, stone, 12.5in high, private collection. See Sidney Geist: 1978.
127 A. Rodin: *The Kiss*, 1886, marble, Musée Rodin, Paris
128 Quoted in H.P. Roche: "L'Enterrement de Brancusi", *Homage de la Sculpture à Brancusi*, Paris, 1957, 26f
129 A. Rodin: *Reclining Female Nude*, c. 1900, pencil, 12.2 x 8in, Musée Rodin, France
130 A. Rodin: *Océanides*, 1905, marble, 22in high, Musée Rodin, Paris

around the voluptuousness of eroticism, on the beauty of bodies clasped together in complex poses. Rodin's *The Kiss* is the height of modern figurative sculpture, Michelangelo Buonarroti made heterosexually erotic. Other sculptors produced similarly sensuous, entwined *Kisses*, with the man always on top, always bearing down onto the woman, always enveloping, always controlling the kiss (in M.L. Bégine's *The Embrace*, J. Dalou's *The Kiss*, Edvard Munch's 1897 *The Kiss*, Klimt's *The Kiss*, F. Voulot's *The Kiss,* Pablo Picasso's *The Embrace,* William Zorach's *The Embrace* and E. Derré's *La Grotte d'Amour*).[131]

The different versions of *The Kiss* by Constantin Brancusi aim to depict that intimate erotic experience of lovemaking, symbolized by a kiss. The two people – male and female, of course – are shown kissing face-on, their bodies fused together. It is a modern version of spiritual union, that dream of Plato, the love which is 'two-in-one', and celebrated

through post-classical Western history. The Platonic syzygy or 'two yolks (or souls) in one egg (life)' aspect is underlined by the fact that these *two* lovers are made out of *one* block of stone.

The Kiss is distinctly gendered, with many details that describe the man and the woman not apparent from just a glance. The hair, for instance, is parted on the woman but pulled back on the man; the man's hands are on her shoulders, while hers are pressed against the back of his head; the woman is clearly sexualized by her breasts, as ever in masculinist art; the eyes and lips (there are no ears) seem to be the same, though the man is shorter than the woman. In subtle ways, Constantin Brancusi delineated the psychology of his male and female figures. They are at once flawed individual and generalized (idealized) archetypes.

The variations on *The Kiss* (Constantin Brancusi regarded them all as one work), reveal interesting departures from that first, Craiova *The Kiss*. The 1908 Diamond *The Kiss* is much rougher, in its grey limestone, with the strokes of the chisel still visible, but the eyes bulge, with heavily-lined eyelids. These eyes became so enlarged in the later works they filled up the face until, in the late columns, all you can see is the great orbs of

131 E. Derré: *La Grotte d'Amour,* 1905; Jules Dalou: *The Kiss*, Giraudon; M.L. Béguine: *The Embrace*, 1906; Edvard Munch: *The Kiss*, 1895, private collection; Pablo Picasso: *The Embrace*, 1900; F. Vaoulot: *The Kiss*, 1905; William Zorach: *The Embrace*, 1933, bronze, 66in high, collection: the Zorach children

the eyes, fused together, in *The Gate of the Kiss* and *Column of the Kiss*.[132]

These late *Kisses*, the column and the gate, are monumental versions of the Platonic *syzygy*, the Platonic soul union, but erotic and cosmological versions. The 'eyes' are biological 'cells', as Constantin Brancusi explained. They are the basic form of life, the organic cell, from which all life grows. These 'eyes' are also circles, and in *The Column of the Kiss* and *The Gate of the Kiss*, Brancusi uses the circle as the prime symbol of life. He cuts it in two, and so those two semi-circles become the perfect symbol of the Platonic souls finding their 'other half'. Circles split in two also have sexual associations, hinting at the genitals of men and women. The bisected circle can be, if you like, labia, or testes, or glans, etc. Brancusi explained the meaning of the 'eyes':

> What is left behind when you are no more? It is the memory of the eyes, of your looks that imparted love for man and people. These figures are a representation of the amalgamation of man and woman through love.[133]

It is worth noting, too, that above the pillars of *The Gate of the Kiss* are forty couples inscribed on the surface of the massive lintel. These couples are copulating, they are drawn like the full length bodies on the Montparnasse *The Kiss,* where legs and arms entwine in a Tantric lovemaking. Constantin Brancusi's *The Gate of the Kiss* is thus an epic, monumental poem to erotic, human love, love made cosmic and mythic. The tenderness that writers such as D.H. Lawrence, William Shakespeare, Sappho, Thomas Hardy and André Gide thought of as essential in love is there in Brancusi's *Kissing Gate*, but made vast and monolithic.

The 1912/6 *The Kiss*, in limestone, is a further 'rationalization', as critics say, of the first *The Kiss*. There is a clear line marking the narrow space between the figures, who are shown down to the waist. The 1923-5 limestone *The Kiss* returns to the shortened version of 1908. It is rounded, making the two figures into an oval shape.

In Constantin Brancusi's vision of the supreme erotic

132 C. Brancusi: *The Gate of the Kiss*, 1937-8, banpotoc travertine, 17 ft 3.5in x 21 ft 7.2in x 6 ft 6in, Tirgu Jiu, Romania; *Column of the Kiss*, c.1933, plaster, 18in high, Musée National d'Art Moderne, Paris. See Sidney Geist, 1973, 70-78

133 C. Brancusi, quoted in Barbu Brezianu: *Brancusi in Romania*, op. cit., 143

moment, the *unio mystica* as Catholic mystics and theologians call it, the two figures are clasped together so tightly nothing gets between them. It is a pure fusion of body and soul: their eyes touch, their faces touch, their mouths touch, their bodies touch.

In later versions of *The Kiss*, such as the one in Montparnasse Cemetery, Constantin Brancusi showed the whole body of the two eternal, archetypal lovers.[134] Sidney Geist wrote of the Montparn-asse *The Kiss*:

> The initial innocence of *The Kiss* has given way to the image of pagan frankness. In the total embrace of the Montparnasse *Kiss* we witness a scene so sweet and stately that it is often not recognized for what it is. In all except primitive art, there is probably no representation of the sexual act that is at once so undisguised and so discreet. Although the lovers in this *Kiss* are revealed in a passional act, its intensity is mitigated by a new rigour of design and execution. The broad facade are, for all purposes, identical.[135]

Constantin Brancusi's *The*

Kiss motif has been influential, though not, perhaps, as influential as the *Birds in Space*, the eggs and heads, or the *Endless Column*. Barry Flanagan has produced a sculpture of erotic figures carved into a chunk of square stone that directly recalls Brancusi's *The Kiss*.[136]

Constantin Brancusi's lovers recall the figures in Tantric art, where couples are shown erotically entwined with each other. In Oriental sex yoga and erotic literature, couples are depicted in a series of poses, which demonstrate how the cosmic energies, *yin* and *yang* or *Shiva* and *Shakti* fuse together in an erotic-religious embrace. Brancusi's *The Kiss* makes the ephemeral nature of eroticism permanent: it is carved not in marble or bronze, but in stone, which gives the work a heavy, earthy, durable feel.

The Kiss is a sculpture that is meant to represent by its solid mass a timeless erotic union. *The Kiss* is nothing less than a representation of that central 'act' of culture – making love. It is a cosmic vision of togetherness, a vision that goes down to the fundamental, organic levels of life. Constantin Brancusi used the image of two halves melding into one in his

134 C. Brancusi: *The Kiss*, 1909, stone, 35.2in high, Montparnasse Cemetery, Paris
135 Sidney Geist, 1978, 51.
136 B. Flanagan: *Tantric Figures*, 1973, collection: E.J. Power, London

monuments at Tirgu Jiu. Asking
the American sculptor Malvina
Hoffman what she thought of
the columns, she said: 'I see the
forms of two cells that meet
and create life. The beginning of
life…through love. Am I right?'
Brancusi replied,

> Yes, you are…and these
> columns are the result of
> years of searching. First
> came this group of two
> interlaced, seated figures in
> stone…then the symbol of
> the egg, then the thought
> grew into this gateway to a
> beyond.[137]

---

137 M. Hoffman, 1939, 53

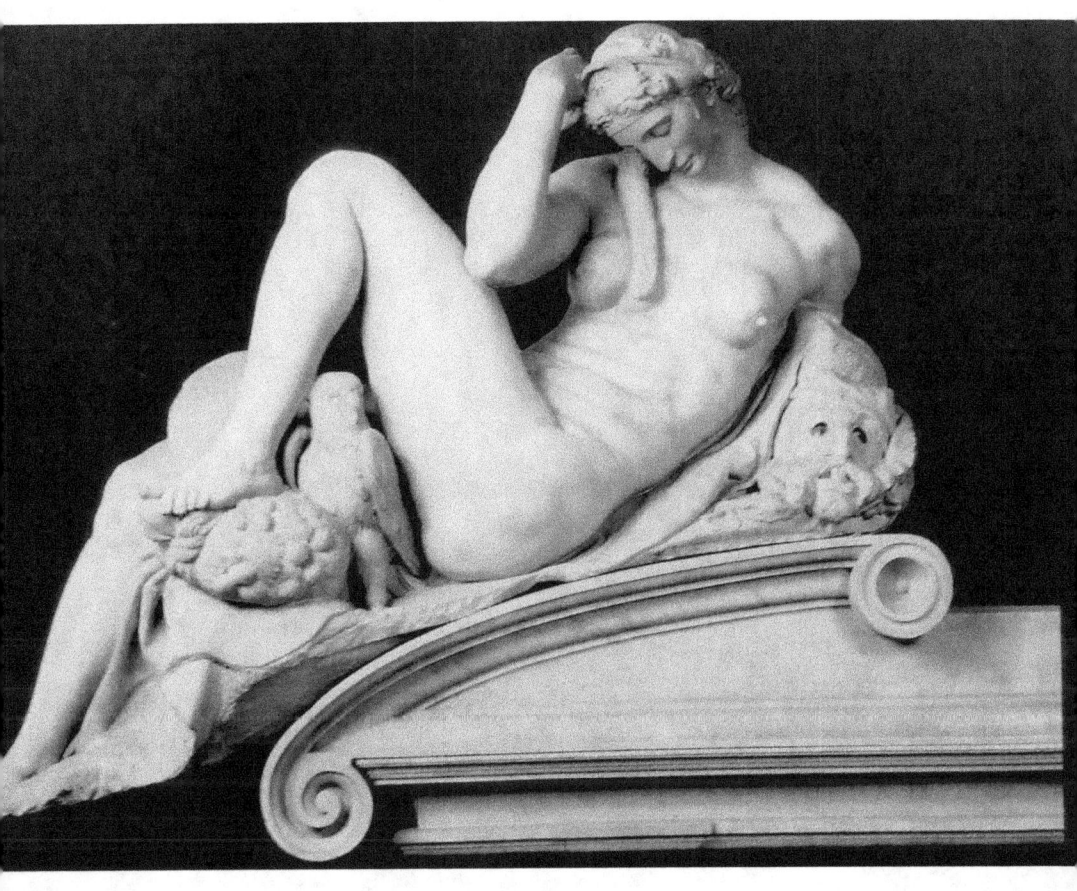

Michelangelo, Night, Medici Chapel, Florence

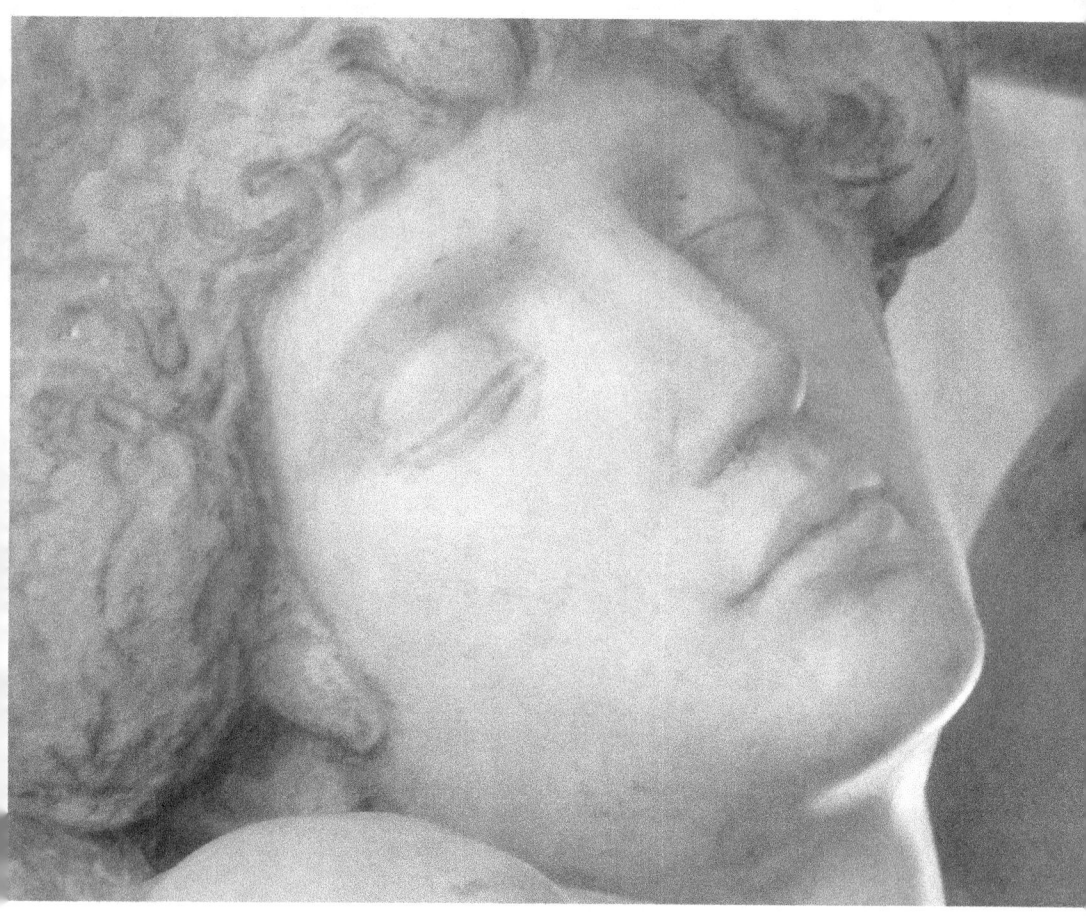

The Dying Slaves by Michelangelo in the Louvre Museum,
this page and following pages (photos: author)

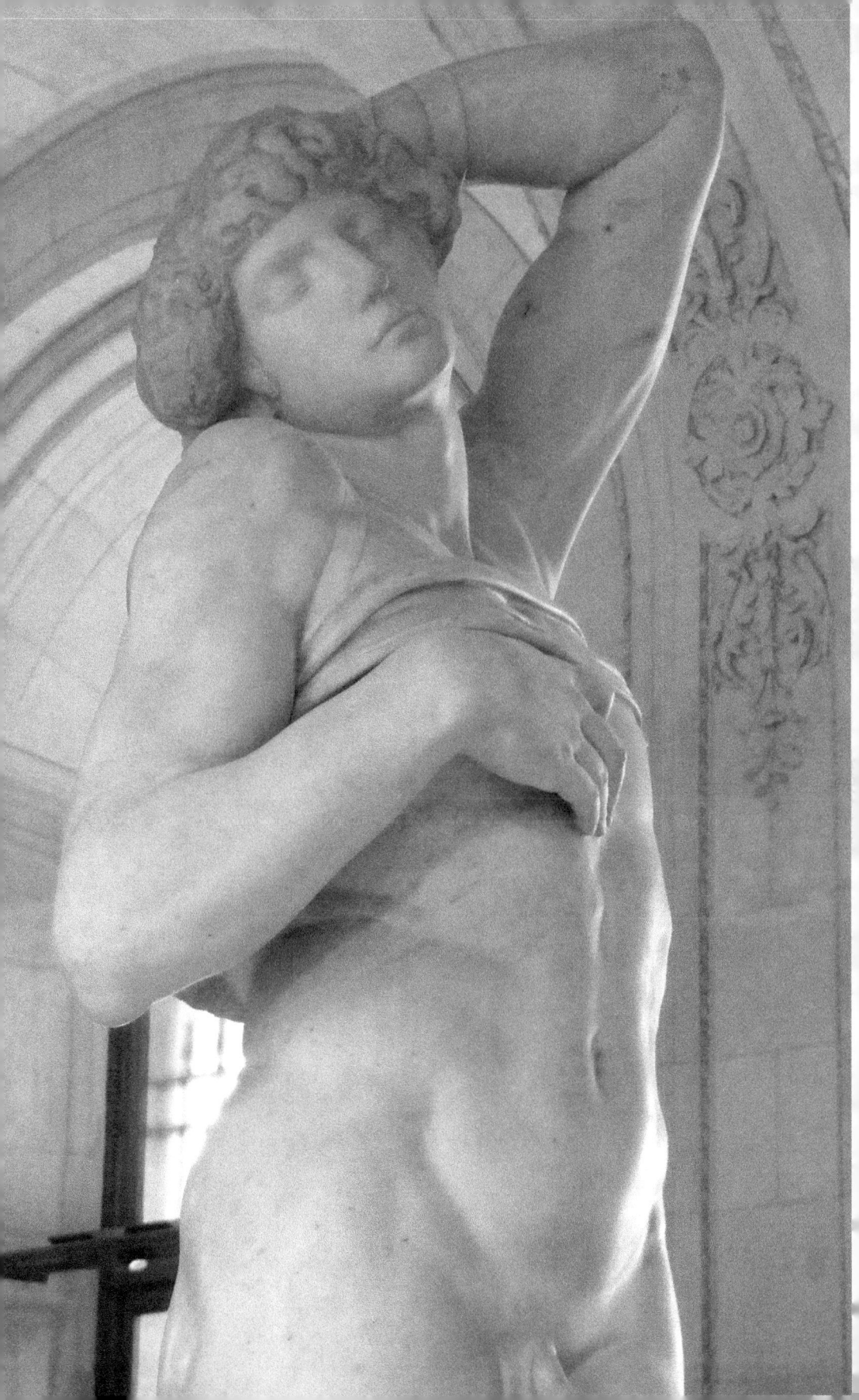

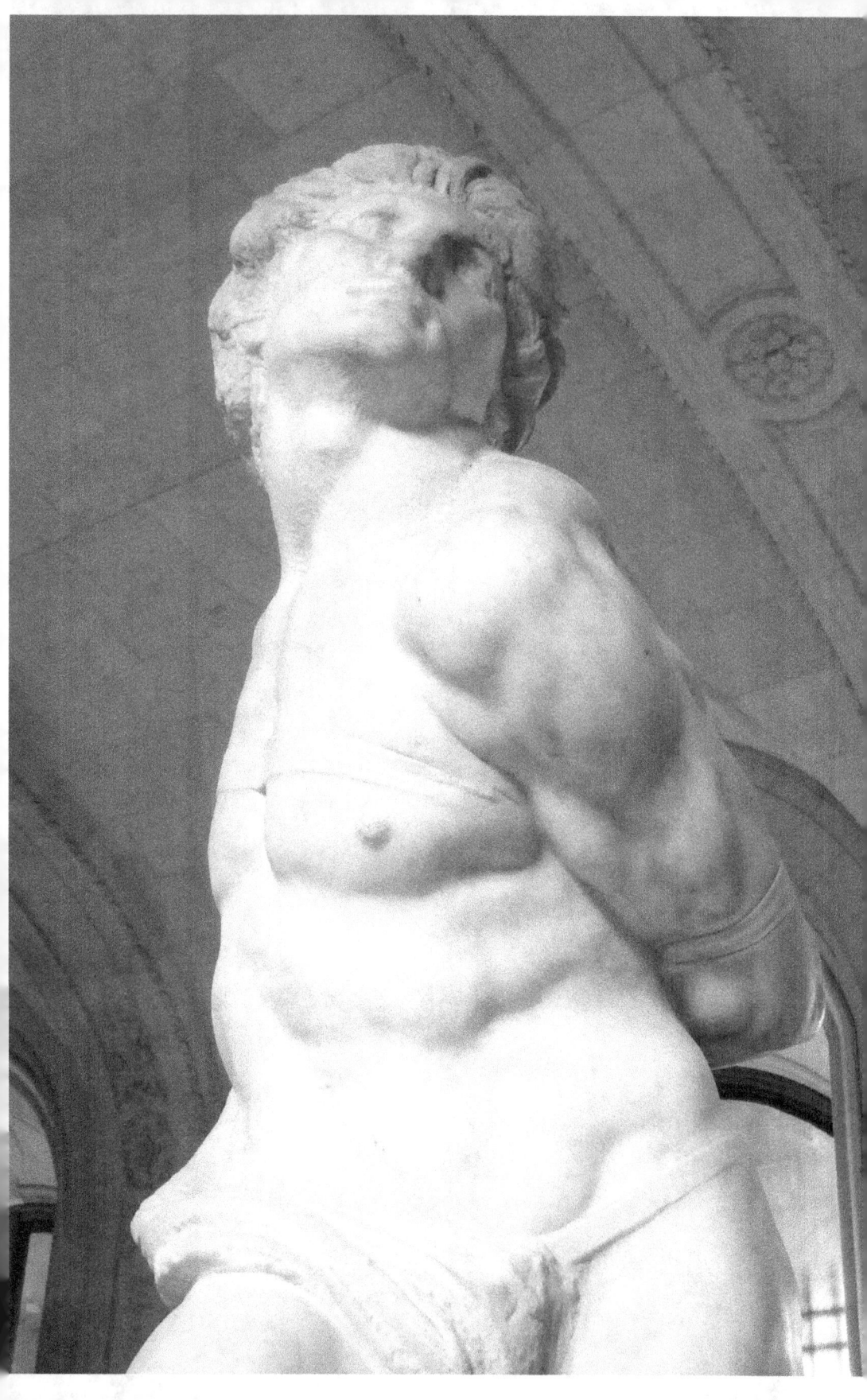

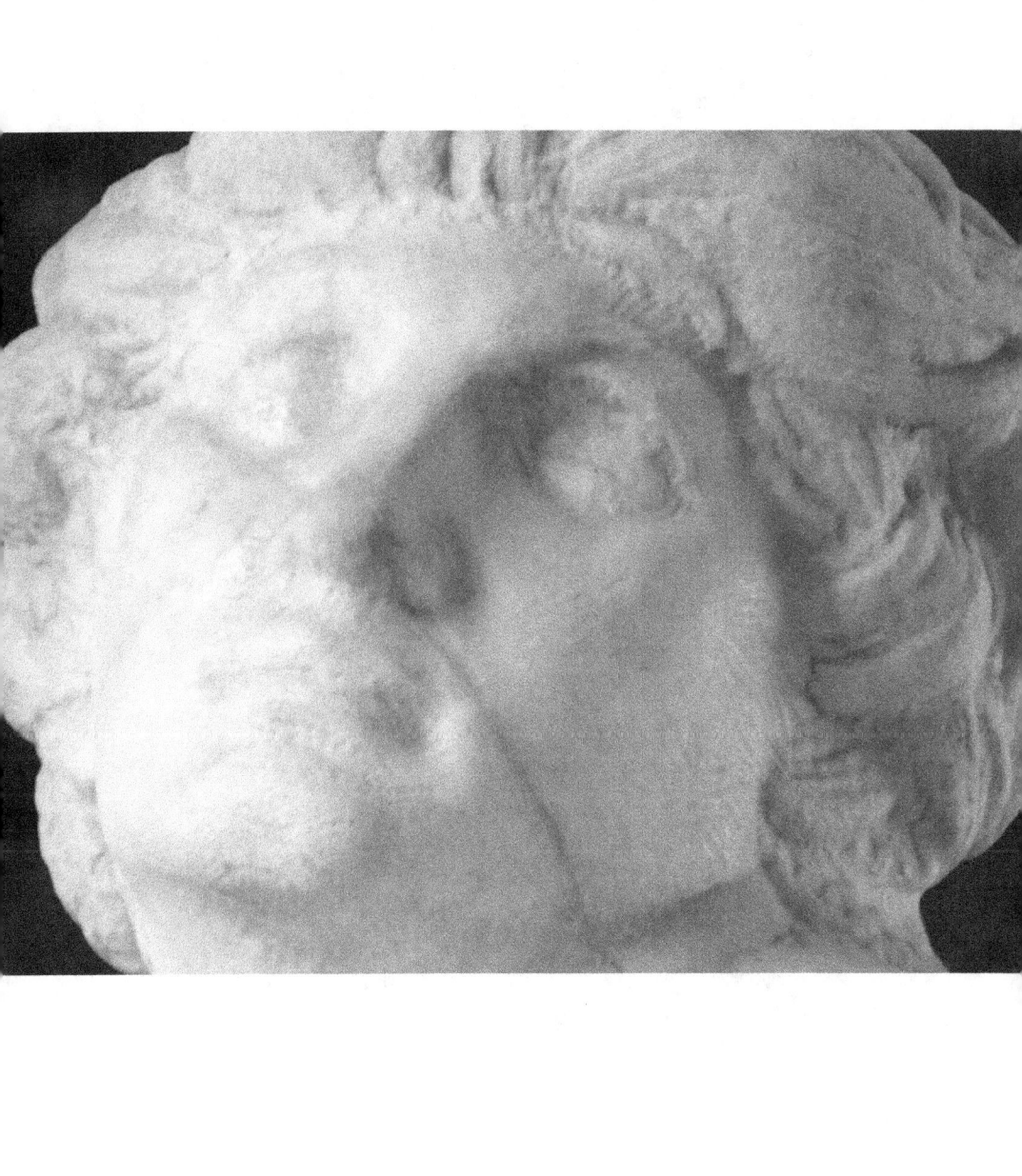

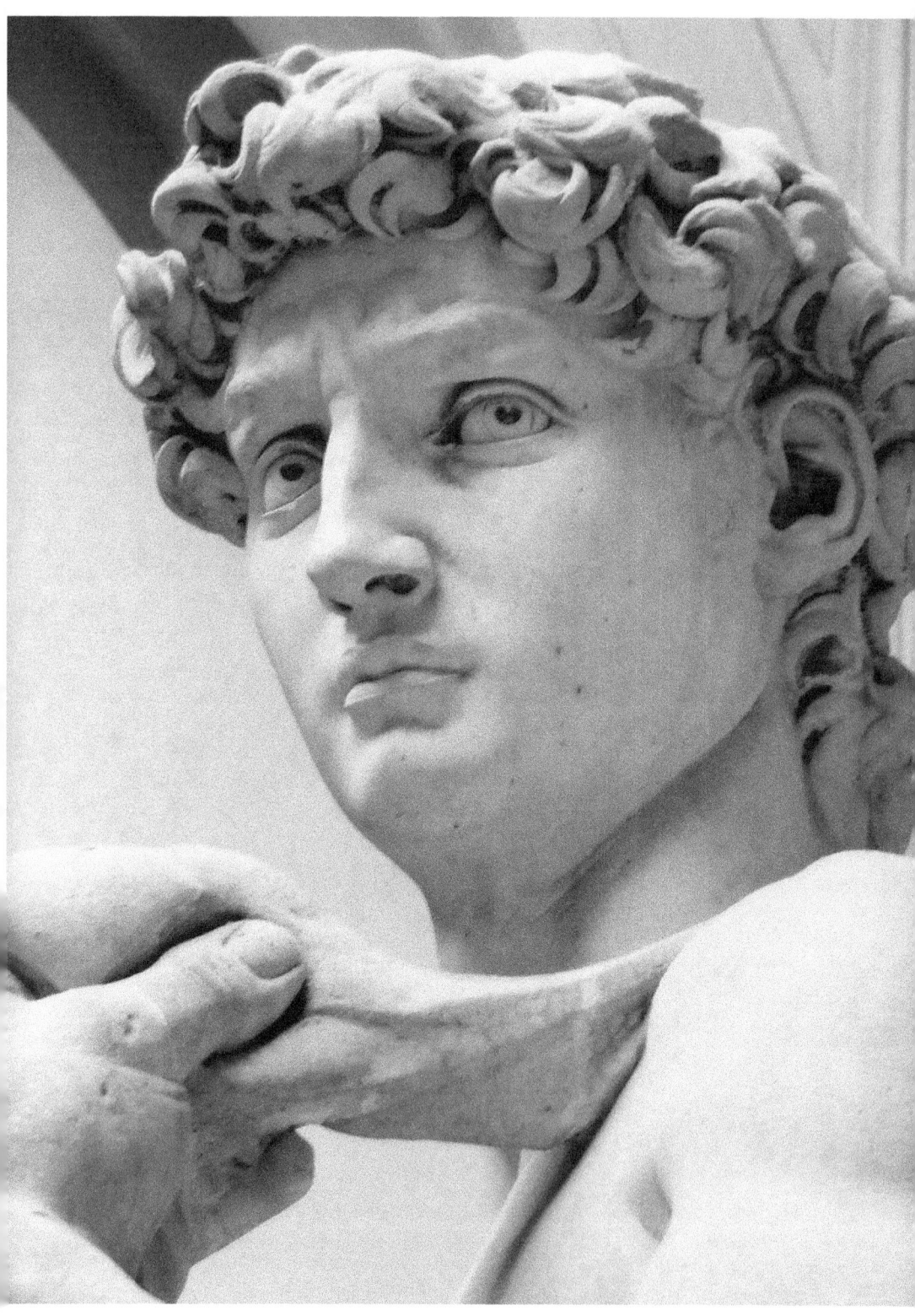

Michelangelo Buonarroti, David, 1501-04

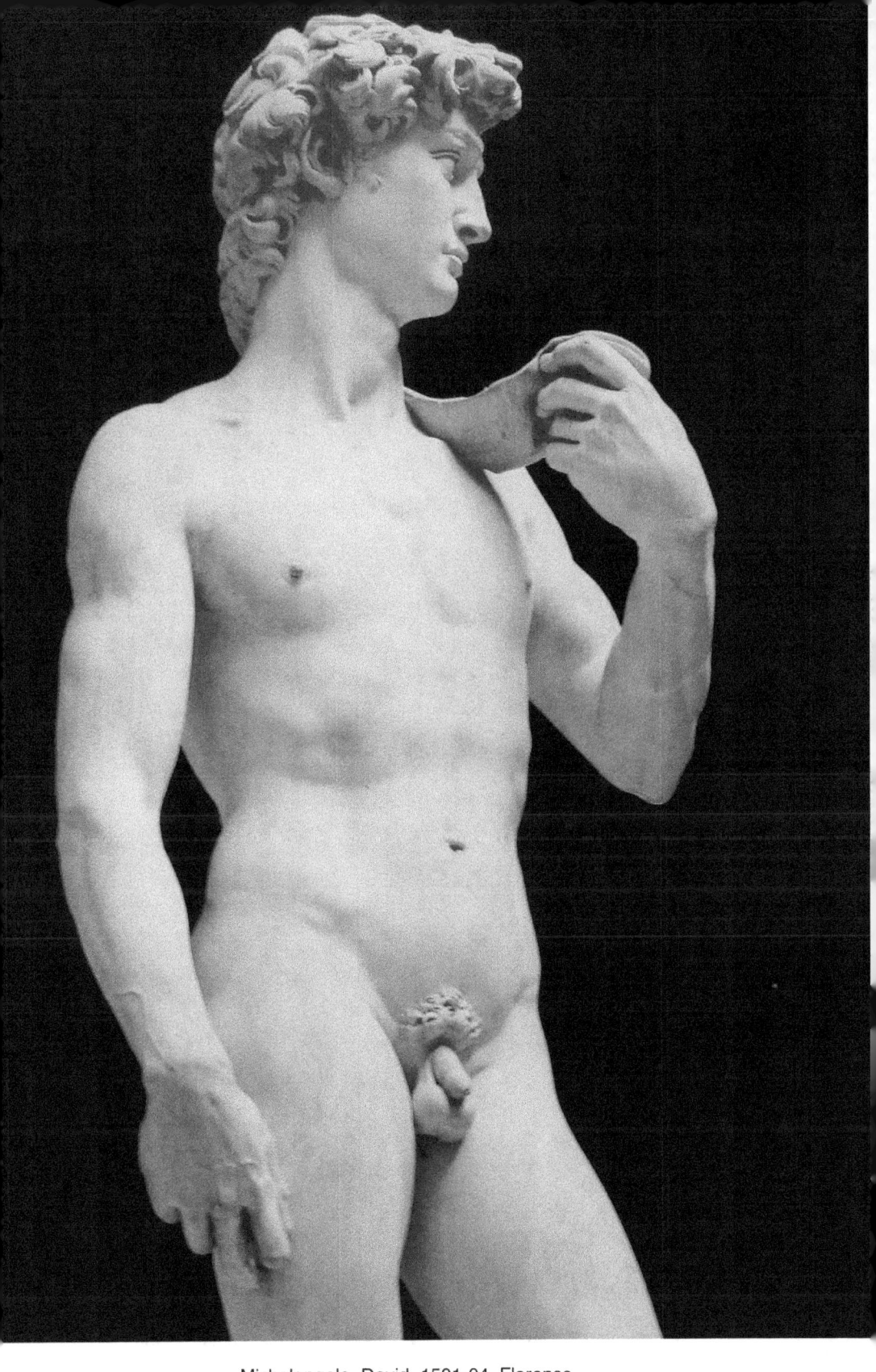

Michelangelo, David, 1501-04, Florence

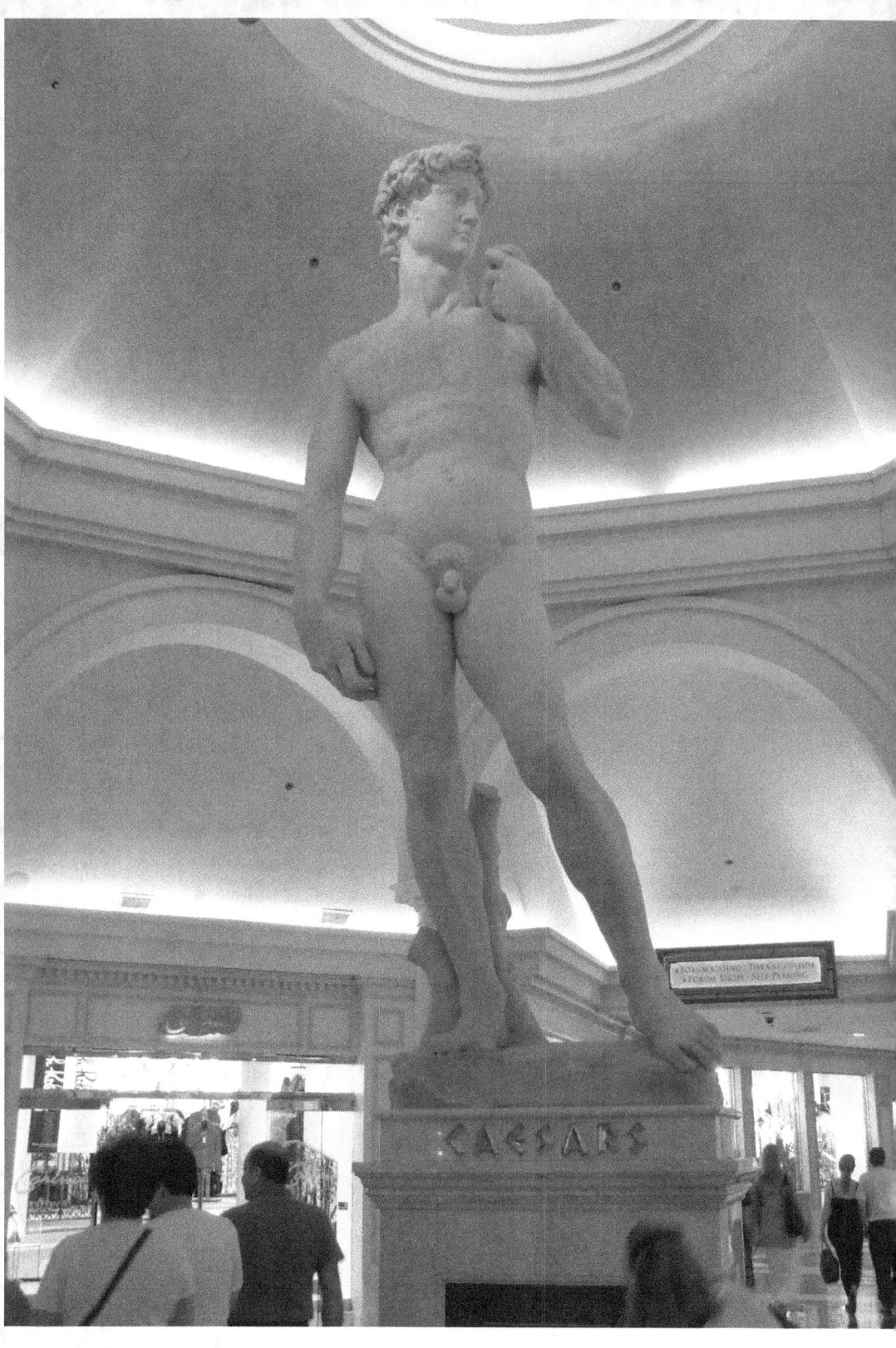

Michelangelo's David in Caesar's Palace, Las Vegas (photo: author)

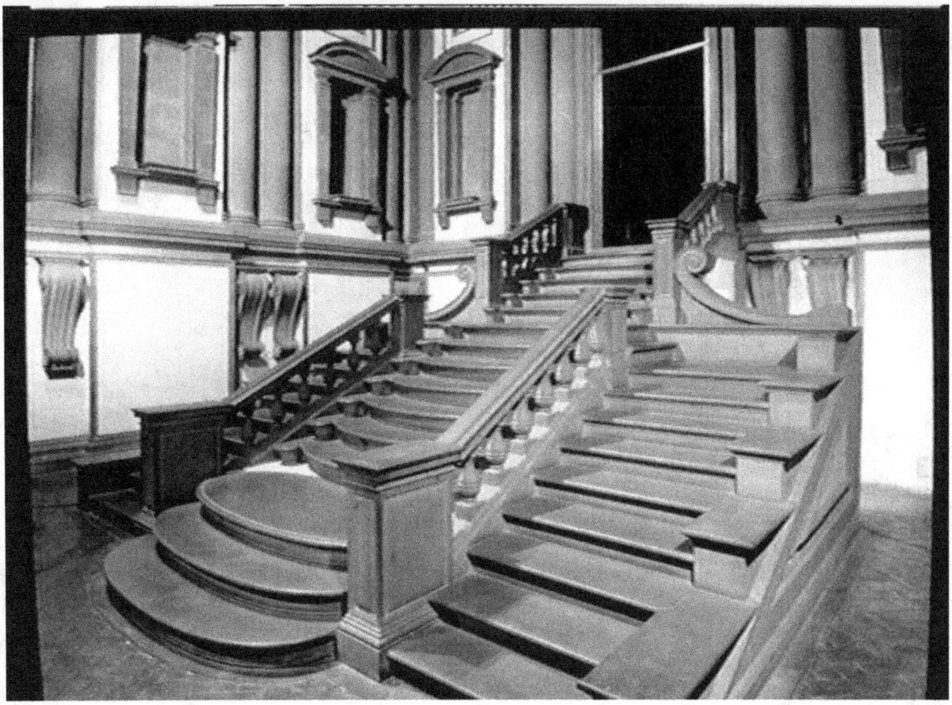

Michelangelo's Medici Library in Firenze. 1524-26

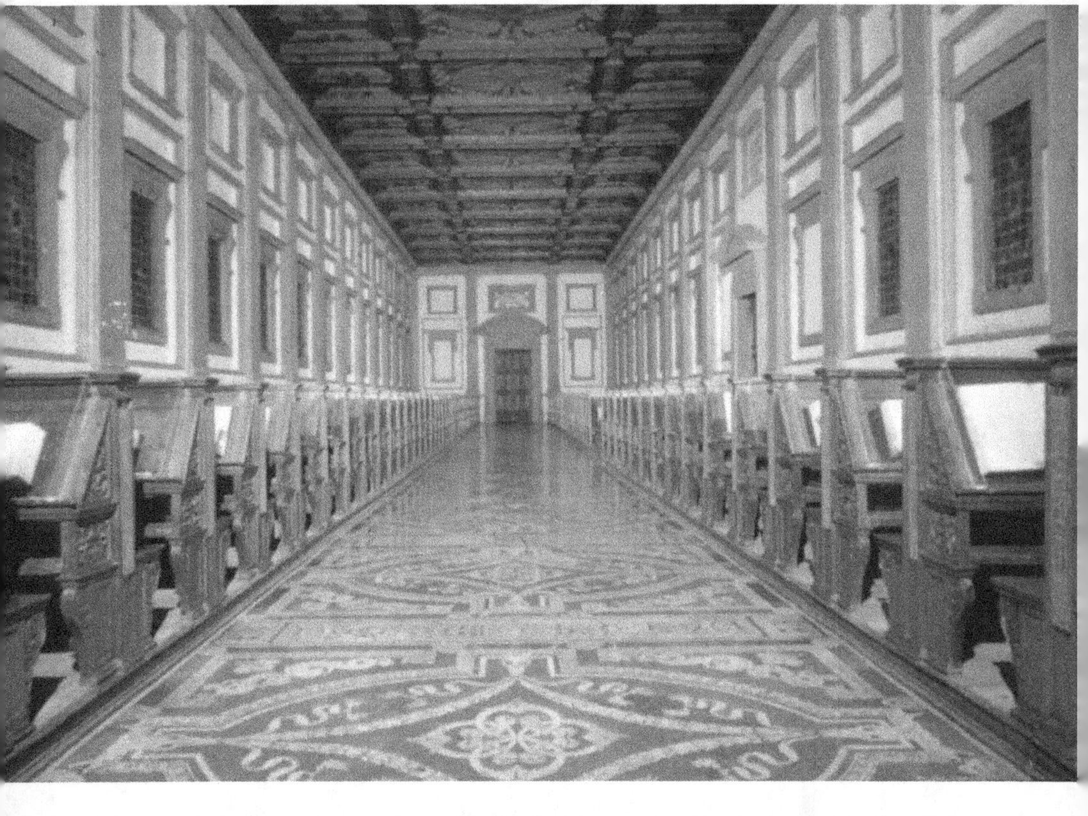

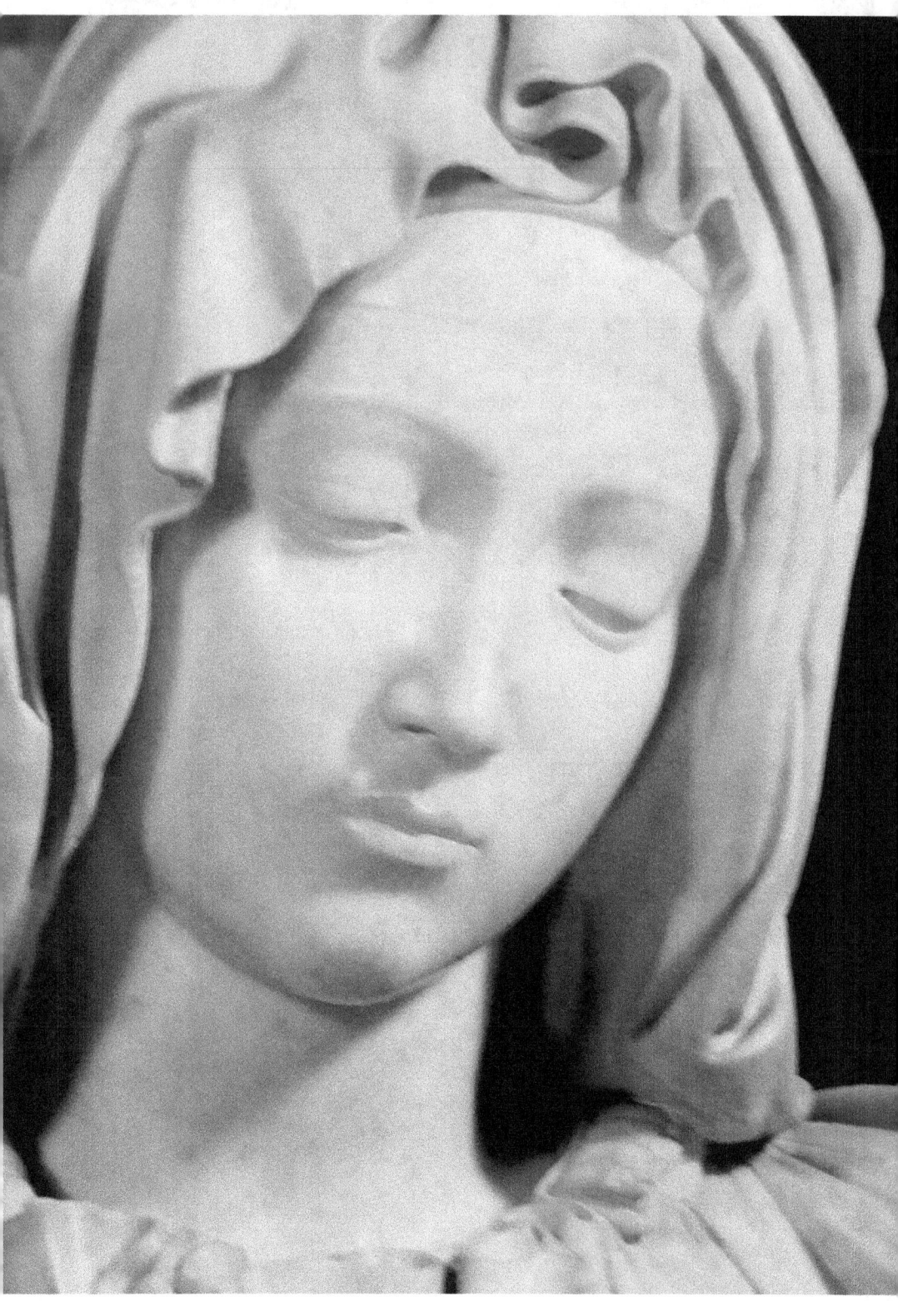

Michelangelo, Pietà, detail, Vatican, Rome

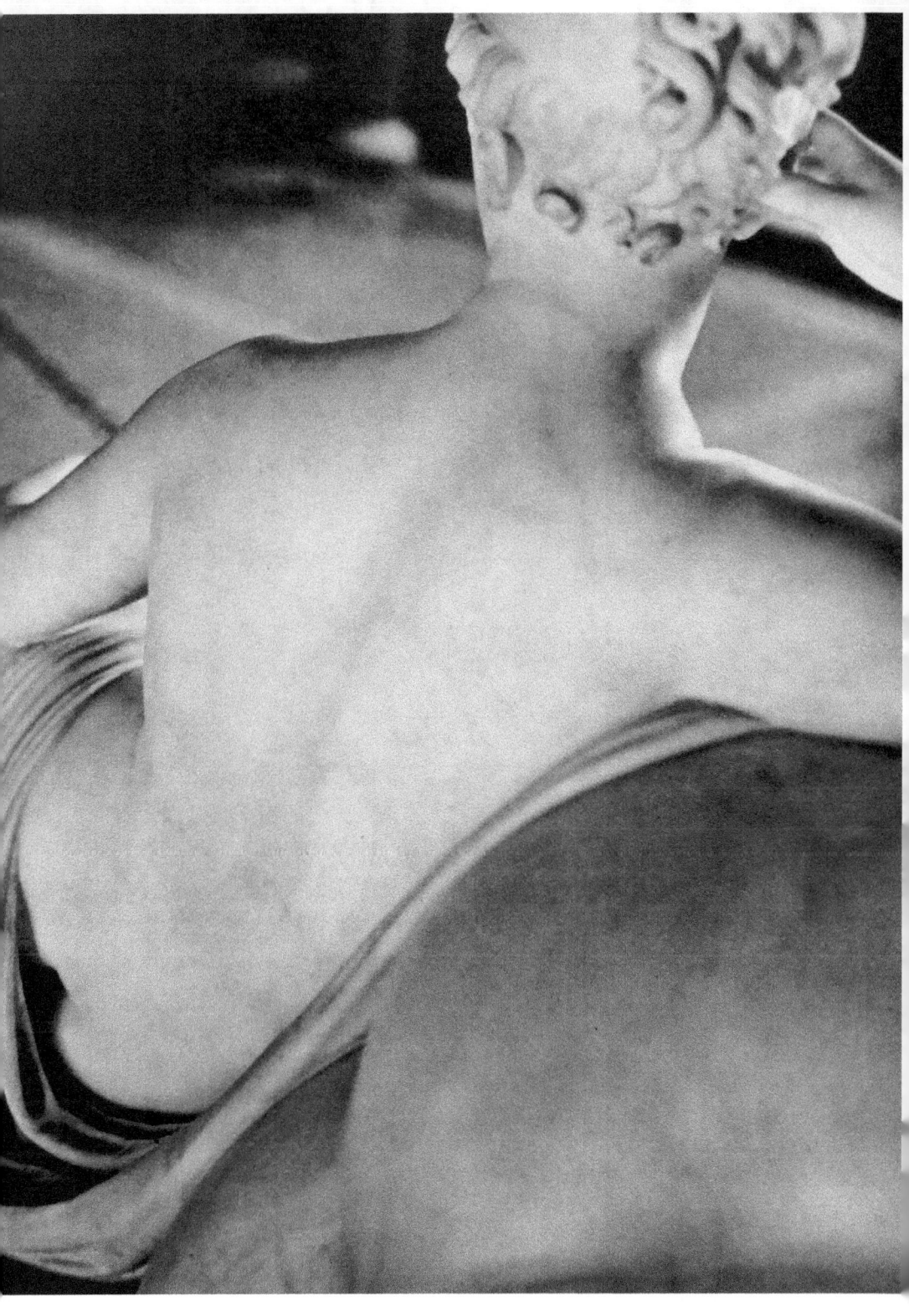

Antonio Canova, Venus Victorious, 1808

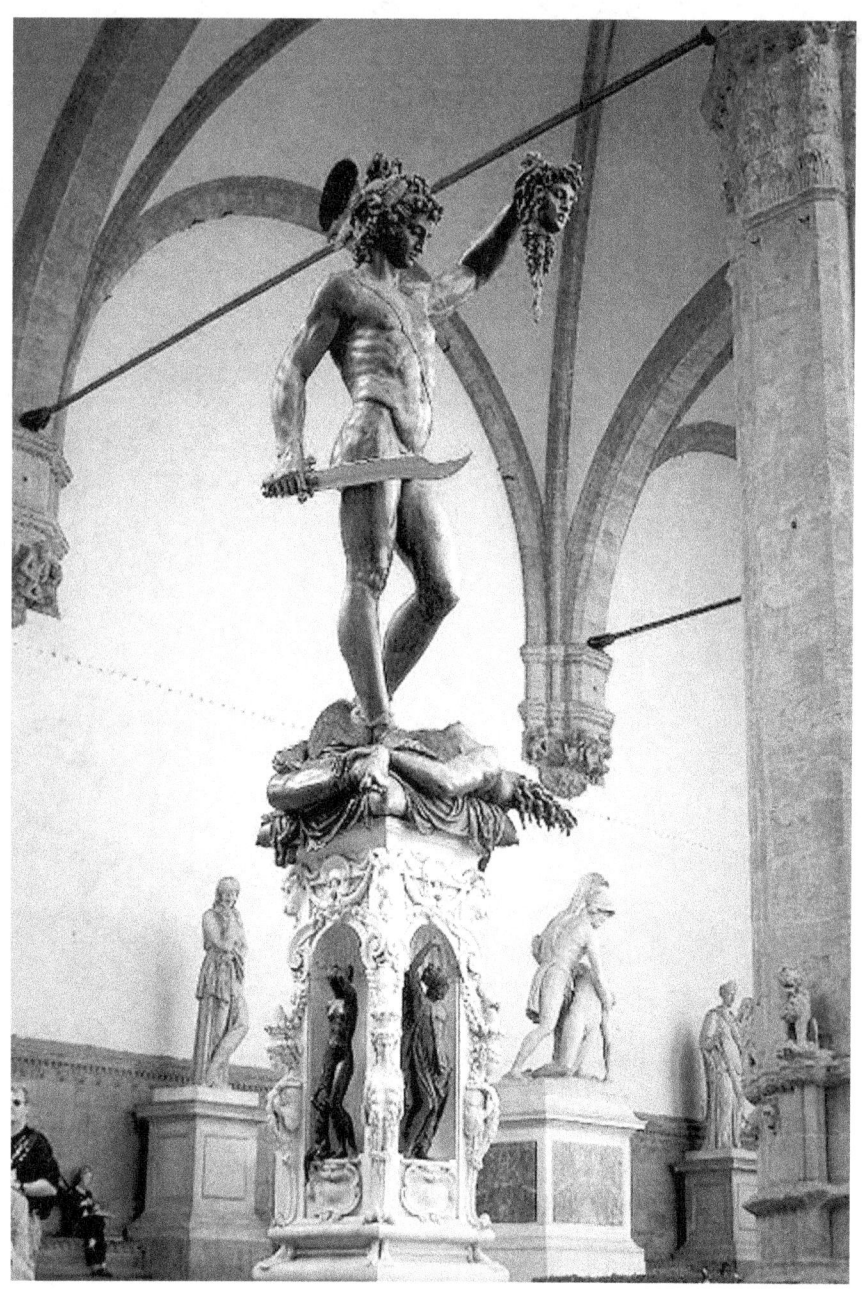

Benvenuto Cellini, Perseus, Florence

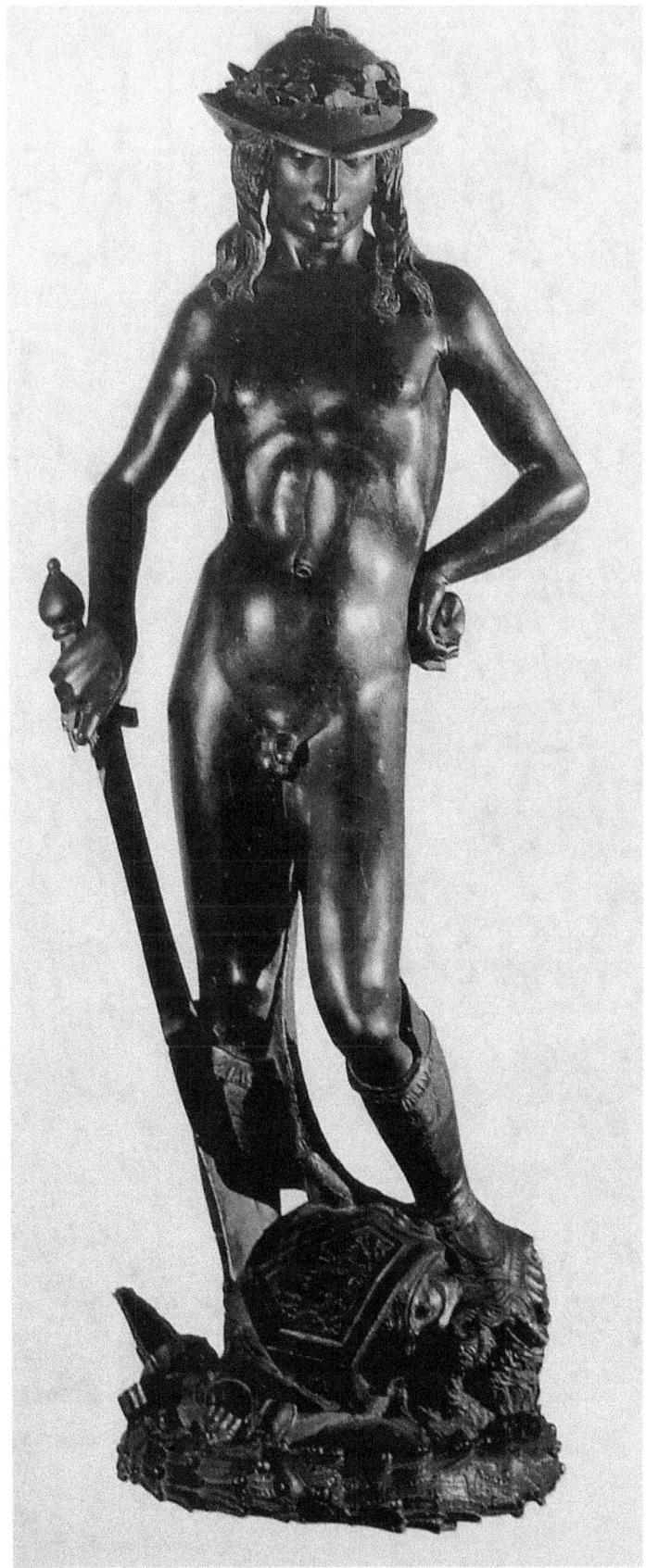

Donatello's ultra camp David, 1433, Florence

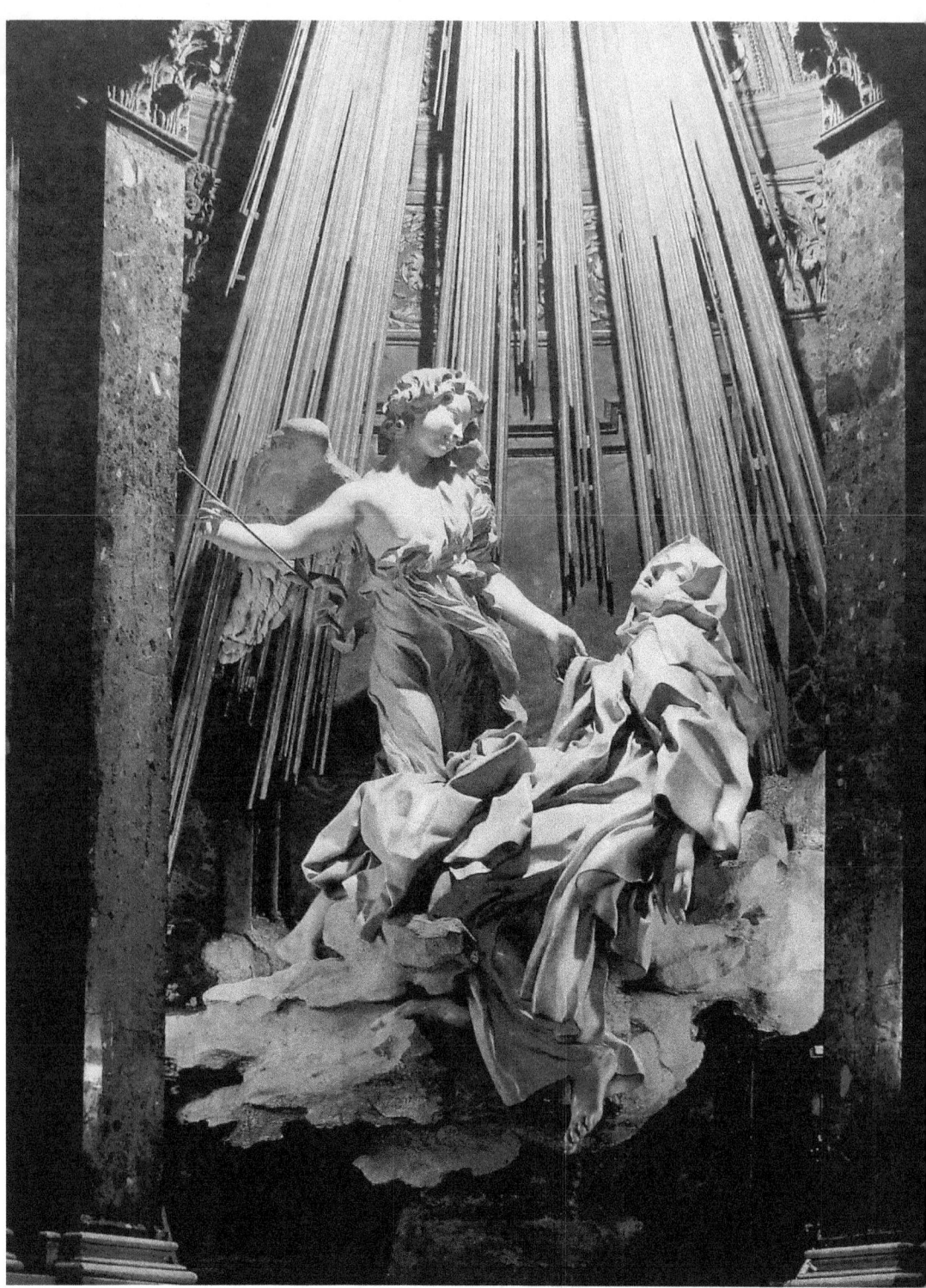

Gianlorenzo Bernini, The Ecstasy of St Theresa, 1652, Rome

8

Jasper Johns
and Joseph Cornell

*The problem is not doing
something, the problem is
knowing what one wants to
do.*

Jasper Johns[1]

Jasper Johns (b. 1930) is known
as a painter: but, like Robert
Rauschenberg and Frank Stella,
Johns works in three dimensions. He often adds objects to
his paintings. He is a painter
questioning painting, and often
crosses over into sculpture.
Similarly, sculptors such as
Nancy Graves paint their
sculptures.

Jasper Johns is one of the
most erotic of all contemporary
artists in his manipulation of
paint and texture and surface.
He does not depict naked
women or men or the usual
trappings of erotic art. His
eroticism stems from, as with
much sculpture, his surfaces. In
fact, there are no nude women
or men in his art, bits of bodies,
yes – a handprint, the cast of a
leg, masks, critics' mouths – but
not the usual sex objects of
Western art. (Although Johns
did make an image of his own
'genitalia and buttocks' in *Skin I*
and *Skin II*.)[2]

Jasper Johns' incredible
surfaces are made of oil and
wax or encaustic, spread thickly
on the canvas. Paintings such as
White Flag, Highway, Canvas and
Scent are really exquisite works,
so intensely tactile and

2 J. Johns: *Skin I*, 1973, charcoal on
paper, 25.5 x 40.25in, collection:
the artist; *Skin II*, 1973, charcoal
on paper, 25.5 x 40.25in,
collection: the artist. See Mark
Rosenthal, *Jasper Johns: Work Since
1974*, New York, NY, 1989, 18

1 J. Johns, quoted in Daniel
Wheeler, 139

sumptuous.3 Johns' drawings with ink are just as deluxe – ink is drawn onto plastic, so the colours swirl and merge into each other, in effects akin to marbling.4

A sense of space is crucial for Jasper Johns, as it is for all sculptors. 'As well as I can tell,' he says,

> I am concerned with space. With some idea about space. And then as soon as you break space, then you have things.5

OIL AND WAX

Like, a sculptor, Jasper Johns works very closely with his paintings, becoming absorbed totally in the surfaces, as a critic wrote:

> when he is working, Jasper is totally concentrated on those surfaces. He lives in those surfaces. The surfaces are his whole world, they are everything. He loses himself in them. They are everything.6

Jasper Johns' tactile surfaces are built up using wax – the thick impasto of oil and wax is one of the keys to his textures, for when the wax cools, you can paint on top of it very soon, instead of waiting for the paint to dry.7 Johns used encaustic and oil because he wanted evidence of the gestures he made *before* and *after*, that is, a finished painting which would reveal its making. Many sculptors in the contemporary era have made works which reveal their means of production. Johns said:

> It was very simple. I wanted to show what had gone before in a picture, and what was done after. But if you put on a heavy brush-

3 *White Flag*, 1955, encaustic and collage on canvas, 199 x 307cm, Collection: the artist; *Highway*, 1959, encaustic and collage on canvas, 190.5 x 154.9cm, Collection: Mrs Leo Castelli, New York; *Scent*, 1973-4, oil and encaustic on canvas, 182.9 x 320.6cm, collection: Ludwig Aachen; *Canvas*, 1956, encaustic and collage on canvas with objects, 76.2 x 63.5cm, Collection; the artist. See Robert Bernstein: *Jasper Johns' Paintings and Sculptures 1954-1974,* Ann Arbor, Michigan 1985, Richard Francis: *Jasper Johns,* New York 1984, Max Kozlof: *Jasper Johns,* New York 1969
4 Johns: *Untitled*, 1983, ink on plastic, 24.8 x 36.2in, Museum of Modern Art, New York; *Perilous Night*, 1982, ink on plastic, 31.6 x 40.8in, collection: the artist; *Untitled*, 1983-4, ink on plastic, 26.2 x 34.5in, collection: the artist
5 Quoted in Peter Fuller: 'Jasper Johns Interviewed", *Art Monthly*, no 18, July 1978, 12

6 Quoted in Michael Crichton: *Jasper Johns*, 21
7 J. Johns, quoted in M. Crichton, 28

stroke in paint, and then add another stroke, the second smears the first under the paint unless the paint is dry. And paint takes too long to dry. I didn't know what to do. Then someone suggested wax. It worked very well as soon as the wax was cool I could put on another stroke, and it would not alter the first.[8]

Marcel Duchamp and Kurt Schwitters are usually cited as precursors of Jasper Johns' mixed media explorations. Robert Rauschenberg and Johns rewrote the notion of painting-as-object by sticking objects onto it. Schwitters is often cited as a major exponent of multi-media formalism. Schwitters explained how he came to do it:

I simply could not see any reason why old streetcar tickets, driftwood, coat checks, wire and wheel parts, buttons, junk from the attic and heaps of refuse should not be used as material for paintings, any less than colours made in a factory.[9]

For Jasper Johns, the use of objects and quotes became modernist and ironic. Before Roy Lichtenstein had aped the Abstract Expressionists, writes

David Anfam in his study of Abstract Expressionism, Johns had been making ironic art-about-art statements:

Well beforehand, however, Johns had multiplied such ironic displacements and his *Field Painting* (1963-64) condenses a decade of them. Item by item, ideals from the past generation are processed into alien disguises: their symbolic chiaroscuro calls forth a light switch in a darkly painted passage (above left of centre), the encounter with materials yields several pots and brushes, lettering replaces noumenal chroma and depth gapes through a central break, the passive antitype of Newman's heroically virile 'zip'. Literary parallels to this replacement of a humanized vision by one of mirrored textual codes and signifiers were William Gaddis's novel *The Recognitions* (1955) and the overall drift into post-modernity announced in the fictions of John Barth and Thomas Pynchon (V, 1963).[10]

---

8 J. Johns, quoted in Daniel Wheeler, 134-5
9 K. Schwitters, quoted in Roh, 133

10 David Anfam: *Abstract Expressionism*, 202-3

FLAGS AND TARGETS

The Johnsian motifs – the targets, flags, numbers, maps – are merely patterns or shapes which free the artist to explore other things. He is not interested in maps or flags or ale cans or numbers, but in plasticity, surface, colour, texture, form and other painterly concerns. As Johns says:

> Take an object
> Do something to it
> Do something else to it
> " " " " "[11]

The motifs take care of certain elements in a work, so that the artist is free to look at other aspects. The aim is to create 'things which are seen and not looked at', Jasper Johns said, and explained further:

> Using the design of the American flag took care of a great deal for me because I didn't have to design it. So I went on to similar things like the targets – things the mind already knows. That gave me room to work on other levels.[12]

The flags and targets are disarmingly simple forms, a formal reductionism that allows æsthetic expansion in other areas. As Max Kozloff wrote in "Pop Culture, Metaphysical Designs and the New Vulgarians", the flags and targets were

> merely so many abstract forms upon which social usage has conferred meaning, but which now, displaced into their new context, cease to function socially. From this tremendous insight alone have sprung the momentum of Pop Art and the huge quantities of abstraction that is emblematic in character.[13]

Jasper Johns' famous American *Flag* is a complex work that opens up the way into Pop Art. *Flag* can be read in a number of ways, which seemingly conflict with each other. Johns explores the notions and relations between presentation and representation, between image and actuality, between iconography and abstraction. Johns' *Flag* is at once a banal icon (though for the America of the 1950s, as now, feelings of U.S.A. nationalism, embodied in the American Stars and Stripes, are

11 Jasper Johns: "Sketchbook Notes", in *Art and Literature*, 4, Lausanne, Spring 1965, 192
12 In Leo Steinberg: "Jasper Johns: The First Seven Years of His Art", in *Other Criteria: Confrontations with Twentieth-Century Art*, Oxford University Press, New York 1972, 31

13 Max Kozloff: "Pop Culture, Metaphysical Designs and the New Vulgarians", *Art International*, March, 1962, 34-6

still running high). and a complex piece of formal abstraction. With Johns' *Flag*, everyday signs and images, taken for granted, are treated with a grandeur of style and technique formerly employed by the great painters, the Old Masters. Johns uses the gestures of Abstract Expressionism, which aspire for grandeur and monumentality in painting, and gives them an ironic, self-reflexive twist. Johns produced a new sense of space which the art object inhabits. Rosalind Krauss remarked in *Passages in Modern Sculpture*:

> Johns's *Targets* or *Ale Cans*, in negating the internality of the abstract-expressionist picture, simultaneously rejects the innerness of its space and the privacy of the self for which that space was a model. His was a rejection of an ideal space that exists prior to experience, waiting to be filled, and of a psychological model in which a self exits replete with its meanings prior to contact with its world. (259)

The key to Jasper Johns' reworking of formalism and abstraction in the flags, targets, numbers and alphabets was precisely the sensuality of his art. It was the way he so powerfully employed the techniques of the Old Masters, of great art, that made his flags and targets so successful. For critics could not see Johns' banal signs culled from popular culture as trivial art, because Johns used one of the key elements in high art, the sensual, heavily impastoed surface. Johns' art could not be dismissed by critics, then as now, because its surface is as sensual and painterly as Rembrandt van Rijn, Diego Velásquez, Edouard Manet or Titian. William Rubin discusses Johns' *Flag*:

> his flag pictures and some of the other images he made were the first paintings in which the field of the pictures is absolutely identical with the motif of the picture: the boundaries of the pictures are identical with the boundaries of the flag. The flag Is laid out as a flat pattern on the surface, and although Johns is a representational painter in that sense and Frank [Stella] became an abstract painter, I think the notion of making the motif identical with the shape of the field, even though that shape remains rectangular in Johns' flag, lurks somewhere behind what would become the principle of Frank's shaped canvas. And that principle is, if I can define it in its simplest way, essentially that the boundary of the picture is going to be determined by

the governing pattern of the surface, and that there will be an absolute reciprocity between the outer shape of the picture, which might be considered simply the outside line of a pattern that operates over the entire surface.[14]

JOSEPH CORNELL

One modern sculptor who defies categorization, who cannot be pigeon-holed as a sexist artist, who produced works that can truly have the word 'unique' applied to them, is Joseph Cornell (1903-73). He is one of those artists whose works employ the techniques of both painting and sculpture, like Frank Stella or Anselm Keifer. Like Marcel Duchamp and Kurt Schwitters, the two early gurus of mixed media constructs, and like Robert Rauschenberg and Jasper Johns who developed the ideas of Duchamp and Schwitters further, Joseph Cornell uses real objects in his art. He gathers together trinkets, toys, signs, buttons, bangles, marbles, glasses, jars, adverts, postcards, butterflies, pipes and dried flowers. He places them inside small handmade wooden boxes which have a glass front. Already, by the very use of this small wooden box, with its dark and varnished wood and glass front, Cornell has set up a sense of something being treasured, being put in a treasure box, like a box of jewels or ornaments; Cornell is making something precious out of the quotidian detritus of life. An art of memory, re-invention, rediscovery. Cornell's boxes have this atmosphere of the

14 Rubin, in De Antonio & Tuchman, 138-9

treasure trove, of a boxed, contained world. They are supremely mysterious, some of the most mysterious objects in all sculpture.15 They are unlike anything else in sculpture.16 Other artists have set objects in boxes (since the 1990s it has become an increasingly popular sub-genre of art), but no one has done it quite like Cornell. His boxes create a poetry of objects, so that a clay pipe is set beside a tiny glass bottle, and creates an enigmatic juxtaposition.

It's not possible, perhaps, to say *exactly* what Joseph Cornell is aiming for, as with Constantin Brancusi or Barbara Hepworth. Cornell's boxes, like Louis Nevelson's walls of painted wooden boxes, evoke a myriad of responses and meanings. The mystery Cornell generates is not that of the Surrealists, of René Magritte, say, who juxtaposed objects *ad nauseam* (but rather simplistically, I've always

thought. Which's perhaps why Magritte, like Salvador Dali, appeals to students and teens). Cornell's mystery is more like that of Giorgio de Chirico, who created empty sunlight squares in his paintings which were perennially mysterious (de Chirico's art is a poetry of sunny emptiness, spaces of the modern Existential poet alone, spaces where something has happened earlier that day, but now everybody has vanished).

---

15 Joseph Cornell: *Medici Slot Machine*, 1942, mixed media, 15.5 x 12 x 4.8in, private collection; *Central Park Carrousel – 1950, in Memoriam*, 1950, wood, mirror, wire netting, paper, 20.3 x 14.5 x 6.8in, Museum of Modern Art, New York; *Pipe and Glass Box (Eclipse Series)*, mixed media, private collection.
16 Joseph Cornell's *Untitled (Hotel Eden)*, 1945, National Galery of Canada, Ottawa, for instance, with its bird, spiral, music box and paper scraps, defies simple explanations.

9

Painting and Sculpture

FRANK STELLA

There are many other contemp-
orary painters, apart from Jasper
Johns, who have developed an
acute, sometimes sculptural
sense of surface and texture.
Among the more successful are
painters such as Christopher Le
Brun, Anselm Keifer (such as in
his *Wayland's Song*[17]), Thérèse
Oulton, Lance Smith, Hughie
O'Donoghue, R. B. Kitaj, Jim
Dine and Richard Diebenkorn.

One of the contemporary
painters who have 'gone
sculptural' is Frank Stella (b.
1936), who since the 1970s and
his *Indian Birds* series has been
building his paintings out from
the wall, so that they become
deliriously three-dimensional
(though Stella claims they remain
'paintings', not sculptures).
Stella's new works are as
exuberant and as colourful as art
can be. They are so startling in
their sheer pleasure and
enthusiasm that some people
must be put off by them,
observing them with suspicion
(the lack of angst and neurosis is
immediately apparent). Works
such as 1982's *Thruxton 3X* are
explosions of light, colour,
texture, shape, pattern, volume,
space and multi-media

17 Anselm Keifer: *Wayland's Song
(With Wing)*, 1982, oil, emulsion,
straw on photo, on canvas with
lead

extravagance.[18] Pieces like
Diavolozoppo (1984) are
constructed out of as many
materials as the painter can get
his hands on.[19] *The Try Works*
(1988) employs huge slabs of
aluminium pressed into elaborate French curves, layered over
each other, painted in wild red,
blues and pinks.[20]

Frank Stella's massive mixed
media structures are truly wild,
unfettered eruptions of paint,
metal, fibreglass, ink and crayon.
No one can deny that Stella has
very decisively and joyfully
exploded the traditional easel
kind of painting, where everything sits neatly within a box-like
frame, on a flat, illusionistic
surface. Stella's new pieces
systematically demolish the
traditional, academic notion of
painting as a rectangle of illusion.
For there is no illusion in Stella's
works: they are not depicting
anything other than themselves,
with their squiggles and zigzag
patterns, their fluorescent pinks
and lurid greens, their splotches

and dabs and overpainting. Stella
sai din 1964:

> My painting is based on the
> fact that only what can be
> seen there *is* there. It really
> is an object...All I want
> anyone to get out of my
> paintings, and all I ever get
> out of them, is the fact that
> you see the whole idea
> without any confusion...
> What you see is what you
> see.[21]

Frank Stella dislikes the
flatness of modern painting, and
of abstraction in particular: the
smooth flatness of Barnett
Newman or Jules Olitski or
Morris Louis. Much as he
admires other abstract painters,
Stella aims to move beyond
them by destroying the
solemnity of the flatness of
modern painting. He writes in
Working Space, his major artistic
credo:

> The result of modern
> painting's restrictive view of
> flatness has been a negative
> reaction to the yielding
> surface of painting. Paint-
> ing today is trying to be
> deliberately messy in order
> to deny the fragility and

18 Frank Stella: *Thruxton 3X*,
1982, mixed media on etched
aluminium, 75 x 85 x 15 in,
Shindler Collection, Honolulu
19 Frank Stella: *Diavolozoppo*,
1984, oil, urethane enamel,
fluorescent alkyd, acrylic, and
printing ink on canvas, etched
magnesium, aluminium and
fibreglass, 139 x 170 x 16in,
collection: the artist
20 F. Stella: *The Try Works (B-6,
2X)*, 1988, mixed media on cast
aluminium, 281.3 x 235 private
collection

21 F. Stella, radio broadcast, 1964,
in Gregory Battock, ed, 158. See
Robert Rosenblum, 1971, William
S. Rubin, 1970; "Frank Stella:
Portrait of the Artist as an Image
Administrator", *Art in America*,
Feb 1985, 94-107; "Frank Stella
and the Simulacrum", *Flash Art*,
Feb-March 1986, 32-5,

limits of the surfaces available to art. (51)

Aesthetically, the explosion into chaos and mess helps to renew the connection, as Frank Stella says, with the eroticism of texture, with the sexuality of texture and the sensuality of surface, which has always been a large part of art. Think of ancient Greek sculpture: the smoothness of the marble and stone is crucial to the overall experience of the statue. Similarly with Italian Renaissance painting, with all that punched and embossed gold, which provides the spaceless, divine background to Jesus and the Virgin in so many altarpieces and panels.

Jasper Johns' art, like that of Robert Ryman, Leonardo da Vinci, Titian or Rembrandt van Rijn, is founded on the sensuality of paint, of surfaces, of the eroticism of texture. We come back to this again and again in art criticism, this sensualism of surface. As Lynda Nead writes of art critic Kenneth Clark:

Clark reads brush marks and lines as though they are part of a symbolic language of sensual impulses, telling traces of sexual desire.[22]

Donald Judd moved, like Frank Stella and Robert Rauschenberg, from painting to sculpture, although Judd had painted figurative works, as had Barnett Newman and Mark Rothko before they turned to abstraction. Stella, however, has always worked in abstraction. Judd described his move to three dimensions thus:

First, I did the pipe relief and kept it on the floor. It was a big thing when sitting on the floor. I left it on the floor, and that didn't seem to bother it much. It was meant to go on the wall, but it looked all right on the floor. And then the whole situation of the wall so tired of low relief... And I didn't want it to sit back against the wall. A piece that was completely three-dimensional was a big event for me.[23]

There are many artists who use multiple panels or 3-D paintings that more than rival Frank Stella's recent 'maximalist paintings': Anselm Keifer sticks bits of straw onto his oil

22 Lynda Nead: "Getting down to basics: art, obscenity and the female nude", in Isobel Armstrong, ed, 206
23 "Donald Judd: An Interview with John Coplans", 21-23, in B. Haskell: Donald Judd, 1148

paintings.24 Elizabeth Murray produces marvellous shaped panels, which are more like sculptural reliefs than traditional paintings: the third dimension, the depth from the wall on which the painting hangs, becomes an added element.25 Sam Gillam creates complexly shaped 'paintings' which, like Stella's constructs, gleefully smash the primacy of the traditional rectangle in painting;26 Robert Mangold explores colour and architecture in his multi-panelled paintings which often contain a unifying element of drawing;27 and Judy Pfaff's multi-media installations are riots of colour and materials which sometimes out-distance Stella in scale and madness.28

What this shows, this emphasis on the sensuality of surface, colour and other formal elements of painting, is that painting's eroticism is crucial to its effect, just as much as in sculpture. Without this eroticism of colour, surface, texture, shape, pattern and form, painting loses much of its impact. Art historians call this eroticism of form 'beauty', that old Platonic word for all that is desirable. What 'beauty' means is precisely this experience and the relation of the eroticism of the painting-as-object. The word 'beauty' too is distinctly femin-ized in art criticism, for the 'beauty' of a painting is a 'feminine' quality; the painting is thus equivalent to a woman, to 'women'. The more a painting or sculpture reveals its sensuality, the more 'beautiful' it will be. It is the same when people look at women: women and paintings are thus equated in fine art criticism: the painting is stared at and enjoyed, as is the woman. The female nude, then, com-bines the two erotic pleasures, of art and women, of art and sex (with looking as the basis of the exchange). 'Beauty' is thus a neat Platonic term that

24 A. Keifer: *Margarethe*, 1981, oil and straw on canvas, 9'2" x 12'6", Saatchi Collection, London; *Nürnberg–Festspiel–Weise*, 1981, oil, straw, mixed media on canvas, 9'2" x 12'6", collection; Eli & Edythe L. Broad, Los Angeles
25 Elizabeth Murray: *Simple Meaning*, 1982, oil on two canvases, 107 x 96in, collection: Jerry & Emily Spiegel, New York; *Fire Cup*, 1982, oil on canvas, each canvas 92 x 82in, Paula Cooper Gallery, New York. See Paul Gardner: "Elizabeth Murray Shapes Up", *Ârt News*, Sept 1984, 47-55; Roberta Smith, 1987.
26 Sam Gillam: *Like Today*, 1985, acrylic on canvas with aluminium construction, 55 x 67 x 4in, Monique Knowlton Gallery, New York
27 Robert Mangold: *Four Color Frame Painting no. 1*, acrylic and pencil on canvas, 111 x 105in, collection: Martin Sklar, New York

28 Judy Pfaff: *N.Y.C.–B.Q.E, 1987*, painted steel, plastic laminates, fibreglass and wood, 15 x 35 x 5 feet, Max Protetch Gallery, New York

incorporates many forms of erotic looking or pleasure. The art object is that 'beautiful' thing that gives pleasure, like 'woman' in cultural discourse.

ANDY WARHOL, CLAUS OLDENBURG, ROBERT RAUSCHENBERG

Eroticism abounds in contemporary art, where the æsthetic of materialism, of junk, of mass culture, of design and printed reproduction, dominates art. Andy Warhol is the high priest of contemporary art, of Pop Art, of art that embraces anything and everything. Everything can be included in contemporary art: ashtrays, car crash victims, Coke cans, bland skyscrapers, whatever is around can be used. This is the 'pop æsthetic'.[29] The artist who throws anything onto the picture plane is Robert Rauschenberg[30] (see his many 'combine' paintings, mixed media extravaganzas. Rauschenberg has the magical ability, as with Joseph Cornell or Max Ernst, for taking

29 See Bob Colacello: *Holy Terror: Andy Warhol Close Up*, New York 1990; Andy Warhol: *POPism: The Warhol 60s*, New York 1980; Carter Ratcliff: *Andy Warhol*, New York 1983

30 See Robert Hughes: "The Arcadian as Utopian", *Time*, 24 Jan 1983, 74, 77; Roni Feinstein: "The Early Work of Robert Rauschenberg: The White Paintings, the Black Paintings, and the Elemental Sculptures", *Arts*, September 1986, 28-37; Charles F. Stuckey: "Reading Rauschenberg", *Art in America*, April 1977, 74-84; Calvin Tomkins: *Off the Wall: Robert Rauschenberg and the Art World of Our Time*, New York 1980.

everyday objects and giving them a new, uncanny allure. It's just paint, canvas and a few items culled from antique stalls or dumpsters, but somehow Rauschenberg alchemically transforms them, as in *Canyon* and *Odalisque*).31 Claes Oldenburg's soft telephones and toilets far outdo Rauschenberg for pure oddness. Oldenburg goes much further than Warhol in questioning the holy notion of 'Art' with a capital 'a'.32

Contemporary art has to have three dimensions in its specifications, it seems. The picture plane, which had been so scrupulously flat throughout the European Renaissance (ignoring the embossed and punched gold), suddenly bursts open in contemporary art. As Clement Greenberg put it: '[p]ictorial space has lost its "inside" and become all "outside".'33 Sculpture in the 1960s lost some of its 'inside': Robert Morris's and Donald Judd's cubes, for instance, do not offer any 'inside', any 'essence'. Of course, some contemporary artists asserted the flatness of the picture plane even more fervently: Morris Louis with his stained, furled canvas, Frank Stella with his black stripes done with housepaint direct onto cotton duck, Mark Rothko with his cloud-like shapes, Agnes Martin with her finely pencilled squares, and Sol LeWitt with his spacious walldrawings. Lucio Fontana, though, destroyed the flatness of the canvas in a phallic, penetrative fashion: he slashed the canvas.34 Fontana explained his seemingly violent, nay, pornographic act in terms of space, thus:

> I want to open up space, create a new dimension for art, tie in at the cosmos as it endlessly expands beyond the confining place of the picture. With my innovation of the hole pierced through the canvas in repetitive perforations, I have not attempted to decorate a surface, but, on the contrary, I have tried to break its dimensional limitations. Beyond the perforations a newly gained freedom of interpretation awaits us, but also, and just as inevitably, the end

31 R. Rauschenberg: *Canyon*, 1959, combine painting, 219.7x 179 x 57.8cm, Sonnabend Gallery, New York; *Odalisque*, 1955-8, wood, material, wire, grass, paper, photographs, metal, stuffed rooster, 4 lightbulbs, 205 x 44 x 44cm, Museum Ludwig, Cologne.
32 Oldenburg: *Soft Toilet,* 1966, vinyl filled with kapok, painted with liquitex, and wood,132 x 81 x 76.2cm, Whitney Museum of American Art, New York; *Soft Pay-Telephone*, 1963, vinyl filled with kapok, mounted on painted wood, 118.1 x 48.2 x 23cm, Guggenheim Museum, New York
33 Greenberg: *Art and Culture*, Beacon Press, Boston 1961, 134

34 Lucas Fontana: *Tela tagliata*, c. 1960, private collection

of art.35

Everyone apart from the Minimal artists, though, was throwing everything they could lay their hands on at the canvas. Typical contemporary works employ a plethora of media and techniques, including wood, plastic, acrylic, oil, pencil, metal, wire, fur, stone, leaves, cotton and glue. There is certainly an element of eroticism in this chaotic use of multiple medias. Contemporary art sometimes looks like that of adults regressed to kids and let loose on a mound of materials. Pop Art in particular is highly energetic in its appropriation of every sort of material.

In the work of many contemporary artists, gesture is crucial, and erotic in its sensuality. It is central to Jackson Pollock's dripped paintings, to Franz Kline's arcane, thick black brushstrokes, to Pablo Picasso's bronze sculptures, and to Willem de Kooning's wild expressionism.36

It's easy to spot the cases

of erotica in contemporary high art. In Allen Jones' fetishized, half-naked sculptures of characterless women who become chairs or the legs of a table. Jones' painted fibreglass women, with their high heels, stockings and elbow-length gloves are pure pornography.37 They are pure fetish-objects, like Hans Bellmer's *Doll,* or Thomas Rowlandson's erotic drawings. Several Pop artists featured the phallus, and the Rolling Stones used giant wieners on stage on one of their tours: Brigid Polk with her *Cock Book*, Claes Oldenburg in his *Capric Monument,* Andy Warhol with his prints from *Blue Movie,* and Robert Rauschenberg with his *Carnal Clock.*

The 'original' Pop Art image, by Richard Hamilton (*Just what is it that makes today's homes so different, so appealing?*),38 depicts a muscleman carrying a huge lollipop. The red sphere and stick of the lollipop is a phallus, an image of the phallus which has been reduced to idiocy, to mere candy. Most of Pop Art, and contemporary art,

35 L. Fontana, quoted in Jan Van der Marck, *Lucas Fontana,* catalogue, Walker Art Center Minneapolis 1966
36 J. Pollock: *Blue Poles,* 1952, enamel, aluminium, glass on canvas, 41 x 106in, collection: Joseph H. Hazen; de Kooning: *Door to the River,* 1960, 203 x 179cm, Whitney Museum, New York; Kline: *Wotan,* 1950, oil, 201 x 150cm, collection: A. I. Sherr, New York

37 Allen Jones: *Table,* 1969, *Chair,* 1969, both painted fibre-glass, leather and hair, life-size, Neue Galerie, Aachen
38 Richard Hamilton: *Just what is it that makes today's homes so different, so appealing?,* 1956, collage, 26 x 25cm, Kunsthalle Tübingen, Tübingen

is wildly phallic, from a feminist point-of-view; that is, inundated with phallic lust, with phallic desires, phallic objects (cars, guns, machines), and phallic values (the values of capitalism; accumulate, accumulate, grab, grab, grab).

There is no escaping erotica/ porno in contemporary art, it seems. It is everywhere – from the less well-known (in the German sculptor Gustav Seitz's *The Chooser*,[39] where three women stand waiting to be 'chosen' by a man), to the most famous icons of Andy Warhol or David Hockney.

Like Jasper Johns and Robert Rauschenberg, Robert Longo incorporates some of the formal aspects of sculpture in his paintings. As with David Salle and Eric Fischl, Longo uses the imagery of porn, though his multi-media approach makes the irony more obvious, as in his *Still*, for instance.[40] Francis Bacon's few depictions of lovemaking emphasized the brute physicality of bodies clashing together.[41] Bacon's Expressionist view of sex is the familiar one of patriarchy: that sex is an aggressive, violent 'act', a view found in much of Western art and literature.

39 Gustav Seitz: *The Chooser*, 1956
40 Robert Longo: *Still*, 1984, acrylic on silkscreen on wood; charcoal and graphite on dyed paper; oil and copper leaf on hammered oak; oil on hammered lead, 248 x 732cm, private collection
41 F. Bacon: *Two Figures*, 1953, oil on canvas, 5 x 3'10", private collection

10

Contemporary Sculpture

BOMBASTIC SCULPTURE

Contemporary sculpture has out-dazzled painting in many ways. However exciting a painting by, say, Julian Schnabel, Anselm Keifer, Jasper Johns, Robert Longo, Eric Fischl or David Salle may be, sculptures by artists such as Nancy Graves, Rebecca Horn, Robert Morris, Tony Smith, Mark di Suvero, Eva Hesse, Lucas Samaras and Louise Nevelson out-dazzle the painters.

Contemporary sculpture is, on the whole, really extra-ordinary. While Renaissance painting may represent the apotheosis of high art, and ancient Greek sculpture may be the height of 'high sculpture', contemporary sculpture really is startling. Part of the reason is, of course, scale. Contemporary artists, of all kinds, have made massive art, sometimes achieving the truly 'monumental' effect beloved of art critics. David Smith's *Wagon I* and his *Cubi* sculptures are huge, heavy, chunky, truly colossal pieces which dominate their surroundings.42 Donald Judd wrote: '[t]his scale is one of the most important developments in

42 David Smith: *Wagon I*, 1963-4, painted steel, 308.6 x 162.6 x 224.8cm, National Gallery of Scotland

twentieth century art'.43 The Abstract Expressionists may still have made 'easel paintings' despite claiming they didn't (Barnett Newman argued on this matter), but they made gigantic paintings. Helen Frankenthaler, Mark Rothko, Franz Kline and Newman produced huge paintings, which swallow up the spectator when s/he moves close to them. Similarly, contemporary sculptors have made massive works. Artists such as the Christos created pieces that were 24 miles long (such as their *Running Fence*).44 Even medium-sized pieces, such as Donald Judd's wooden boxes, are sometimes seen as monumental. A critic on *The New York Times* called Judd's 1977 installation at the Heiner Friedrich Gallery a 'majestic and finely measured presence'.45

The bombastic, 'monumental', massive and brash sculpture in contemporary art was not made exclusively by

male artists. Mary Miss created a 5-acre scale work in Illinois, while Nancy Holt produced gigantic *Sun Tunnels*, 18 foot long pipes that were 9 feet high with many holes punched in the side, to let light in.46 Helen Escobedo has created some huge concrete and steel sculptures which 'attempt to fuse hard-edge geometric forms with nature's organic manifest-ations' as she puts it. Works such as *Snake* rise impressively from the Earth, celebrating the flux and movement of organic forms.47

Many of the celebrated products of contemporary 'sculpture', however, have been made by male artists: Donald Judd's 'specific objects', those blocks of aluminium and Plexiglass that 'climb' gallery walls,48 Tony Smith's monumental cubes with their *thereness*, the primacy of

43 Donald Judd: *Complete Writings 1959-1975*, 200f
44 Christo: *Running Fence*, 1972-6, steel poles, steel cables, woven nylon, 18 ft high, 24.5 miles long, Sonoma & Marin Counties, California
45 "Donald Judd", *The New York Times*, 1 April 1977, C20. See Donald Judd: *Complete Writings, 1959-1975*; William Agee, 1975, 40-49; P. Carlson: "Donald Judd's Equivocal Objects", *Art in America*, Jan 1984, 114-8; Donald Kuspit, 1985; Barbara Haskell, 1988; Brydon Smith, 1975.

46 Mary Miss: *Field Rotation*, 1981, wood, steel, gravel, earth, 5-acre site, central well 60 ft square and 7 feet deep, Governors' University, Park Forest South, Illinois; Nancy Holt: *Sun Tunnels*, 1973-6, concrete, each pipe 18 ft long, 9 ft high, Great Basin Desert, near Lucin, Utah
47 Helen Escobedo: *Snake*, 1980-1, painted steel, 49 ft high, National University of Mexico Cultural Centre
48 Donald Judd: *Untitled*, 1968, ten units, each 9 x 40in x 31in, height 14'3", Nelson A. Rockefeller Empire State Plaza Art Collection, New York.

presence, not effect,[49] Dan Flavin's[50] mesmeric fluorescent tubes,[51] Sol LeWitt's Conceptual cubes, Richard Serra's huge 'walls' or slabs of steel,[52] and Carl Andre's plates of steel, copper and zinc.[53]

One of the most exciting developments of contemporary sculpture and art is the installation, the taking-over of a whole space or environment – the floor, walls and ceiling. The installation is pretty much the default position for any contemporary art exhibition these days. Examples of installation art include: Rebecca Horn's *Ballet of the Woodpecker* of the mid-1980s, a room full of mirrors, or Sylvia Stone's *Crystal Palace* of the early 1970s.[54]

49 Tony Smith: *Die*, 1962, 72 x 72 x 72in, Paula Cooper Gallery, New York. See Lucy Lippard, 1972, Gene Baro, 1967, 27-31, E. Greene: "Morphology of Tony Smith's Work", *Artforum*, April 1974, 54-9

50 See Ira Licht, 1968, 50-57, William Wilson: "Dan Flavin: Fiat Lux", *Art News*, Jan 1970, 48-51; Jack Burnham:, 1969, 48-55

51 Dan Flavin: *Untitled (to the "innovator" of Wheeling Peachblow)*, 1968, 96.5 x 96.5 x 5.7in, Museum of Modern Art, New York; *Untitled*, 1976, pink, blue, green fluorescent light, 96in high, Saatchi Collection, London.

52 Richard Serra: *Clara-Clara*, 1983, Cor-Ten steel, installation, Jardin des Tuileries, Paris. See Rosalind E. Krauss:, 1972, 38-43, Douglas Crimp: "Richard Serra: Sculpture Exceeded", *October*, Fall 1981, 67-78

53 Carl Andre: *Lead Piece (144 Lead Plates)*, overall 75 x 144.8 x 145.5in, Museum of Modern Art, New York. See Kenneth Baker, 1980, 88 -94, Diane Waldman: "Holding the Floor", *Art News*, Oct 1970, 60-2, 75-9, Phyllis Tuchman, 1978, 29-33; Enno Develing, 1969

54 Sylvia Stone: *Crystal Palace*, 1971-2, Plexiglass, 6.5 x 14 x 16 ft, Andre Emmerich Gallery, New York; Rebecca Horn; *Ballet of the Woodpecker*, 1986-7, room installation with mirrors, small hammers and a painting machine,330 x 230cm (4 mirrors), 330 x 125cm (4 mirrors), Eric Franck Gallery, Geneva; Red Grooms & Mimi Gross: *The City of Chicago*, 1967, mixed media, c. 12 x 25 x 25 ft, Art Institute of Chicago

ALEXANDER CALDER AND BARNETT NEWMAN

There is an undisputed eroticism in Alexander Calder's (1898-1976) mobiles. Calder's constructions are delicate filaments of wire, with the distinctive 'leaf' or circle shape at the end of each tendril (they are delicate even when they're constructed on a giant scale). The actual construction of the mobiles is dazzling in itself. In *Thirteen Spines* (1940), Calder fixes one wire to another, near the end, forming a chain of spines rather like the quills of some mechanical armadillo.[55]

Alexander Calder's mobiles mystify with their extraordinary balancing acts. We take the mobile for granted now, so obvious does its construction seem. We see mobiles every-where, with teddies, whales, fairies, clowns, stars, moons, cars, trains and Pierrots hanging from them. Yet, before Calder, there were no mobiles – not in the form we know them today.

Sculptors before Alexander Calder have employed balance in sculpture. When an object balances it sets up an immediate, physical tension. Barnett Newman traded on this mystifying, gravity-defying aspect of sculpture in his *Broken Obelisk* (1963-67). This is a pillar balancing on the tip of a pyramid.[56] The balancing of the steel pillar is a technical *tour-de-force*, a piece of bravado that seems macho because Newman conceived of the two forms as masculine and feminine. Guess which one is on top: the male. In a similar way, Constantin Brancusi conceived his *Adam and Eve* sculpture as one form on top of the other. Guess which one was on top. In Newman's and Brancusi's sculpture, the male element is nearer the sky, it is spiritual, transcendent, ascendant, superior. The feminine element is underneath, close to the earth, a squat, nurturing figure which holds up the male's balancing act which seems like showing off.

Like so many of Barnett Newman's paintings, his *Broken Obelisk* is conceived as an act of faith, a flame in the darkness. Like Constantin Brancusi's *Birds in Space*, Newman's sculpture aims to soar heavenward in some ultimate act of earthly transcendence. The religious aspect of Newman's sculpture is a part of his overall religious sensibility: he used elements of the *Qabbalah* (Jewish mystic-

55 Alexander Calder: *Thirteen Spines*, 1940, sheet steel, rods, wire and aluminium, 84 in, Wallraf-Richartz Museum, Cologne

56 Barnett Newman: *Broken Obelisk*, 1963-7, Cor-Ten steel, 26 ft high, Institute of Religion and Human Development, Houston

ism), he created a *Stations of the Cross* series, and his paintings have titles such as *Vir Heroicus Sublimis, Cathedra* and *Onement*.[57]

What is most exciting about Alexander Calder's skeletal mobiles, though, is their motion. The mobiles drift slowly, each arm moving in a different manner from the others. Calder's mobiles shift in the wind. They are powered by the random, natural energy of the breeze. The balancing acts of Calder's mobiles are playful – the sculptures set alight the space around themselves with their gravity-shaping design and movement, as if drawing in space. All sculpture exists in a space, whether virtual, artificial or actual. Norbert Kricke created sculptures which looked like frozen lightning strikes, all spikey and angular, the thin rods of steel being set at different angles to each other.[58] Calder does not have a monopoly on thin, spindly sculptures made of steel: David Smith, Hans Uhlmann, Eduardo Chillida, Nancy Graves, Jean Tinguely, Alberto Giacometti, and Norbert Kricke all produced sculptures in this manner.

57 See Harold Rosenberg: *Art on the Edge*, Macmillan 1975; Lawrence Alloway: "The Stations of the Cross and the Subjects of the Artist", in *Barnett Newman: The Stations of the Cross: Lama Sabacthani*, Guggenheim Museum 1966; E.C. Goossen: "The Philosophic Line of B. Newman", *Art News*, Summer 1958
58 Norbert Kricke: *Space Sculpture*, 1958-9, stainless steel, 9.4 ft high, Municipality Leverkusen, Germany

KINETIC SCULPTURE

Alexander Calder's mobiles, no matter what the scale, extend far beyond themselves, by virtue of their construction and motion. Like optical and light sculpture, Calder's mobiles create spaces around themselves which act on the viewer in a palpable manner, quite distinct from the relatively staid and stolid approach to sculpture of, say, Antonio Canova or Luca della Robbia. This is not to say that pre-20th century sculpture is immobile: far from it. Take Giovanni da Bologna's *Mercury* (1564), for instance: as the winged messenger of mythology, a static depiction of Mercury or Hermes would be a mistake, and da Bologna's statue is full of movement.[59] Gianlorenzo Bernini's *David* (1623) is similarly kinetic: the man's body is twisting, ready for battle, ready to carry out one of the most celebrated acts of murder in the history of art.[60]

The kinetic dimension would be out of place in the sombre religiosity of Barnett Newman's or Constantin Brancusi's sculptures. There are some sculptors' work which just seems to be static and rock solid. Indeed if Michelangelo Buonarroti's statues of *Moses* or the *Pietà* were kinetic, it would be utterly out of keeping with the tone and theme of these sculptures. Other sculptors, though, actively developed motion in sculpture, especially in the modern era: Naum Gabo with his *Kinetic Construction*, with its oscillating rod, Len Lye's magnetized steel *Loop* and his *Fountain*, which wafts from side to side, Marcel Duchamp with his *Rotorelief*, which span, creating a circle, and George Rickey with his swaying rods of steel, as in *Peristyle III*, 1966.[61]

But the master of kinetic sculpture must be the rebellious Jean Tinguely (1925-91), whose motorized sculpture gleefully and mischievously create chaos. Tinguely's sculptures don't just move – in all directions – they are very noisy, with clatterings, bangs, pants, grinds and wheezes. The most famous was

59 Giovanni da Bologna: *Mercury*, 1564, Museo Nazionale, Florence
60 Gianlorenzo Bernini: *David*, 1623, Galleria Borghese, Rome

61 Naum Gabo: *Kinetic Construction*, 1920, metal rod with electric vibrator, 24.2in high, Tate Gallery, London; Len Lye: *The Loop*, 1963, stainless steel, 60 x 6in, Art Institute, Chicago, *Fountain II*, 1959, steel, motorized, 7.5 ft high, Howard Wise Gallery, New York; George Rickey: *Peristyle III*, 1966, stainless steel, 40.5 x 102.5 x 60.2in, Corcoran Gallery of Art, Washington DC; Marcel Duchamp: *Rotorelief (Revolving Glass)*, 1920, three strips of painted glass on metal frame, 4 x 6 ft, Yale University Art Gallery, New Haven

Hommage à New York of 1960, a sculpture 'created for self-destruction'.62 Daniel Wheeler describes some of the actions of Tinguely's monster machine:

> the machine was supposed to beat a steady, thundering din on the bassinet and washing-machine drum, switch on the radio at maximum volume, and send a horizontal roll of paper down a sheet-metal trough, there to be attacked by two large brushes held by an elaborately constructed painting arm and then blown into the audience by the electric fan. Meanwhile ten armatures of bicycle parts were to strike the piano's keys in sequence, at the same time that two pairs of spindles would wind and then rewind scrolls of writing. Adding to the syncopated clamor were to have been a bell and the Addressograph machine, whose ringing and clatter would help to set off numerous other things, such as the stink- and smoke-producing chemicals stored in the bassinet, the silver-dollar "thrower" contributed by Robert Rauschenberg, the orange balloon exploding atop a 2-foot mast, and, at the end, a wheeled, flag-waving, cable-drum carriage careering forward to drown in the reflecting pool reigned over by Maillol's monumental female nude personification called *The River*. Few of these particular "events' ever took place, owing to immediate and chronic breakdown, which almost invariably happened in Tinguely's Meta-matic performances, but all kinds of other wonders did come to pass, which, being, unexpected, struck Tinguely as far superior to anything he had programed. (239-240)

62 Jean Tinguely: *Hommage à New York*, 1960, mixed media, motorized, Sculpture Garden of the Museum of Modern Art, New York

CRAGG, HANSON, DE ANDREA AND OTHER SCULPTORS

There is eroticism in Tony Cragg's steel vessels, or Anne and Patrick Poirier's long, elegant *Archæological Model*, or Jannis Kounellis' *Cotton Sculpture*, a mass of cotton stuffed into a large steel container – a sculpture of contrasts between the softness of the cotton and the rigidity of the steel, or Jackie Windsor's *Burnt Piece*, a 3 foot cube made of concrete, wire and burnt wood.[63]

British artist Tony Cragg has spoken of having 'an erotic response to the external world', something which, it seems, all artists have, or have to have, to be truly great artists.[64]

In the figures of realist or hyperrealist sculpture we see people frozen in often bizarre attitudes and poses, as in Duane Hanson's *The Tourists and other works* (1970).[65] Hanson's figures are vicious and ironic, exploiting the eerie otherness of the life-size dummy and waxwork, while George Segal's explore the alienation of modern life (it's as if Hanson only has to reproduce what people really wear and really carry and really look like to make a powerful artistic statement about the unreality of contemporary life).

Anthony Donaldson has produced a truly horrible *Girl Sculpture* (1970), a plastic red and gold model of a woman – naked, of course – set in a 'streamlined' mould, rather like the 3-D logos beloved of entertainment organizations, where the letters are drawn in exaggerated perspective.[66] Sculpture as capitalist commodification.

John De Andrea also explores 'the resignation,

63 Tony Cragg: *Instinctive React-ions*, 1987, cast steel, 8 x 21 x 15 ft, Lisson Gallery, London; Jackie Windsor: *Burnt Piece*, 1977-8, concrete, wire and burnt wood, 36in cube, Paula Cooper Gallery, New York; Jannis Kounellis: *Cotton Sculpture*, 1967, steel and cotton, 3.9 x 3.9 x 4.9 ft, collection: the artist; Anne & Patrick Poirier: *Archaeological Model*, 1986, Bath International Festival. See Terry A. Neff, 1987; Ben Jones: "A New Wave in Sculpture: A survey of recent work by ten younger sculptors", *Artscribe*, 8, September 1977, 16; Lisa Ponti: "Tony Cragg", *Domus*, 611, Nov 1980, 50-51; Isabelle Lamaître: "Interview with Tony Cragg", *Artefactum*, 2, Dec 1985, 7-11; Germano Celant: "Tony Cragg and Industrial Platonism", *Artforum*, 20, 3, Nov 1981, 40-46

64 Tony Cragg, quoted in D. Wheeler, 324
65 Duane Hanson: *The Tourists*, 1970, polyster resin, polychrome glass fibre, National Gallery of Scotland, Edinburgh; *Bunny*, 1970, fibreglass, life-size, O.K. Harris Gallery, New York
66 Anthony Donaldson: *Girl Sculpture "Red 'n' Gold"*, 1970, 75 x 448cm, Rowan Gallery, London

emptiness and loneliness'[67] of contemporary life, that emotional territory of Middle America that Raymond Carver so successfully explored in his short stories. But De Andrea's nudes turn out to be just as negatively pornographic as other high art nudes.[68] Take his *Reclining Woman* (1970),[69] which is a Superrealist version of the high art 'reclining nude', a life-size and seeming 'life-like' rendition of a person. There are differences of æsthetic approaches in the Superrealist plastic doll-woman and the female nude of high art sculpture, but, essentially, both are works of porn, and De Andrea's work is no different than sculptures such as Fritz Klimsch's *Eos*, a woman posing in voluptuous fashion, arms behind her head, hips thrown to one side, a pin-up sculpted nude.[70] But De Andrea's reclining woman recalls the blow-up doll sex toy. Reg Butler's bronzes of women – naked, of course – are 'exquisitely crafted', to use terms typical of art criticism,[71] but in fact turn out to be very sexist representations of women.[72]

67 John De Andrea, quoted in Le Normand-Romain, 241
68 John De Andrea: *Couple*, 1971, acrylic on polyester and hair, man 5.7 ft high, woman 5.1 ft high, Musée d'Art Moderne, Paris
69 John De Andrea: *Reclining Woman*, 1970, life-size, David Bermant Collection
70 Fritz Klimsch: *Eos*, 1904
71 Edward Lucie-Smith: *Sculpture since 1945*, 33
72 Reg Butler: *Girl on Red Base*, 1968-72, painted bronze, 32 x 43 x 63.5in, Pierre Matisse Gallery, New York

SUGARMAN, NOGUCHI, POMODORO, SAMARAS

George Sugarman's flowing sculptures tend towards eroticism, like Lynda Benglis's or Gio Pomodoro's. With their twisting, entwined forms painted in red, white, green and yellow,[73] Sugarman creates a series of objects, interlinked spatially and thematically, set end to end, a chain of mysterious forms. Sugarman's seemingly disparate collections of objects are united in part by his use of colour. Taking his cue from Stuart Davis, Sugarman used colour spatially. In Sugarman's art, the flat colour – all-over red, or yellow, or green – tends to suppress the irregularity of his peculiar shapes. This use of colour to flatten gives a collection of objects a unity is found also in Tony Cragg's *New Stones*, where all the kitchen utensils, household items, children's toys and bits and pieces are painted with the colours of the spectrum in a uniform manner, going from red through yellow to blue. When bright, primary colours are employed in sculpture, as in the grand scale of Minimal sculpture, such as on Isamu Noguchi's huge *Red Cube*, the result has a formal purity that borders on the childlike. How simple and 'right' seem these bold, bright colours seem when combined with the simplicity, boldness and exactness of basic geometric shapes such as cubes, or spheres, cones or pyramids. You might see this indulgence in purity and precision combined with vivid colouration as an erotic pleasure. You find this simplicity of colour and formal purity in Philip King's orange and green painted blocks (*Call*), the powder colour on Anish Kapoor's semi-organic shapes (*Half*), and the green lacquer on John McCracken's *Untitled*, although Minimal/ Conceptual sculptors such as Sol LeWitt only permitted themselves white.[74]

Gio Pomodoro's sculptures are crumpled sheets of fibreglass which directly recall the fields of unbroken colour of the Abstract Expressionists, in particular Barnett Newman,

---

73 George Sugarman: *Bardana*, 1962-3, polychromed wood, 8 x 12 x 5.1 ft, Galerie Renée Ziegler, Zurich

74 Isamu Noguchi: *Red Cube*, 1969, painted welded steel and aluminium, 28 ft high, 140, Broadway, New York; Anish Kapoor: *Half*, 1984, polystyrene, cement, earth, acrylic medium and pigment, 5.6 x 3.1in, Barbara Gladstone Gallery, New York; John McCracken: *Untitled*, 1967, fibreglass and lacquer, 7.9 x 1.2 x 0.1 ft, Saatchi Collection; Philip King: *Call*, 1967, fibreglass and painted steel, two pieces each 14.5 x 0.5 x 0.5 ft, two pieces each 5 x 6 x 3 ft, Juda Rowan Gallery, London

Franz Kline and Mark Rothko.[75] Pomodoro moves away from the flatness of much of Abstract Expressionism and Minimalism, introducing curves and hollows in his sheets of fibreglass which suggest the subtle, lyrical changes in colour and tone associated with the colourfield works of Rothko and Morris Louis.

Lucas Samaras' pieces are the flipside of George Sugarman's sensual forms. Samaras deliberately subverts the eroticism of sculpture by furnishing his sculptures and assemblages with pins, nails, razor blades, knives and scissors, as in his vicious *Book 4*, which is stuffed with knives, nails and razor blades.[76] For Samaras, as for so many (male) artists from Dante Alighieri through the Marquis de Sade to Georges Bataille, sex (pleasure) is intermixed with death, or, as Samaras puts it: 'I cannot separate beauty from pain.'[77]

LAND ART

Land art (a.k.a. earth art/ earthworks/ environmental art) have proved to be among the most phallic and patriarchal of contemporary productions, from a (second wave) feminist viewpoint.[78] I have already mentioned Christo, who wraps buildings or stretches curtains across valleys or surrounds islands with 1000s of yards of tarpaulin.[79] Other domineering works of land art in this vein (many from the 'golden age of land art, the 1960s-1970s), include Michael Heizer's famous *Double Negative* of the late 1960s, where he (and a team – he didn't do it with his bare hands!) carved two chunks out of the earth, a gigantic mark on the planet.[80] Heizer's other works include gouging huge holes in the ground and putting

75 Gio Pomodoro: *Tensione*, 1959, black fibreglass, 5.9 x 4.2 x 1.9 ft, David Anderson Gallery, Buffalo
76 Lucas Samaras: *Book 4*, 1962,5.5 x 8.8 x 11.5in, Museum of Modern Art, New York
77 quoted in Diane Waldman: "Samaras", *Art News*, Oct 1966, 56

78 See Alan Sonfist, ed: *Art in the Land: A Critical Anthology of Environmental Art*, New York 1983, John Beardsley, 1984
79 Christo: *Surrounded Islands, Biscoyne Bay, Greater Miami*, 1980-3, 6 million square feet of polypropylene fabric; *Valley Curtain*, synthetic fabric, 417m long, 1970-2, Grand Canyon, Colorado
80 Michael Heizer: *Double Negative*, 1969-70, 1,500 x 50 x 42 feet, Mormon Mesa, Nevada. See Julia Brown et al: *Michael Heizer: Sculpture in Reverse*, Museum of Contemporary Art, Los Angeles 1984, Gregoire Müller: "Michael Heizer", *Arts Magazine*, Dec 1969, 42-5

great chunks of rock in them, and also creating geometric holes in the ground (such as can be seen at DIA in Beacon in upstate New York, one of the great collections of contemporary art anywhere in the world).[81]

Walter de Maria made a similarly deep mark in the earth when he cut a 4.5 mile long scar in the desert in Nevada (the desert, especially in the South-West, was a favourite stamping ground for the American land artists, and also the American Minimal artists). The ultimate in ithyphallic, masculine land art has to be de Maria *Vertical Earth Kilometer*. At a cost of $500,000, de Maria (and an industrial team – he didn't do it with his bare hands!), sunk a brass rod a kilometre (0.6 mile) into the planet. Nothing can be seen of it except a 2 inch brass disc on the ground.

There's no denying the sensuality and eroticism of land art and earthworks. In another famous piece, Walter de Maria filled a gallery with black soil, and the effect is undoubtedly sensual (de Maria's *New York*

Earth Room[82] can still be seen in Gotham, operated by DIA – highly recommended. You can also visit de Maria's *Broken Kilometer* not far away in Lower Manhattan. Both are free).

More spectacular (and just as masculine and phallic in its connotations of male creativity, sperm, fire, power and shamanism), is Walter de Maria's *Lightning Field*, a grid of 400 stainless steel poles, each about 20 feet high, set in the New Mexico desert. (there are two versions of this famous earthwork)[83] The sheer size of some of the works of land artists or earth artists is itself visceral and erotic. De Maria's *Lightning Field*, for instance, attracts lightning, and a storm, as anyone knows, is one of the most erotic phenomenon in nature (as well as dangerous).[84] Many poets have written of the eroticism of nature, among

---

81 Michael Heizer: *Displaced, Replaced Mass*, 1969, Silver Springs, Nevada

82 Walter de Maria: *The New York Earth Room*, 1977, 250 cubic yards of earth and earth mix (peat and bark), covering 3,600 square feet to a depth of 22 inches, installation, Dia Art Foundation, New York.
83 *Lighting Field*, 1971-7, 400 stainless steel poles, in a rectangular grid, 16 x 25, spaced 220 feet apart, average pole height 20'7", New Mexico. See David Bourdon, 1968, 39-43, 72, Malcolm Winton: "Sculptures That Blow Away", *Ark*, Spring 1970, 18-19, Roberta Smith: "De Maria: elements", *Art in America*, May 1978, 102-5
84 See Peter Redgrove: *The Black Goddess; The Clypoean Mistress*, Bloodaxe, 1993

them John Wolfgang von Goethe, Sylvia Plath, John Keats, Arthur Rimbaud, and Emilys Brontë and Dickinson. In many poems, British poet Peter Redgrove has written of the eroticism of nature, and especially of thunderstorms. This is from 'The Pale Brows of Lightning':

> And lightning opens its
>   shutter but an instant,
> When it catches you burn
>   like a candle,
> What is that lambent
>   shadow fluttering into
>   the woods
> In its own blue light that
>   illuminates primrose
> The ripped tree's flesh?[85]

Lightning Field assumes some of its impact from the fact that it is interacting directly with *real* storms, not storms constructed in an art gallery, and it is outside in the world, not built in a city.

Joseph Beuys produced a startling piece in the mid-1980s entitled *Lightning*: a gigantic chunk of bronze, thin at the top, splaying out towards the bottom, as if he is trying to make manifest the bolt of energy leaping down to the earth.[86]

Robert Smithson's famous *Spiral Jetty* is another monumental earthwork, though the use of the spiral motif has connotations with the ancient symbols of the Goddess.[87] Of his *Spiral Jetty*, Smithson writes:

> As I looked at the site, it reverberated out to the horizons only to suggest an immobile cyclone while flickering light made the entire landscape appear to quake. A dormant earthquake spread into an immense roundness. From that gyrating space emerged the possibility of the Spiral Jetty. No idea, no concepts, no systems, no structures, no abstractions could hold themselves together in the actuality of that phenomenological evidence.[88]

Not all of land and earth art has been (or is) of the phallic and bombastic kind. Richard Long speaks for many British sculptors when he writes:

> In the sixties there was a feeling that art need not be a production line of more objects to fill the world. My interest was in a more thoughtful view of art and nature, making art both visible and invisible, using

85 Peter Redgrove: *The Man Named East and other new poems*, Routledge & Kegan Paul 1985
86 Joseph Beuys: *Lightning*, 1982-5, bronze, Anthony d'Offay Gallery, London

87 See Marija Gimbutas; Monica Sjoo, Shirley Nicholson
88 R. Smithson" "The Spiral Jetty", unpublished MS, quoted in R. Krauss, 282. See Robert Hobbs, 1981

ideas, walking, stones, tracks, water, time, etc, in a flexible way...It was the antithesis of so-called American "Land Art," where an artist needed money to be an artist, to buy real estate to claim possession of the land, and to wield machinery. True capitalist art.[89]

The circle motif, one of the primæval symbols of eternity, cycles, time, rebirth, etc, is employed throughout the work of many land artists, including Richard Long, Robert Smithson, Nancy Holt, Robert Morris and Dennis Oppenheim, Alice Aycock and Herbert Bayer. Long's circles,[90] made from slate, timber or by walking in a circle, are gentler, more eco-friendly kinds of sculpture.[91] The circle shape itself speaks of organic forms, and, in some religions, speaks of the 'feminine' and the Goddess.

Circular sculptures of the land art and Minimal kind include Donald Judd's two steel bands, 180 inches diameter, as well as a concrete circular 'wall'.[92] Robert Morris produced gigantic circular works, such as his *Observatory*,[93] which is a huge earthwork recalling the megalithic structures of ancient times, such as Avebury stone circle, while his *Labyrinth*[94] is a maze-size sculpture, the kind of maze one finds in theme parks and country houses, except that Morris's *Labyrinth* uses the ancient pattern of the Cretan labyrinth, itself a motif some see as distinctly feminine, speaking

89 R. Long, quoted in Suzi Gablik: *Has Modernism Failed?*, Thames & Hudson 1984, 44
90 See J. Poinsot: "Richard Long: To Build the Landscape", *Art Press*, Nov 1981, 9-11, Michael Compton: *Some Notes on the Work of Richard Long*, British Council 1976, Gabriella Jeppson: *Richard Long*, Fogg Art Museum, Cambridge, Mass., 1980, Nancy Foote: "Long Walks", *Artforum*, Summer 1980, 42-7, Simon Field: "Touching the Earth", *Art and Artists*, April 1973, 14-19, John T. Paoletti: "Richard Long", *Arts Magazine*, Dec 1982, 3; Richard Long: "Richard Long replies to a critic", *Art Monthly*, 68, July 1983, 20-21; Rudi H. Fuchs: "Memories of Passing: A Note on Richard Long:, *Studio International*, 1987, 965, April 1974, 172-3.

91 Richard Long: *Circle in Alaska*, driftwood on the Arctic Circle, Bering Strait 1977; *Untitled*, 1987, mud on paper, Anthony d'Offay Gallery, London; *Mountain Lake Powder Snow*, 1985, Lapland.
92 D. Judd: *Untitled*, 1971, concrete, min. height 36 in, max. height 48in, external radius 150 in, collection: Philip Johnson; *Untitled*, 1971, hot-rolled steel, outer circle: min. height 24in, max. height 32.8in, radius 90in, Guggenheim Museum, New York
93 Robert Morris: *Observatory*, 1971, earth, grass, wood, steel, granite, diameter c. 300 feet, Oosterlijk Flevoland, Holland.
94 *Labyrinth*, 1974, painted mason-ite, plywood & two-by-fours, 96 x 360in, Institute of Contemporary Art, University of Pennsylvania, Philadelphia.

of Goddess mysteries; Robert Smithson's *Closed Mirror Square*[95] is like a Aztec ziggurat, while his *Amarillo Ramp* recalls the gigantic embankments found at Neolithic earthworks such as Britain's Maiden Castle.[96] Some artists have produced stone circles which look very much like Stonehenge, such as Nancy Holt's monumental *Stone Enclosure: Rock Rings*.[97] These Minimal sculptures are ambivalently related to ancient monuments, however, as Samuel Wagstaff remarks of Tony Smith's works:

> They are related to early cultures intentionally or through sympathy − menhirs, earth mounds, cairns... [and] to this culture with equal sympathy − smokestacks, gas tanks, dump trucks, poured concrete ramps.[98]

Constantin Brancusi, Richard Long, Bill Woodrow

and many sculptors have spoken of the importance of materials in their work, how they learn from their materials, and 'follow' their materials. Tony Cragg speaks of 'works in which I learnt from the materials'.[99]

Wolfgang Laib dusts the earth (or gallery floor) with pollen, to form an enormous square layer of brilliant yellow.[100] Andy Goldsworthy and Laib collect leaves, berries, pollen, honey and other natural elements and weave sensuous artifacts that are ephemeral and intricate. Dennis Oppenheim worked with snow and circles in his *Annual Rings*, a series of concentric circles that straddle the Canadian/ American border, and with burning circles onto grass in his *Branded Mountain*.[101]

Other intriguing and sensual land artists include David Nash,[102] who has built a number of stoves and hearths, out of

95 Robert Smithson: *Closed Mirror Square*, 1969, rock salt, mirrors and glass, Blum Helman Gallery, New York.
96 *Amarillo Ramp*, 1973, red sandstone shale, 1800in diameter, estate of the artist. See also Maurice Berger, 1989.
97 Nancy Holt: *Stone Enclosure: Rock Rings*, 1977-8, hand-quarried schist, outer ring 40 feet, inner ring 2 feet across, ring walls 10 feet high, Western Washington University, Bellingham
98 Quoted in Lucy Lippard: "Tony Smith", 26

99 Quoted in Norbert Lynton, introduction to *Tony Cragg*, Fifth Triennale India, British Council 1982, 2
100 Wolfgang Laib: *Hazelnut Pollen*, Dokumenta 8
101 Dennis Oppenheim: *Annual Rings*, 1968, 150 x 200 feet, Fort Kent, Maine and Clair, New Brunswick; *Branded Mountain*, 1969, 30 ft diameter, San Pablo, California
102 See Alan McPherson: "Interview with David Nash", *Artscribe*, 12, June 1978; Hugh Adams: "The Woodman", *Art and Artists*, 12, April 1979; *Sixty Seasons: David Nash*, Third Eye Centre, Glasgow, 1983; David Nash: "David Nash", *Aspects*, 10, Spring 1980

natural materials – snow, slate, wood.[103] Nash's 1978 *Wooden Boulder* is exactly that – a huge, near-spherical chunk of oak. Nash tipped the boulder into a stream near his studio at Blaenau Ffestiniog, Wales. His idea was for the sculpture to make its way to the ocean. Instead, it stayed put in a pool (but moved over the years), and now it interacts continually with the environment.[104] Nash's art is gentle and based firmly in a reverence for nature.

Crucial in land art is the concept and reality of change and transience, for these works in wood, snow, ice, leaves, water, slate, grass, etc, do not stay. They are not 'permanent', in the way that, say, bronze, marble, steel or stone can be. We have bronze and marble sculptures still looking remarkable from the Græco-Roman period, and stone figurines from the Palæolithic period. One cannot see how Andy Goldsworthy's leaves could last very long, or Richard Long's clusters of stones on remote mountainsides. Indeed, ephemerality, transiency and change are key components in land art, and many land artworks take transience as the guiding principle. As Barry Flanagan said in 1969:

> Truly sculpture is always going on. With proper physical circumstances and the visual invitation, one simply joins in and makes the work... there is a never-ending stream of materials and configurations to be seen, both natural and man-made, that have visual strength but not object or function apart from this. It is as if they existed for just this physical, visual purpose – to be seen.[105]

Sculpture is never-ending, like all of art – like life itself.

103 David Nash: *Slate Stove*, 1988, Blaenau Ffestiniog, Wales; *Wood Stove*, 1979, Maentwrog, Wales; *Snow Stove*, 1982, Kotoku, Japan. 104 Nash: *Wooden Boulder*, 1978, oak, Maentwrog, Wales

105 Quoted in Gene Baro: "Sculpture made visible: Barry Flanagan in discussion with Gene Baro", *Studio International*, 178, 915, October 1969, 122; See Charles Harrison: "Barry Flanagan's sculpture", *Studio International*, 175, 900, May 1968, 266-8; Judith Russi Kirshner: "Barry Flanagan", *Artforum*, 23, 10, Summer 1985, 112

11

Sculpture In Great Britain

I'm fed up with objects on pedestals. I'd like to break down the graspability of sculpture. Sculpture is terrifically tangible, but a painting, however concrete, is partly in the realm of illusion.

Anthony Caro[106]

British sculptors, those of St Martin's School of Art, the 'New Generation' and others, benefited from the openness and freedom of American sculpture. 'America made me see that there are no barriers and no regulations', wrote Anthony Caro, the influential British sculptor (in ib.). According to William Tucker, contemporary or modern, post-Cubist sculpture 'could be made from anything, about anything.'[107] Caro described a mood that was common in the æsthetics of the 1960s, in painting as much as in sculpture, the idea that sculpture should not be on pedestals, but on the floor; that there are no barriers.

The big (and little) statements in British sculpture include: Anthony Caro's welded steel constructions, which are abstract but also emotional, such as *Early One Morning;* • Philip King's flamboyant steel and fibreglass pieces, such as his *Genghis Khan*, which speak of a direct apprehension of the object in itself, in the manner of Constantin Brancusi and Frank Stella's art;[108] • Tony Cragg's coloured spreads of found objects arranged in lines on the

106 Anthony Caro: in Lawrence Alloway: "Interview with Anthony Caro", *Gazette*, 1, 1961, 1

107 William Tucker: "An Essay on Sculpture", *Studio International*, 177, 907, January 1969, 13
108 Philip King: *Genghis Khan*, 1963, fibreglass and plastic with steel support, 41 x 56.5 x 34.5in, Tate Gallery, London

floor (such as his *New Stones*),109 which are works of found objects, all manner of objects, each given the same status, in a non-hierarchical fashion, laid out on the floor; • Richard Long's slate, wood, mud and stone circles (see below); • William Tucker's hard-edged and organic forms, which aim for maximum 'visibility' and physicality (see below); • Tim Scott's segments of circles in glass, perspex and acrylic sheets;110 • Stephen Cox's Kleinian, post-Renaissance reliefs;111 • Anish Kapoor's erotic, mysterious painted objects, which are bizarre yet wholly believable departures from natural forms – a pitted surface like that of a black-currant fruit, interfolding petals like those of a rose, multi-part spirals, cones made of shapes like the folds in robes (but the most startling thing about Kapoor's forms are their colours, powdery blues, lemon yellow and scarlet, at once seductive and unreal, simul-taneously, like all sculpture, inviting touch and repelling it, perhaps by being indifferent to

it);112 • Richard Deacon's poetic, open-forms,113 sculptures which are 'drawn in space', setting space alive in a Rilkean manner, in the Rilkean sense of space being deep and alive, and as in the poet's 'song' (the poem) setting alive space, like, Rainer Maria Rilke said, fruit filling your mouth, where the song, and breathing, is equated, in Orphic fashion, with life itself (see the famous sonnet on the *Archaic Torso of Apollo* by Rilke (quoted earlier), where the statue comes alive, though not in the manner of Pygmalion and his statue, or Hermione at the end of William Shakespeare's *The Winter's Tale*, where Leontes takes the reborn Hermione's hand and gasps 'o, she's warm!/ If this be magic, let it be an art/ Lawful as eating'); • Bill Woodrow's wonderful remaking and remingling of everyday found objects – a post-industrial sculpture with a lot of humour – for instance, structures such as flowers of branches sprouting from the smashed car door of a Porsche 928, and *A Passing Car, A Caring Word*, another car door, this time fixed against a decayed double bed base, with a cross on the floor made by tearing the

---

109 Tony Cragg: *New Stones*, 1982, Marian Goodman Gallery, New York
110 Tim Scott: *Quinquereme* 1966, Tate Gallery
111 Stephen Cox: *The Fiery Kind*, 1982-3, marble, 100 x 110cm, British Council, London

112 Anish Kapoor: *Six Secret Objects*, 1983, mixed media, 115 x 425 x 60cm, Lissom Gallery, London
113 Richard Deacon: *Turning a Blind Eye no. 2*, 1984-5, High Museum of Art, Atlanta, Georgia

bed's cloth, while in front of the car door is a 'microphone' on a stand, connected by a ribbon of steel torn from the door, with a gun connected to the door, lying on the floor; the resulting sculpture is a meditation, perhaps on violence, oppression, and death;[114] • Barry Flanagan's witty, seemingly naïve semi-figurative works, such as his bronze hares, or his *Soprano*, which is a bronze bird, mouth wide open, singing like an opera diva, with a gilded arrow through her breast; • Tim Head's *State of the Art*, a collection of phallic objects, stacked up like a Louis Nevelson wall sculpture: Head places a host of dildos and vibrators next to electronic calculators, model aircraft, tape players, computers, computer games, deodorants, and hair sprays, all the panoply of consumer items; • And David Nash's environmentally-friendly interactions with nature.[115]

The influence of British landscape on British sculpture is apparent in many, but by no means all, of British sculptors.

Specifically *British* landscape, as opposed to other kinds of landscape occur in the art of Andy Goldsworthy, David Nash, Hamish Fulton, David Tremlett, Roger Ackling and Richard Long, as you might expect. It was Carl Andre who noted, quite rightly, that the British landscape is 'one vast earthwork'.[116]

---

114 Bill Woodrow: *Winter Jacket*, 1986, mixed media, collection: Anne MacDonald Walker, San Francisco
115 Barry Flanagan: *Soprano*, 1981, bronze, 80 x 66 x 57cm, Arts Council of Great Britain; Tim Head: *State of the Art*, 1984, colour photograph, 183 x 274cm, collection: the artist; David Nash: *Fletched Over Ash Dome*, 1977, Caény-Coed, Maentwrog, Wales

---

116 Carl Andre, quoted in Andrew Causey: "Space and Time in British Land Art", *Studio International*, 193, 986, March-April 1977, 126

12

Richard Long

A story current at the time
[1967] told of Caro con-
fronted by an arrangement
of twigs in the exhibition
hall of the St. Martin's
sculpture department. A
conversation ensued. Caro:
"What's this?" Long: "it's
one part of a two-part
sculpture." Caro: "So show
me the other half." Long:
"It's on top of Ben Nevis."
Caro: "So how can I assess
it when I can't see all of it?"

Charles Harrison[117]

Crucial, too, is the sense and delicacy of touch in land art. Richard Long (b. 1945) sprinkles snow in a circle, or smears mud, often from the River Avon near his home in England, in huge circles on walls, or he makes marks on grass using his feet. The sense of touch, of gesture and of sensuality is crucial in Long's circles, lines, cairns and routes. Often the 'touch' in Richard Long's art is the foot. The touch of the feet on grass, rock, soil, water, mud. The walk itself is an artistic 'statement' in Long's work. The walk is a mark, a gesture, an interaction of artist and 'material', the 'material' being the world.

There is a historical and human dimension to Richard Long's walks, for he is always aware of the personal and social history of a place, even when it is a wilderness.

A walk is just one more layer, a mark laid upon the thousands of other layers of human and geographic history on the surface of the land.[118]

Richard Long talks in terms of walking as a kind of palimpsest, where one layer is written upon the next, a notion explored in Lawrence Durrell's *The Alexandria Quartet*, stories

117 C. Harrison, in Terry Neff, ed,
32

118 R. Long, quoted in D. Wheeler,
264

with successive layers of meaning. Long is aware of re-activating history as he walks through landscapes. He walks in time as much as space. His works also emphasize the temporal, historical dimension: for instance, Long will pick up a stone for a mile then drop it, or spend a certain length of time building a sculpture before moving on.

Everywhere the human 'touch' is present in Richard Long's sculpture, as in all sculpture. The shapes might be 'organic' – circles, spirals, zigzags – but the appearance of Long's sculpture in their wilderness settings is always of some sophisticated (not archaic) human gesture at work.

Like Bruce Chatwin, who also spoke lovingly of walking, wandering, nomads and wild-ernesses, Richard Long has travelled to some wild places: Lappland, Africa, Australia, Peru, Bolivia, Alaska and the Hima-layas. It's easy to see his art as simply pure Romanticism, a 'back to the land' art that utterly ignores political, societal, ideological, racial, economic and gender issues. True. His art is not concerned with the urban real world at all. And it looks very odd to see his work in galleries in cities. Rather, Long's sculpture is deeply poetic, personal, subjective and

romantic. It is *all* about a response to nature, about getting into connection with nature, as with Andy Golds-worthy and David Nash. Like Goldsworthy, Long works with his hands too – touches of the hand not to be seen, perhaps, in the walks or the lines of stones amidst rocky valleys – but seen in the circles of mud smeared on gallery walls.[119] The eroticism of such mud-smeared works is obvious, as is the sensuality of rites such as mud dancing (and today, echoing mud rituals).

The personal details of each sculpture in land art are import-ant, and artists catalogue them-selves meticulously. It is curious to visit a Richard Long exhibition and be confronted by lots of large pieces of paper with Long's documentation of his walks or sculptures printed on them.

An archetypal Long artwork is Richard Long's *Three Moors, Three Circles* of 1982 – a walk in his beloved Southwest British terrain. The whole artwork is a large piece of paper (you can buy it framed or unframed if you like). There are three concentric rings of words, printed in red, which read: *Three miles on Exmoor, two miles on Dartmoor, one mile on Bodmin Moor.* The words are printed in circles clearly to indicate a

119 R. Long: *Avon Mud Circle*, 1986, installation, Guggenheim Museum, New York

number of things – the walk itself, on the earth, in circles, and stone circles, and circles in general, as symbols and as Long's primary motif. The next line, also in red, is the title: *Three Moors, Three Circles*. The next line of type, in black, reads: *A 108 mile walk from Bodmin Moor, to Dartmoor, to Exmoor, walking around three circles along the way*. The next three lines read: *Liskeard to Porlock, Richard Long, England 1982*.

That's it. That's the whole artwork, a cursory, matter-of-fact description of the walk. The words on the paper, though, have little if anything to do with the actual experience of walking on England's very wild moors, with their sudden rainfalls out of nowhere, their amazingly impenetrable mists, their vast marshes, and their utter solitude. Long's bits of paper are word games which only hint at the reality of walking in wildernesses. They are semiotic games which point towards the powerful nature of Long's 'landscape of the soul'. The 'reality' of Long's work is clearly 'out there', in the world, in the landscape. Yet much of his art is conceptual, fictive, representations of representations. There is much ambivalence in his importing of 'natural' forms and materials into the urban space of the art gallery. The walks themselves are the reality of his art. Everything else is secondary, something for the punters and art critics, something, perhaps, to do on cold Winter evenings in between walks and trips and travels to wildernesses.

The relationship between titles/ documentation and artworks is precarious in land art, because the photography, the documentation and the title and description of the artwork is often all that remains of it. Richard Long's cairns or lines made by flattening grass will soon be lost. Similarly, Andy Goldsworthy's ridges of sand are blown away, the ice melts, but we have the photographs.

Richard Long speaks in poetic, religious terms of his art – 'art should be a religious experience'.[120] Although his sculptures alter the world – no *object* can avoid altering the world – he maintains that he takes his cue from the landscape, instead of imposing on it 'from outside', as it were: 'I use the world as I find it'.[121] Bill Woodrow, a contemporary of Long's, also 'uses' the world as he finds it: he trawls the world for materials with which to make sculptures:

---

120 Quoted in D. Wheeler, 264
121 R. Long: *Five, six, pick up sticks/ Seven, eight, lay them straight*, 1980, Anthony d'Offay Gallery, September 1980

My choice of objects is dictated, I think in the first instance by what is available, what I come across in the streets, on dumps... What I find more interesting about the work, is that these items are material for me that is found in my environments...[122]

Richard Long's views have something in common with Zen Buddhism, Taoism, shamanism and Western magic.[123] The sculpture and the place are one, in a mystical relationship, as Long points out in his writings:

> The material and the idea are of the place; sculpture and place are one, the same. The place is as far as the eye can see from the sculpture. The place for a sculpture is found by walking. Some works are a succession of particular places along a walk, e.g. *Milestones*. In this work, the walking, the places and the stones all have equal importance.[124]

Richard Long has evoked the *participation mystique* with the earth, with places and atmospheres and organic materials, that the archaic peoples of the world had (and have). It is a pre-institutionalized, pre-pagan and pantheistic rapport with the world, deliberately eschewing dogma, doctrine and manifestos. It is also part, as many commentators have noted, of a British Romantic tradition, that feeling for nature found in the art of William Blake, J.M.W. Turner, Lord Byron, Percy Bysshe Shelley, John Constable, etc.[125] Lynne Cooke writes (in "Between Image and Object: The 'New British Sculpture'"):

> by the early 1970s, Long's work had become increasingly interpreted in terms of an atavistic archetypal content, with the artist assuming the mantle of spiritual wanderer. Allusions to a rural, pastoral tradition, often couched in a language of almost Georgian naïveté, were gradually replaced by a more universal statement, one in which the concept of the timeless, unchanging order of nature was pre-eminent. Referring to prehistoric artifacts, like menhirs and leylines, introduced a megalithic symbolism and an engagement with cosmic forces fully in keeping with the way in

122 B. Woodrow, quoted in *Objects and Sculpture*, Institute of Contemporary Arts, 1981, 37
123 See Anne Seymour: "El Estanque de Basho – una nueva perspectiva", in *Piedras Richard Long*, Ministerio de Cultura, Dirección general de Bellas Artes y Archivos and the British Council 1986
124 Long, quoted in Lucie-Smith: *Sculpture Since 1945*, 121
125 See Anne Seymour, op.cit., Suzi Gablik, op.cit.

which the stone sculptures
in the gallery or the
photographs of stone and
stick circles and lines in
remote, untouched sites
postulated not a linear,
historical sense of time but
chthonic time, the time of
the earth's functioning. All
evidence of contemporary,
and especially of urban,
existence was therefore
eliminated. By establishing
this ahistorical tempor-
ality, and by eliciting a
symbolic order from chaos
and formlessness through
the imposition of pure
geometric forms, Long was
felt to have posited an
alternative to modern
man's sense of alienation.
The grandeur and monu-
mentality in works such as
Slate Circle or the photo-
sculpture *Stones in the
Sierra Nevada, Spain* attest
to the shift in his work from
a pastoral mood and a
concern with the *genius
loci* in which a harmonious
unity between man and
nature is intimated... to a
heroic statement centred
on the notion of a sacred
site or a site with mystical
meaning, a *locus con-
secratus*.[126]

---

126 Lynne Cooke: "Between Image
and Object: The 'New British
Sculpture'", in T. Neff, 40

13

Andy Goldsworthy

Andy Goldsworthy (b. 1956) seems particularly gentle and sensitive in his handling of materials: thus, every Goldsworthy sculpture might be regarded as an 'erotic object': he stitches together leaves to form lines, often placed in water, or makes circular slabs of snow, or entwines twigs in an arc.[127] He creates a delicate spiral of chestnut leaves, called *Autumn Horn*; he pins bright yellow dandelions on willowherb stalks in a circle, on bluebells; he makes lines and cairns, like Richard Long, of pebbles; he fashions hollow, circular structures, like igloos, from slate, leaves, driftwood and bracken;[128] he carves long wavy ridges in Arizona desert sand; he builds arches, globes, hollow spheres, slabs, spires, spirals and star-shapes out of snow and

---

127 Andy Goldsworthy: *Japanese maple leaves stitched together to make a floating chain*, 21 November 1987, Ouchiyama-mura, Japan; *Slate Stack*, 1988, Scaur Water Valley, Penpont, Dumfriesshire, Scotland; *Circular stalks in a lake*, 29 April 1987, Yorkshire Sculpture Park
128 Goldsworthy: *Autumn Horn*, Nov 1986, chestnut leaves, Penpont, Dumfriesshire; *Dandelion Flowers*, 1 May 1987, 'flowers pinned to willowherb stalks laid in a ring held above bluebells with forked sticks', Yorkshire Sculpture Park, West Bretton; *Line and Cairn* 31 May & 1 June 1985, pebbles, St Abbs, the Borders

ice.[129] Very impressive it all is. The sculptures made of sticks, for instance, stuck together in an arch, or a line, reflected in the mirror-like water of Derwent Water in Cumbria, are indeed wonderful.[9] Or the globe made from oak leaves in different states of autumnal decay, superb stuff.[130] Or the globe built out of snow, and perched amidst some young trees, or the slabs of snow, set up in a line with slits cut in them.[131] Or his most dramatic work, *Touching North*, four circular arches or tunnels made of snow, which is dramatic partly because its location, that space so thoroughly a masculine 'wild zone', the place of macho adventures, colonization and courage, the North Pole.[132]

Paul Nesbitt wrote of Andy Goldsworthy's art in 1990:

> Throughout these works the dominant theme is one of working with nature, to reveal nature itself – physical, chemical and biological. Goldsworthy uses nature's materials – rock, water (snow and ice, rain and mist), earth and the plants and animals which inhabit these; he uses nature's properties – structure, shape, form and colour; he uses nature's forces which together create, alter and animate those materials and properties – forces of light, heat, wind and gravity.[133]

The ethics of Andy Goldsworthy are those of Richard Long, David Nash and other British land artists: a mystical feeling for the landscape, expressed by an exquisite sensitivity of *touch*, that all-important component in the eroticism of sculpture:

> Movement, change, light, growth and decay are the lifeblood of nature, the energies that I try to tap through my work, I need the shock of touch, the resistance of place, materials and weather, the earth

---

129 [*Cairns*], made of plane leaves, 19 Oct 1988, Castres, France, slate, Summer 1987, Stonewood, Dumfriesshire, bracken, 13 February 1988, Borrowdale, Cumbria, driftwood, 29 November 1987, Kinagashima-cho, Japan; [*Waves of Sand*], 21 Nov 1989, 'fine dry sand', Arizona; *Ice Arch*, 1-2 Dec 1982, Brough, Cumbria; *Stacked Ice*, 28 Dec 1985, Hampstead Heath
130 [*Oak Globe*], 15 September 1985, branches and oak leaves, Jenny Noble's Gill, Dumfriesshire
131 Goldsworthy: *Slits cut into frozen snow*, 12 February 1988, Blencathra, Cumbria; *Snowball in Trees*, February 1980, Robert Hall Wood, Lancashire
132 A. Goldsworthy: *Touching North*, 24 April 1989, North Pole

133 Paul Nesbitt: "A Landscape touched by Gold", in Graham Hughes: *Arts Review: Yearbook 1990*, Arts Review Magazine 1990, 49

as my source.[134]

Andy Goldsworthy says, like Richard Long and any number of sculptors, that the personal touch, of hand on materials, is crucial:

> The work itself determines the nature of its making. I enjoy the freedom of just using my hands and 'found' tools – a sharp stone, the quill of a feather, thorns. I am not playing the primitive. I use my hands because this is the best way to do most of my work.

Many sculptors have spoken of the importance of the *making* of the sculpture, its actual construction, with real (and sometimes organic, living) materials (for instance, Alison Wilding).

Andy Goldsworthy's sculptures are marked by a number of elements familiar in land art: transience, domination, penetration, circular forms (globes, circles, spirals, snakes, cones) and nature mysticism. The ephemerality of the pieces, for instance, is a key component. Snow and ice will melt away, leaves will disintegrate, stones will be blown over. Each Goldsworthy sculpture has a date printed with its title. Not just a year, as in the usual artwork, but a specific day. Thus, one of his finest pieces, the delicious poppy covered boulder, has the title: *Poppy petals wrapped around a boulder held with water* (Sibobre, France, June 6, 1989). The petal-covered rock, with its brilliant red colour, nestles in some mossy boulders, looking very much like one of Constantin Brancusi's 'cosmic eggs'.

Andy Goldsworthy speaks of '[r]hythms, cycles, seasons in nature working at different speeds'.[135] Each date records a particular day (September 24, 1982, December 30, 1987, February 9, 1981, March 11, 1984, October 19, 1988); each day has its own weather, atmosphere and events, which are important for the artist. Goldsworthy records personal details, sometimes, like Richard Long, in his titles: *Slits cut into frozen snow / stormy / strong wind / weather and light rapidly changing*, or *Fine dry sand/ edges and ridges/ softened by the breeze.*

Andy Goldsworthy says he is not against long-term art:

> That art should be permanent or impermanent is not the issue. Transience in my work reflects what I find

134 A. Goldsworthy: *Andy Goldsworthy*, no page numbers. All Goldsworthy's quotes are from this edition.

135 A. Goldsworthy: *Touching North*, Fabian Carlsson Gallery, London 1989

in nature and should not be confused with an attitude towards art generally. I have never been against the well-made or long-lasting.

Domination and *penetration*. These are familiar terms describing patriarchal actions or constructions or ideologies used by feminists. Is Goldsworthy, seemingly so delicate in his touches, dominating nature? He says he isn't: '[b]y working large, I am not trying to dominate nature. If people feel small in relation to a work, they should not assume that there is an intention to make nature itself small.' Yet, clearly, Goldsworthy, and Richard Long, and the American earthworks artists (Michael Heizer, Walter de Maria, Robert Smithson, Charles Simonds) do dominate nature. Smithson's *Spiral Jetty* or Heizer's gigantic *Double Negative*, probably the two signature works of land art, will clearly be around for a long time, unless someone or something destroys them. Goldsworthy's stone pieces, too, like Long's, may indeed stay around for a while. There is a sense of gloating when Goldsworthy says:

Fourteen years ago I made a line of stones in Morecambe Bay. It is still there, buried under the sand,

unseen. All my work still exists, in some form.

Daring not to change or affect nature, land artists do just that, all the time. They 'interact' with nature, but their 'interactions', however small scale, can't help changing nature.

Andy Goldsworthy, like Richard Long, Michael Heizer, Walter de Maria and Robert Smithson, has made some huge pieces of sculpture, such as the long 'snake' and the 'pool' or maze, in Country Durham, large works which take up a lot of space, and certainly *dominate* the surrounding landscape.[136] In a forest, Goldsworthy, 'helped by students and friends', created another snake-like sculpture out of pine trees, pinned together to form a huge structure weaving between the trees.[137] Goldsworthy's large-scale works, like Long's or Heizer's or de Maria's, are monumental works, which sprawl across the landscape.

Mysticism is emphasized in Andy Goldsworthy's writing, as in Richard Long's would-be 'enigmatic' statements. Goldsworthy's æsthetics are those of a neo-pagan, shamanic, native Native American, pantheistic, nature worshipping kind, the sort of beliefs that some other

---

136 *Leadgate and Lambton Earthworks*, 1989, County Durham
137 *Snow and Wind Damaged Pine Trees*, Spring 1985, Grizedale forest

people call Goddess worship. For Goldsworthy and Long speak of the earth's energies and atmospheres. Goldsworthy writes:

> The energy and space around a material are as important as the energy and space within. The weather – rain, sun, snow, hail, mist, calm – is that external space made visible. When I touch a rock, I am touching and working the space around it.

This talk of earth energies naturally recalls ley lines, the so-called 'dragon lines' or *feng shui* of Chinese geomancy. The spiral and snake employed by so many land artists down the ages (in ancient Peru, or on the doors of Neolithic tombs, or in the mid-west of America) is associated with the Goddess and with the energies of life. The circles and spirals of Goldsworthy, David Nash, Robert Smithson and Richard Long are clearly those of the Goddess, the ancient Earth Mother.

Land artists, then, make marks upon the earth. Andy Goldsworthy speaks inadvertently of phallic penetration when he says: 'I want to get under the surface... At its most successful, my 'touch' looks into the heart of nature.' Land artists penetrate or cut into nature – by Michael Heizer

gouging vast chunks out of the American desert, by Walter de Maria thrusting a kilometre-long brass rod into the earth, and Goldsworthy, seemingly so gentle, has cut trenches into the earth, or smashed slabs of slate or pebbles or leaves, to make lines of broken, shattered material on the earth. He has torn leaves apart to form a line, and has smashed pebbles, making a line, like a fault line in geological structures. These are violent gestures, destroying the organic make-up of the natural forms he so adores.[138] All land artists, all artists, must break up and re-form materials,.

Land and earth artists often use circular forms, which hide the violence of their gestures. The spiral or circle is a 'kind', organic, even gentle shape, seemingly in tune with 'earth energies'. Circular structures (igloos, huts, stone circles, tombs, earthworks, pools), seem to be in harmony with nature, echoing the circle shapes of the planet itself, or suns, eyes, blood cells, orifices, orbits. The circular structures speak of primitive, archaic more

138 A. Goldsworthy: *Leaves torn in two*, 2 Nov 1986, Glasgow Green; *Broken Pebbles*, 12 April 1987, Scaur Water, Dumfriesshire; *Trench*, 6-7 August 1987, 'trench edged with clay supported by sticks', West Bretton, Yorkshire Sculpture Park; *Slate Crack Line*, Feb 1988, Little Langdale, Cumbria

'authentic' ethics, the 'back to nature' syndrome. There is, then, not only a mystical side to land art, to the art of Andy Goldsworthy, Richard Long, David Nash, Robert Smithson and Walter de Maria, but also a nostalgic element (nostalgia is a key element in any religion). Looking *back* to the land, the earth and land artists also look *back* to a former, even ancient era which was, patently, better. This is the hidden subtext in the writings of the land artists, this nostalgia for the better times of archaic cultures, when people lived 'in harmony' with the earth. This is, of course, a widespread nostalgia, not backed up by the evidence, which is that for ancient and prehistoric peoples life was as hard, if not harder, than it is now.

14

Minimal Sculpture

With the rise of Minimal, 'cool', Process and Conceptual sculpture, in the 1960s, sculpture became all 'object'.[139] 'Objecthood' became crucial, the 'thing-in-itself', as the Existentialist philosophers such as Jean-Paul Sartre and Edmund Husserl put it.[140] Inner and outer space became one, objects were simply what they are, without referring to anything outside themselves. Barbara Rose writes in "ABC Art", that the 'thing... is not supposed to be suggestive of anything other than itself'.[141] It was Frank Stella who had emphasized the object-in-itself of art, and of his paintings in particular. His paintings are objects which display openly their 'objecthood' (such as his *Ophir* (1960-61), one of his shaped canvas, a zig-zag shape with striped paint).[142] 'What you see is what you get', he famously said, and Stella influenced many of the key artists of the 1960s: Donald Judd, Carl Andre, Sol LeWitt,

140 See Corinne Robbins: "Object, Structure or Sculpture: Where Are We?", *Arts Magazine*, vol. 40, no. 9, Sept-Oct 1966, 33-37; Michael Fried: "Art and Objecthood", *Artforum*, vol.5, no. 10., June 1967, 12-23
141 Barbara Rose: "ABC Art", *Art in America*, Oct-Nov 1965, 66
142 Stella: *Ophir*, 1960-1, copper oil paint on canvas, 250.2 x 210.2cm, private collection

Robert Morris.[143] Stella was an important artist in the creation of 1960s Minimal sculpture: '[t]he idea that a painting is primarily a thing-in-itself has been around for a long time,' wrote Mel Bochner, 'But before Frank Stella not much was done about it'.[144]

The influence of Constantin Brancusi is also apparent in Minimal sculpture. Robert Morris, Donald Judd, Carl Andre and Dan Flavin acknowledged Brancusi's art, in particular his *Endless Column*.[145] Andre's early work *Last Ladder* is particularly reminiscent of Brancusi's *Endless Column*.[146] The Brancusi ethics, of simplicity, purity, smoothness, interiority, organic form are found in the Minimal sculptors, as well as the Constructivist notion of working with materials in a 'natural' way, so that the material dictates the form you create with it. Barry Flanagan has commented that sculpture works directly with materials:

The convention of painting has always bothered me.

There always seemed to be a *way* of painting. With sculpture, you seemed to be working directly, with materials and with the physical world inventing your own organisations.[147]

Minimal sculpture[148] is marked by the extremely hard edges, creating angular forms (the cube is highly favoured). Minimal sculpture, Barbara Rose remarked, looks 'machine-made, industrial, standardized, materialized or stamped out as a whole'.[149] Other aspects of Minimal sculpture include the multiplicity of sculptural material (fluorescent lights, Plexiglass, fibreglass, formica, chrome, plastic), simplicity, surface, and the insistence on the environment and contextual space.

Minimal sculptures are not set on pedestals, like

143 See Bruce Glaser: "Questions to Stella and Judd", in *Art News*, ed. Lucy Lippard, no. 5, September 1966, 55-61

144 Mel Bochner, 1966, 40

145 Constantin Brancusi: *Endless Column*, 1918, 80 x 9.8 x 9.8in, Museum of Modern Art, New York

146 Carl Andre: *Last Ladder*, 1959, wood, 214 x .6 x 15.6cm, Tate Gallery, London

147 Flanagan, quoted in catalogue of *Entre el Objeto y la Imagen: Escultura Británica Contemporánea*, Palacio de Velásquez, Madrid, 1986, 233

148 On Minimalism, see M. Tuchman, *American Sculpture of the Sixties*; Frederic Tuten: "American Sculpture of the Sixties", *Arts Magazine*, vol. 41, no. 7, May, 1967, 40-44; Irving Sandler: "The New Cool-Art", 96-101; Richard Wollheim: "Minimal Art", *Arts Magazine*, vol. 39, no. 4, January 1965, 20-1; D. Mayhall: *The Minimal Tradition*, 1979; Rosalind Krauss, 1973, 43-53; Barbara Reise, 1969, 166-172; Phyllis Tuchman, 1988.

149 Barbara Rose: "New York Letter", *Art International*, 15 Feb 1964, 41

Renaissance or Greek sculpture; they sit on the floor, or
lean against walls (as in Robert
Morris's *Floor Piece*, or Carl
Andre's *Cedar Piece*).150 Minimal
sculptures exist in the same
space, on the same plane (the
floor) as the viewer. They are,
as Morris said, in an in-between
cultural space, somewhere
between being monuments and
being ornaments, between being
architecture and jewellery.151 In
Minimal sculpture, surfaces are,
typically, smooth, utterly
smooth and 'pure'. Simplicity is
exalted, as is repetition, seriality,
process, flatness as well as
volume and space. The many
materials are flattened out and
depersonalized, and gestures, so
important to certain kinds of
sculpture, such as that of
Michelangelo Buonarroti, are
suppressed. Indeed, the flatness
of the surfaces, whether in the
art of Robert Morris, Donald
Judd, Dan Flavin, Carl Andre,

Ronald Bladen or Tony Smith, is
crucial, and some commentators call Minimal sculpture
'boring'.152 The boringness
becomes a part of the metaphysics of Minimal sculpture, so
that Lucy Lippard writes: '

> The exciting thing about...
> the "cool" artists is their
> daring challenge of the con-
> cepts of boredom, mono-
> tony and repetition... their
> demonstration that intens-
> ity does not have to be
> melodramatic.153

Boring art for some is
exhilarating art for others, just as
erotic art for some is pornography for others. Thus, James
Mellow wrote that a Donald
Judd's shows was 'one of the
most provocative of the
season',154 while Barbara Rose
described Judd's art as 'our
most radical sculpture, if not
perhaps our fullest'.155 Certainly

150 Carl Andre: *Cedar Piece*,
1959/64, 68.7 x 36.3in, Öffentliche
Kunstammlung Basel; Robert
Morris: *Floor Piece*, 1964, 17 x 17
x 288in, Green Gallery, New York
1964; Robert Morris wrote: '[t]he
ground, not the wall, is the necess-
ary support for the maximum
awareness of the object. (in
"American Quartet", *Art in
America*, Dec 1981, 95).
151 Robert Morris: "Notes on
Sculpture", *Artforum*, October
1966, 20-3. See also: Phil Patton:
"Robert Morris and the Fire Next
Time", *Art News*, vol. 82, no. 10,
December 1983, 84-91

152 See Irving Sandler, *American
Art*, 245f; Lucy Lippard: "An Impure Situation", *Art International*,
20 May 1966, 62; Robert Morris:
"Notes on Sculpture", op.cit.;
Kynaston McShine: *Primary Structures*, 1966; Richard Lund: "Why
Isn't Minimal Art Boring?", *Journal
of Aesthetics and Art Criticism*, vol.
45, no. 2, Winter 1986, 195-7
153 Lucy Lippard: "New York
Letter: Recent Sculpture as
Escape", 50
154 James Mellow: "New York
Letter", *Art International*, 20 April
1966, 89
155 Barbara Rose: "Looking at
American Sculpture", *Artforum*, 3,
February 1965, 34

Judd's wall reliefs are beautiful, especially when made in brass or copper.[156] Judd combined the sensuality of these industrial materials with cool geometric patterns. Judd, like other Minimal sculptors, combined austerity with sensuality, producing 'minimal forms at the service of glamorous, hedonistic effects of light' (Hilton Kramer).[157] As Barbara Haskell writes in *Donald Judd*:

> By coupling these luxurious materials with spare forms, he exploited their inherent "language". The opposition between the inert and rigorous geometry of his forms, and the opulent hedonism and shimmering color effects of his surfaces accounted for the unexpectedly exultant lyricism of his work. (72)

One of the triumphs of Minimal art was to make seemingly dead and uninteresting materials such as steel and plastic sensual. On 'boringness', Robert Morris wrote (in "Notes on Sculpture") that sculpture is found 'boring' by those who desire 'specialness':

> Such work which has the feel and look of openness, extendibility, accessibility, publicness, repeatability, equanimity, directness, immediacy, and has been formed by clear decision rather than groping craft would seem to have a few social implications, none of which are negative. Such work would undoubtedly be boring to those who long for access to an exclusive specialness, the experience of which reassures their superior perception.[158]

Minimal artists such as Donald Judd, Robert Mangold, Sol LeWitt and Robert Morris explored the notions of 'boringness' and 'interestingness'. 'Boring art is interesting art', writes Frances Colpitt in her book on Minimalism (121). Judd, the chief explicator of Minimal æsthetics, wrote: 'I can't see how any good work can be boring or monotonous in the usual sense of those words', adding: '[a]nd no one has developed an unusual sense of them.'[159] Clearly, the Minimal sculptures thought they were making 'interesting' art. Or at least, *they* were interested in it. If art's

156 D. Judd: *Untitled*, 1978, brass, 10 units, 6 x 27 x 224in, Indiana University Art Museum, Bloomington; *Untitled*, 1969, brass and red fluorescent Plexiglass, 10 units, 6.2 x 24 x 27in, Hirshhorn Museum and Sculpture Garden, Washington
157 Hilton Kramer: "Display of Judd Art Defines an Attitude", *The New York Times*, 14 May, 1971, D48
158 Robert Morris: "Notes on Sculpture", part 3, *Artforum* 5, 10, Summer 1967, 29
159 D. Judd, in Kynaston McShine, 1966

good, it can't be 'boring', said Judd, claiming that 'a work needs only to be interesting'. The discussion of 'interesting', 'boring' and 'value' becomes a quagmire of semantics and the metaphysics of meaning. Language soon fails to describe the kinds of intentions that artists have, and the kind of responses that critics have to works. Robert Mangold said:

> I certainly know whether I'm interested in the work or whether I'm not interested in the work.[160]

Sol LeWitt explained his view thus:

> I wouldn't say that I wanted to like uninteresting things or to dislike interesting things. I think that's one way that you measure your response, if it interests you. 'Interests' means that it somehow makes a bridge between you and it, you and the object, you and the art object. If it hits home, it means that it's of interest.[161]

You might see Robert Ryman's white-on-white paintings as unsensual, flat, 'boring'. In fact, Ryman's paintings are very erotic. As Ad Reinhardt painted black-on-black

squares, so Ryman explores the mysticality of white-on-white, as Kasimir Malevich had done.[162] Paintings such *Untitled,* a small painting by contemporary standards (53.5 inches square), or the very small *Untitled* of 1961 (12 inches square), display a sense of the tactile to rival Jasper Johns. The surfaces themselves are highly poetic, but Ryman also moves towards the state of sculpture, like Frank Stella, with his use of many different materials, from wood to steel, from fibreglass to Plexiglass, from cardboard to copper.

Similarly, the archetypal Minimal painter, Agnes Martin, might appear to be quite 'uninteresting'. Her paintings, though, are deeply poetic. They are, like Robert Ryman's and Ad Reinhardt's, flat squares in a human-scale (five foot square, for instance). They have poetic titles: *Mountain II, Drift of*

---

160 Quoted in F. Colpitt, 121
161 Quoted in F. Colpitt, 121

162 R. Ryman: *Department,* 1981, oil on aluminium, 60 x 60in, collection: Rhona J. Hoffman, Chicago. See Carlo Huber: *Robert Ryman,* Kunsthalle, Basel; Nancy Grimes: "Robert Ryman's White Magic", *Art News,* Summer 1968, 86-92; Carter Ratcliff: "Robert Ryman Making Distinctions", *Art in America,* June 1986, 92-97

Summer and *Night Sea*.[163]
Martin's white paintings are not
all they seem at first, as with
Robert Ryman's work. They are
in fact covered with a faint but
strictly controlled grid, usually
made with a pencil. 1963's *Night
Sea* is, unusually in Martin's
oeuvre, a light blue, hinting at
nature, at skies and seas.
Martin's painterly reductionism
seems austere, but in fact
poeticizes the world, as with
Ryman or Marden. Martin
writes:

> My paintings have neither
> objects, nor space, nor
> time, not anything – no
> forms. They are light,
> lightness, about merging,
> about formlessness,
> breaking down forms.[164]

Agnes Martin's paintings go
beyond being simply graphs
made in graphite on oil paint;
they shimmer, phosphoresce,
they are, as Martin says, about
lightness and formlessness. They
embrace a physicality of light
and are not 'abstract' in the
sense of being 'unreal'. Rather,
they are grounded in reality, in
nature, as with the oil and wax
panels of Brice Marden.

By limiting himself to white,
Robert Ryman frees himself up
for an exploration of different
media, for he paints in white on
many kinds of material: canvas,
linen, cotton, wood, paper, steel,
copper, aluminium, mylar,
fibreglass, Plexiglass, cardboard,
etc, and with different sorts of
media: oil, baked enamel, paper,
vinyl acetate emulsion, etc. As
Ryman says, typically of so
many contemporary artists:
'[t]here is never a question of
what to paint, but only how to
paint' (in D. Wheeler, 207).

It would be hard to see Sol
LeWitt's cuboid, mathematical,
conceptual sculpture as sensual.
LeWitt's angular objects – the
frames of cubes painted while –
seem to be the antithesis of
sensual art.[165] His art is all about
ideas the initial idea, the con-
ception, is everything. As
LeWitt said: 'all of the planning
and decisions are made beforehand and the execution is a
perfunctory affair. The idea
becomes a machine that makes

163 Agnes Martin: *Night Sea*, 1963,
oil and gold leaf on canvas, 72 x
72in, Saatchi Collection, London;
Drift of Summer, 1965, acrylic and
graphite on canvas, 72 x 72in,
Saatchi Collection, London;
Mountain II, 1966, oil and pencil
on canvas, 72 x 72in, collection: R.
Solomon, New York
164 Agnes Martin, quoted in Peter
Schjedahl, 26

165 Sol LeWitt: *Untitled Cube*,
1968, 15.5 x 15.5 x 15.5in, Whitney Museum of Art, New York;
Open Modular Cube, 1966,
painted aluminium, 5 ft cube, Art
Gallery, Ontario. See Ann Sargent
Wooster: "Sol LeWitt's Expanding
Grid", *Art in America*, vol. 68, no.
5, May 1980, 143-7

the art.'[166] Much of contemporary sculpture consists of hard-edged cubes or rectangular slabs. Whether this use of such stark mathematical forms as cubes is rational or intuitive, it takes a scientific, numerical approach to art to extremes. The idea, Donald Judd wrote, is to simply do 'the next thing': 'one thing after another'. It is a strategy that is not called a strategy, a systemless system. Of Frank Stella's paintings, Judd wrote that the 'order is not rationalistic and underlying, but is simply order, like that of continuity, one thing after another.'[167] The notions of Minimalism – seriality, succession, progression, repetition, permutation – have been around for a long time. Leonardo da Vinci, you might say, painted the same picture in different ways, often abandoning projects before completion, while J.M.W. Turner seemed to be painting the same sky, attacking it from thousands of different viewpoints and different locations, from every coastline of Britain, to France, Switzerland, Italy and Germany.

But, whether the system is serial or modular, whether there is progression or simply repetition, the notion of Donald Judd's, 'doing the next thing', 'one thing after another', explains so much of Minimalist art. It explains so much of Judd's work, for instance, those 'ladders' of forms ascending to the ceiling in bronze or plastic, and those long lines of curved shapes set on a wall.[168] It also describes how artists simply go on making work, as variations, or repetitions, or progressions, like Mark Rothko with his many canvases that explore different combinations of purple or yellow clouds floating on oceans of red or blue, or Ad Reinhardt's seemingly repetitious but actually methodical explorations of five foot square black canvases. Minimal ethics can produce some extremes of mathematics and seriality. Carl Andre's *37 Pieces of Work* is a good example of Minimal æsthetic permutations taken to extremes:

Taken as a whole *37 Pieces*

166 Sol LeWitt: "Paragraphs on Conceptual Art", *Art Language*, May 1969. See *Sol LeWitt*, Gemeentemuseum, The Hague 1970, Lucy Lippard: "Sol LeWitt: Non-Visual Structures", *Artforum*, April 1967, Roberta Smith: "Sol LeWitt", *Artforum*, Jan 1975, Ann Sargent Wooster: "LeWitt's Expanding Grid", *Art in America*, May 1980
167 Donald Judd: "Specific Objects", *Arts Yearbook*, 8, 1965, 82
168 D. Judd: *Untitled*, 1970, copper, 5 x 69 x 8.8in, private collection; *Untitled*, 1969, steel with blue Plexiglass, ten units, each 9 x 40.3 x 31.2in, at 9.2in intervals, Norton Simon Museum of Art, Pasadena

of Work consists of 1,296 plates, 216 each of aluminium, copper, steel, magnesium, lead and zinc. Each metal appears alone in individual six-foot square plains. Then alternates with another, checkerboard fashion, in every possible permutation. Since each of the six metals in the large piece was laid out in the alphabetical order of its chemical symbol, alternating successively with the others, there are two versions of each combination.[169]

Some might see this kind of Minimal, Conceptual or mathematical art as too abstract, too unreal, too dry and clinical. But critics such as Robert Rosenblum claim that Conceptual art can be 'awesome'. Of LeWitt's art, Rosenblum writes in 1978 that it

> elicits…an immediate awe that…has to be translated by the same feeble words – beautiful, elegant, exhilarating – that we use to register similar experiences with earlier art.[170]

You might see Minimal sculpture as so 'cool' it's lifeless.

Yet, despite the profusion of smooth white surfaces, which hint of clinics and hospitals, there is much sensuality in Minimal sculpture. Carl Andre's works are extremely sensuous, with their shiny or dull surfaces of copper, zinc, steel or aluminium.

In Minimal sculpture, the object and its 'objecthood' is primary. As William Tucker wrote, it

> is the matter-of-fact 'objectness' of sculpture that has become in recent years its prime feature.[171]

The notion of 'objecthood' is problematic, theoretically and artistically, for the world is full of objects, it is a continuum of objects. As critics have noted, much of what makes sculpture sculpture is that the object is contextualized, physically as well as æsthetically and psychologically, as a sculpture. Context is crucial, says Julia Kristeva. Thus, a pile of bricks on a building site is…a pile of bricks. A pile of bricks in an art gallery is… sculpture. This is what Carl Andre explored. The *response*, affected by so much of culture, socialization, physical context, education, etc, makes objects sculptures. As Garth Evans

169 David Bourdon: *Carl Andre: Sculpture 1959-1977*, 56. See Mel Bochner: "Serial Art Systems: Solipsism", 39-43
170 Robert Rosenblum: "Notes on Sol LeWitt", in *Sol LeWitt*, Museum of Modern Art, New York 1978, 15-16
171 William Tucker: "An Essay on Sculpture", *Studio International*, vol. 177, no. 907, January 1969, 12-13

writes:

> What happens to a sculpt-
> ure is determined largely by
> factors outside of itself. The
> fact of its being thought of
> as a sculpture is more
> critical to its existence, its
> life, than any other facts
> about it. This is a funda-
> mental distinction between
> objects and sculpture.[172]

Artists of this century have
explored this area between
'everyday' or 'ordinary'
'objects', and the 'art object' –
Marcel Duchamp with his
readymades, Kurt Schwitters'
multi-media pieces, and, later, by
Jasper Johns and Robert
Rauschenberg, who stuck
objects onto their paintings and
further explored the blurred
region between painting and
sculpture.[173]

Minimal sculpture is
certainly austere – 'cool', as it
was dubbed. It is very cool,
ascetic, restrained, flat, exact,
with its smooth surfaces and
precise square edges and angles.
Body has been erased from this
cool Minimal art. There is no
space for the body, and the
spectator is also 'erased', in
some way. The ruthless

asceticism of Minimal art denies,
like early Christianity, the body.
Rosalind Krauss writes:

> The art of [Auguste Rodin
> and Constantin Brancusi]
> represented a relocation of
> the point of origin of the
> body's meaning – from its
> inner core to its surface – a
> radical act of decentring
> that would include the
> space to which the body
> appeared and the time of
> its appearing. What I have
> been arguing is that the
> sculpture of our time con-
> tinues this project of
> decentring through a voc-
> abulary of form that is
> radically abstract. The
> abstractness of Minimalism
> makes it less easy to recog-
> nize the human body in
> those works and therefore
> less easy to project our-
> selves into the space of that
> sculpture with all of our
> settled prejudices left
> intact. Yet our bodies and
> our experience of our
> bodies continue to be the
> subject of this sculpture –
> even when a work is made
> of several hundred tons of
> earth. (279)

You can see the body
written into, say, Andy
Goldsworthy's delicate leaf
sculptures, or Constantin
Brancusi's extraordinary egg
shapes, but not, perhaps, in the
giganticism of Michael Heizer's
Double Negative. Yet, even here,
the human body is present – if

172 Garth Evans: "Sculpture and
Reality", Studio International, vol.
177, no. 908, February 1969, 62
173 Marcel Duchamp: Bottle Rack,
1914, readymade, galvanized iron,
25.5in, Galleria Schwarz, Milan;
Kurt Schwitters: Picture, 1925,
Sammlung Janlet, Brussels

only by the way it is violently dwarfed by the scale of Heizer's earthwork.

Much of contemporary sculpture has been thoroughly traditional, and patriarchal, in its orientation and expression. Take Henry Moore, one of the most celebrated of Western sculptors. His nudes, though, are no different from the conventional 'female nude lying down', found in so much of high art from the Renaissance onwards.[174] Moore's polished wood surfaces, so softly rounded and enigmatic, seem so enchanting. But, despite his formal innovation, Moore is as sexist a sculptor as is Francis Bacon as a painter. Contemporary figurative sculpture has rarely escaped the usual confines of patriarchal art. David Smith's bronze sculpture *The Rape* depicts a woman being raped by a canon, a phallic gun which climbs over her.[175] It is meant to be a savage and ironic comment on violation, but it isn't ironic enough, as with Aristide Maillol's relief of a man assaulting a woman, entitled –

what else? – *Desire*.[176] Edward Kienholz's quasi-Surrealist *Back Seat of a '38 Dodge* is a re-assembled car with all manner of bits added to it and inside it, two people tup.[177]

But when sexuality is addressed, contemporary sculptors have rarely been ironic, or critical. Usually, the norms of male/ female, active/ passive, culture/ nature, good/ evil are exalted. The great or celebrated names in contemporary sculpture – Alberto Giacometti, Henry Moore, David Smith, David Hare, Eduardo Chillida, Pablo Picasso, Isamu Noguchi, Mark Di Suvero, Jean Tinguely – rarely tackled notions of sexuality in major works of sculpture. When Picasso incorporates eroticism, it is invariably heterosexist, as in his *Bust* with its gigantic breasts, echoing the "Stone Venuses" of yore.[178] The great works of contemp-orary sculpture – David Smith's *Cubi XXVII,* Alexander Calder's mobiles, Richard Serra's chunks of metal, John Chamberlain's squashed cars – seem to

---

174 Henry Moore: *Reclining Figure,* 1945-6, elmwood, 75in long, collection: Humana Corp, Louisville; *Three Piece Reclining Figure: Draped,* 1975, bronze, 14 ft 8in long, Henry Moore Foundation
175 David Smith: *The Rape,* 1945, bronze, 9 x 5.75 x 3.5in, private collection
176 Aristide Maillol: *Desire,* 1903-5, lead relief, Musée Nationale d'Art Moderne, Paris
177 Edward Kienholz: *Back Seat of a '38 Dodge,* 1964, the Kleiner Foundation, Los Angeles
178 P. Picasso: *Bust of a Woman,* 1932, bronze, 25.1in high, estate of the artist

eschew issues of sexuality.[179]
Not much of mainstream or
'malestream' contemporary
sculpture concerns itself with
eroticism.

However, as the next
chapter demonstrates, many
women artists and feminist
artists have directly tackled
issues of sexuality and gender,
with an emphasis on criticism,
irony, and a highly educated
exploration of the issues.

[179] David Smith: *Cubi XXVII*,
1965, stainless steel, 9.2 ft high,
Guggenheim Museum, New York;
Alexander Calder: *Red Flock*, c.
1949, hanging mobile, metal, 2.8 x
5.5 ft, Phillips Collection, Washington DC; John Chamberlain: *Toy*,
1961, welded auto parts and
plastic, 4 x 3.1 x 2.6 ft, Art
Institute, Chicago; Richard Serra:
Prop, 1968, 96in high, sheet 60 x
60in, Whitney Museum of Art, New
York

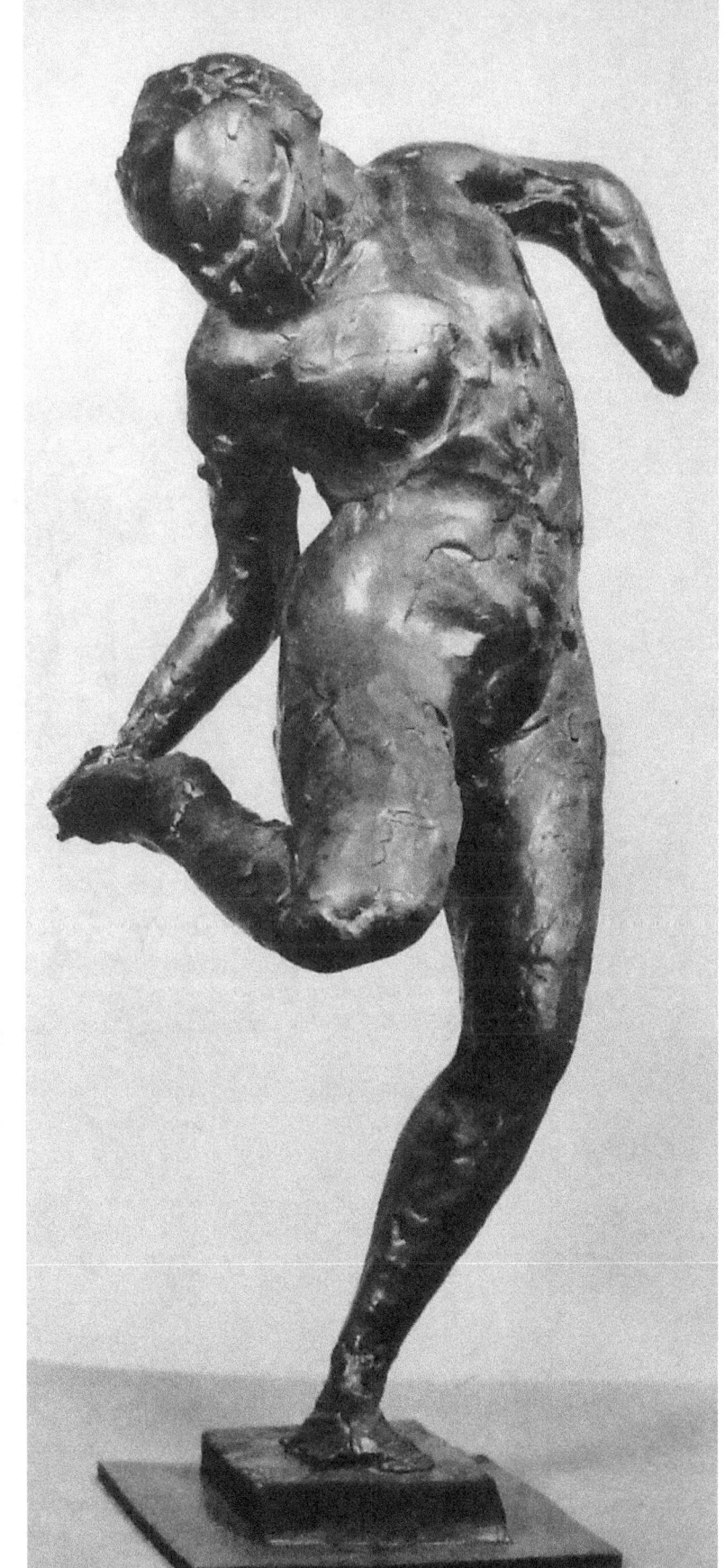

Edgar Degas,
Dancer Looking At
the Sole of Her
Right Foot, 1882-95,
New York

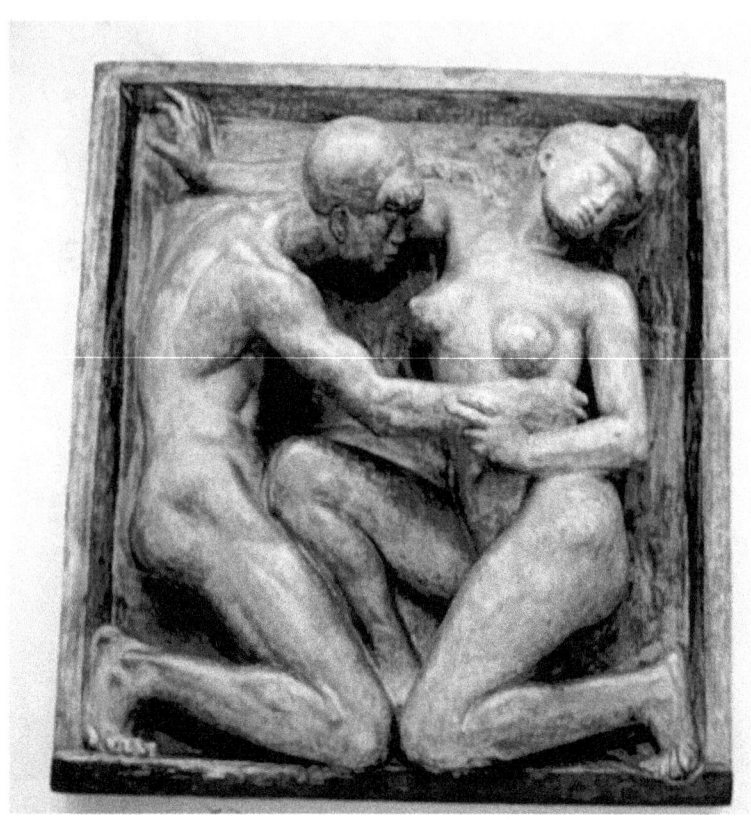

Aristide Maillol, Desire, 1908

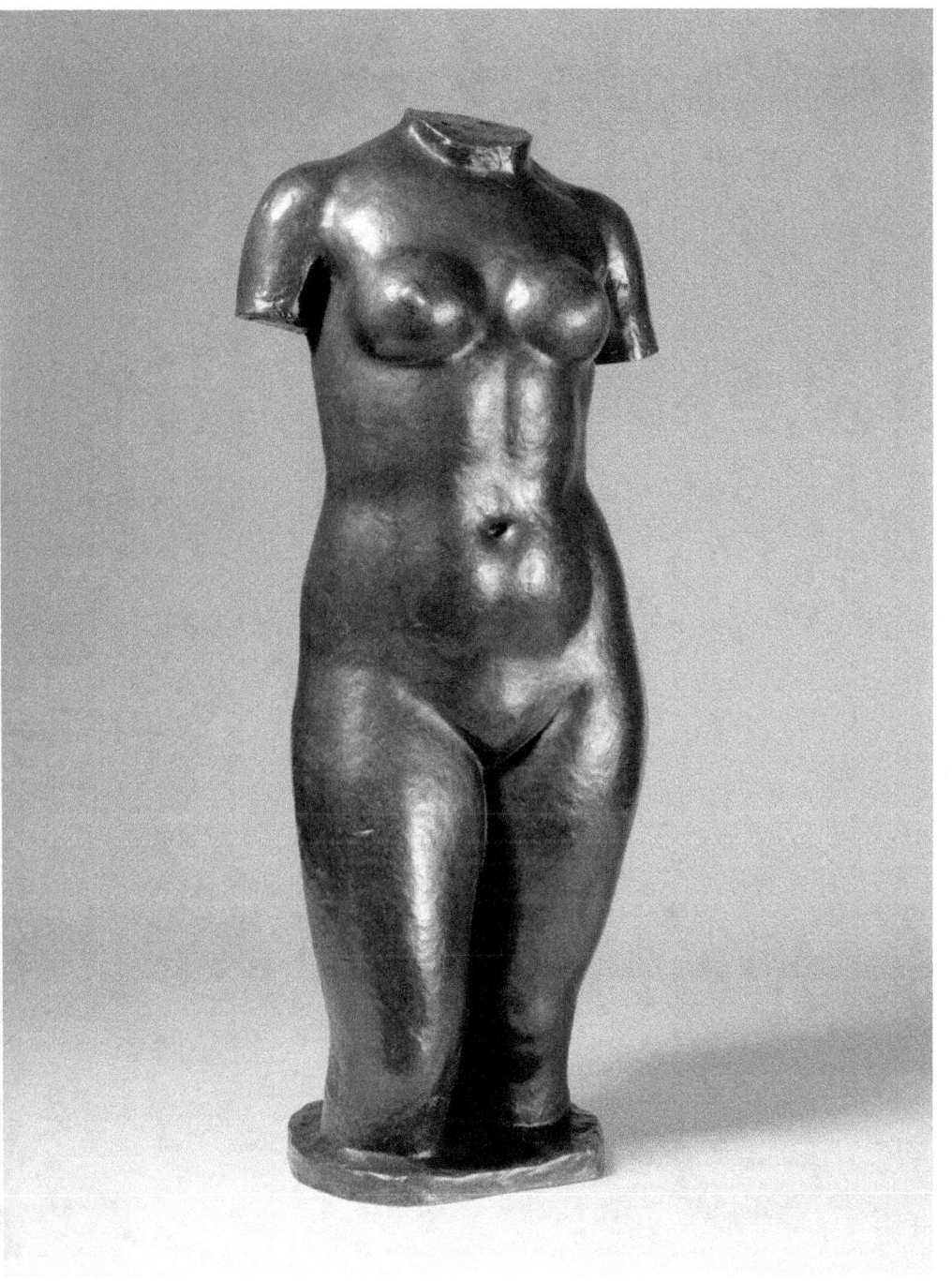

Aristide Maillol, Torso of a Young Woman, 1935,
Montreal Museum of Fine Arts

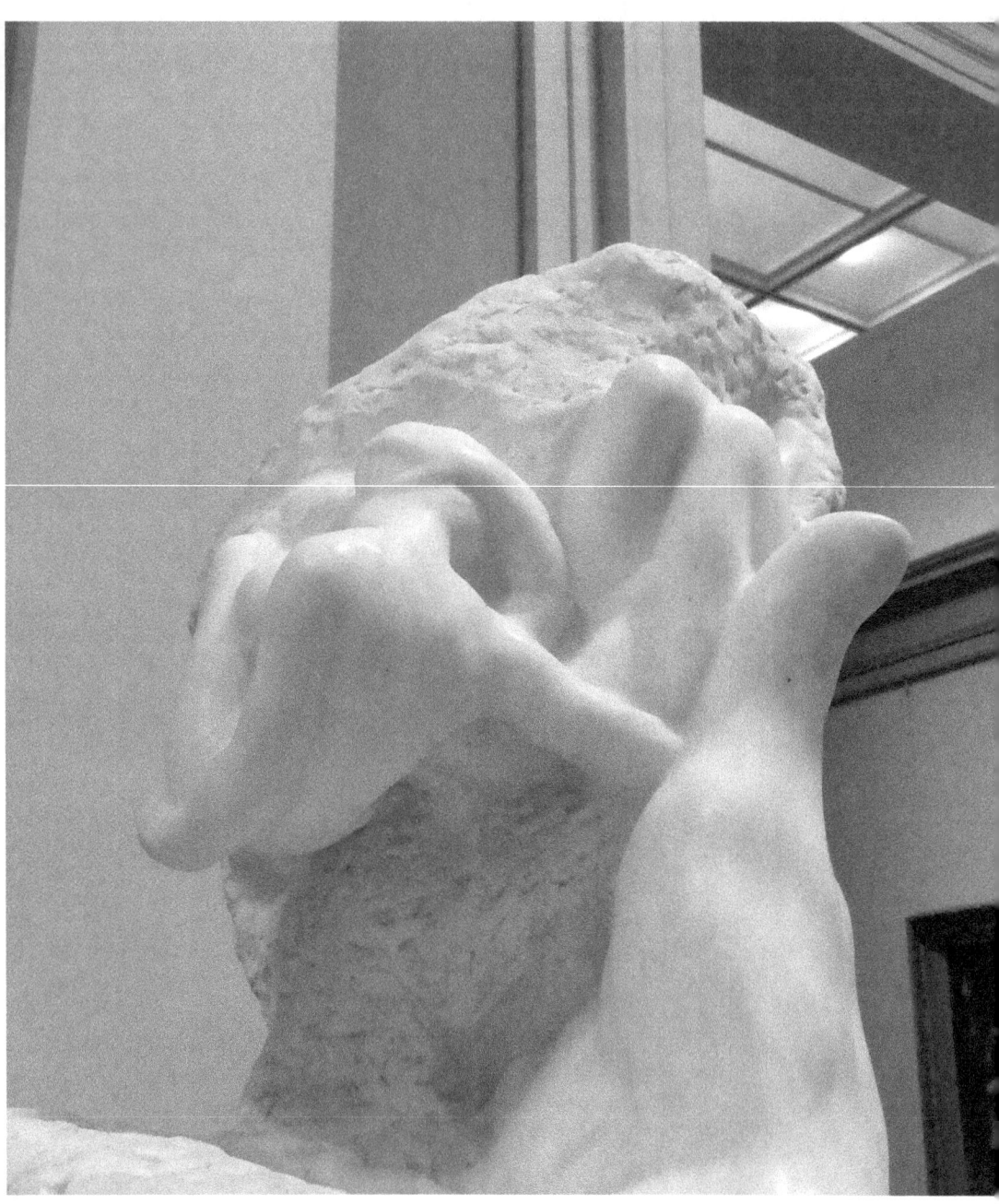

Auguste Rodin, Hand of God, 1907, Metropolitan Museum of Art, New York City

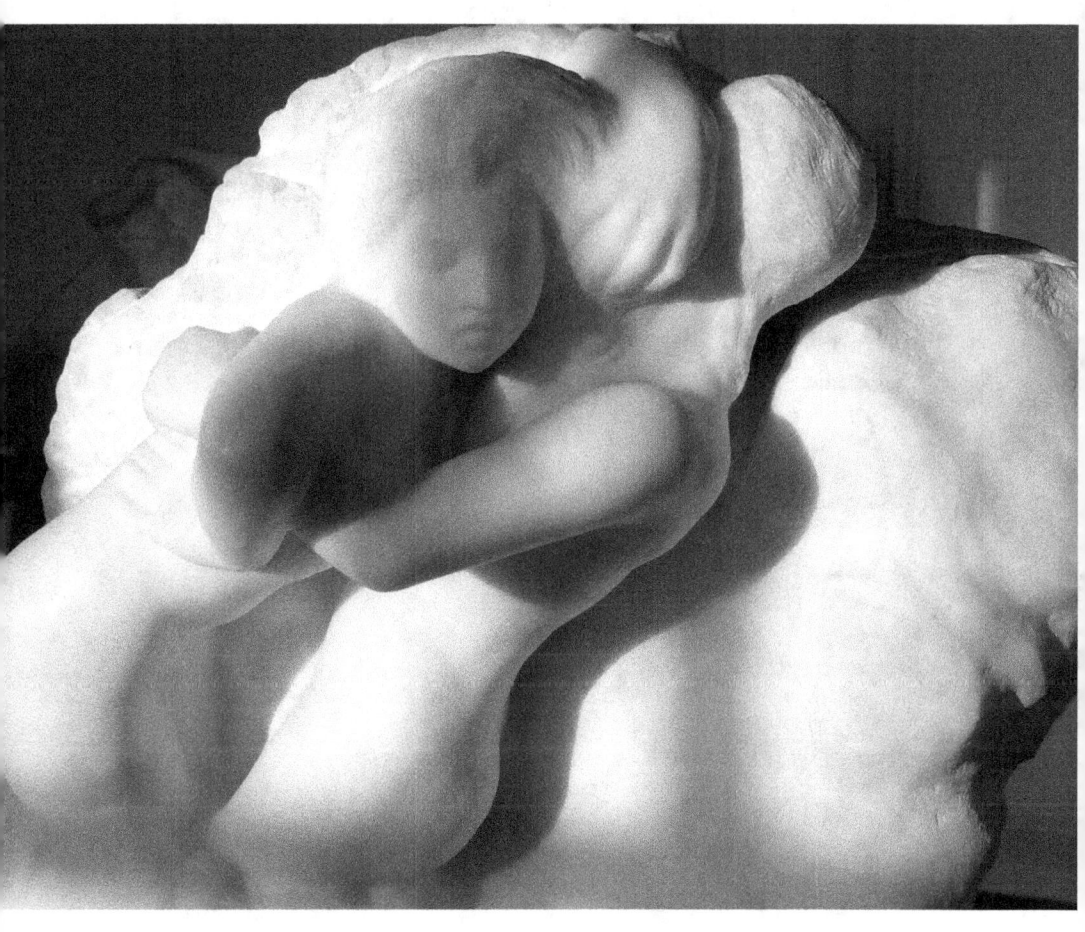

Auguste Rodin

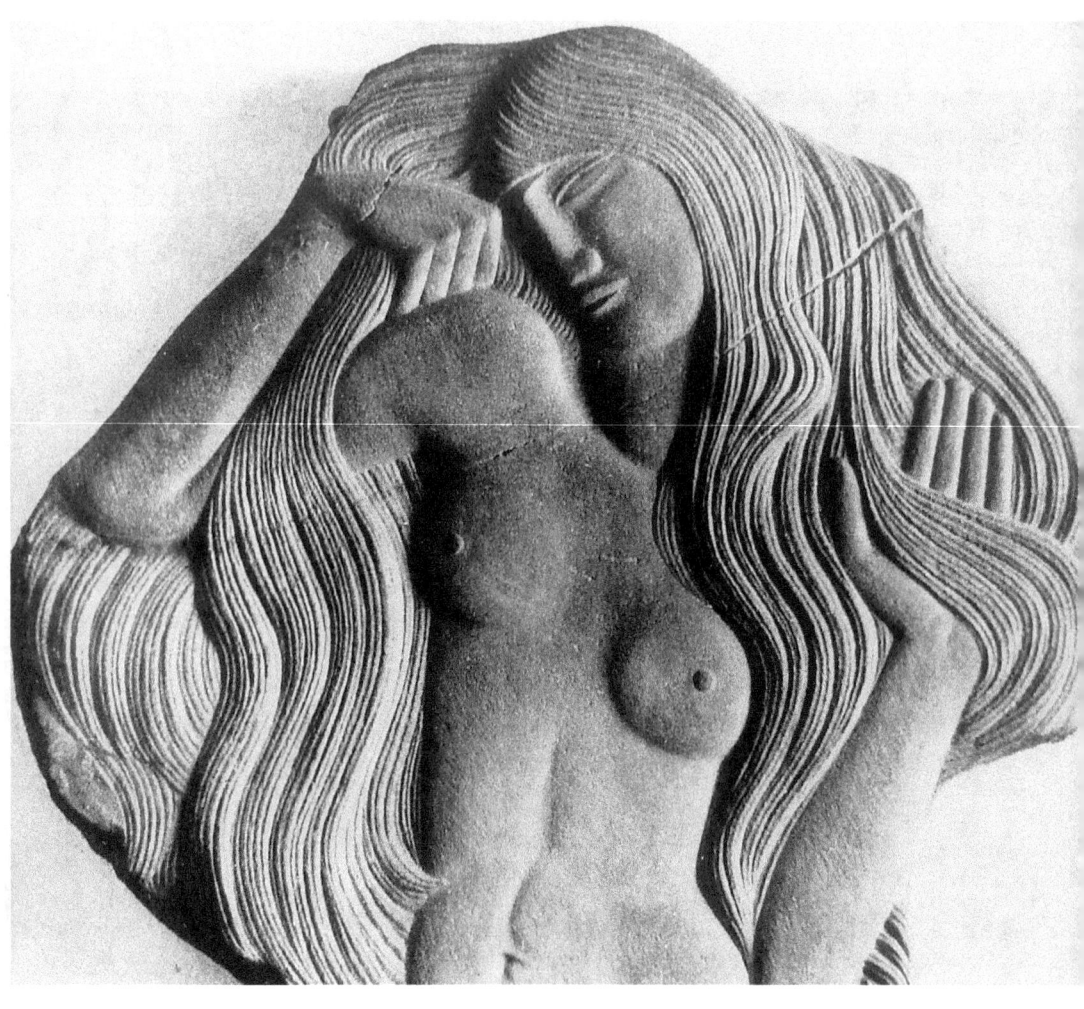

Eric Gill, Nude Girl With Hair, 1925

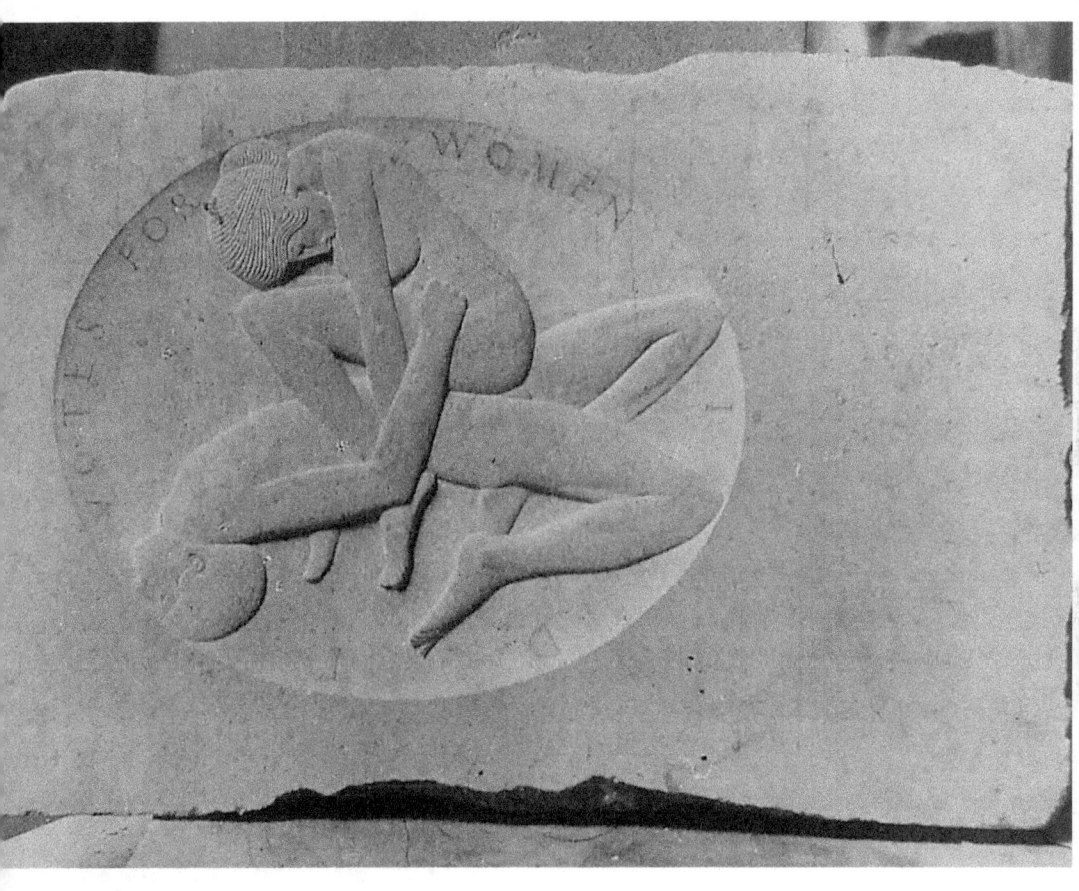

Eric Gill, Votes For Women, 1911 (whereabouts unknown)

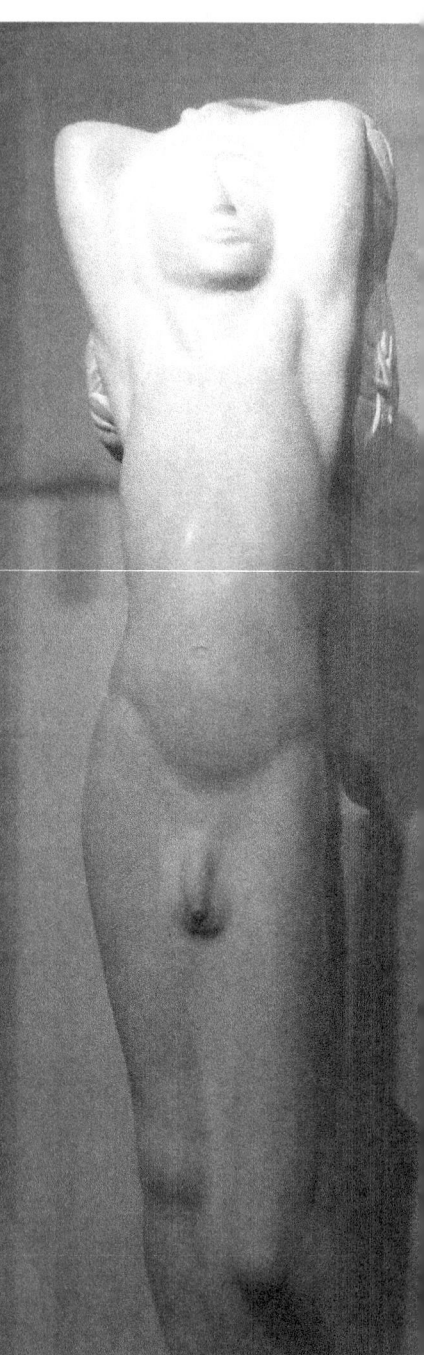

Eric Gill, St Sebastian,
1920, Victoria & Albert Museum,
London

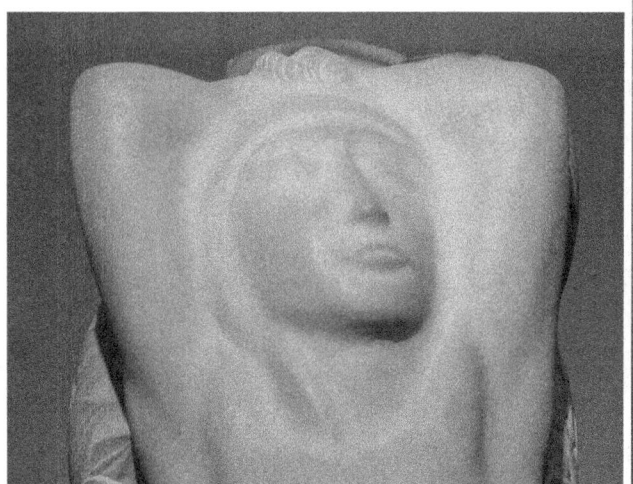

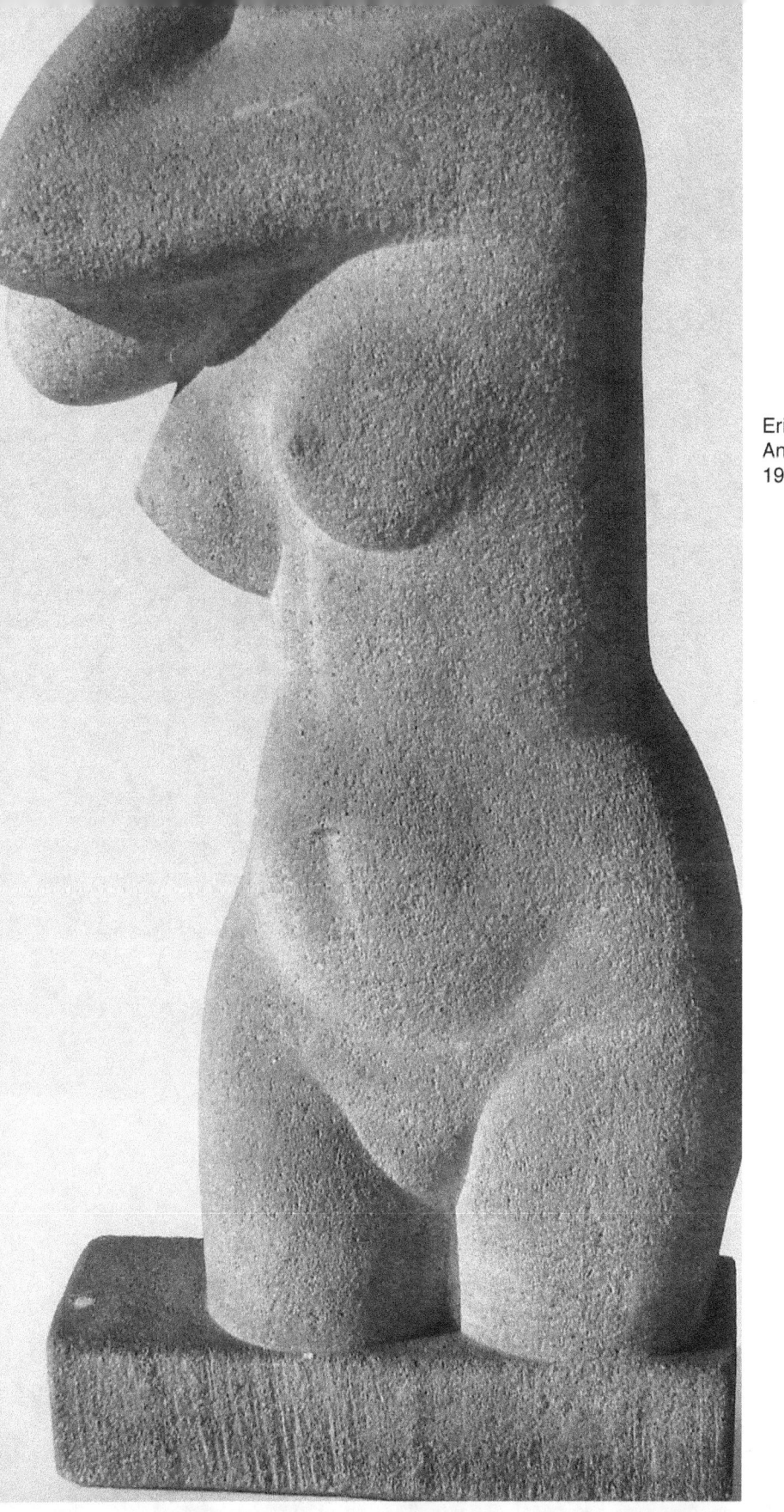

Eric Gill,
Anadyomene,
1920

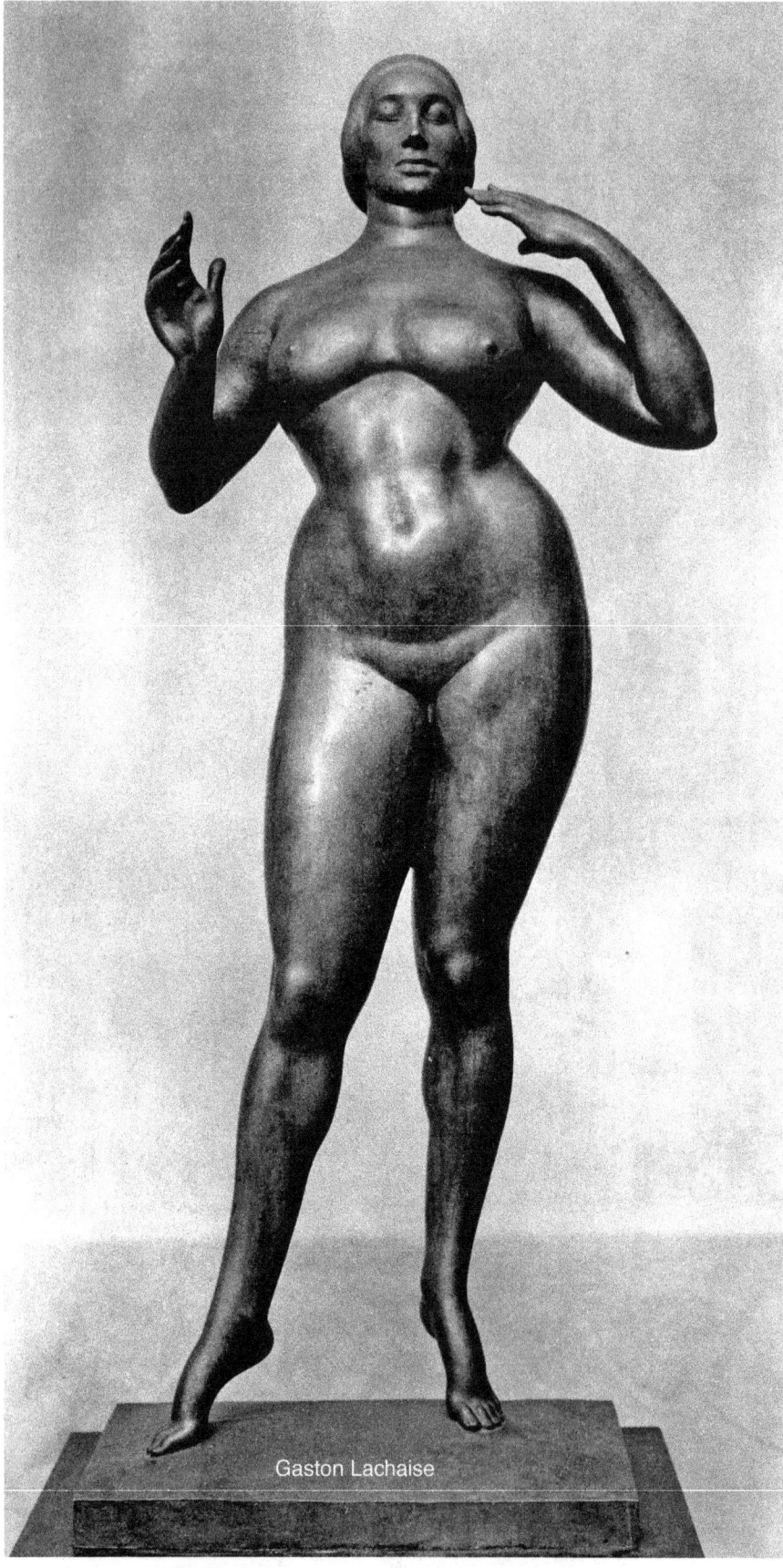

Gaston Lachaise

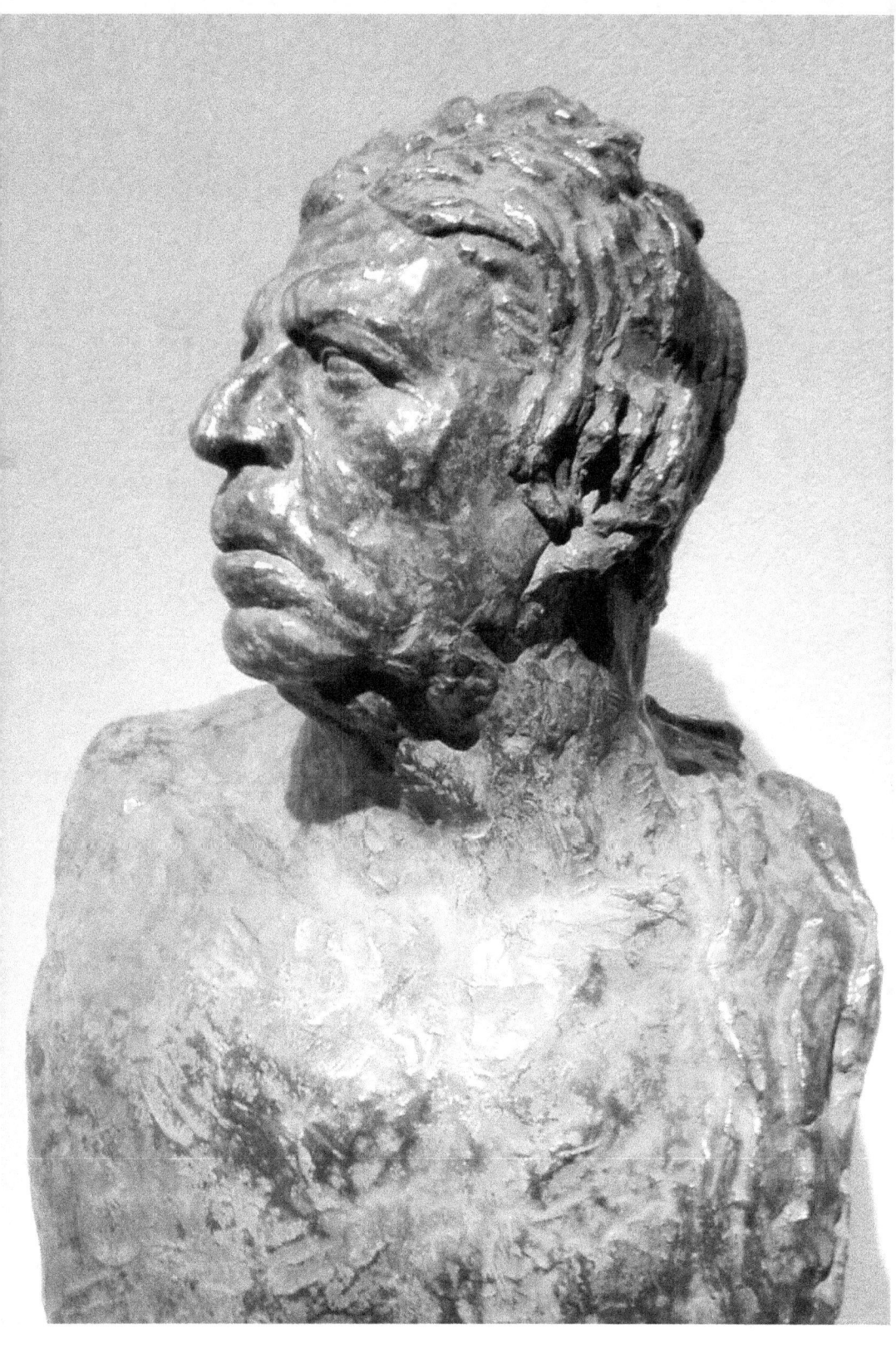

Antoine Bourdelle, Ingres, Musée Antoine Bourdelle

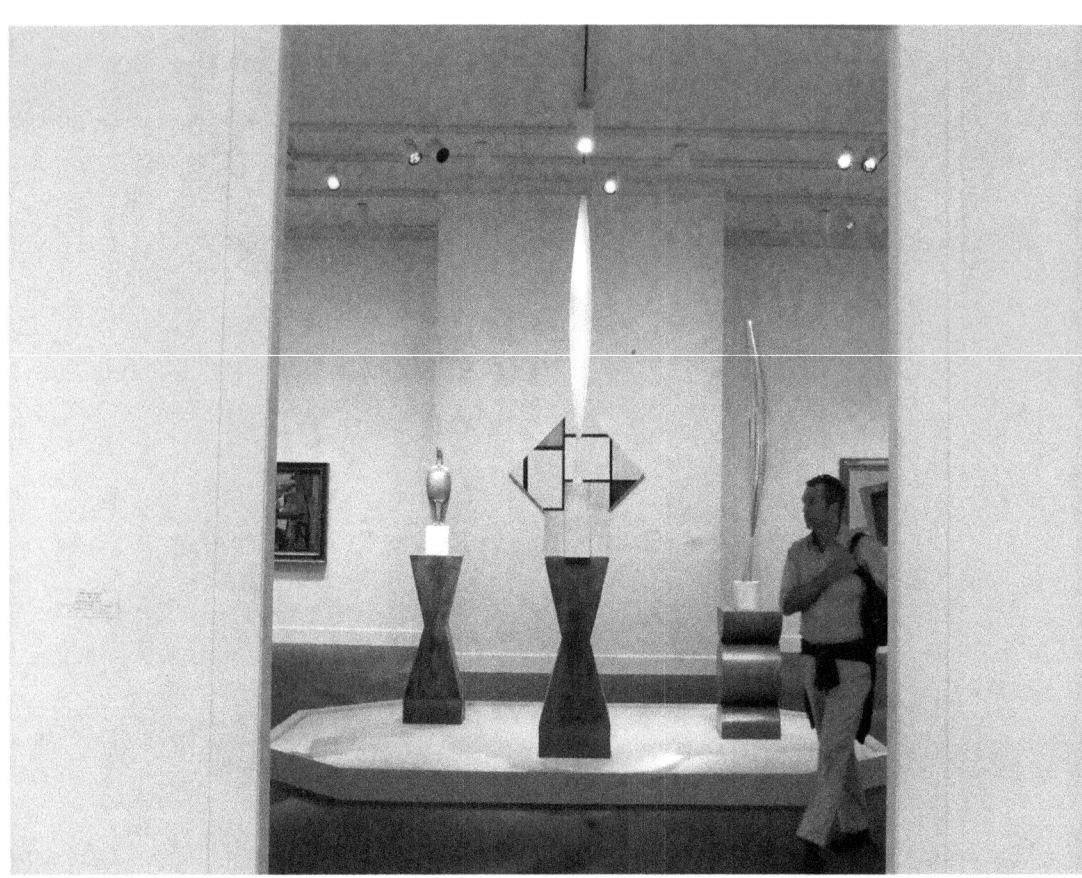

A display of Constantin Brancusi's works in Washington, DC,
at the National Gallery of Art

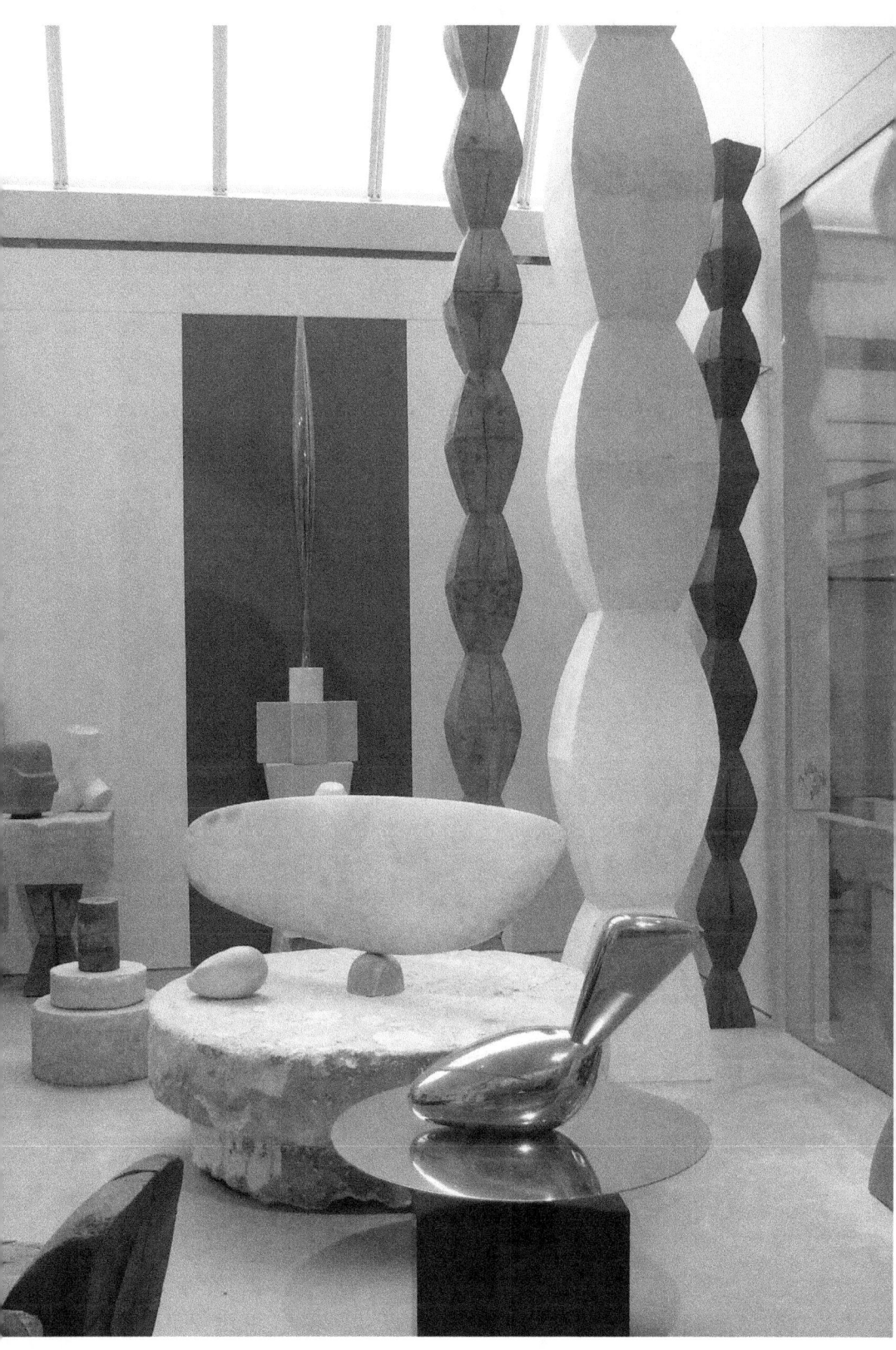

The Brancusi Studio in Paris

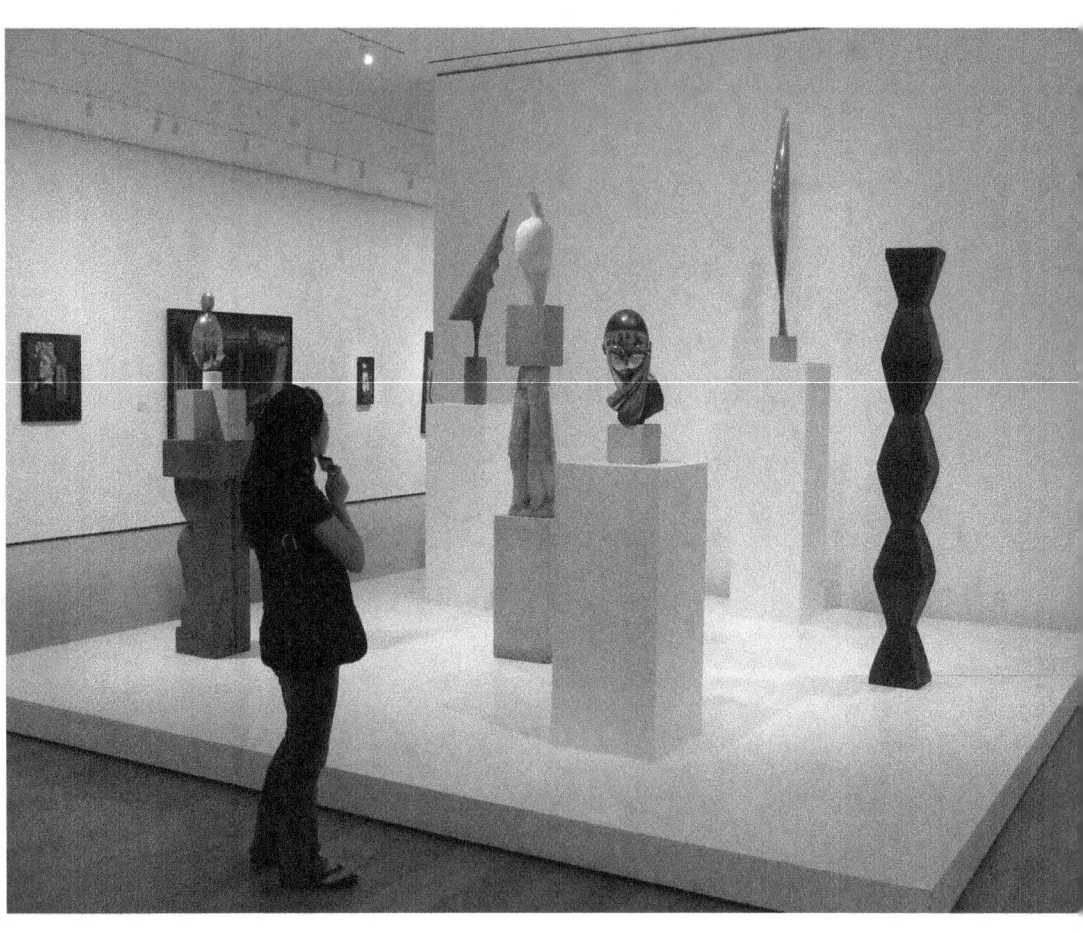

Constantin Brancusi display, Museum of Modern Art, Gotham

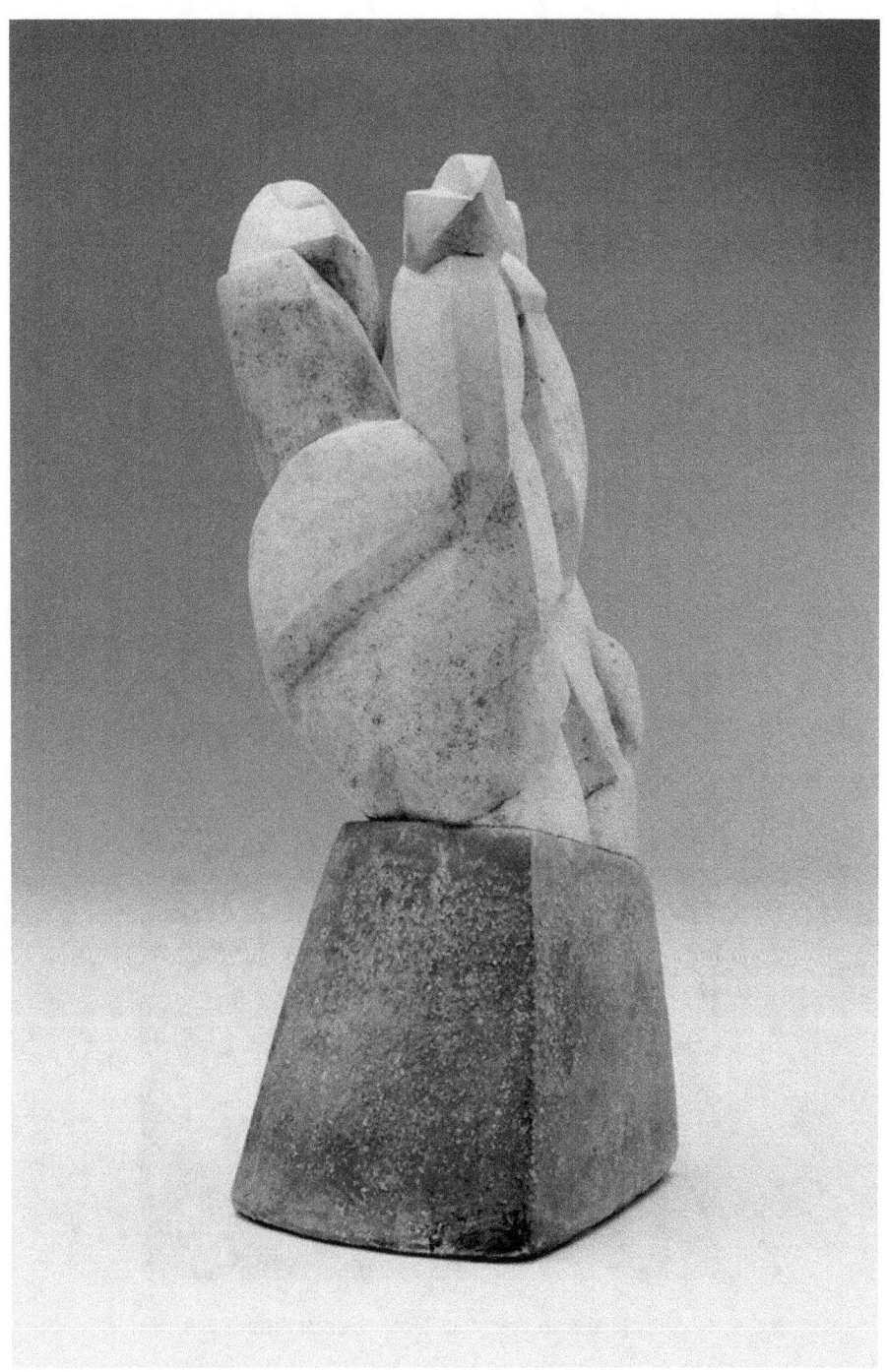

Henri Gaudier-Brzeska

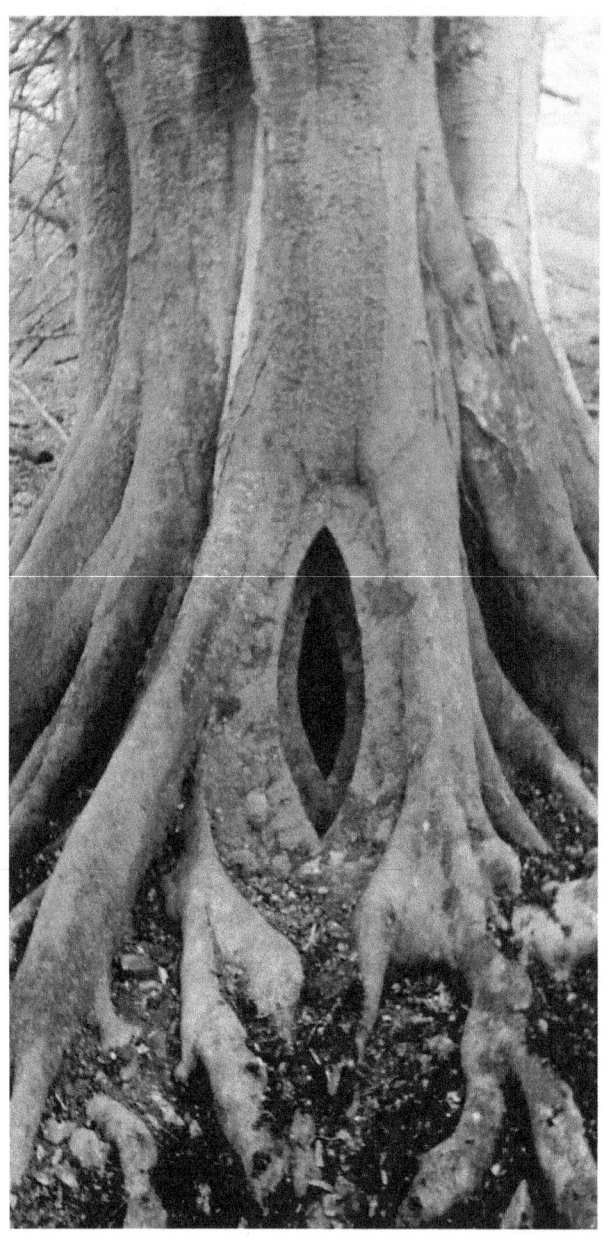

Andy Goldsworthy, Mud, Moss, Beech Tree, 1999

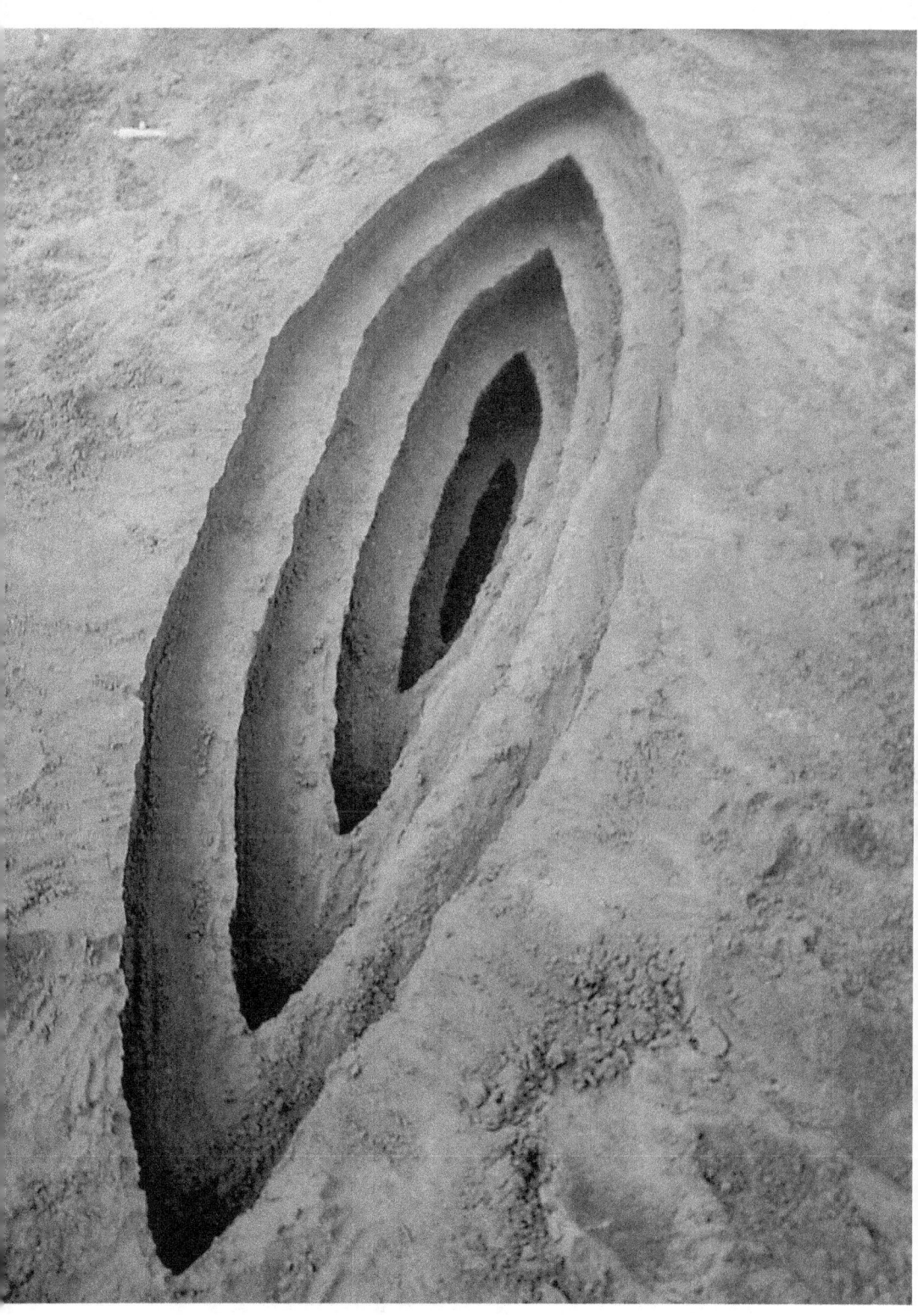

Andy Goldsworthy, Hard Sand Carved Out With a Stick, 1991,
Australia

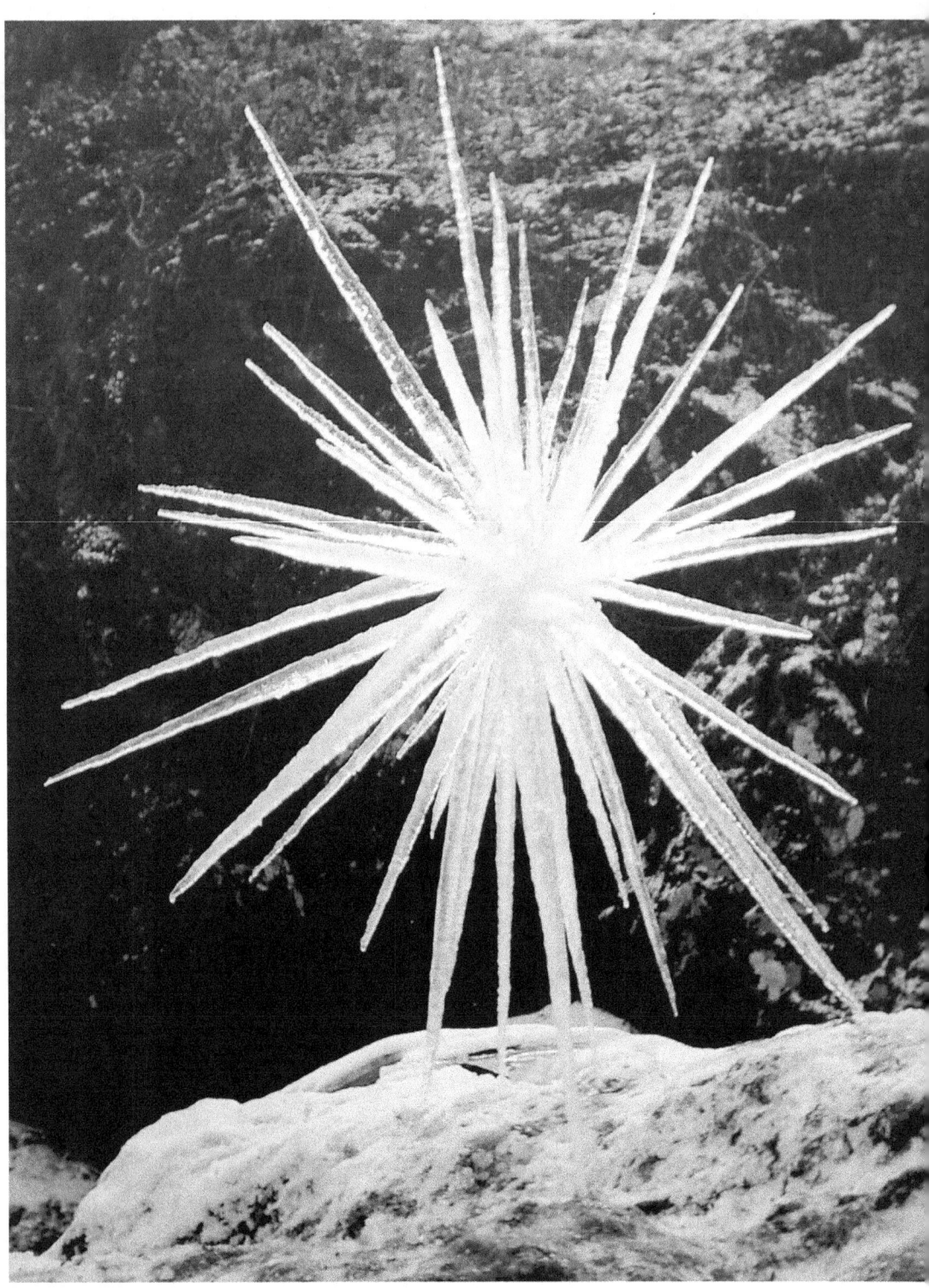

Andy Goldsworthy, Icicles, 1987

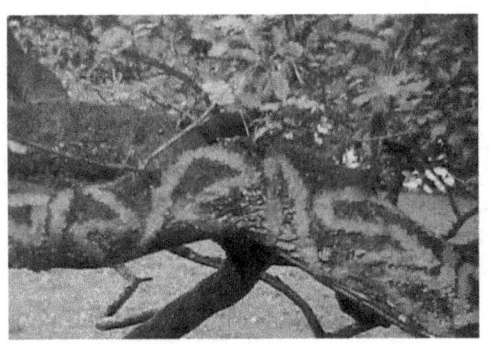
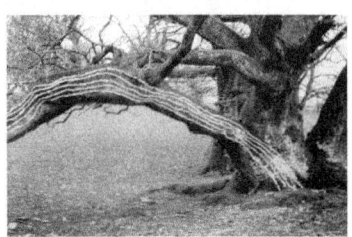
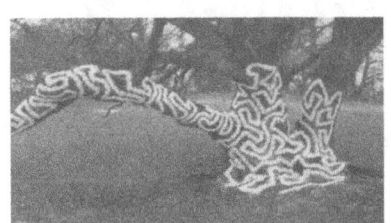
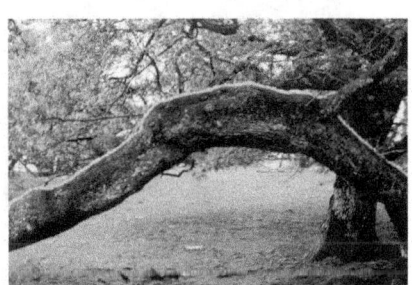

Andy Goldsworthy, from the Capenoch Tree series, 1994-96

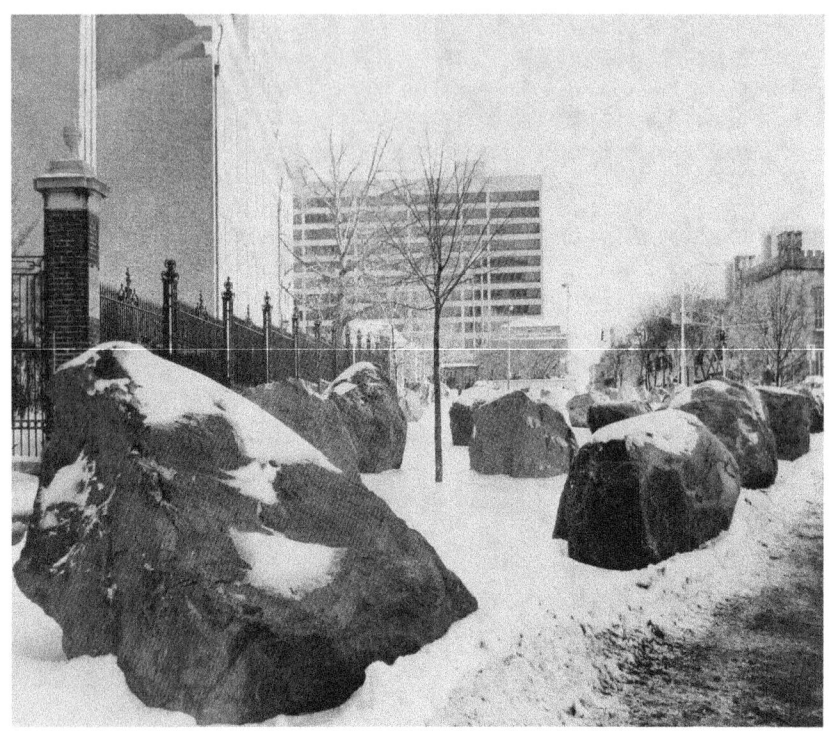

Carl Andre, Stone Field, 1977

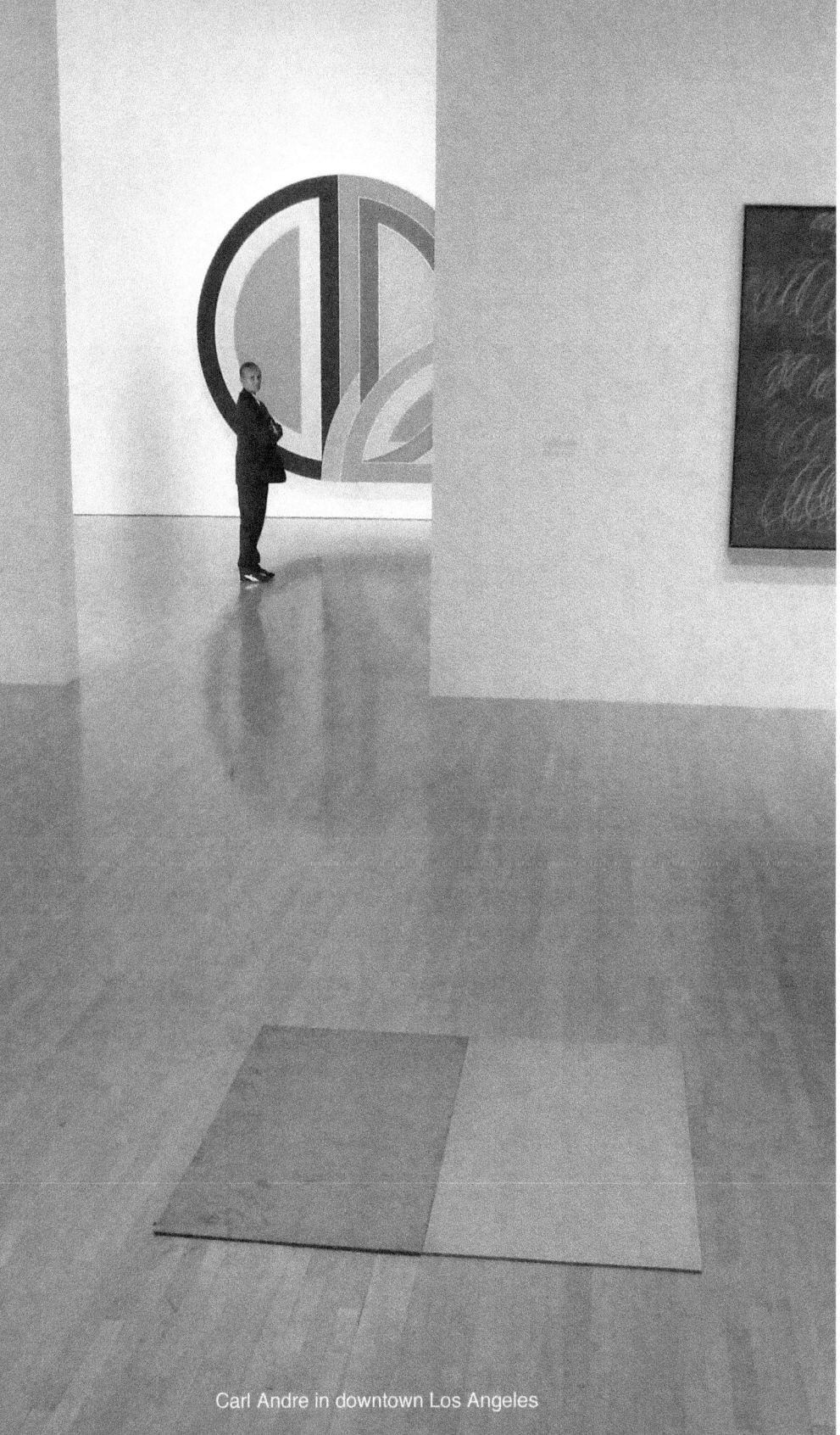

Carl Andre in downtown Los Angeles

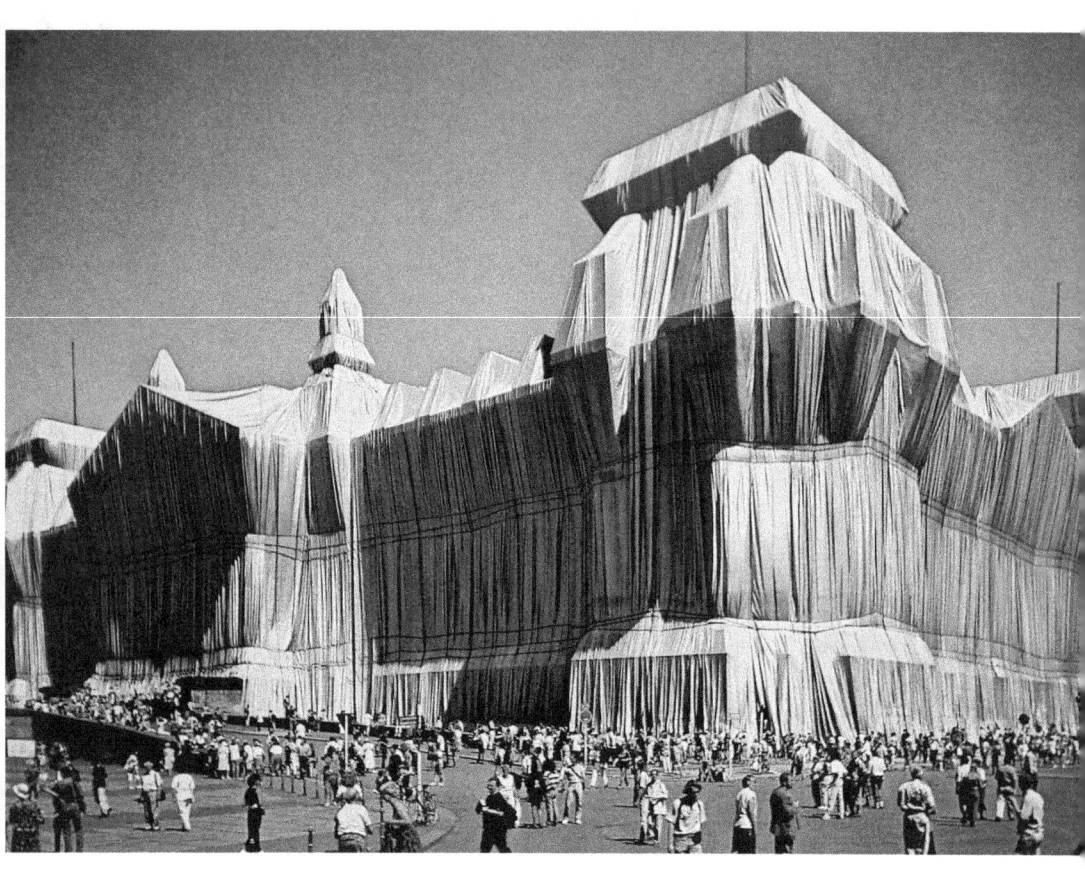

Christo, Wrapped Reichstag, 1997

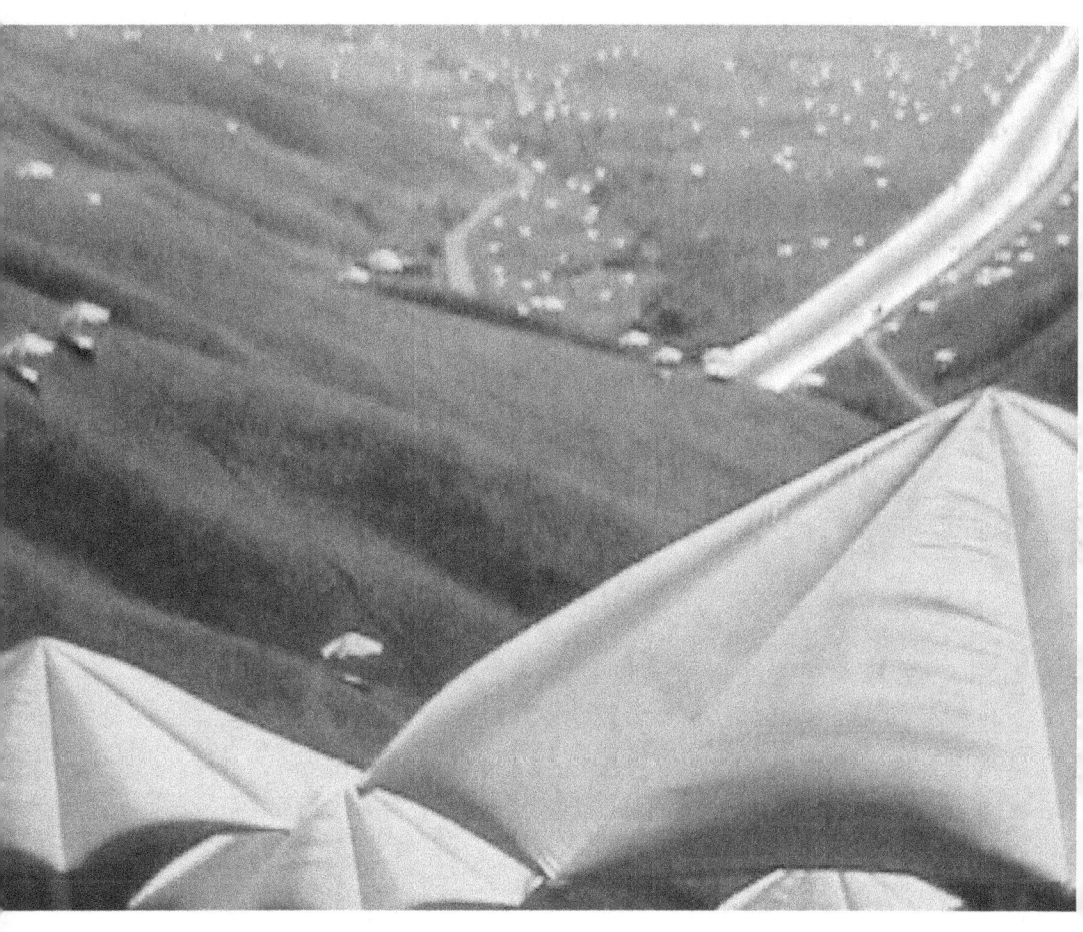

Christo, Umbrellas, 1976

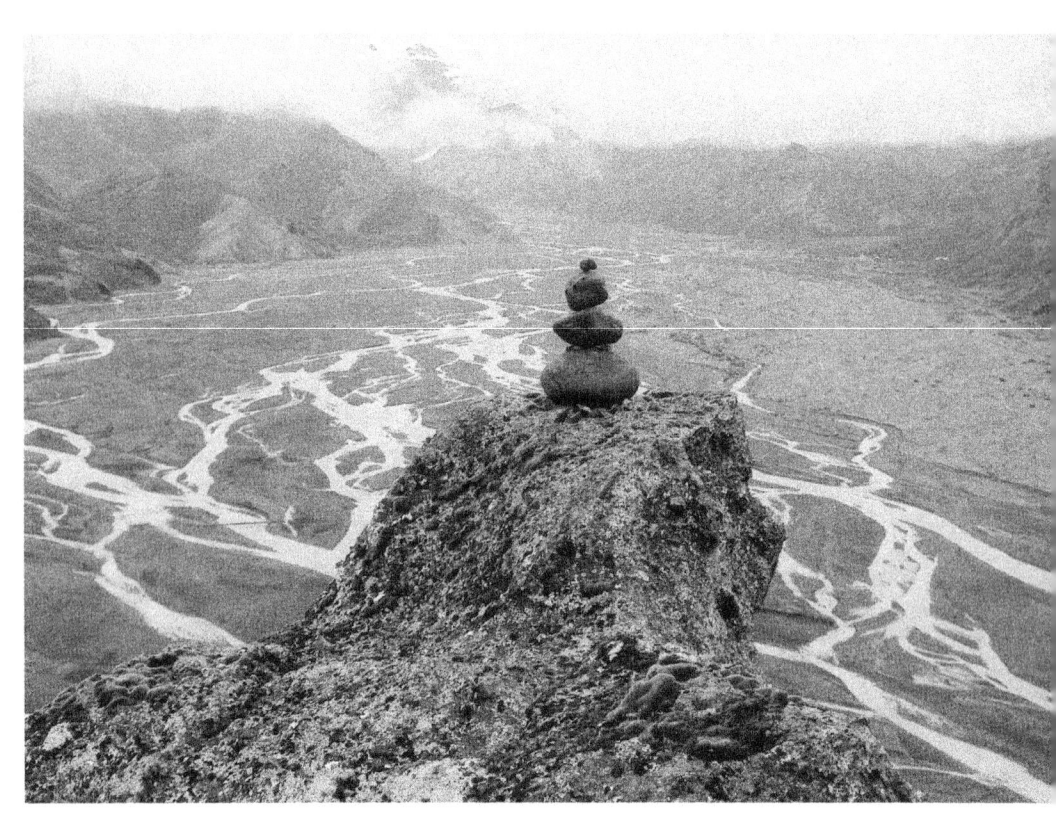

Chris Drury, Cairn

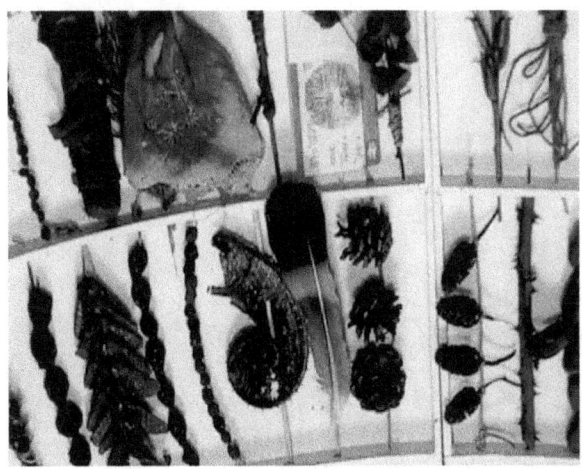

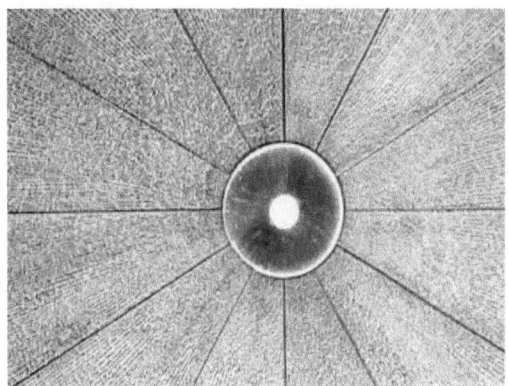

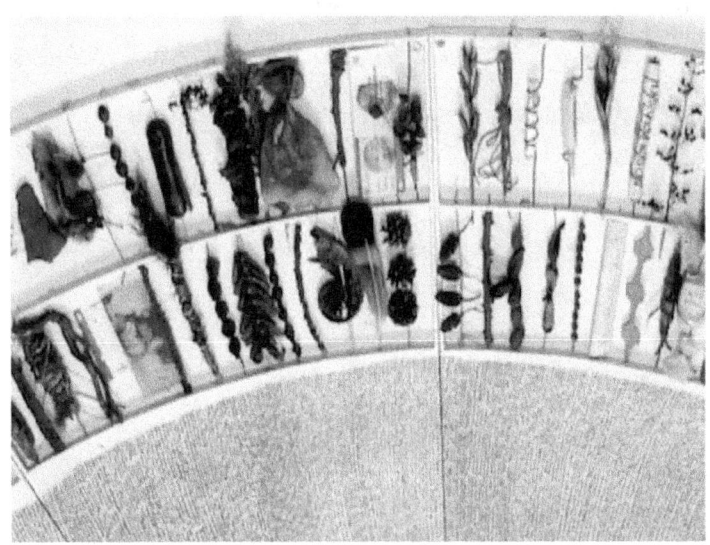

Chris Drury, Medicine Wheel, 1983

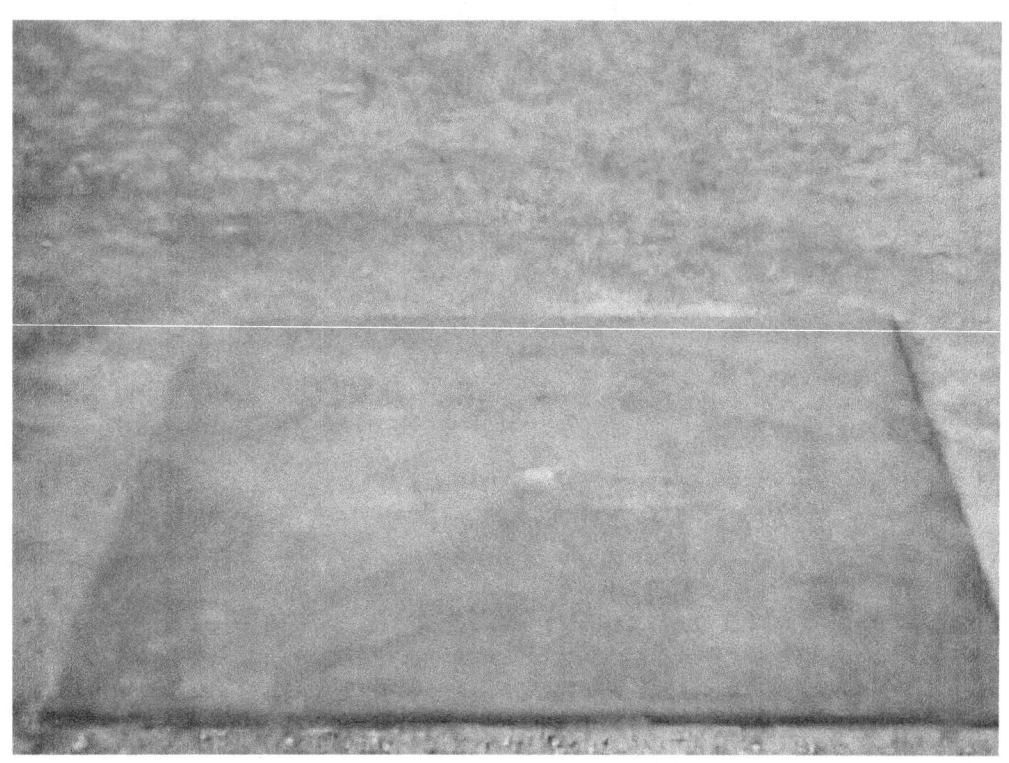

Walter de Maria, Vertical Earth Kilometer, 1977

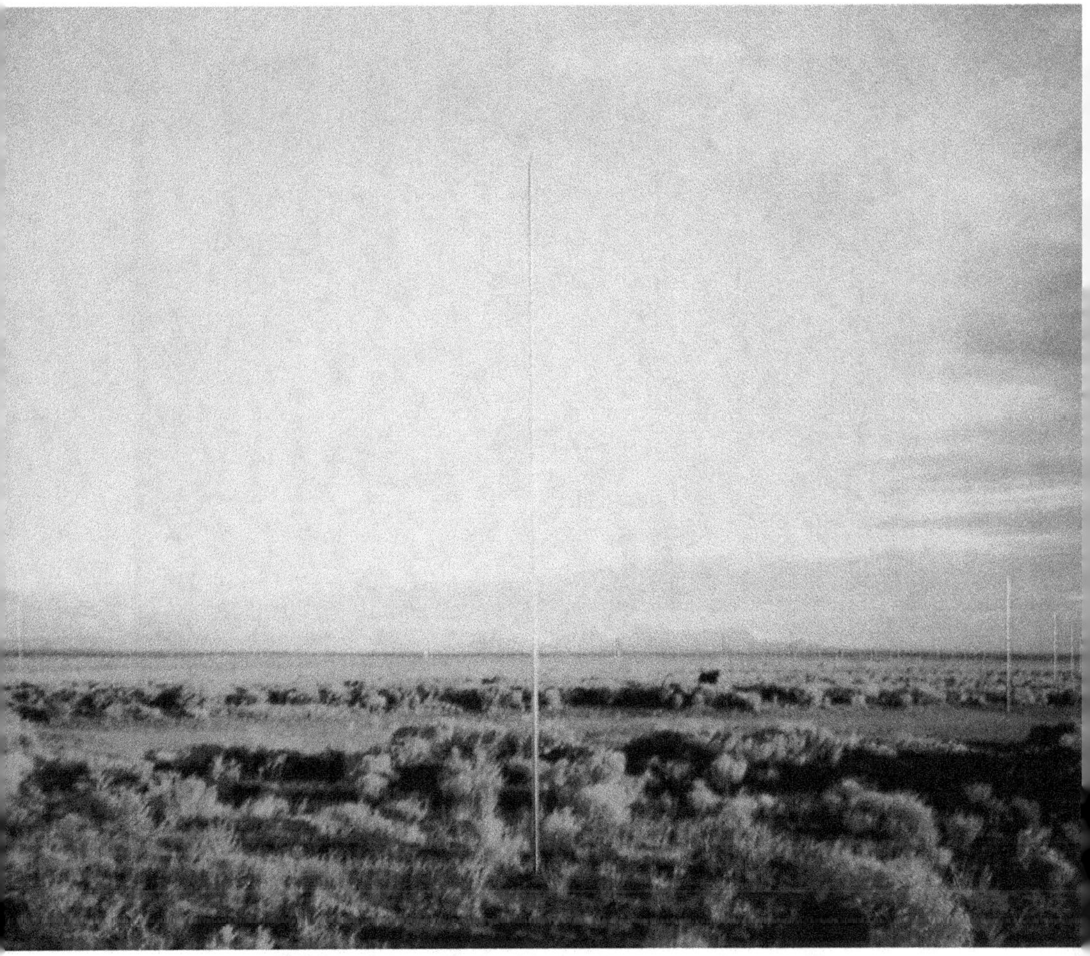

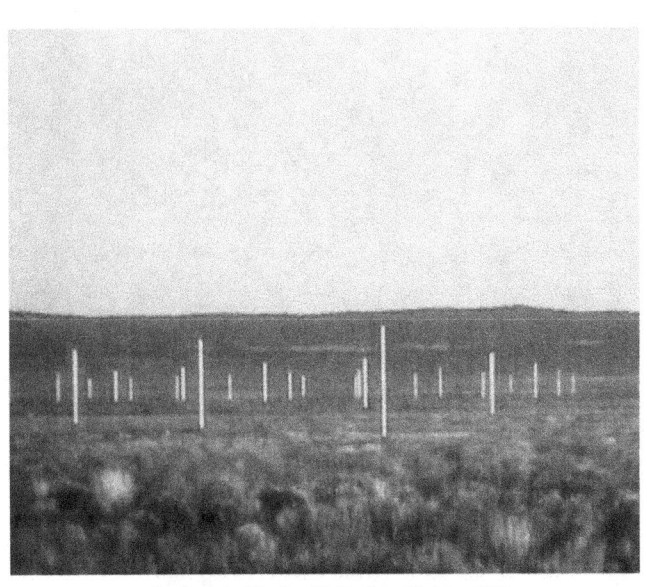

Walter de Maria, Lightning Field, 1977

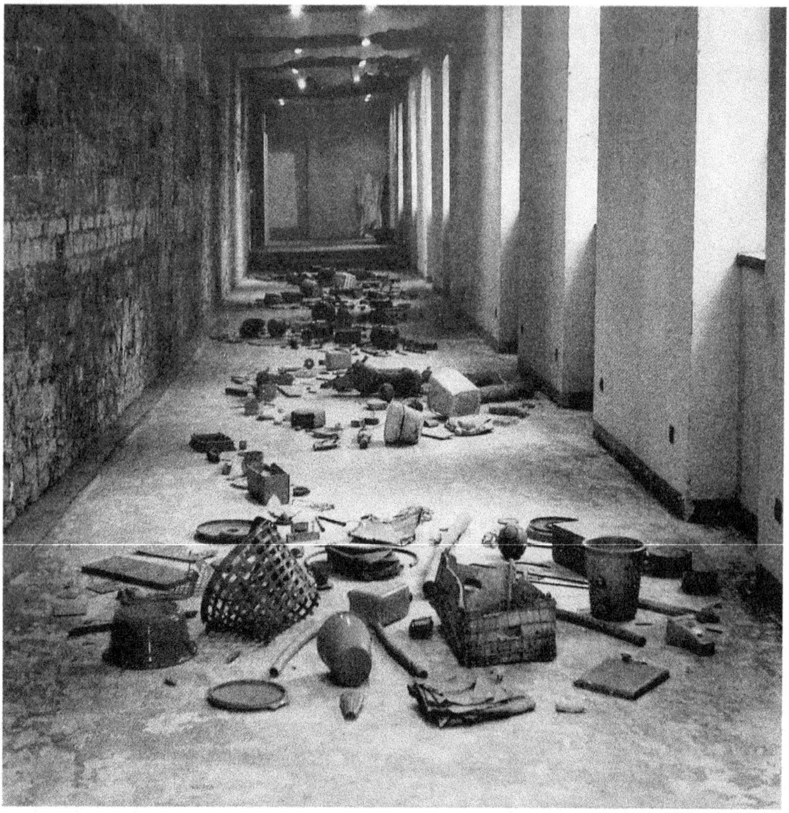

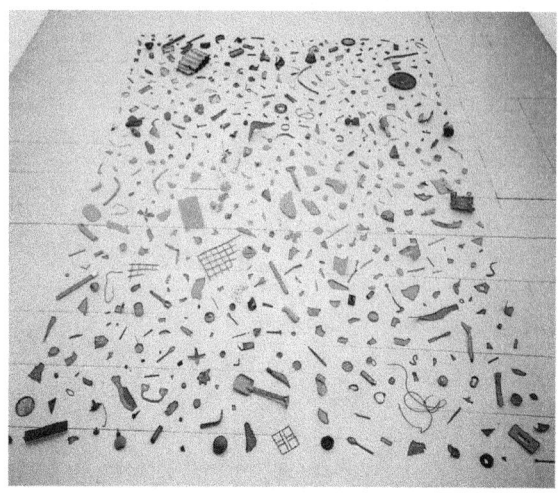

Tony Cragg

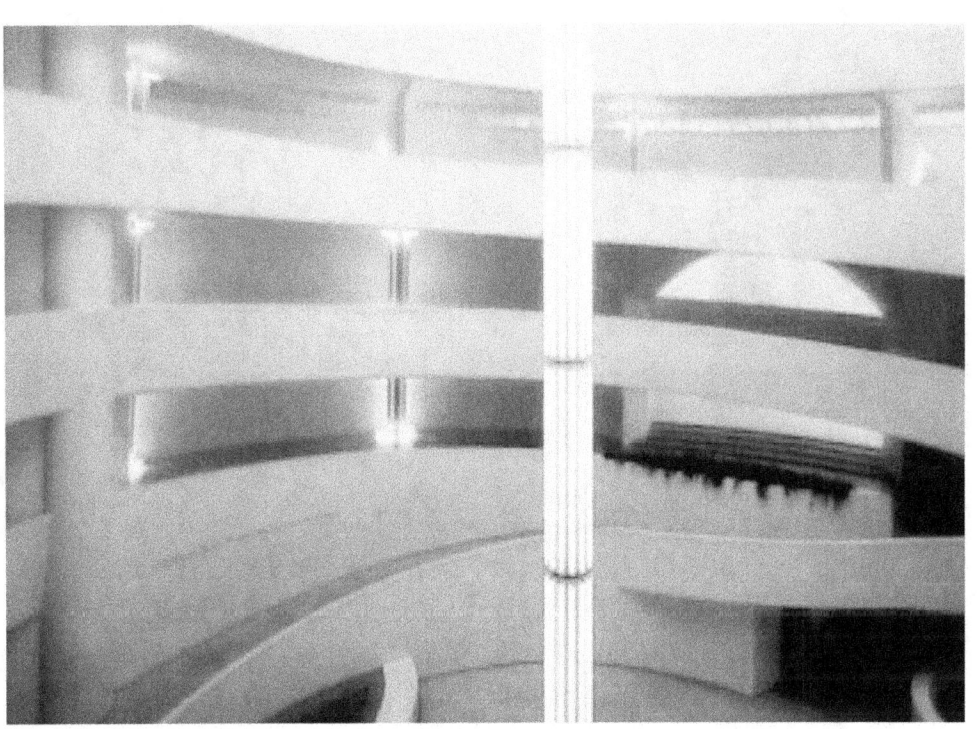

Dan Flavin, Untitled (To Tracy, To Celebrate the Love
of a Lifetime), 1992

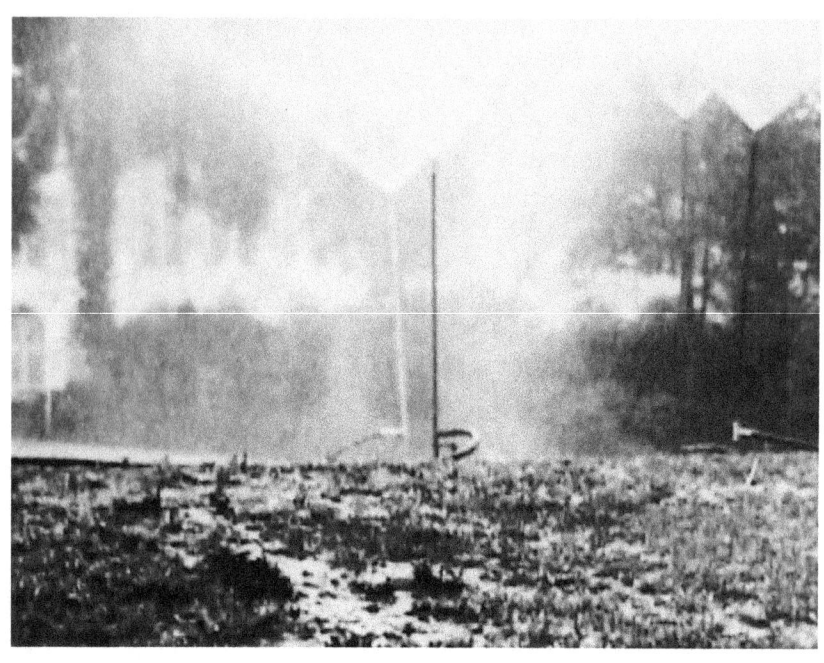

Hans Haacke, Fog, Flooding and Erosion, 1969

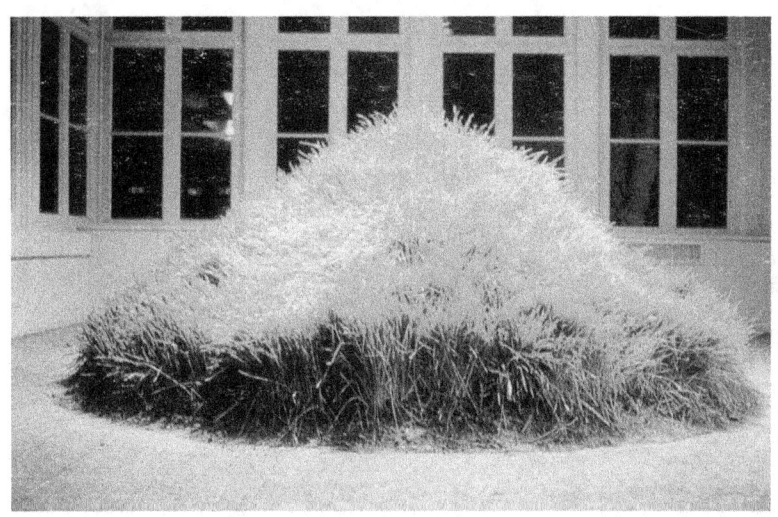

Hans Haacke, Grass Grows, 1969

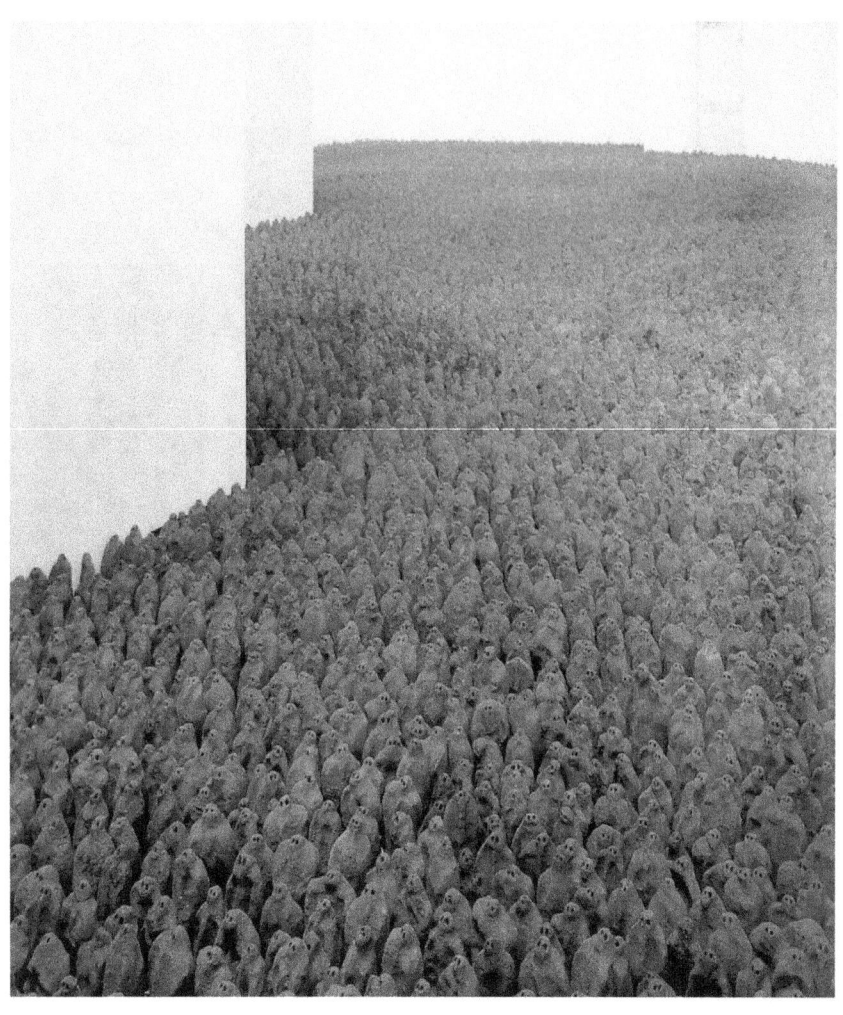

Anthony Gormley

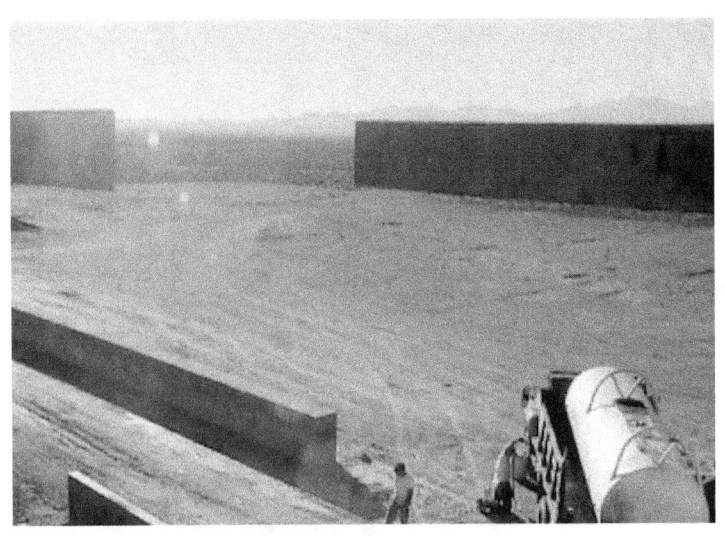

Michael Heizer, Complex One, 1972

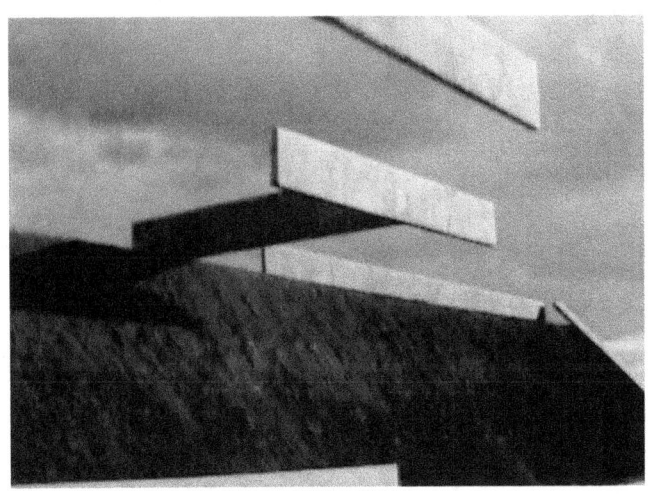

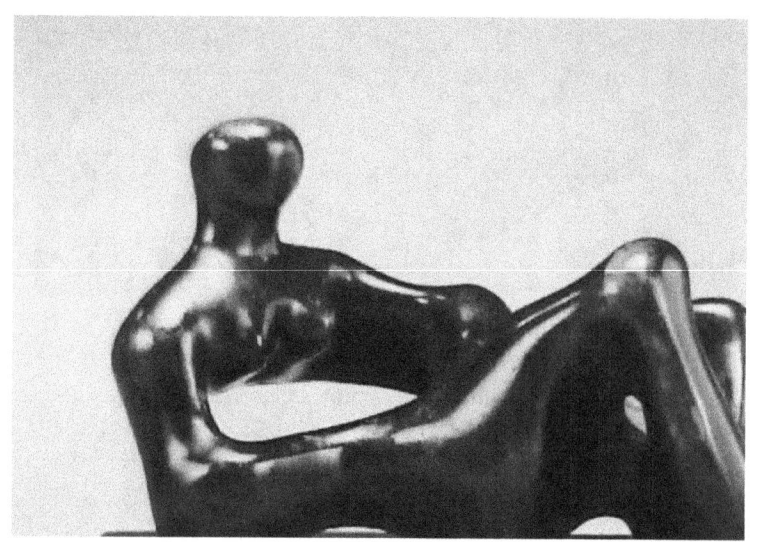

Henry Moore, Maquette For Recumbent Figure, 1938

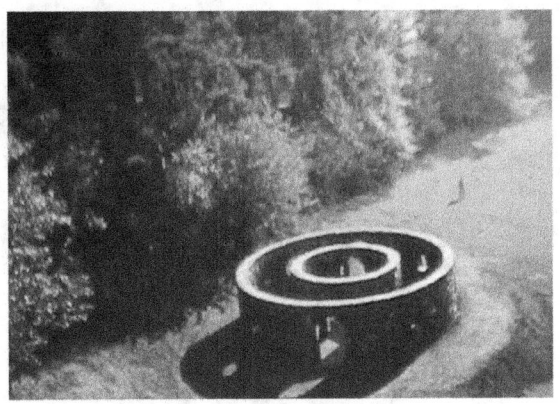

Nancy Holt, Stone Enclosure - Rock Rings, 1977-78

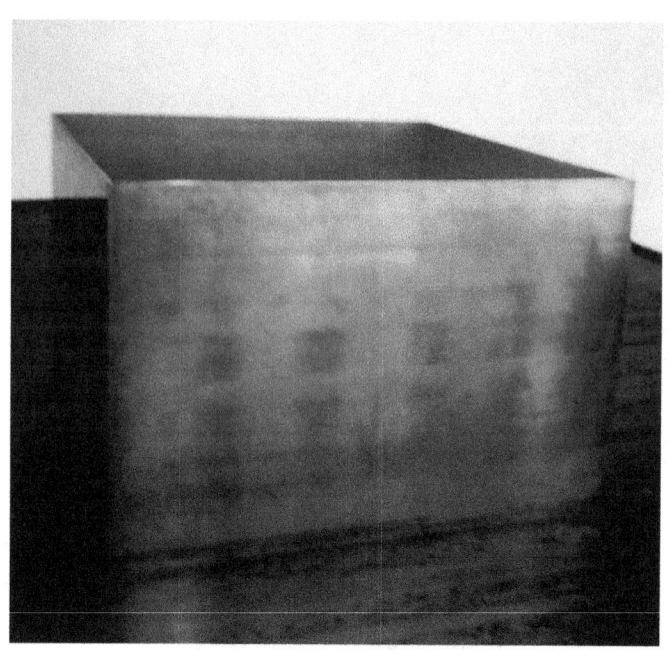

Donald Judd's Minimal
sculptures from the 1970s

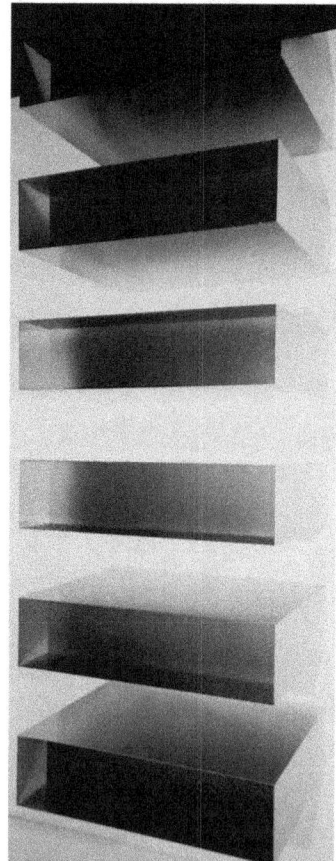

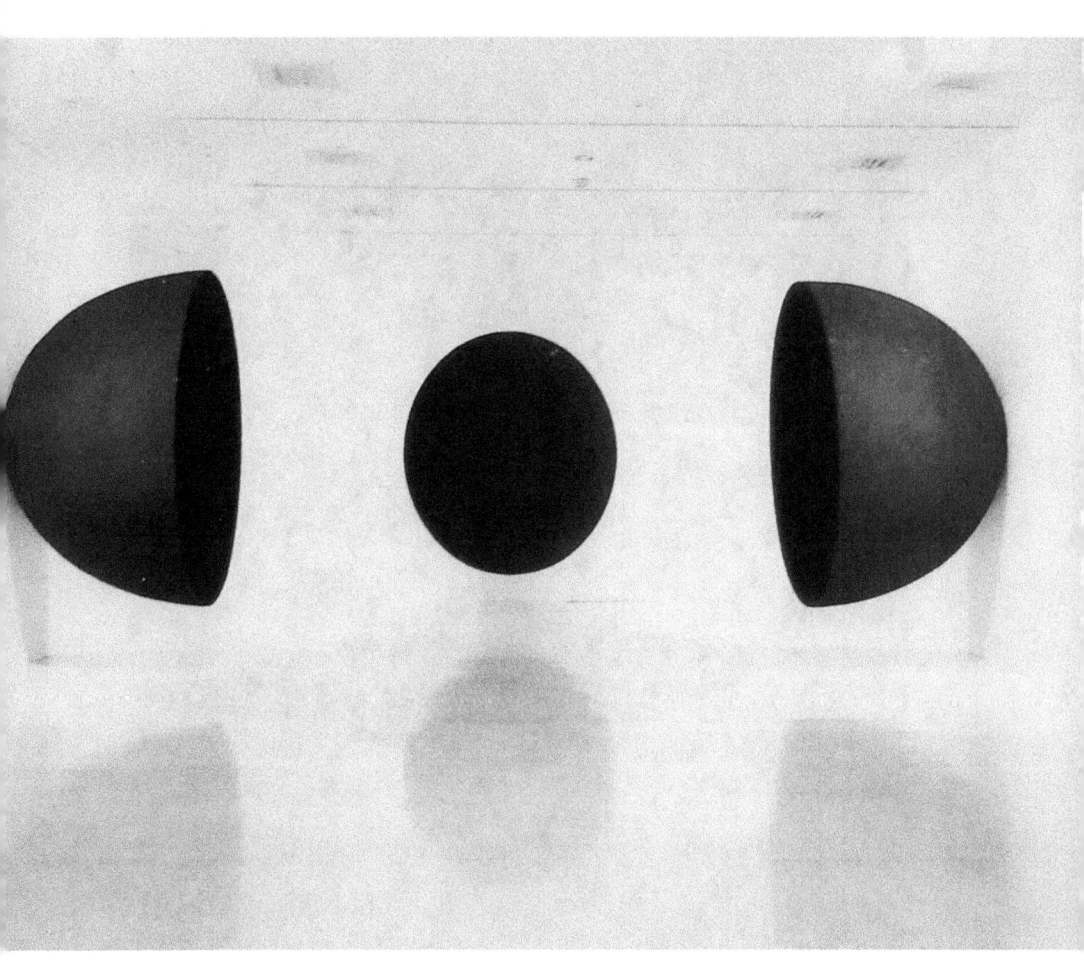

Anish Kapoor

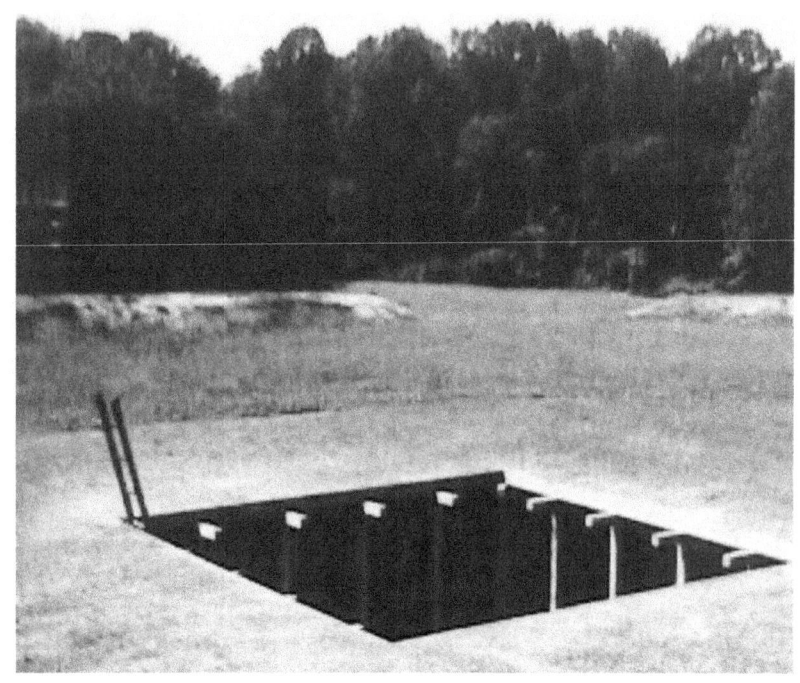

Mary Miss, Perimeters/ Pavilion/ Decoys. 1978

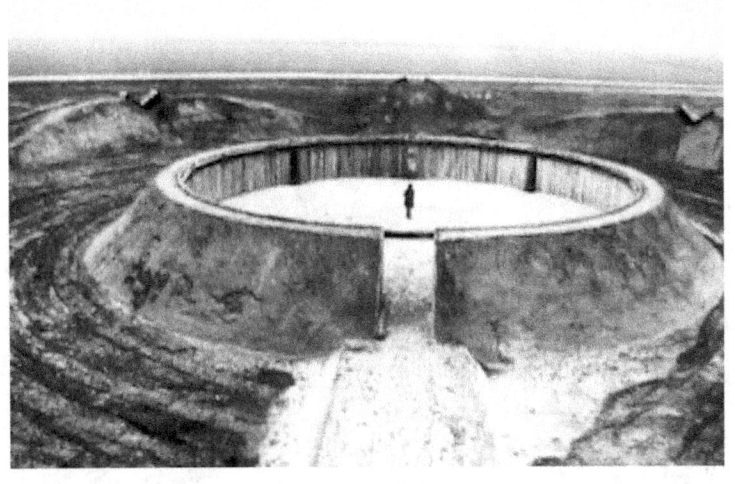

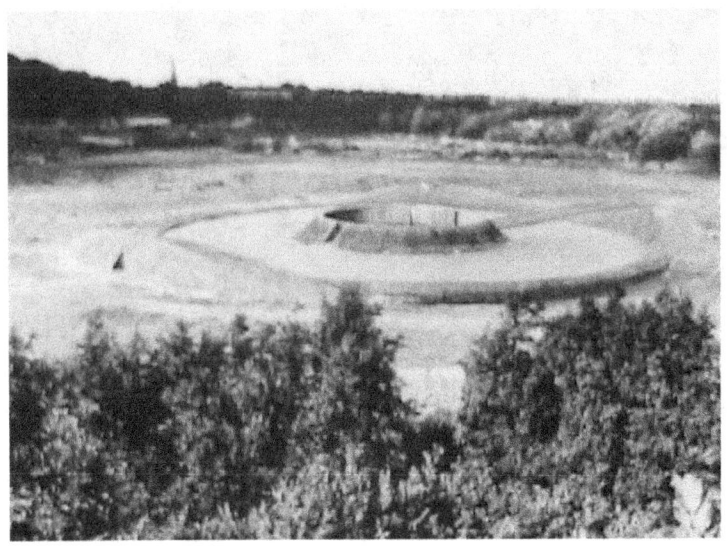

Robert Morris, Observatory, 1971

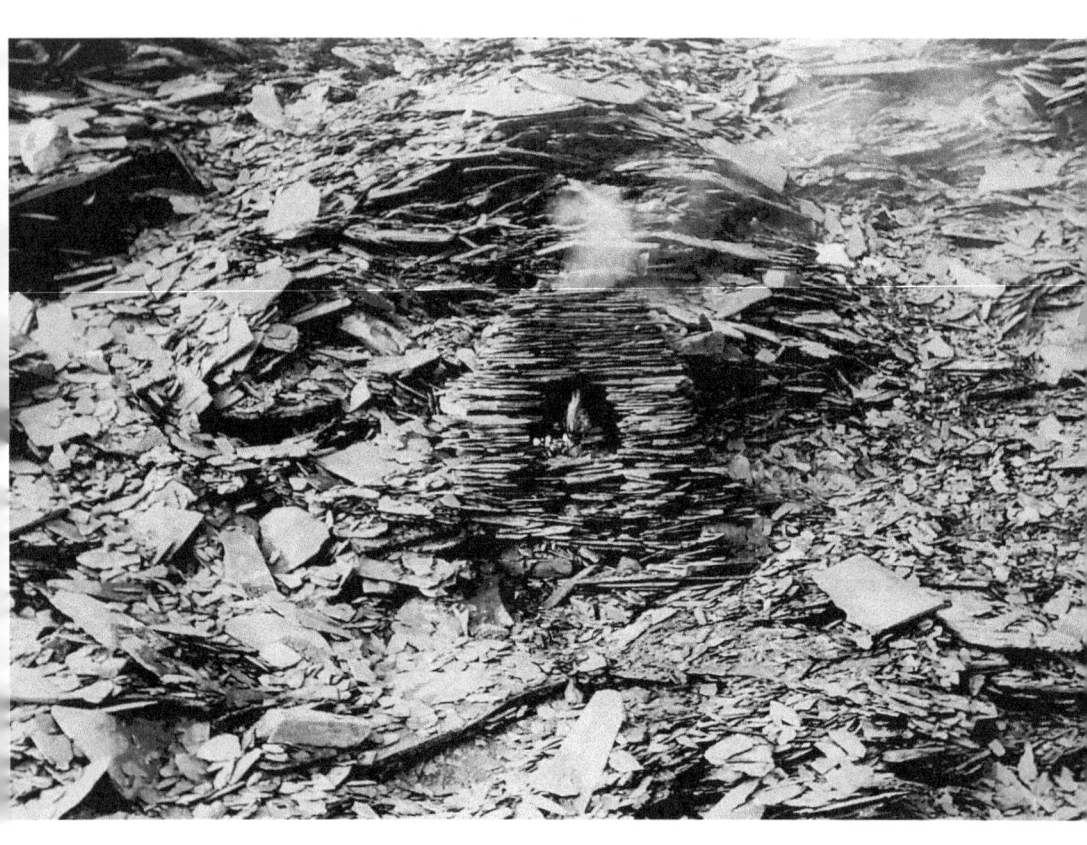

David Nash, Slate Stove

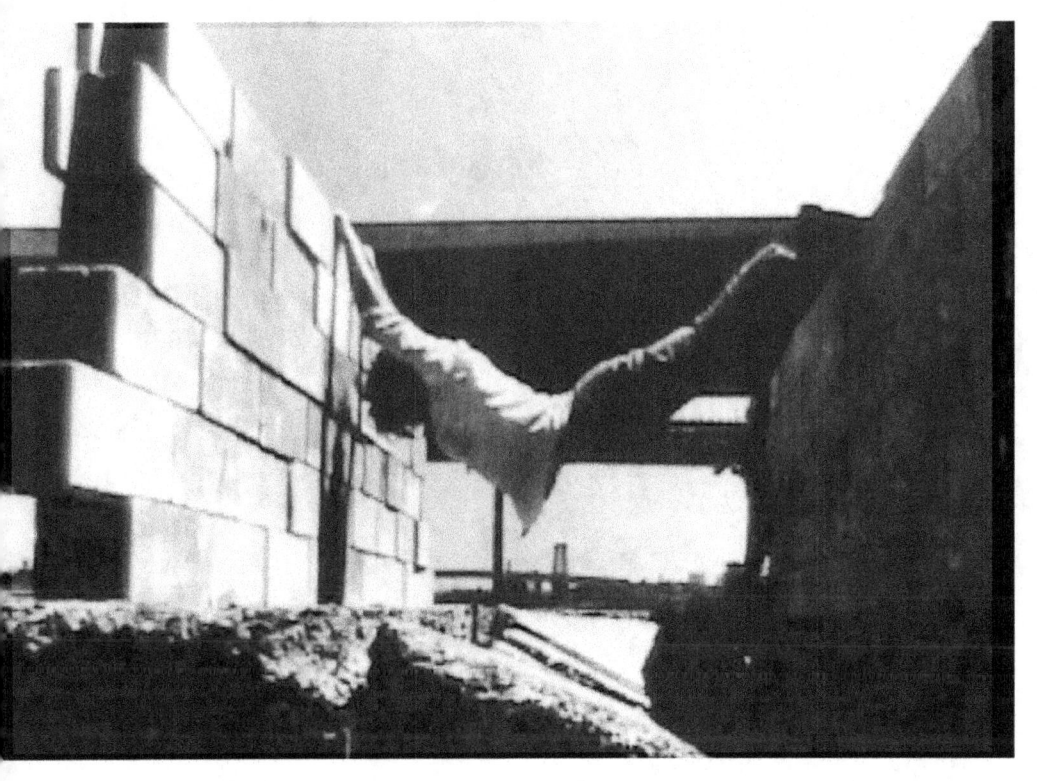

Dennis Oppenheim, Parallel Stress, 1970

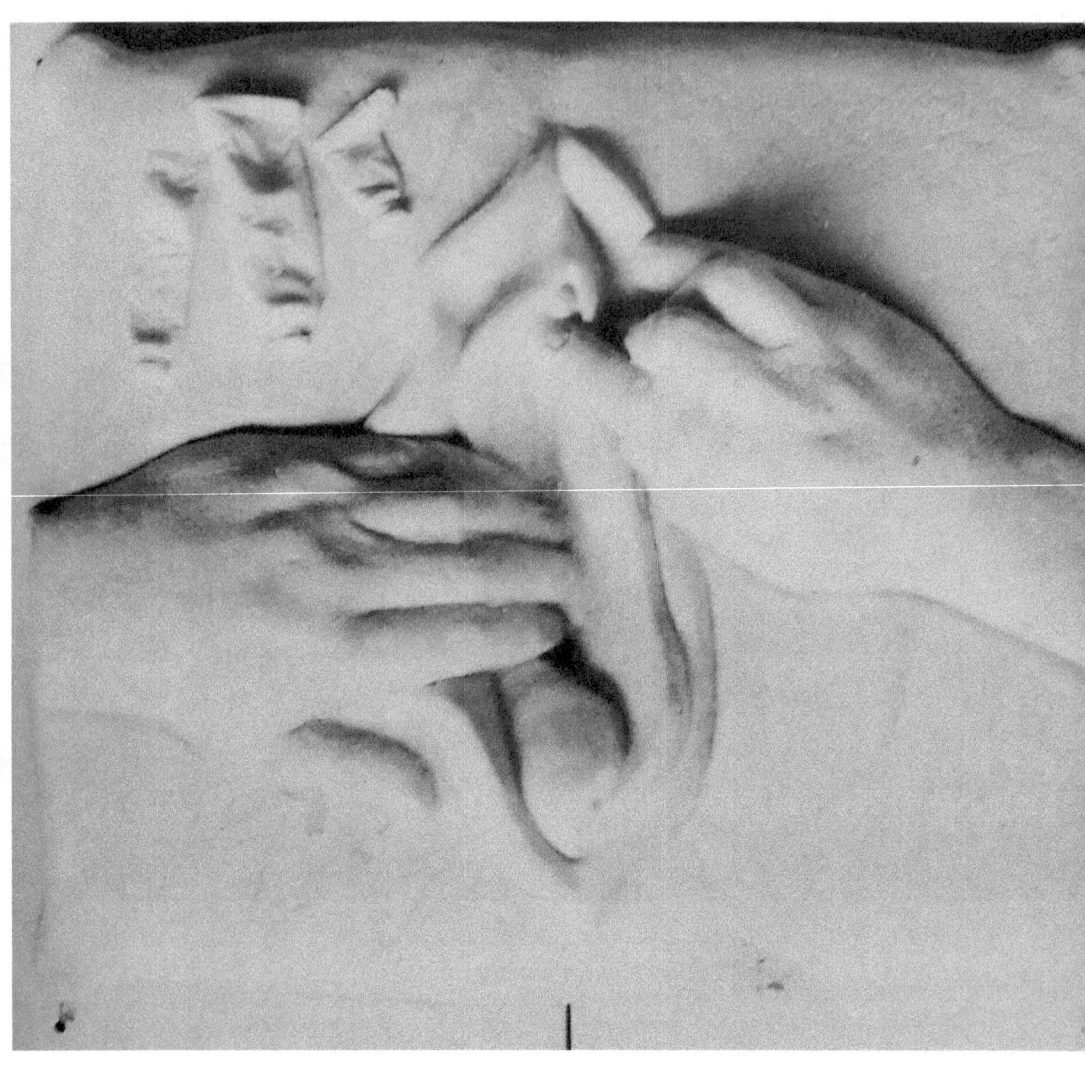

Otto Dressler, Sitzbild No. 2

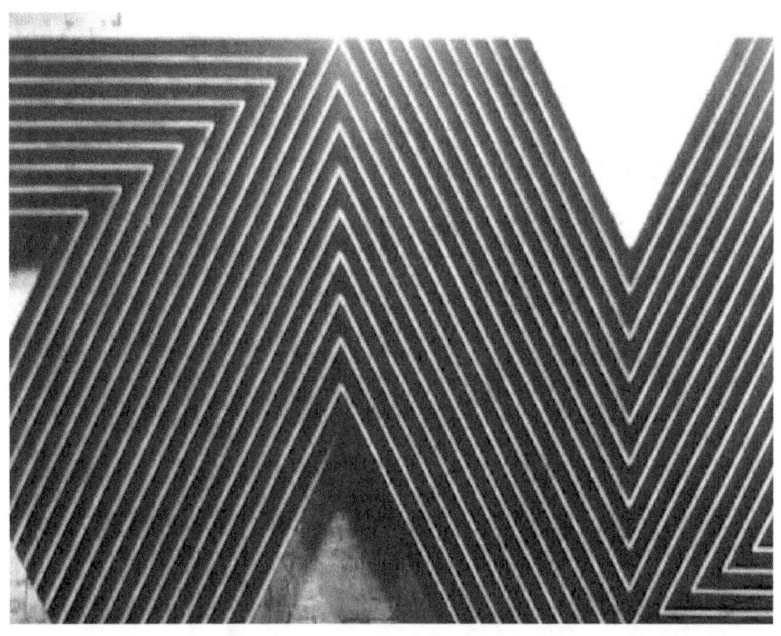

Frank Stella

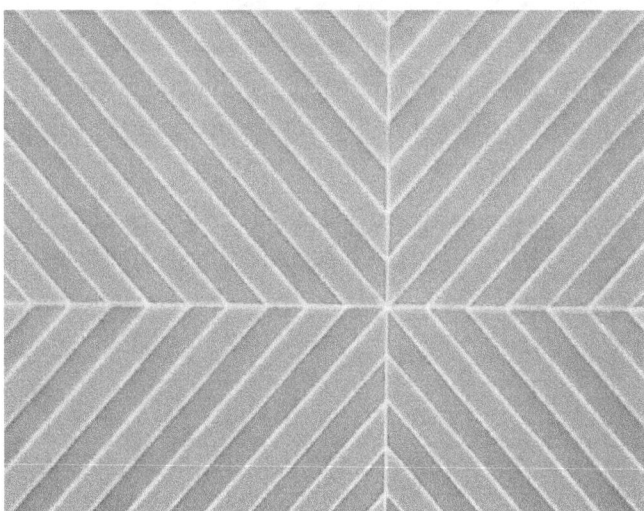

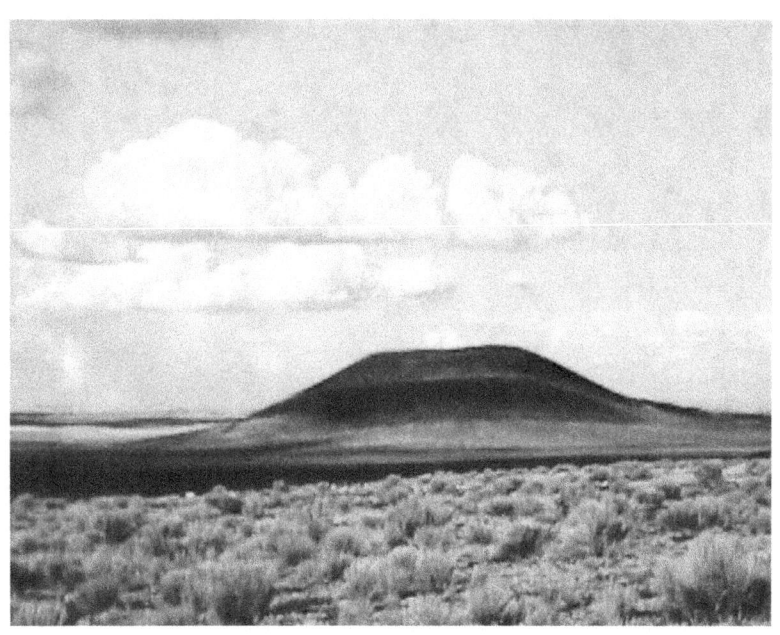

James Turrell, Roden Crater, 1974-

15

Women's Art

Many feminists and comment-ators have studied the history of women's art and women artists. Where are the great women painters, feminists ask, the artists who can stand alongside Édouard Manet, Michelangelo Buonarroti, Sandro Botticelli and Peter Paul Rubens? So feminists have been discovering, redis-covering, excavating and re-writing art history. It turns out there have been many, many brilliant women artists: Artemisia Gentileschi, Sofonisba Anguissola, Gwen John, Mary Cassatt, Berthe Morisot, Suzanne Valadon, Käthe Kollwitz, Frida Kahlo, Paula Modersohn-Becker, Ch'en Shu, Barbara Longhi, Natalia Goncharova, Gabriele Münter, Dorothea Lange, Julia Margaret Cameron, Harriet Hosmer, Ma Shou-Chen, Anna Bilinska, Elisabeth Vigée-Lebrun, Françoise Duparc, Rosalba Carriera, Angelica Kauffmann, Georgia O'Keeffe, Diane Arbus, Judith Leyster, Sonia Delaunay, Kuan Tao-Sheng, Ts'ao Miao-Ch'ing, Clara Peeters, Catharina van Hemessen, and a host of contemporary artists: Miriam Schapiro, Leonor Fini, Niki de Sant-Phalle, Judy Chicago, Mary Beth Edelson, Barbara Hep-worth, Helen Frankenthaler, Cindy Sherman, Jennifer Bartlett, Elizabeth Catlett, Alison Wilding, Barbara Kruger, Mary Duffy, Jo

Spence, Lyn Malcolm, Agnes Martin, Elizabeth Murray, Judy Rifka, Louise Bourgeois, Nancy Graves, Katherine Porter, Susan Rothenberg, Eva Hesse, Louise Nevelson, Lynda Benglis, Lee Bontecou, Sherrie Levine, Rebecca Horn, Magdalena Abakanowicz, Judy Pfaff, Pat Steir, Catherine Murphy, and Audrey Flack.

Many images made by women artists have become widely celebrated: Artemisia Gentileschi's marvellous *Judiths*, empowered women at the cutting edge of proto-feminism, and her luminous, extraordinary *Self-Portrait*; Gentileschi seemingly effortlessly refined the art of Michelangelo Merisi da Caravaggio to a striking degree, demonstrating to all that women painters can do everything that male painters can do, *and then some*; Käthe Kollwitz's emotionally-charged sculptures; Georgia O'Keeffe's elegant, semi-abstract close-ups vulva-shaped flowers; Barbara Hepworth's holed forms; Mary Cassatt's independent form of Impressionism; Elisabeth Vigée-Lebrun's royal portraits, and so on. These works by women, though, are still not as highly regarded by the art world as, say, Jasper Johns' *American Flag* or Eugène Delacroix's *Sardanapale*.

One of the problems that

feminists have addressed with regard to women's art is: can there be a truly 'female' or 'feminine' or 'women's' art, or a 'women's' sculpture? Is art made by women (women's art) ever completely free of patriarchal influences, structures, forms? Can there be a women's art that exists in its own 'female' space, away from patriarchy and masculinist ideas and experiences? French feminist Julia Kristeva is pessimistic on this contentious issue. For her, there has been no 'female writing' thus far in our culture. She says:

> If we confine ourselves to the *radical* nature of what is today called 'writing', that is, if we submit meaning and the speaking subject in language to a radical examination and then reconstitute them in a more polyvalent than fragile manner, there is nothing in either past or recent publications by women that permits us to claim that a specifically female writing exists.[1]

For Hélène Cixous, most writing, by men or women, is masculine. She writes: '[m]ost women are like this; they do someone else's – man's –

1 "A partir de *Polylogue*", interview with Françoise van Rossum-Guyon, *Revue des sciences humaines*, vol. XLIV, no. 168, tr. Seán Hand, Oct-Dec 2977, 495f

writing, and in their innocence sustain it and give it voice, and end up producing writing that's in effect masculine.'[2] The notion of 'écriture féminine' of Luce Irigaray and Hélène Cixous is much discussed in feminist literary criticism.[3] It is rejected by Monique Wittig. Wittig also rejects the notion of 'man' and 'woman'. For her, 'woman' is a historical, political, ideological and cultural construct. She writes that "woman' has meaning only in heterosexual systems of thought and heterosexual economic systems'.[4]

Camille Paglia, one of the more outspoken of feminist critics, is not so optimistic about female artists:

> One of the many lies of women's studies is that European art history was written by white males and that feminism has conclusively rewritten that history by discovering and restoring major female artists excluded from the pantheon by patriarchal conspiracy. But European art history was not just written but created by white males. We may lament the limitations placed on women's training and professional access in the past, but what is done cannot be undone. The last 20 years of scholarship have brought many forgotten women artists to attention, but too often their presentation has been marred by anachronistic feminist rhetoric: feminism has not found a single major female painter or sculptor to add to the canon.[5]

The discussion of women's art and women artists is, though, many feminists feel, crucial to feminism. After all, we know what male artists are like, and we are utterly familiar with male art. We are surrounded, embedded, drenched, choked, smothered by patriarchal art and culture, by male-orientated, even if not specifically male-made, culture. Male projections, often onto women, have become dogma. Masculinist fear of the body, and sexuality, have been projected onto women, so

2 H. Cixous: "Castration or Decapitation?", *Signs*, 7, 1, 52
3 Arleen B. Dallery: "The politics of the body: écriture féminine", in Alison M. Jaggar & Susan R. Bordo, eds: *Gender/ Body/ Knowledge: feminist reconstruction of being and knowing*, Rutgers University Press, New Brunswick, 1989; Deborah Cameron, 1990; Jan Montefiore: *Feminism and Poetry: Language, Experience, Identity in Women's Writing*, Pandora 1987; Andrea Nye: "The voice of the serpent: French feminism and the philosophy of language", in Ann Garry & Marilyn Pearsal, eds: *Women, Knowledge and Reality: explorations in feminist philosophy*, Unwin Hyman 1989
4 M. Wittig: "The Straight Mind, *Feminist Issues*, I:1, 110

5 Camille Paglia: "New Sexism for women", *The Guardian*, 30 September 30, 1993

that the vagina becomes a hell hole, the 'gateway to Hell'. As Luce Irigaray writes: men's *'fantasies lay down the law'*.6

PRIMACY OF MASCULINITY

Feminists have, rightly, a lot to complain about. Look at any art history book or account of art history anywhere: nearly all the names, either of artists or critics, are male. Books such as *Techniques of the World's Great Painters*, are typical. *All* the fifty painters featured in this book are male. Published in 1980, i.e. in the age of second wave feminism, around the time of Griselda Pollock and Rozsika Parker's study *Old Mistresses: Woman, Art and Ideology* and Karen Petersen and J.J. Wilson's book *Women Artists* were published, books such as *Techniques of the World's Great Painters* should have known better.

There are hundreds of art books which feature the same roll-call of male artists: in Robert Goldwater and Marco Treves' anthology *Artists on Art From the 14th to the 20th Century* (1975), there are no women artists in amongst the quotes from one hundred and forty-one male artists. In Waldemar Januszczak's *Techniques of the World's Great Painters*, we find the usual litany of holy male artists: Giotto, Duccio, Jan van Eyck, Piero della Francesca, Leonardo da Vinci, Hieronymous Bosch, Titian, Michelangelo Merisi da Caravaggio, El Greco, Diego

6 Luce Irigaray: *Parler n'est jamais neutre*, tr. David Macey, in *The Irigaray Reader*, 94

Velásquez, Peter Rubens, Rembrandt van Rijn, Jan Vermeer, Antoine Watteau, Joshua Reynolds, John Constable, Jean Auguste Dominique Ingres, Éugene Delacroix, J.M.W. Turner, Jean François Millet, Gustave Courbet, Édouardo Manet, Clauded Monet, Pierre Renoir, Edgar Degas, Vincent van Gogh, Edvard Munch, Paul Cézanne, Paul Gauguin, Henri Matisse, Pablo Picasso, Wassily Kandinsky, Pierre Bonnard, Edward Hopper, Salvador Dali, Paul Klee, Piet Mondrian, Max Ernst, Jackson Pollock, Jasper Johns, Frank Stella, Roy Lichenstein, and David Hockney.

These are the great names, the great surnames, of Art. They form a religion of art, a cult which decisively excludes women and the female voice. High art is distinctly a male preserve, an area presided over and fiercely guarded by men and male ideology. Gwen John, Berthe Morisot, Georgia O'Keeffe and Barbara Hepworth are allowed into art history occasionally, perhaps because their art is not deemed to be threatening.

Of course, the reasons why there are so few exalted women artists in the art world are many and complex, having to do with economy, power, politics, law, ideology, sexuality, identity, etc. The guardians of high art are also male: the critics and reviewers. The 'great' critics have always been male: Vasari, Bernard Berenson, Titus Burckhardt, Kenneth Clark, John Ruskin, Walter Pater, Friedrich Nietzsche, Leon Baptista Alberti, and Benvenuto Cellini. (Maybe you can name ten great female artists, but can you name ten great female art critics?).

WOMEN'S ART?

Is there a true 'women's art'? Is there feminist art? What is the relation of 'feminist' to 'masculinist' art? Does 'feminist art' have to be made by women? These questions go to the heart of feminism and feminist cultural criticism. Feminist art is not simply all women's art', all women's 'experience' in/ of art, some feminists state: '[f]eminist art is not the same as any art which emphasizes women's experience.'[7] Shoshana Felman has criticized french feminist Luce Irigaray's writings on 'women's' art and 'feminist' æsthetics:

> Is [Irigaray] speaking *as* a woman, or *in the place of* the (silent) woman, *for* the woman, *in the name of* the woman? Is 'speaking as a woman' a fact determined by some biological *condition* or by a strategic, theoretical *position*, by anatomy or by culture? What if 'speaking as a woman' were not a simple 'natural' fact, could not be taken for granted?[8]

But what is the relation of the 'feminine' qualities of the woman artist to her work? Is not all art, of any kind, produced *within* patriarchal culture? Is it possible to make art that is utterly *outside* of patriarchy? Is the 'female tradition' of women artists simply patriarchal art made by women? If men, or masculine culture, has defined everything in culture, how can there by a truly 'feminine art'? These are important questions, that require much debate and analysis.

'Feminist art', then, aims to question all manner of notions of æsthetics, attitudes, assumptions, traditions, representations, meanings and mythologies. As Gisela Ecker writes in *Feminist Aesthetics*:

> We have to be aware of the paradox that there cannot be any certainty about what is feminine in art but that we have to go looking out for it.[9]

Creating (a) 'feminist æsthetics' means writing/ rewriting language, art, culture, notions of knowledge and ontology, of identity and politics, all manner of things. For Julia Kristeva, there is no 'other place' in language (and therefore also for sculpture), for, as the Austrian philosopher Ludwig Wittgen-

7 Michele Barrett: "Feminism and the Definition of Cultural Politics", *Feminism, Culture and Politics*, ed. Rosalind Brunt & Caroline Rowan, and in Eagleton, ed, 163
8 Shoshana Felman: "The critical phallacy", *Diacritics*, Winter 1975, 3

9 Gisela Ecker: *Feminist Aesthetics*, Women's Press 1985

stein said, the world we live in is a world circumscribed by language. In effect, language 'writes' the world: to go beyond it is the quest for the 'wild zone', the utterly Other Place. For Kristeva, revolution must occur *within* symbolic (that is, patriarchal) language.[10] Women's writing or art becomes a literature of absence, of negative capability, revealing by what it does not reveal, forever outside yet also inside patriarchal discourse. As the Marxist-Feminist Literature Collective write:

> Women, who are speaking subjects but partially excluded from culture, find modes of expression which the hegemonic discourse cannot integrate. Whereas the eruptive word cannot make the culturally inaccessible, it can surely speak its absence.[11]

Women sculptors who wish to make non- or extra-patriarchal art, then, have to find new ways of making art, new methodologies which are not those of traditional sculpture, of Michelangelo Buonarroti, Antonio Canova, Gianlorenzo Bernini, Auguste Rodin, or Constantin Brancusi.

Julia Kristeva asks questions which are central to feminist æsthetics and 'women's' art. Will there be a visionary feminism which takes women's art (French feminists use the term 'writing' to cover cultural/creative activities) into a new era?

> Or is it, on the contrary and as avant-garde feminists hope, that having started with the idea of difference, feminism will be able to break free of its belief in woman, Her power, her writing, so as to channel this demand for difference into each and every element of the female whole, and, finally, to bring out the singularity of each woman, and beyond this, her multiplicities, her plural languages, beyond the horizon, beyond sight, beyond faith itself?[12]

Julia Kristeva is very positive, though, despite her insistence on absence. She is uncompromising: in "Freud and Love" she says she believes in the 'notion of emptiness, which is at the heart of the human

10 See Julia Kristeva: *Desire in Language*; *Révolution du language poétique*, Seuil, Paris 1974
11 Marxist-Feminist Literature Collective: "Women's Writing: *Jane Eyre, Shirley, Villette, Aurora Leigh*", in Francis Barker et al, eds: *1848: The Sociology of Literature*, in Eagleton, ed. *Feminist Literary Theory: A Reader*, 197

12 J. Kristeva: *Women's Time*, in *The Kristeva Reader*, 208

psyche'.[13] Yet she is optimistic, too. Her philosophy is founded on absence, yet she often writes of the possibility that a 'wild zone' or otherness has been neglected, that there maybe a nighttime space, of the unconscious, of magic or otherness.

And, again from *Women's Time*, Julia Kristeva argues for aspects of female subjectivity that could exist outside of patriarchy:

> As for time, female subject-ivity would seem to provide a specific measure that essentially retains *repet-ition* and *eternity* from among the multiple modul-aties of time known through the history of civilizations. On the one hand, there are cycles, gest-ation, the eternal recurr-ence of a biological rhythm which conforms to that of nature and imposes a temporality whose stereo-types shock, but whose regularity and unison with what is experienced as extra-subjective time, cosmic time, occasion vert-iginous visions and un-nameable *jouissance*. On the other hand, and per-haps as a consequence, there is the massive pres-ence of a monumental temporality, without cleav-age or escape, which has so

little to do with linear time (which passes) that the very word 'temporality' hardly fits: all-encom-passing and infinite like imaginary space, this temporality reminds one of Kronos in Hesiod's mythology, the incestuous son whose massive presence covered all of Gaea in order to separate her from Ouranos, the father.[14]

The notion of Kristevan 'absence' being carved out of Lacanian 'desire' has a correl-ation with sculpture's continual denial and affirmation of pres-ence, its eternal dialogue with the presence/ absence con-figuration. As Rainer Maria Rilke noted of Auguste Rodin's art, sculpture pivots around the dialogue between idea and actuality, between the Platonic forms and physical materials, between presence and absence, or, in Lacanian/ Kristevan terms, desire and lack. The sculpture-as-object, then, is that reassuring affirmation of presence, the 'fret' or 'worry' blanket that children have to lull themselves to sleep, like sucking their thumb.

It is not a simple act of substituting feminism for mascu-linism, women for men, female for male. Griselda Pollock writes in "Feminism and Modernism":

13 J. Kristeva: *Histoires d'amour*, Denoël, Paris, 1983, and in *The Kristeva Reader*, 242

14 J. Kristeva: *Women's Time*, in *The Kristeva Reader*, 191

Feminism in culture cannot be reduced to substituting *women's* for men's subjectivities in an otherwise unchanged notion of art as self-expression. It is not, therefore, the fact that activities or representations are undertaken by *women* which renders them feminist. Their feminism is crucially a matter of *effect*. To be feminist at all work must be conceived within the framework of a structural, economic, political and ideological critique of the power relations of society and with a commitment to collective action for their radical transformation.[15]

The problems stem, partly, from accepting and using systems and approaches of criticism, philosophy, psychology and politics that are male-made or masculinist. It's all very well, feminists comment, using the vulva or womb as a powerful image of the feminine, as artists such as Judy Chicago has done in many works (one of Chicago's ceramic pieces is entitled *The Cunt as Temple,*

Tomb, Cave and Flower),[16] or Ana Mendieta with her body art and performance art, in which vulvic forms are prominent (as well as the naked female body – the artist's own body, in Mendieta's case – so that a real living body becomes a kind of 'Ultimate Sculpture'), but this very notion plays into the hands of men and patriarchal attitudes, which so often reduce women to sex objects, so that the body becomes mere 'cunt'.[17]

And a female artist such as Nancy Grossman, who employs the imagery of bondage, S/M and fetish pornography, seems to be wholly phallic and patriarchal. Her images depict cult, kitsch gear, such as leather, zips, straps, chains, guns in erotic contexts.[18] Her views on art are patriarchal and phallic, those of the Marquis de Sade, Charles Baudelaire, Georges Bataille, Wilhelm Reich, and Henry Miller: she wishes to get rid of taboos:

---

15 Griselda Pollock: "Feminism and Modernism", in R. Parker, 1987.

16 Judy Chicago: *The Dinner Party,* 1975-9; *The Cunt as Temple, Tomb, Cave and Flower,* c. 1974, china pencil on porcelain, collection; the artist; *Female Rejection Drawing,* 1974, coloured pencil on paper, 30 x 40in, collection: the artist; *Earth Birth,* from *The Birth Project,* 1982-3, sprayed fabric paint and quilting, 152 x 365cm, ACA Gallery, New York
17 See Lisa Tickner, 236-51; also Lynda Nead: *The Female Nude,* 65f
18 Nancy Grossman: *Figure,* 1970, ink on paper, 45.5. x 34.5in, Princeton Art Museum, Princeton

to have a head and no
feelings, to have a vagina
and not fill it, to have a
penis and not stick it in –
that is not living.[19]

19 Nancy Grossman, quoted in
Tilly, 74

16

Women Sculptors

EVA HESSE

Among women artists, Eva Hesse (1936-1970) is especially powerful. Her lyrical, enigmatic and sometimes perplexing artworks hang from ceilings, or in rows, on the floor, or linked by ropes between the floor and the wall, made of rubber, latex, cloth, wire, fibreglass, evoking organic forms in ambivalent, sensual and occasionally disturbing ways.[20] Pieces such as *Ingeminate* offer up a mysterious affirmation of life in the form of two coils of cord connected by a long piece of surgical hose. *Sans II,* meanwhile, is a dozen rectangular 'compartments' made from fibreglass and set on the wall, which hints at some obscure systematization of flesh and organic form.[21]

Eva Hesse wrote: '[i]f I can name the content…it's the total absurdity of life.'[22] Her sculptures retain that sense of

20 Eva Hesse: *Contingent*, 1969, reinforced fibreglass and latex over cheesecloth, each of 8 units, 9.5-14 x 3-4 ft, Australian National Gallery, Caberra; *Aught,* 1968, double sheets of latex rubber, polyethylene plastic inside, 4 units, each 78in high, collection: the artist; *Ice Piece*, 1969, fibreglass and wire, 62 x 1in, Xavier Fourcade Gallery, New York
21 See Bill Barrette: *Eva Hesse's Sculpture*: Catalogue Raissonné, New York 1989; Rosalind Krauss & Eva Hesse, 1979; Cindy Nemser, 1973, 12-13.
22 Cindy Nemser, 1970, 62.

mystery and presence that marks Constantin Brancusi's eggs and severely compressed forms. Like Brancusi, Hesse maintained a sense of openness in her art, which would not be tied down to reductive meanings, to, say, psychoanalytic meanings, or socio-political meanings. 'My attitude toward art is most open,' she said. 'It is totally unconservative – just freedom and willingness to work.'[23]

LOUISE NEVELSON

Louise Nevelson (1899-1988) produced huge reliefs or structures which are like Cubist or Constructionist altarpieces full of objects: different articles made of wood, all painted in one colour, black, white or gold: chair legs, railings, door knobs.[24] Her sculptures are like magical cupboards, vertical dreamscapes made of boxes stacked on top of each other.

Louise Nevelson's sculptures recall the flattened dreamscapes of Surrealists Max Ernst and Yves Tanguy. They are three dimensional, but they are always set out against a wall, each box or set of drawers is placed side by side, so the result is more like a relief, or a chunky painting. The use of monochrome paint smooths over the irregularities of each object, so that Nevelson's sculptures have a unified look, as with Tony Cragg of Anish Kapoor. The objects Nevelson collects vary with each work. Sometimes Nevelson's wall sculptures recall Donald Judd's modular reliefs, sometimes made of steel or wood: Judd's pieces, such as the 1969 *Untitled* or the 1975

23 E. Hesse, quoted in D. Wheeler, 259

24 Louise Nevelson: *Royal Tide IV*, 1960, wood, 1 x 14 ft, Ludwig Museum, Cologne; *Sky Cathedral – Moon Garden Plus One*, 1957-60, black painted wood, 9.1 x 10.1 x 1.6 ft, collection: A. & M. Glimcher, New York

installation in Ottawa,[25] are cool, unadorned, and machine-like, while Nevelson's are full of subjective marks and gestures speaking of a personal mythology.

The huge wall of boxes, *Homage to 6,000,000 I*, is fairly selective in the objects it includes in the boxes,[26] while *Sky-Cathedral–Moon Garden Plus One* features all kinds of objects. Like so many sculptors, such as Eva Hesse, Constantin Brancusi, Barbara Hepworth, Gianlorenzo Bernini and Michelangelo Buonarroti, Louise Nevelson produces sculptures that are quite distinct from any other work anywhere in the world. These black walls of wooden boxes are not found in the work of any other sculptor. And with Nevelson, as with Hesse or Brancusi, there aren't even sculptures that are similar. These works stand on their own, creating their own spaces.

BARBARA HEPWORTH

In Barbara Hepworth's (1903-1975) work, organic forms are not sexualized, as they are in so many other (male) sculptors. As with Constantin Brancusi, Hepworth's art hovers between subjectivity and objectivity, between natural form and æsthetic abstraction (as in her *Two Forms*, for example.)[27] Like Brancusi, Hepworth maintained that she always returned to nature, and took her inspiration from nature. For her, nature meant the (Cornish) landscape, and the human body. 'We return always to the human form – the human form in landscape', she said.[28] Her sculpture stems from emotion and expression, from feeling: 'I rarely draw what I see – I draw what I feel in my body', she commented.[29]

Barbara Hepworth's distinctive forms, with their smooth curves and holes, are

25 Donal Judd: *Untitled*, 1973, plywood, six units, 77 x 77 x 77in, National Gallery of Canada, Ottawa; *Untitled*, 1969, galvanized iron, 57 units, 21 x 21 x 120in each, collection: the artist
26 Nevelson: *Homage to 6,000,000 I*, 1964, wood, Jewish Museum, New York

27 B. Hepworth: *Two Forms*, 1937, marble, 26in high, private collection
28 Barbara Hepworth: *Pictorial Autobiography*, Praeger, New York, 50-3
29 Quoted in A. Hammacher, op.cit., 98

clearly sensual objects.[30] Hepworth acknowledged the sensuality of sculptural forms (see the quote, above). In 1969 Elizabeth Catlett took the holed form of Hepworth and suppressed the erotic dimension to produce a political work that celebrated 'the struggle for liberation by black women in this country and everywhere' (K. Petersen, 142).

KÄTHE KOLLWITZ

Käthe Kollwitz's (1867-1945) monumental pieces are heavy with life, heavy with grave feelings, the weight of life on one's shoulders. This emotional gravity is apparent in powerful sculptures such as her *Pietà*, where Christ lays in his mother's lap, as in Sandro Botticelli's *Pietàs*, or those of the Flemish school.[31] Her body encircles the dead Christ, like the *Madonna della Misericordia* of Piero della Francesca. Here, the Mother encircles the Son. The Madonna, though, is brooding on her fate, not just the death of her child, but on the whole meaning of the cycle of events which brought her from being the 'handmaiden of the Lord', as a young woman, to this final, terrible point, with her grown child dead on her lap.

Käthe Köllwitz's *Pietà* is unusual among *Pietàs*, if one thinks of those of the European Renaissance, such as by Michelangelo Buonarroti, Sandro Botticelli and Roger van der Weyden, in that instead of gut-wrenching pain and anguish, which is usual in *Pietàs*, Kollwitz depicts a sombre, contemplative Mother, musing upon the ravages of time and age. Similar deeply parental feelings are

30 Barbara Hepworth: *Porthmeor: Sea Form*, 1958, bronze, 30.5in high, Hirshhorn Museum and Sculpture Garden, Washington DC; *Pendour*, 1947, painted wood, 10 x 27 x 9in, Hirshhorn Museum and Sculpture Garden, Washington DC, *Forms in Movement*, 1956, Barbara Hepworth Museum and Sculpture Garden, St Ives, Cornwall

31 Köllwitz: *Pietà*, 1937, bronze, Staatliche Museen, Berlin

expressed in sculptures such as *Twins* where, again, the mother passionately enfolds her off-spring.[32]

ALICE AYCOCK AND ALISON WILDING

Among contemporary women sculptors who are producing work right now, special mention must be made of Alison Wilding and Alice Aycock. New York sculptor Alison Wilding (b. 1948) directly embraces the potential for sculpture to be supremely sensual. Her abstract forms hint at alchemical trans-formations, intimate experi-ences, investigations of sexuality and the relations between space, imagination, fantasy and the body.[33]

Alison Wilding's sculpture often features two elements, one is often large, the other, small.[34] These two elements are luscious and mysterious, beyond interpretation, though some read them as masculine and feminine elements, the twin poles of heterosexuality, which are involved in some arcane

32 K. Köllwitz: *Twins*, 1935, bronze, Staatliche Museen, Berlin

33 Alison Wilding: *Bare*, 1989-90, Newlyn Art Gallery, *Into the Dark*, 1986, limewood, lead and pigment, Newlyn Art Gallery; see also Hilary Gresty: *Bare*, Newlyn Art Gallery 1993

34 See Alison Wilding's *Nature: Blue and Gold*, 1984, brass, ash, oil and pigment, 47 x 109 x 22cm, British Council Collection, and *Untitled*, 1980, Arts Council of Great Britain, London; *Locust*, 1983, wood, wax, copper, 208 x 71 x 46cm, collection: the artist.

dance or dalliance.[35] Wilding herself stressed the enigmatic nature of her work: '[t]he obverse of making is looking, not telling',[36] and she emphasized, as so many artists do, the making of the sculpture: '[t]he making and doing processes... [are] always the mainspring of the work'.[37]

American artist Alice Aycock (b. 1946), using science as her Muse, has produced some wonderfully fantastical machines, such as *The Angels Continue Turning the Wheels of the Universe,* or the marvellous, massive piece *The Miraculous Machine in the Garen (Tower of the Winds),* which features 268 antenna and bells ringing in a vacuum.[38]

Many of Alice Aycock's installations and sculptures involve underground passages and spaces. In 1972 she constructed a series of underground spaces in *Low Building Made with Dirt Roof (For Mary)* in Pennsylvania. The spectator entered the 20 by 12 feet work through a doorway thirty inches high. The work was experienced by crawling through it. Aycock's intention was to evoke an experience of claustrophia, of being in a cellar.

Alice Aycock wants viewers to be confused, even frightened, by her underground passages and mazes. Aycock did not wish the viewer to be able to get out of her labyrinth easily (it was partially based on a circular Egyptian labyrinth (designed as a prison), the Zulu *kraal* and the Amerindian stockade. Aycock also cited a circular Greek temple at Epidarus, a 'Place of Sacrifice').

Alice Aycock has spoken of the relations between her art and her own childhood dreams and fears. Her works recreate disturbing moments from her childhood, such as when she was trapped in a revolving barrel at an amusement park. Aycock's installations deal with such moments of fear, confusion, strangeness and risk. Aycock also remarked that her structures were inspired by visits to the Pyramids in 1970 and the Greek tombs at Mycenae, and fantasies of being buried alive.

35 See L. Cooke: *Alison Wilding,* Arts Council 1985; L. Biggs: *Between Object and Image,* British Council 1986; Wendy Beckett, 116; Terry A. Neff, 43-5
36 A. Wilding, quoted in W. Beckett, 116.
37 A. Wilding, quoted in T. Neff, 45.
38 Alice Aycock: *One Thousand and One Nights in the Mansion of Bliss,* 1983, mixed media, private collection; *The Miraculous Machine in the Garden (Tower of the Winds),* 1983, mixed media, 16 ft high, private collection

GODDESS ART

Most of the feminist art being produced today is by women. Male artists have only made tentative steps in producing art that radically questions or rewrites patriarchal attitudes, values, ideas, experiences or laws. Much of feminist or women's art celebrates the 'feminine', what is special to 'femininity' or 'womanhood', the being of 'woman' and women.

One aspect of feminist or 'women's' art is embodied by the figure of the Goddess, the ancient and primæval Great Mother of all, celebrated then – and now – as Isis, Ishtar, Astarte, Diana, Artemis, Persephone, Demeter, Kali, etc. The Goddess is now variously interpreted as fact, experience, idea, æsthetic, cult, religion, pagan emblem and many other things by women artists (the Goddess can be whatever an artist wants her to be).

There are a host of artists who have made what we might call 'Goddess art', art that employs the figure of the Goddess as an embodiment of female being or experience. Artists who work in three dimensions in Goddess-related art include: Judy Chicago, Mary Beth Edelson, Miriam Schapiro, Niki de Sant-Phalle, Louis Bourgeois and Helen Chadwick.

Edelson engages in the resurgence of the Goddess, in her *Great Goddess* series.[39] Edelson has also produced a piece on menstruation, entitled, appropriately, *Blood Mysteries*.[40] In a piece of performance art, Catherine Elwes sat in an enclosed studio space and menstruated.[41] Judy Chicago, already mentioned, looked to the flowers of Georgia O'Keeffe, which, she said, 'stand for femininity'.[42] Sutapa Biswas depicts women as incarnations of the Goddess Kali, who beheads men.[43]

The Goddess is a symbol and experience of a new spiritual consciousness that also embraces eroticism. Catholic feminists, such as Meinrad Craighead, have spoken of the need for Christians to embrace eroticism as well as spirituality.[44]

---

39 Mary Beth Edelson: *Great Goddess Series*, 1975, collection: the artist
40 M. Edelson: *Blood Mysteries*, 1973, drawing, 91 x 57 in, collection: the artist
41 Catherine Elwes: "Floating femininity: a look at performance art by women", in S. Kent, 182
42 Quoted in Lucy Lippard, 219; see also Lippard, 1980, 122
43 Sutapa Biswas, interview with Yasmin Kureishi, *Spare Rib*, no. 173, December 1986;
44 See Mary Giles, ed: *The Feminist Mystic*, Crossroad, 1985.

CHADWICK, HORN, BOURGEOIS, SANT-PHALLE

Feminist artists and writers have been putting the erotic dimension back into the Goddess, after thousands of years of desexed deities such as the Virgin Mary. Images such as Piero della Francesca's *Madonna del Parto* are taken up by feminists because here is a depiction of a pregnant Goddess.[45] Goddess art is full of images of menstruation, pregnancy, childbirth, all those things termed by some 'women's mysteries'. Niki de Sant-Phalle (1930-2002) has produced exuberant Goddesses, such as her *Black Venus*, or her marvellous *Pink Childbirth i(1964)*, a Great Mother Goddess made from dolls, toys, tissues and several items collected together like a totem of the prehistoric world,[46] while Sant-Phalle's *Un Ensemble de "Les Nanas"* (1965) is an effervescent – and multi-coloured – representation of female forms, dancing,

cavorting, balancing,[47]

Rebecca Horn's (b. 1944) sculptures are based on natural forms, but also on movement, dance, time and environments. Witty, irreverent, Horn's art explores Existential issues such as mortality, time and individuality. Horn's wonderful *Peacock Machine* is an exuberant activator of space, one of those pieces that aims for the essence of a natural form and captures it: a peacock's magnificent tail.[48]

Helen Chadwick (1953-96) has made a *Madonna and Child* (1985) image with a female Christ Child, complete with labia, placenta and birthcord.[49] Louis Bourgeois (1911-2010) has investigated the female form in many works, using, as so many feminist artists have done, the female body as the site of

45 Piero della Francesca: *Madonna del Parto*, c. 1450-5, fresco, 260 x 203cm, Cemetery Chapel, Monterchi, Arezzo
46 See David Bourdon , 1987; Jean-Yves Mock: *Niki de Sant-Phalle: Exposition Retrospective*, CGP 1980

47 Niki de Sant-Phalle: *Black Venus*, 1967, painted polyester, 110 x 35 x 24in, Whitney Museum of Art, New York; *Pink Childbirth*, 1964, painted relief, 86.24in high, Moderner Museet, Stockholm; *Un Ensemble de "Les Nanas"*, 1965, Archives Galerie Alexandre Iolas, New York.
48 Rebecca Horn: *Peacock Machine*, 1982, installation at Documenta 7, Kassel. See Mina Roustayi: "Getting Under the Skin: Rebecca Horn's Sensibility Machines", *Arts*, May 1989, 58-68; Michael Kimmelman: "A Sculptural Circus of Whips and Suspense", *New York Times*, 23 Sept 1988, C29
49 Helen Chadwick: *One Flesh*, 1986, photocopies, 160 x 107cm, Victoria & Albert Museum, London

feminist explorations.[50] Feminist artists have rewritten, recreated, reviewed the female body. Many feminist artists have used their own bodies as artworks, as living sculptures, challenging radically traditional notions of fine and art criticism.

BODY ART

Feminist artists are using the body to explore political, erotic, pornographic, æsthetic and philosophical discourses. As Lisa Tickner writes in "The Body Politic: Female Sexuality and Women Artists since 1970":

> Living *in* a female body is different from looking *at* it, as a man. Even the Venus of Urbino menstruated, as women know and men forget.[51]

The female nude, for so long the model and image and object of lust in so many high art paintings, has usurped the power relation between artist and art object, and between artwork and spectator. The woman is no longer content to be looked at and lusted after: she is making her own art, employing her body in a radical, challenging way. The 'Old Master/ *Playboy* tradition', as Tickner calls it, has been smashed. Feminists and feminist artists must make sure that the 'Old Master/ *Playboy* tradition' never assumes dominance again.[52]

Feminist body and performance art is a way of

---

50 Louis Bourgeois: *Fragile Goddess*, c. 1970, clay, 10in high, Robert Miller Gallery, New York; *Femme Couteau*, 1982, black marble, 14 x 77.5 x 20.3cm, Robert Miller Gallery, New York

---

51 Lisa Tickner, 239
52 See T. Gouma-Peterson & P. Matthews: "The feminist critique of art history", *The Art Bulletin*, LXIX, 1987, 326-57

repossessing the body, sexuality, identity, power, it is a way of 'rewriting the body'. It can be an act of transgression and subversion, which usurps the power relation between spectator and artwork, so that the (male) viewer's 'cloak of invisibility has been stripped away and his spectatorship becomes an issue within the work', as Catherine Elwes puts it (op. cit., 172).

Displaying the female body, though, can also make it available for being appropriated by men (in whatever context), as some feminists have cautioned.[53] Women artists have to make sure they are not titillating their audience in that way so familiar in porn. The issues raised by feminist body art and performance art are many and complex, basically pivoting around whether body art is truly subversive, or whether it plays into the grasping hands of

patriarchy.[54] As the Editorial Collective of *Questions féministes* write, 'it is also dangerous to place the body at the centre of a search for female identity.'[55] Why? Because it can lead towards biological feminism or essentialism feminism, a central issue in second wave feminism which has been pretty much soundly debunked.

Carolee Schneemann pulls a scroll from her vagina and reads from it, in a famous icon of feminist performance art (you

---

53 See Lynda Nead, 67; Lucy Lippard: "The Pain and Pleasures of Rebirth: European and American Women's Body Art", in *From the Center*, op.cit., 125

---

54 see Henry M. Sayre: *The Object of Performance: the American Avant-garde Since 1970*, University of Chicago Press 1989; Sally Potter: "Our Shows", *About Time: Video, Performance and Installation by 21 Women Artists*, ICA, 1980; Jeannie Forte: "Women's Performance Art: Feminism and Postmodernism", *Theatre Journal*, 40:2, May 1988, 217-35; Elinor Fuchs: "Staging the Obscene Body", *The Drama Review*, 33:1, Spring 1989, 33-58; Janet Wolff: "Reinstating Corporeality: Feminism and Body Politics", *Feminine Sentences: Essays on women and culture*, Polity Press, Cambridge 1990; Claudette Johnson: "Issues Surrounding the Representation of the Naked Body of a Woman", *Feminist Art News*, 3:8, 1991
55 "Variations on Common Themes", *Question féministes*, no. 1, November 1977, quoted in Marks, 218

can see it in documentaries).56 Chila Kumari Burman makes 'body prints'. Performance artist Karen Finley pours 'a can of yams over her naked buttocks', deliberately affirming and denying eroticism, mixing desire with irony. Finley is 'a frightening and rare presence',57 in her *Cut Off Balls* she castrates Wall Street bankers.58 Mary Duffy displays her disabled body in performance and photographic

sequences;59 Jo Spence has photographed the 'unhealthy and ageing female body'.60

---

56 see Carolee Schneemann: *Interior Scroll*, 1975; *More than Meat Joy: Complete Performance Works and Selected Writings*, ed. Bruce MacPherson, Documentext, New York 1979. Schneemann's most famous happening, though, was *Meat Joy* (1964), a kind of orgy which now looks like a bunch of people larking about.
57 C. Carr: "Unspeakable Practices, Unnatural Acts", *Village Voice*, 24 June 1986
58 See Anthony Adler: "Dangerous Woman: Karen Finley", *Chicago Reader*, 26 October 1990; Richard Lacayo: "Talented Toilet-mouth", *Time*, 4 June 1990; Miranda Joseph: "Further Finley", *The Drama Review*, Winter 1990, 13; Kay Larson: "Censor Deprivation", *New York*, 6 August 1990; Catherine Schuler: "Spectator Response and Comprehensions: The Problems of Karen Finley's *Constant State of Desire*", *The Drama Review*, Spring 1990, 131-145; Clive Barnes: "Finley's Fury", *New York Post*, 24 July 1990; Tim Page: "Karen Finley's Tantrum, Amid Choc-olate", *New York Newsday*, 24 July 1990

---

59 Mary Duffy: *Cutting the Ties that Bind*, 1987; *Stories of a Body*, 1990; see Hilary Robinson: "The Subtle Abyss: Sexuality and Body Image in Contemporary Feminist Art", unpublished dissertation, RCA 1987; Mary Duffy: "Cutting the Ties that Bind", *Feminist Art News*, 2:10, 1989, 6-7; Mary Duffy: "Redressing the Balance", *Feminist Art News*, 3:8, 1991
60 Jo Spence and Tim Sheard: *Narratives of Disease*; see Jo Spence: *Putting Myself in the Picture: A Political, Personal and Photographic Autobiography*, Camden Press 1986; Patricia Holland, Jo Spence and Simon Watney, eds: *Photography/ Politics: Two*, Commedia 1986; Darcy Grimaldo Grigsby: "Dilemmas of Visibility: Contemporary Women Artists' Representations of Female Bodies", *Michigan Quarterly Review*, XXIX: 4, Autumn 1990, 584-618

NANCY GRAVES

Among non-figurative, abstract or partially-figurative artists, people such as Nancy Graves (1939-95)[61] are absolutely astonishing, with her superb multi-media constructions.[62] Graves' skeletal, fossil-like works combine fantasy and natural forms in 'one exuberantly open-form, polychrome, freestanding construction after another' (Daniel Wheeler, 303). As with Alexander Calder's mobiles, Graves' constructions defy gravity, sending out spindly arms in all directions. Graves paints her late, bronze sculptures in bright colours – pinks, yellows, blues – colours which add an exuberance to her already ebullient forms, as with Frank Stella's colourful mixed media 'paintings'.

If you want luscious sensuality in sculpture, or a metaphysical, transcendent dimension, or rigorous formalism, or explorative abstraction, then you don't need to go to the revered male 'modern masters' of contemporary art (Tony Cragg, Donald Judd, Sol LeWitt, Philip King, Walter de Maria, or John de Andrea). You can find it aplenty in women sculptors such as Nancy Graves, Jennifer Bartlett, Niki de Sant-Phalle, Mary Beth Edelson, Alison Wilding, Barbara Kruger, Elizabeth Murray, Eva Hesse, Lee Bontecou, Rebecca Horn and Judy Pfaff.

Unfortunately, even decades after some of these female artists produced their best work (in the 1960s and 1970s, for instance), they are still relatively little known.

61 See Avis Berman: "Nancy Graves", *Art News*, Feb 1986, 57-64; Debra Bricker Balken and Linda Nochlin: *Nancy Graves: Painting, Sculpture, Drawing 1980-5,* Vassar College Art Gallery, Poughkeepsie, 1986; E.A. Carmean et al: *The Sculpture of Nancy Graves*, Fort Worth 1987; Amy Fine Collins and Bradley Collins: "The Sum of the Parts [Nancy Graves]", *Art in America*, 1988, 113-8; L. Cathcart: *Nancy Graves: A Survey 1969-1980*, Albright-Knox Gallery, catalogue, 1981
62 Nancy Graves: *Zaga*, 1983, cast bronze with polychrome chemical patination, 6' x 4'1" x 2'8", Nelson-Atkins Museum of Art, Kansas City; *Cantileve*, 1983, bronze with polychrome patina, 999 x 67 x 55in, M. Knoedler & Co, New York.

LYNDA BENGLIS, CINDY SHERMAN AND JUDITH BERNSTEIN

Lynda Benglis (b. 1941) famously appeared in *Artforum* in 1974 nude, holding a big plastic phallus between her legs.[63] Why? Oh, a feminist artistic commentary on the objectification and eroticism of women in art, and a counter-attack on the domination of male artists in the international art market (this was the height of second wave feminism).

Lynda Benglis has produced three dimensional works which develop the ironic objects of Claes Oldenburg, such as her wonderful, twisted *Aldebaran*.[64] Edward Lucie-Smith writes (in *American Art Now*) of Benglis thus:

> Oldenburg's drooping flaccid forms become emblems of impotence. Benglis's rosettes are successors to an earlier group of sculptures in the shape of giant dildos or penises. If we read what she is doing in the context supplied by Oldenburg's work, she still seems to be concerned with sexual issues – her comment is no longer one about men's fears of female aggression, but about women's need to adorn and at the same time 'cheapen' themselves, because they live in a man's world. (57)

The photographer Robert Mapplethorpe produced many pictures of penises: a penis on a pedestal, a black man's penis hanging out of a polyester suit, and so on.[65] These images were heavily contextualized as part of a homoerotic discourse. Women artists, such as Lynda Benglis have taken the phallus, and put it into ironic, satirical contexts. Judith Bernstein (b. 1942) produced thirty-foot high phallic drawings in the late 1960s, entitled *Phallic Screws*. Of these gigantic phalluses, Laurie Anderson wrote: '[t]he scale of Bernstein's seven new drawings, *Phallic Screws*, made Claes Oldenberg look like a minia-turist.'[66] Bernstein's aim was to appropriate some of the power of the phallus, an impossible (as well as undesirable) goal to achieve for some feminists (leave the cult of the phallus and phallic art to men and mascu-linist art, and focus on women's art and women's issues instead). Bernstein wrote: 'I feel the phallus has stood for power for

63 L. Benglis: *Self-portrait*, 1974, advert in *Artforum*
64 Lynda Benglis: *Aldebaran*, 1983, bronze, zinc, copper, aluminium, 167.5 x 134.5cm, Paula Cooper Gallery, New York

65 Mapplethorpe: *Man in Polyester Suit*, 1980, photograph, Estate of Robert Mapplethorpe
66 Anderson: "Judith Bernstein (AIR)", *Art News*, December 1973, 94

so many centuries, and I feel that we women want to be part of that power.'[67] Bernstein's other pieces include *Supercock* (Superman with a penis twice as big as his body), and *Union Jack-Off Series* (flags with penises).

Cindy Sherman has used a Hans Bellmer-like doll, or plastic parts of the (female) body in ironic ways, in works that are, typically, titled *Untitled*.[68] Shermanis best known for her photography, which investigates the female body, often naked, in ever more complex and ironic ways. Her richly coloured photographs quote from movies and create narratives which hover between fear and desire, clarity and ambivalence. Sherman takes the bland furniture and gestures of life and imbues them with a narrative strangeness that engages the spectator in an exploration of æsthetic expectation, identity, perception and tradition. titled *Untitled*.

NANCY HOLT

Land artists, such as Beverly Pepper or Nancy Holt, might also be seen as producing Goddess-orientated art. Pepper's large, curving mirrored slabs of wood buried in sandy beaches (*Sand Dunes*, 1985), might be seen as a type of 'Earth Mother art', art which worships and works with the earth, rather than, as in so much of male land art, cutting or penetrating it, phallically (like Michael Heizer, Robert Smithson and Walter de Maria).[69]

Nancy Holt's (b. 1938) art is more obviously comparable with the male earth artists, with its large, heavy landscaping gestures (such as her *Dark Star Park*).[70] The globes and pools of water, though, are traditional 'feminine' volumes, here given a new, monumental turn. Holt's *Stone Enclosure: Rock Rings* directly recalls the megalithic and astronomical structures of prehistory.[71] *Stone Enclosure* is

67 Bernstein in Jeanie Weiffenback: "Interview with Judith Bernstein", *Criss-Cross Art Communications*, January 1977, 228
68 Cindy Sherman: *Untitled*, 1985, two colour photographs, both 72.5 x 49.5in; and see Laura Mulvey: "A Phantasmagoria of the Female Body: The Work of Cindy Sherman", *New Left Review*, 188, July/August 1991, 136-150; P. Schjeldahl: *Cindy Sherman*, Pantheon Books 1984

69 Beverly Pepper: *Sand Dunes*, 1985, Mylar over wood, approximately 100 ft long, temporary installation for the Atlantic Center for the Arts, New Smyrna Beach, Florida
70 Nancy Holt: *Dark Star Park*, 1979-84, concrete, steel, water, earth, .67 of an acre, Rosslyn, Virginia
71 Nancy Holt: *Stone Enclosure*, 1977-8, hand-quarried schist, 40 ft diameter, inner ring 2 ft diameter, ring walls 10 ft high, Western Washington University, Bellingham

two concentric rings of stone with viewing points for NE, NW, SE and SW emphasized: Holt's *Stone Enclosure* is a modern version of Neolithic constructions such as Britain's Stonehenge and Carnac in France.

The function of prehistoric stone circles is much disputed, but certainly astronomy plays a part. For some feminists, the ancient stones circles and burial sites of the world are 'feminine', founded on Goddess-orientated rituals and themes. For Michael Dames, the great stone circle at Avebury in southern England is an early monument of the Goddess, constructed for Goddess worship.[72] Dames' pseudo-feminist, pseudo-archæological, New Age/ occult/ Jungian/ mythic analysis of Avebury is typical of a certain subjective, conservative, eco-friendly kind of feminism and feminist art. Some Goddess art is like this, evoking some mythic original paradise where people lived in harmony with the earth, worshipping the feminine and marrying in heterosexual bliss.

DECORATIVE ART

Miriam Schapiro (b. 1923) has taken up materials branded 'feminine' by patriarchy (cotton, taffeta, burlap, wool, sequins, buttons, thread), and has created artworks (she calls them 'femmages') that deal with notions of the home, feminist iconography, abstraction and the æsthetics of 'Pattern and Decoration'.[73] Schapiro says: 'I wanted to explore and express a part of my life which I had always dismissed – my home-making, my nesting'.[74]

A number of male artists have explored traditionally 'feminine' notions of pattern, decoration and colour, among them Robert Zakanitch, Lucas Samaras, Robert Kushner, Rodney Ripps, Kim MacConnel, Frank Stella and Ned Smyth. The male-made pieces, such as by Ripps,[75] occasionally approach the flamboyance and intricacy of artworks made by women, such as by Joyce Kozloff, or Valerie

72 Michael Dames: *The Avebury Cycle*, Thames & Hudson 1976; *The Silbury Treasure*, Thames & Hudson 1977

73 Miriam Schapiro: *Heartland*, 1985, acrylic, fabric and glitter on canvas, 7.1 x 7.8 ft, Bernice Steinbaum Gallery, New York
74 Quoted in D. Wheeler, 285
75 Rodloth on wood, 52 x 51 x 8in, Holly Solomon Gallery, New York

Jaudon.[76] The traditional 'women's' arts and crafts of textiles, pattern, sewing, decoration, pottery, etc, are bound up with the economies of labour, race, class, identity, patriarchy, politics and finance. They are modes of production and art that are regarded as secondary by patriarchal culture, not as high art, such as painting or sculpture.

Feminist artists, then, have to tackle not only the images of themselves, whether of patriarchy, the body, or whatever, but also the *production* of the images. The economics of artistic production are embedded with patriarchal slants, just as much as the images themselves. The piece of textiles, the decorative tile, the pot, then, are objects that in the patriarchal system speak of their second-rate mode of production. To make a pot, tile or blanket and to hold it up as a serious artwork, like a painting or a sculpture, the feminist artist has to grapple with the scorn of high art critics, who demean such work. As Catherine King writes, '[m]edia associated with 'malestream' codes, like bronze, marble, or oil, have been

regarded with suspicion' by women artists.[77] The field of sculpture is just one area in which women artists often far excel male artists.

76 Valerie Jaudon: *Caile*, 1985, oil on canvas, 48 x 40in, Sidney James Gallery, New York; Joyce Kozloff: *New England Decorative Arts*, 1985, tile mural, 8 x 83 feet overall, Harvard Square subway station, Cambridge, Mass.

77 Catherine King: "Feminist Arts", in Frances Bonner *et al*, eds, 185

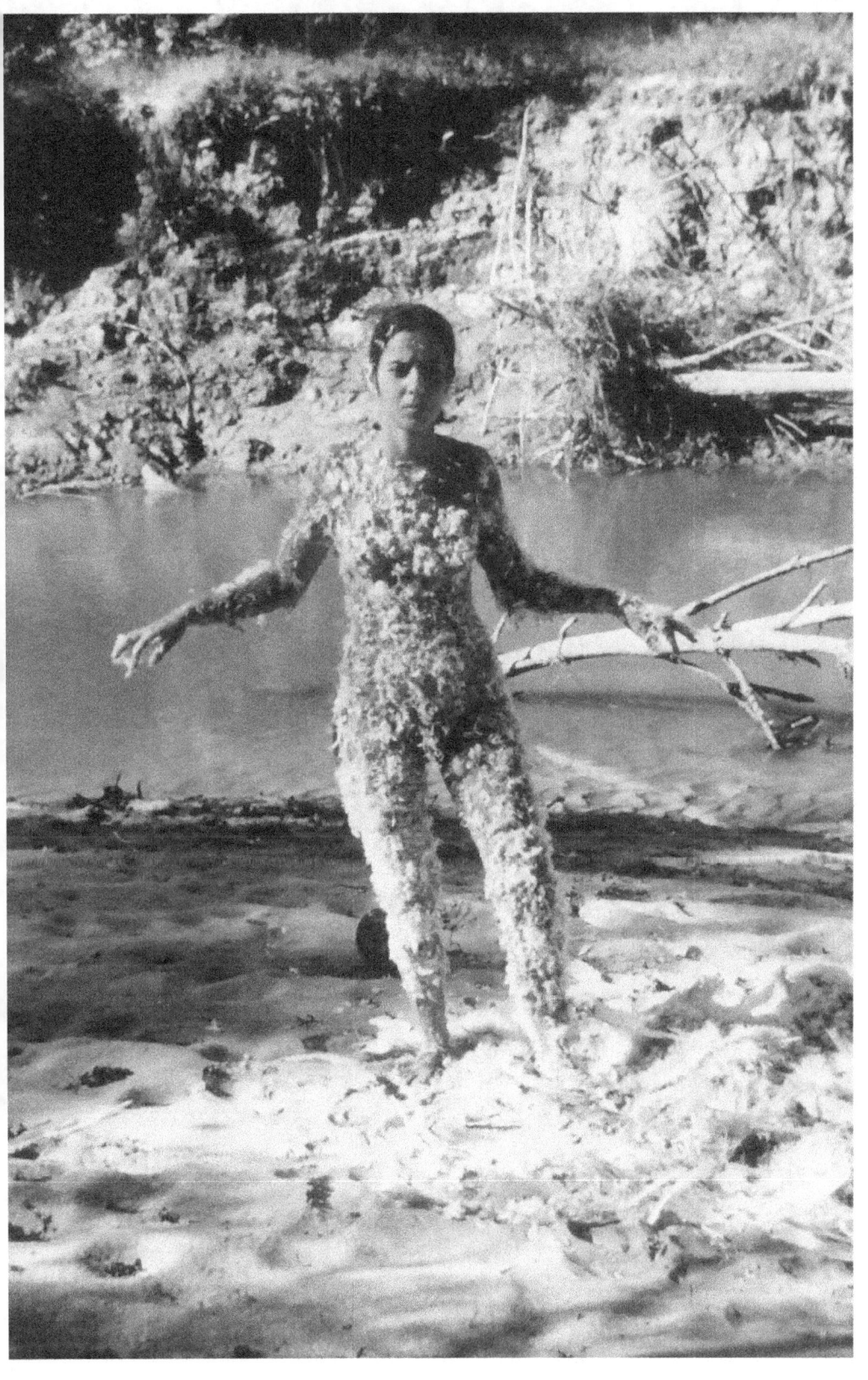

Ana Mendieta, Blood and Feathers, 1974

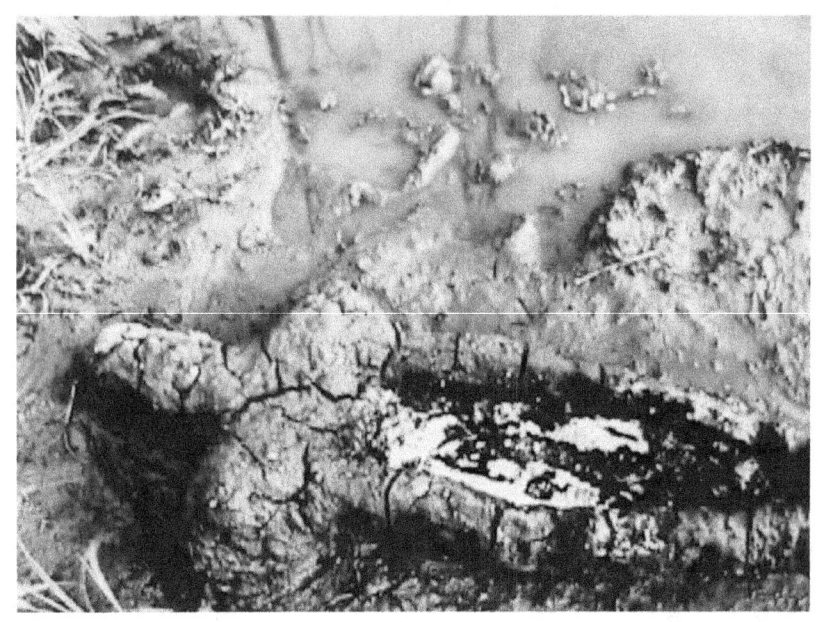

Ana Mendieta, Silueta Series, 1979

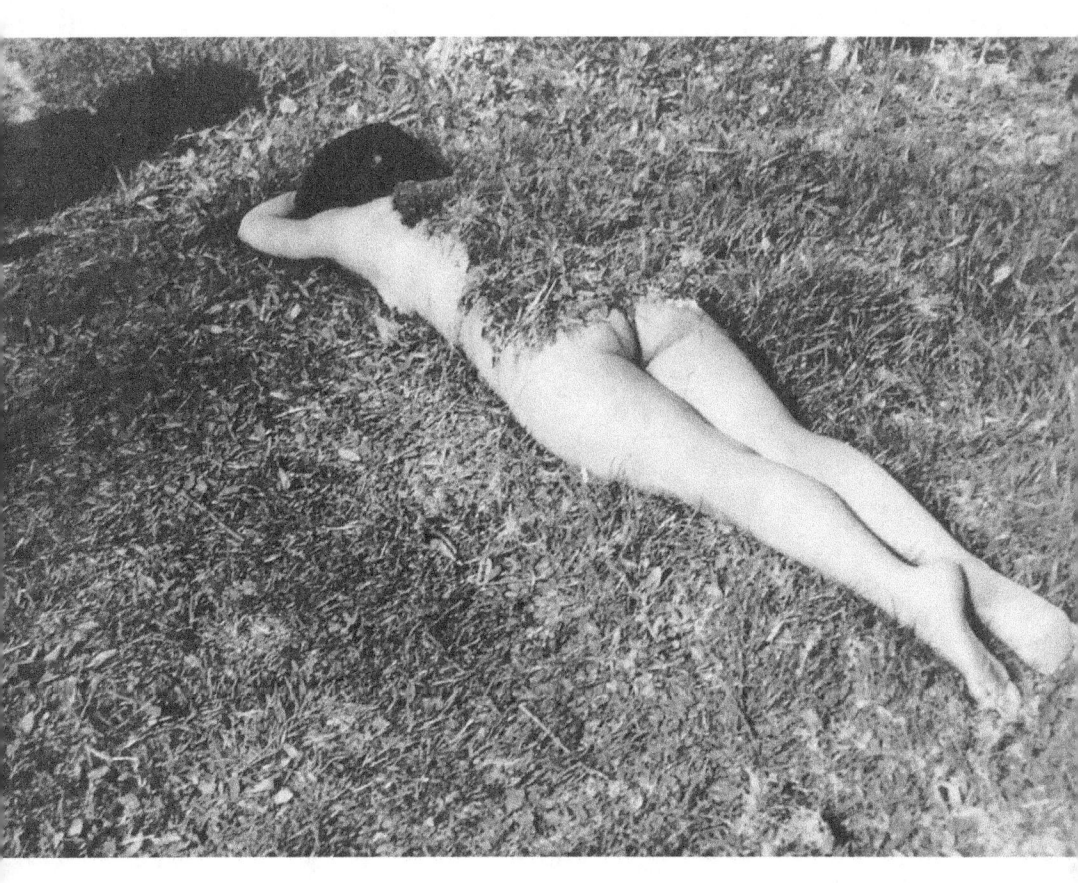

Ana Mendieta, Untitled (Grass On Woman), 1972

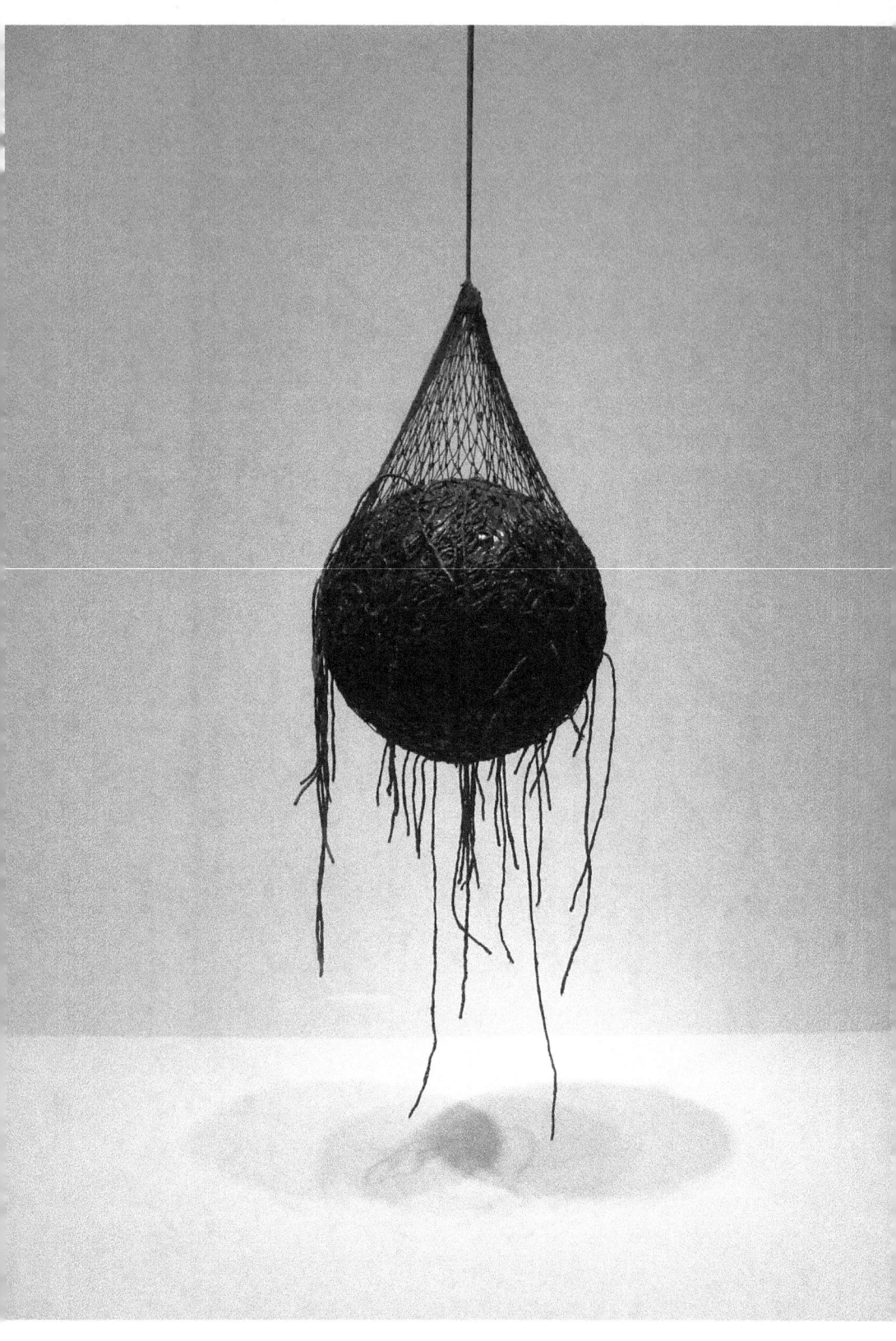

Eva Hesse, National Gallery of Washington, DC

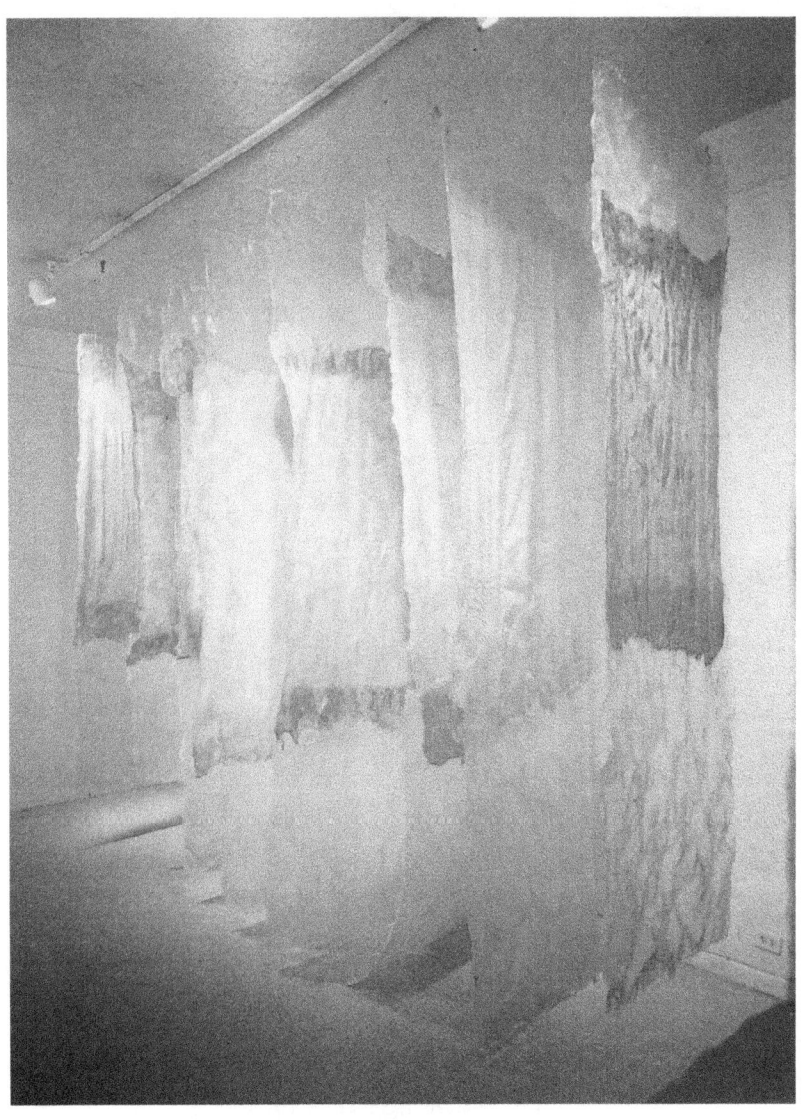

Eva Hesse, Contingent, 1969

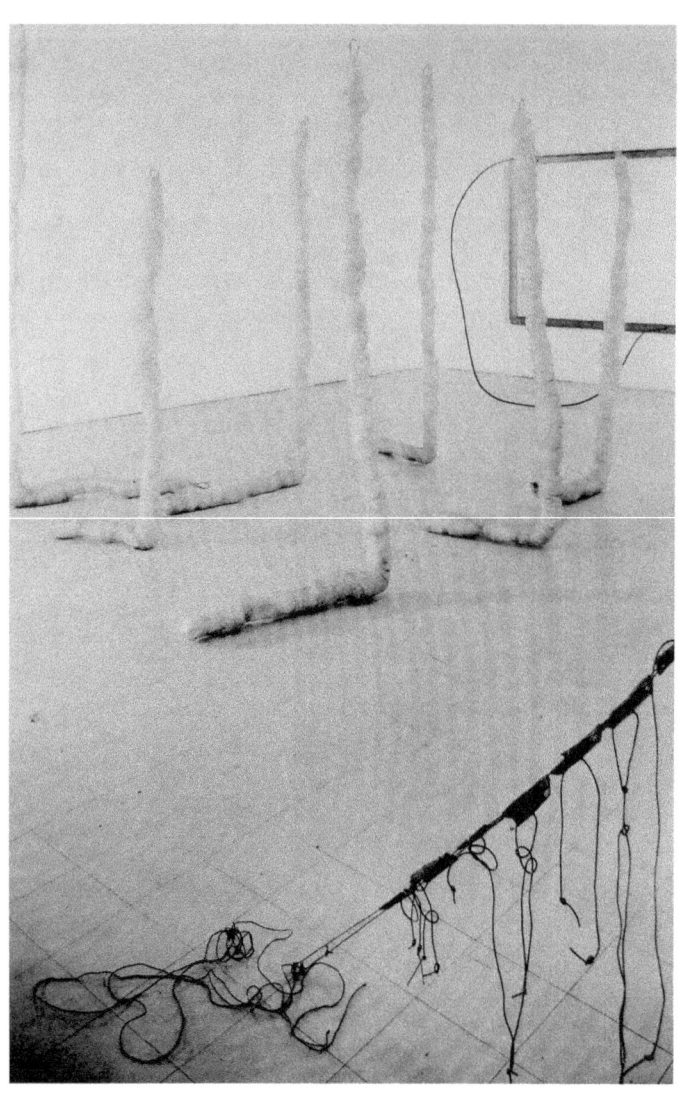

Eva Hesse, installation,1970

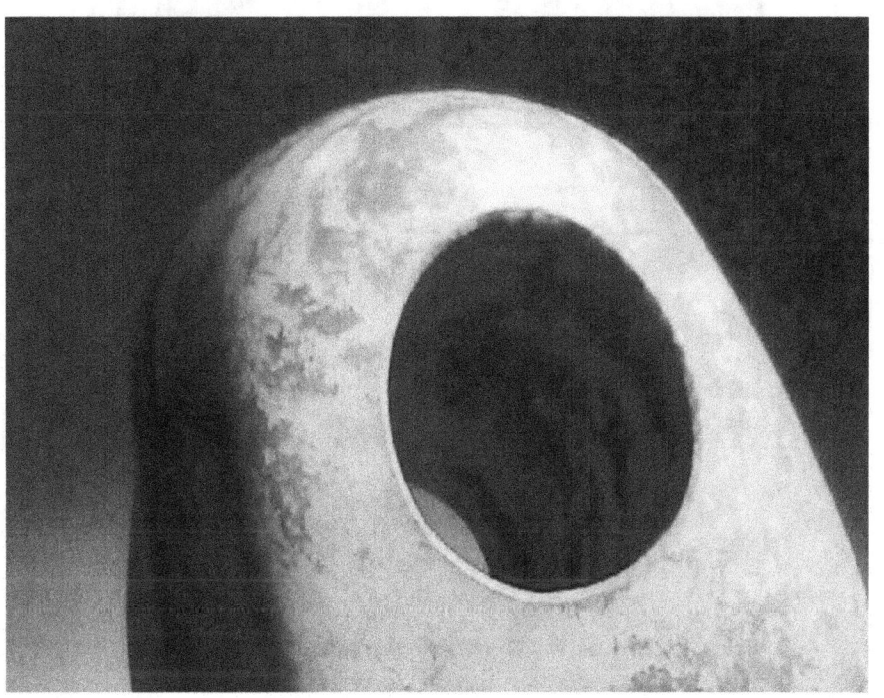

Barbara Hepworth, Pierced Form (April), 1968

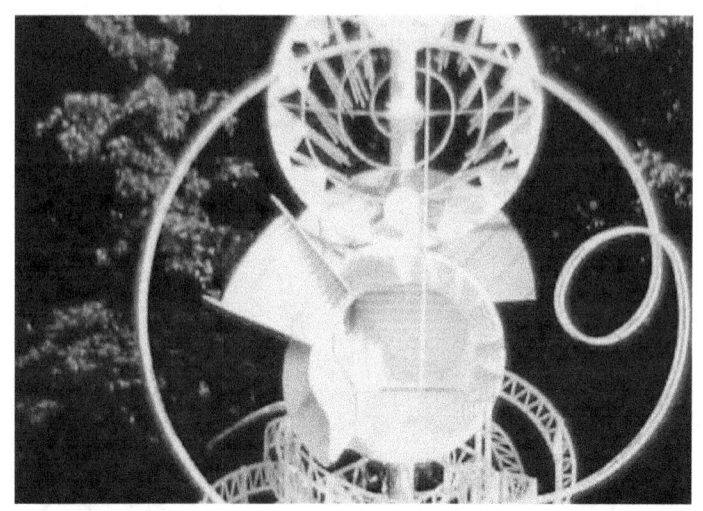

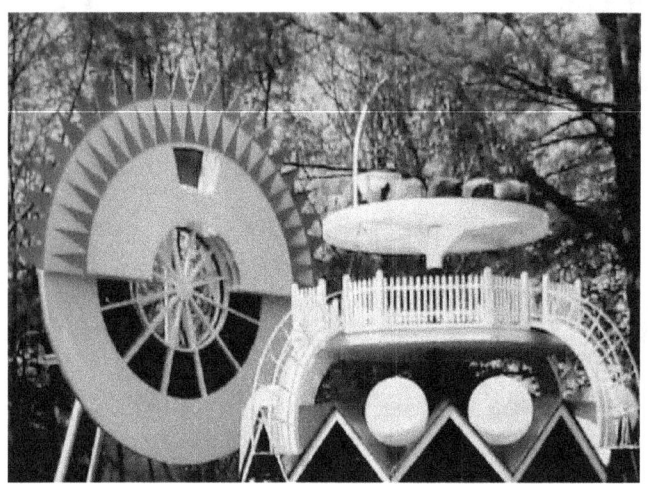

Alice Aycock

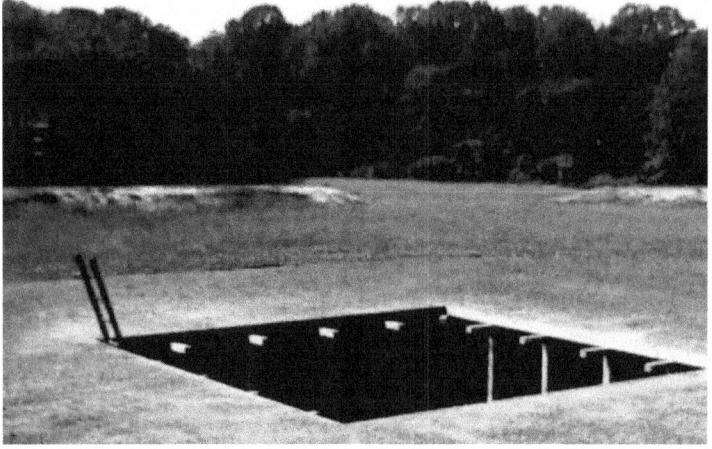

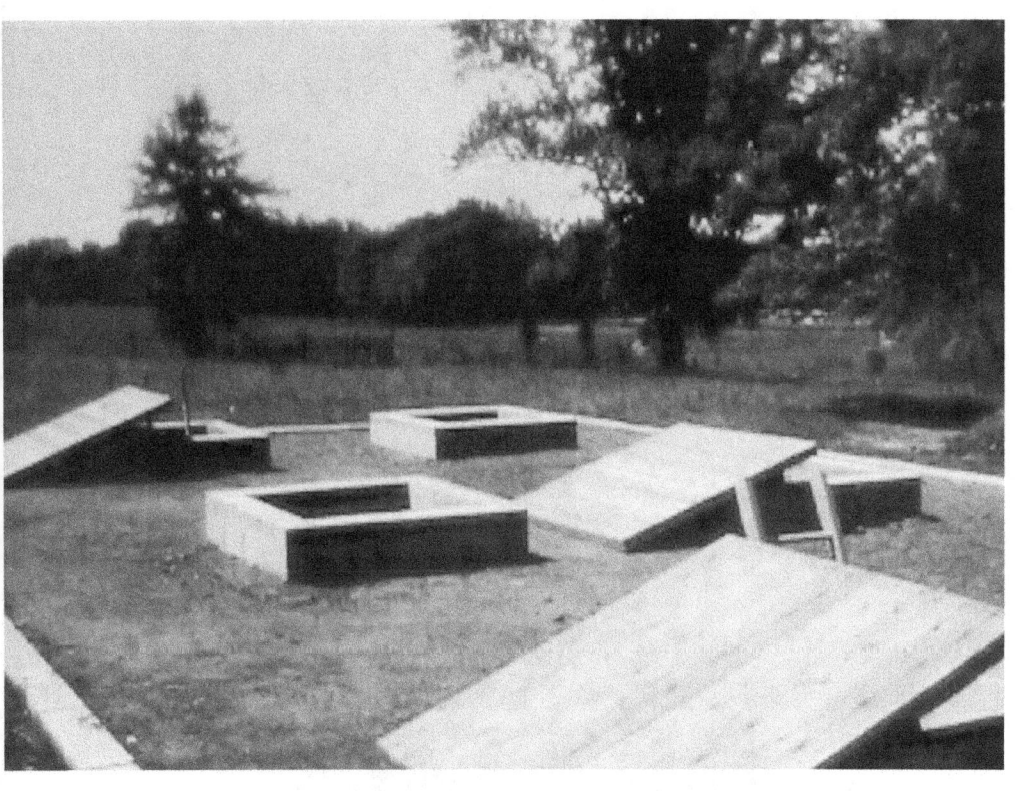

Alice Aycock, A Simple Network of Underground
Walls and Tunnels, 1975

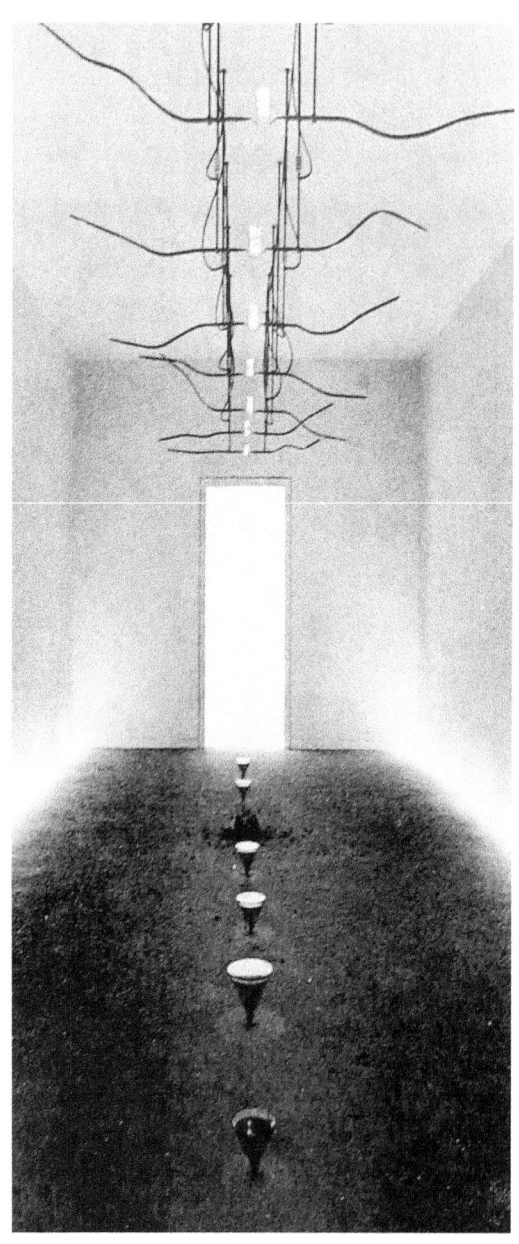

Rebecca Horn

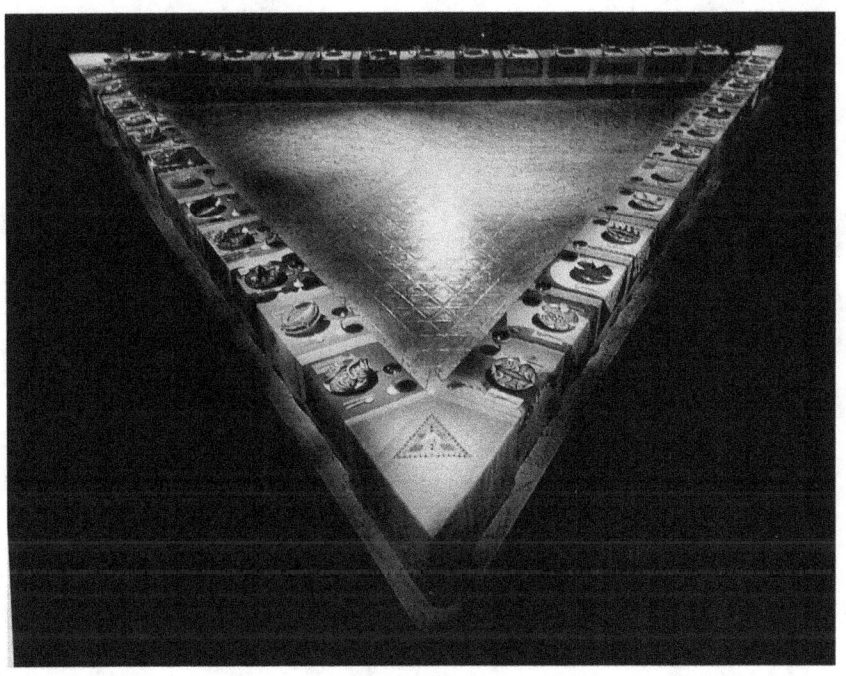

Judy Chicago

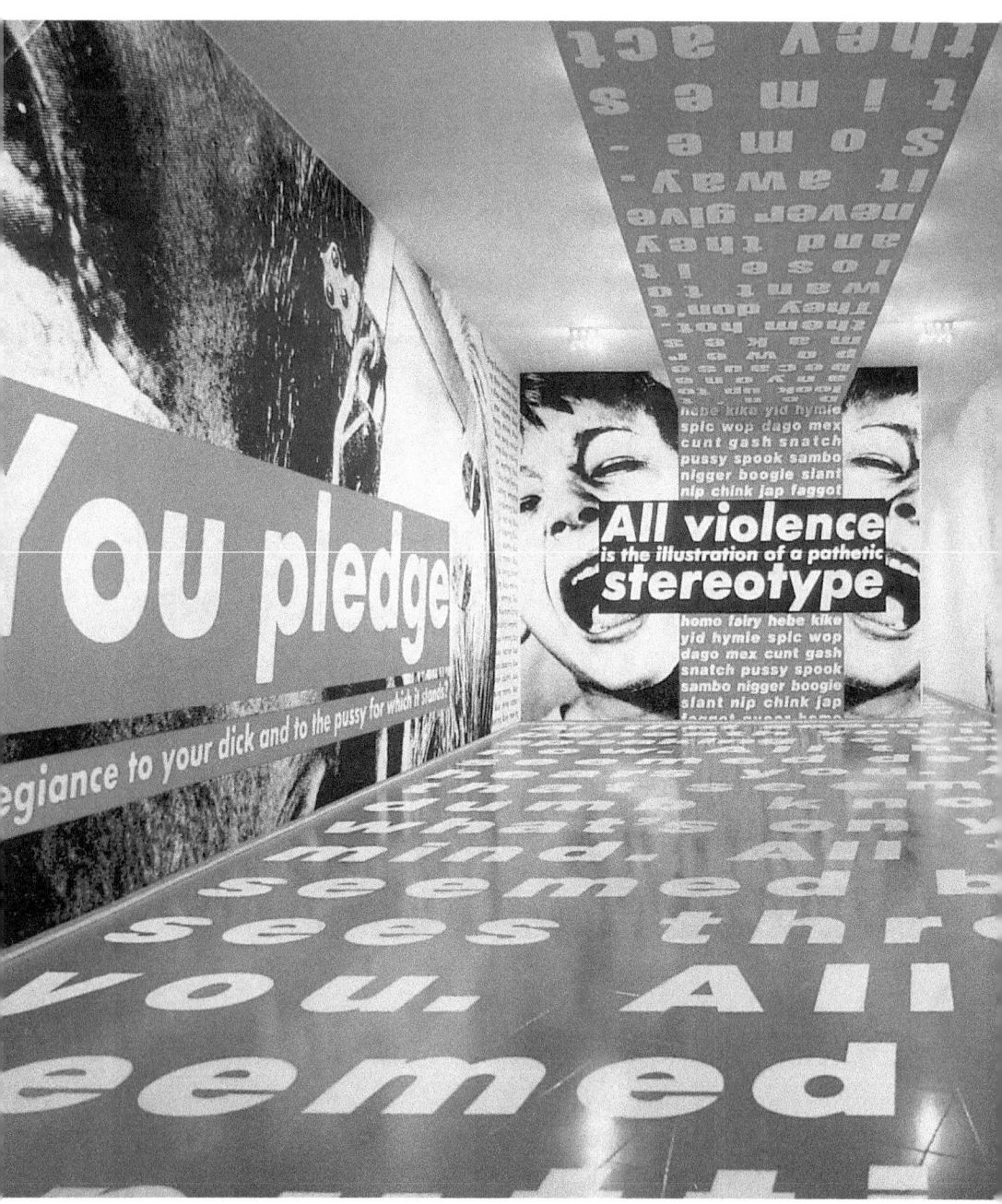

Barbara Kruger, Untitled, 1991

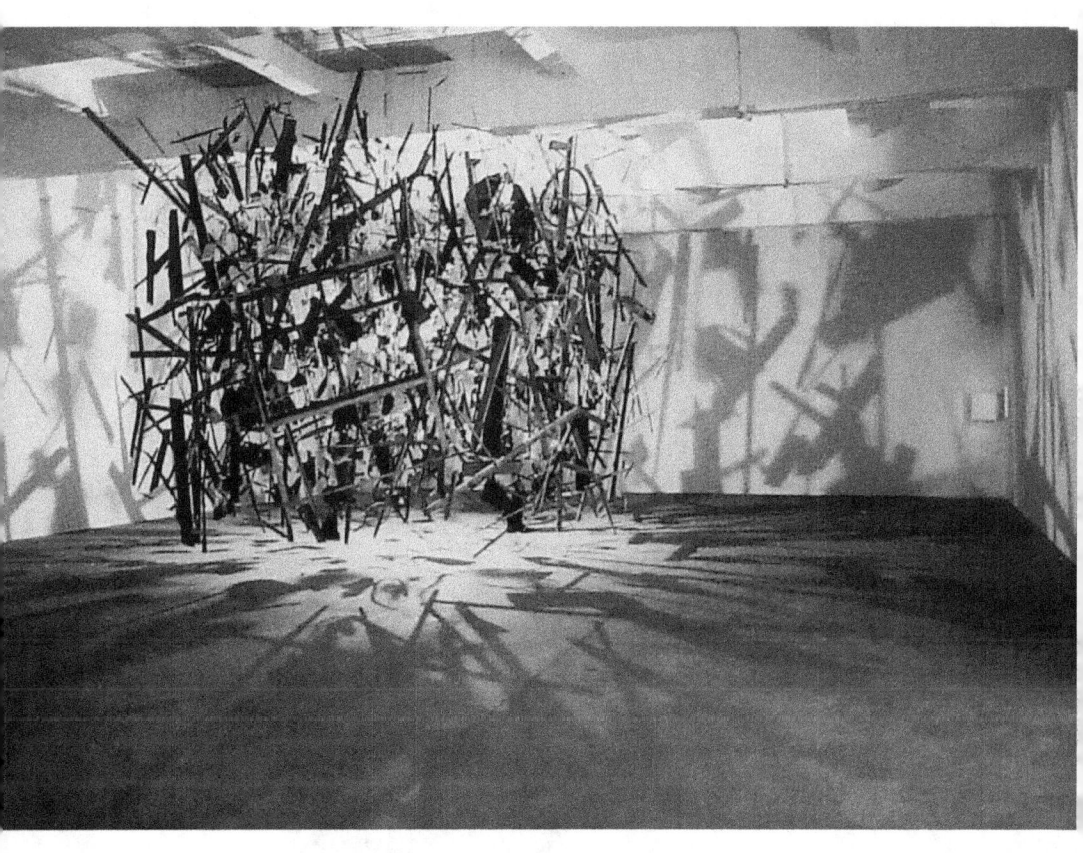

Cornelia Parker, Cold Dark Matter, 1991

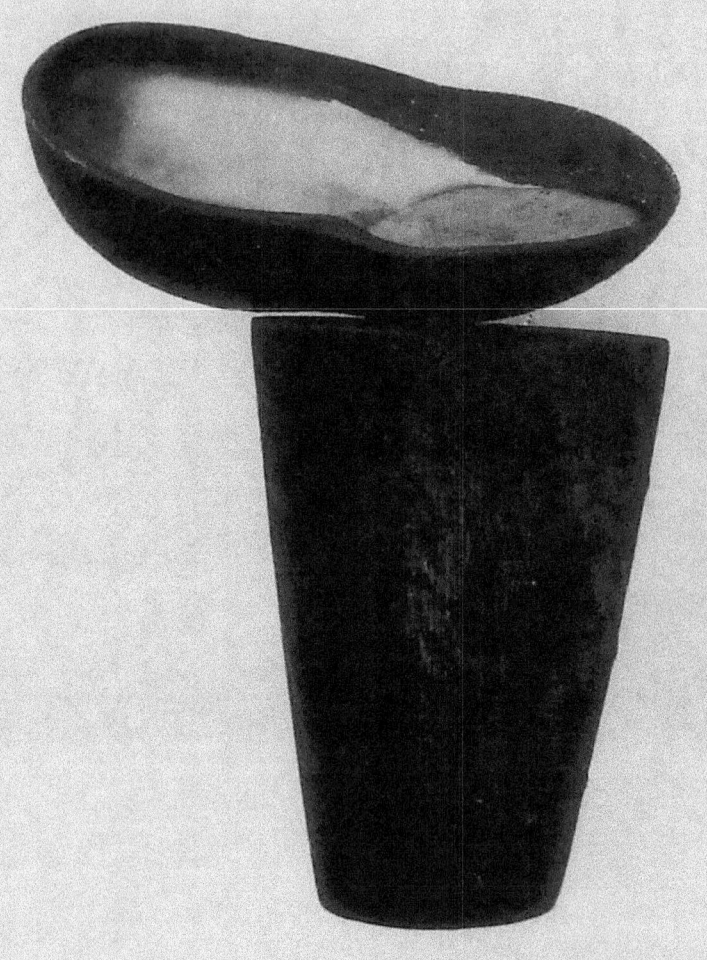

Alison Wilding, Hemlock III, 1986

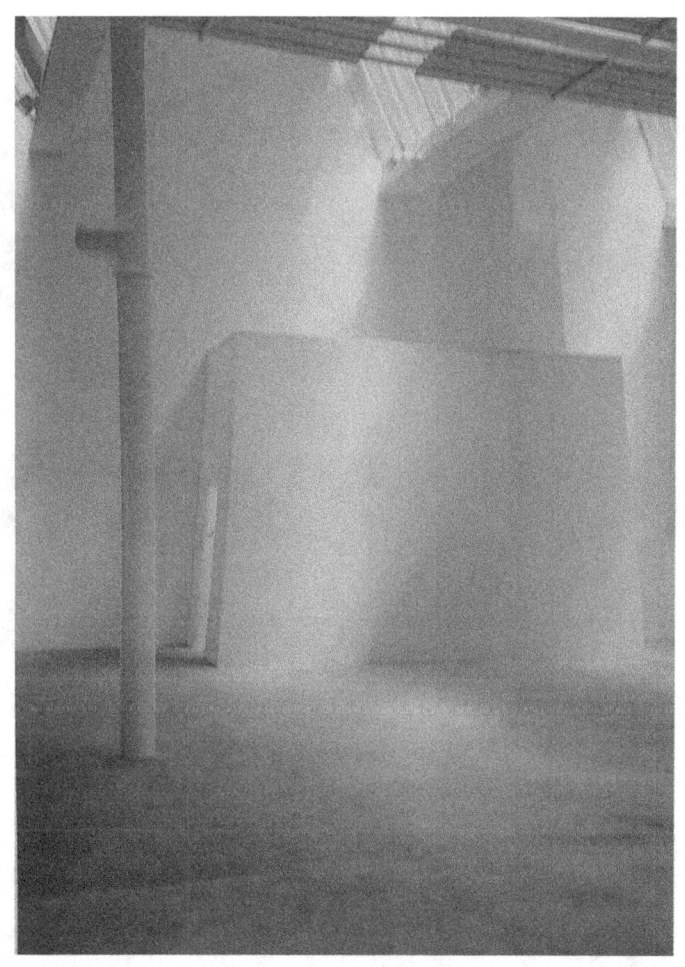

Alison Wilding, Pulse, 1991

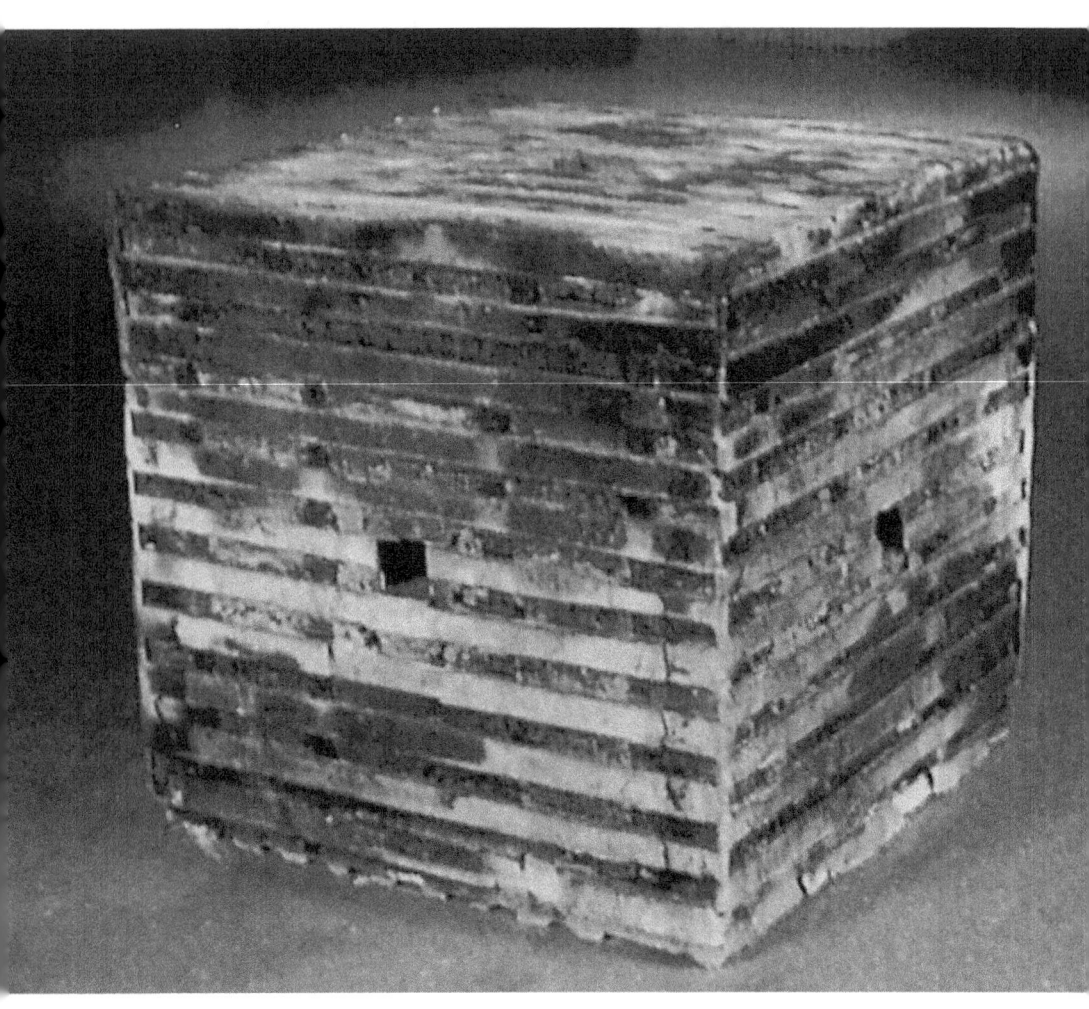

Jackie Winsor, Burnt Piece, 1977

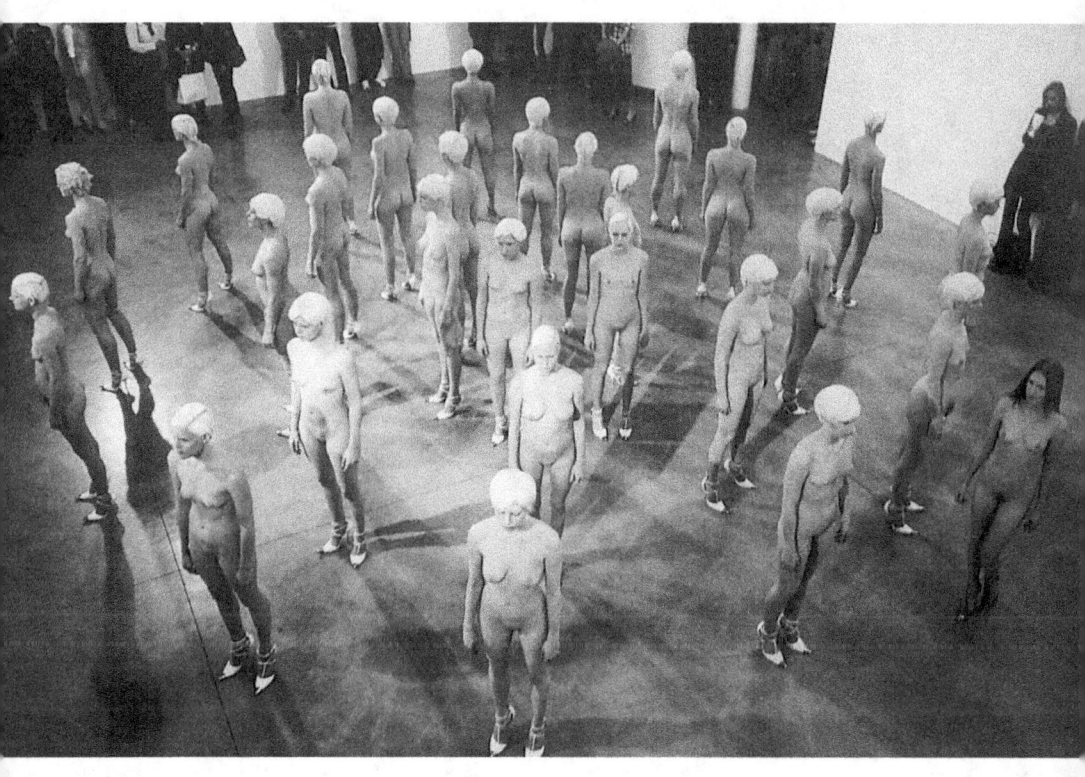

Vanessa Beecroft, VB45.026.ali, 2001

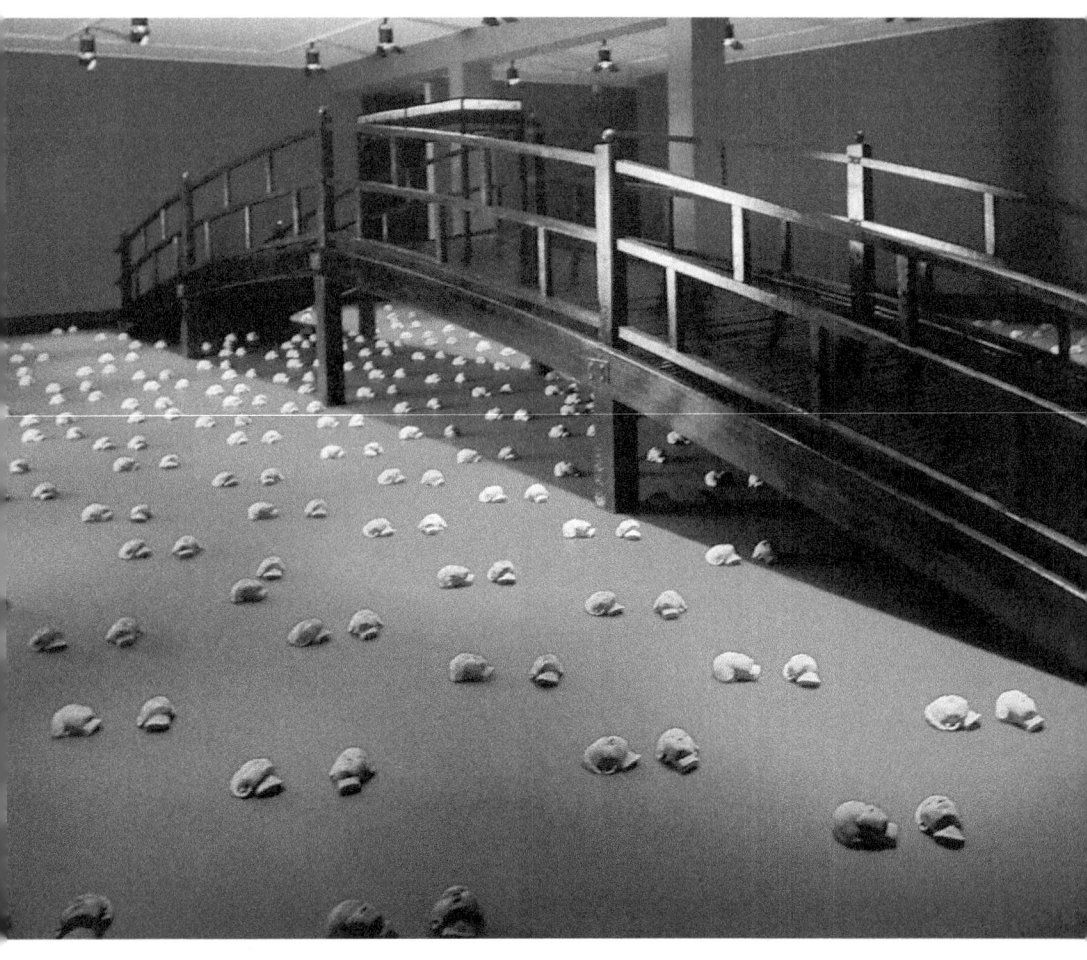

Barbara Bloom, Pictures From the Floating World, 1995

Bibliography

Dorothy Adlow. "Brancusi", *Drawing and Design*, 2 Feb 1927, 37f

W.C. Agee. *Don Judd*, Whitney Museum of American Art, New York, NY, 1968

—. "Unit, Series, Site: A Judd Lexicon", *Art in America*, May 1975, 40-49

—. *The Sculpture of Donald Judd*, Art Museum of South Texas, Corpus Christi, TX, 1977

L. Alloway. "The American Sublime", *Living Arts*, 1, 2, June, 1963

—. *Systematic Painting*, New York, NY, 1966

—. "Residual Sign Systems in Abstract Expressionism", *Artforum*, Nov, 1973

L. Aldrich. *Cool Art: 1967*, Museum of Contemporary Art, LA, CA, 1968

W. Andersen. *American Sculpture in Process 1930/1970*, New York Graphics Society, Boston 1975

C. Andre. "Frank Stella: Preface to Stripe Painting", in Miller, 1959

—. "An Interview with Carl Andre", P. Tuchman, *Artforum*, 8, 10, June, 1970

—. *Carl Andre, Sculpture, 1958-1974*, Kunsthalle, Bern, 1975

—. "Object v Phenomenon", *Sculpture Today*, The International Sculpture Center, Toronto, 1978

—. *Carl Andre: Sculpture*, State University of New York Press, Albany, NY, 1984

—. *Carl-Andre: works on land*, Exhibitions International, 2001

M. Andrews. *Landscape and Western Art*, Oxford Paperbacks, Oxford, 1999

D. Anfam. *Abstract Expressionism*,

Thames & Hudson, London, 1990

E. de Antonio & M. Tuchman: *Painters Painting*, Abbeville Press, New York, NY, 1984

I. Armstrong, ed. *New Feminist Discourses: Critical Essays on Theories and Texts*, Routledge, London, London, 1992

D. Ashton, ed: *Picasso on Art: A Selection of Views*, Viking Press, New York 1972

—. *American Art Since 1945*, Thames & Hudson, London, 1982

—. *Modern American Sculpture*, Abrams, New York, NY, 1968

A. Assiter. *Althusser and Feminism*, Pluto Press, London, 1990

—. & A. Carol, eds. *Bad Girls and Dirty Pictures: The Challenge to Reclaim Feminism*, Pluto Press, London, 1993

P. Bade. *Femme Fatale: Images of evil and fascinating women*, Ash & Grant, London, 1979

E. Baker. "Judd the Obscure", *Art News*, 67, 2, 1968

K. Baker. "Andre in Retrospect", *Art in America*, Apl, 1980a

—. "Reckoning with Notation: The Drawings of Pollock, Newman, and Louis", *Artforum*, 18, 10, Summer, 1980b

—. *Minimalism: Art of Circumstance*, Abbeville, New York, NY, 1988

S. Bann. *Brice Marden: Paintings, Drawings, Etchings 1975-80*, Stedelijk Museum, Amsterdam 1981

G. Baro. "Toward Speculation in Pure Form", *Art International*, Summer, 1967

—. "American Sculpture", *Studio International*, 172, 896, 1968

G. Battock, ed. *Minimal Art: A Critical anthology*, Studio Vista, London, 1969

G. Bazin. *A Concise History of World Sculpture*, David & Charles, Newton Abbot 1981

J. Beardsley. *Probing the Earth: Contemporary Land Projects*, Smithsonian Press, Washington, 1977

—. *Earthworks and Beyond: Contemporary Art in the Landscape*, Abbeville Press, New York, NY, 1984

D. Belgrad. *The Culture of Spontaneity: Improvisation and the Arts in Postwar America*, University of Chicago Press, Chicago, IL, 1998

C. Belsey. *Critical Practice*, Routledge, London, 1980

N. Bennett. *The British Art Show: Old Allegiances and New Directions 1979-1984*, Orbis, London, 1984

M. Berger. *Labyrinths: Robert Morris, Minimalism and the 1960s*, Harper & Row, New York, NY, 1989

M. Bochner. "Art in Process – Structures", *Arts Magazine*, 40, 9, 1966

—. "Primary Structures", *Arts*, June, 1966

—. "Systematic", *Arts Magazine*, 41, 1, Nov, 1966

—. "Serial Art Systems: Solipsism", *Arts Magazine*, 41, 8, Summer, 1967

—. "Mel Bochner on Malevich", interview with J. Coplans, *Artforum*, June, 1974

S. Boettger. *Earthworks*, University of California Press, Berkeley, CA, 2002

F. Bonner et al, eds. *Imagining Women Cultural Representations and Gender*, Polity Press, Cambridge, 1992

D. Bourdon. "The Razed Sites of Carl Andre", *Artforum*, 5, 2, Oct, 1966

—. "Walter de Maria: The Singular Experience", *Art International*, Dec 20, 1968

—"The Mini-Conceptual Age", *Village Voice*, 17 Oct, 1974

—. "You Can't Tell a Painter By His Colors", *Village Voice*, 24 Mch, 1975

—. *Carl Andre: Sculpture, 1959-1977*, Jaap Rietman, New York, NY, 1978

—. et al: *Niki de Sant-Phalle: Fantastic Vision*, Nassau County Museum of Fine Art, Rosyln, New York 1987

T. Burckhardt. *Sacred Art in East and West*, Perennial Book, Middlesex 1967

J. Burnham. *Beyond Modern Sculpture*, Braziller, New York, NY, 1968

—. "A Dan Flavin Retrospective in Ottawa", *Artforum*, 8, 4, Dec, 1969

—. "Robert Morris", *Artforum*, 8, 7, 1970

—. "Haacke's Cancelled Show at the Guggenheim", *Artforum*, June, 1971

N. & E. Calas. *Icons and Image of the Sixties*, Dutton, New York, NY, 1971

D. Cameron, ed. *The Feminist Critique of Language: A Reader*, Routledge 1990

J. Campbell. *The Power of Myth*, with B. Moyers, ed. B.S. Flowers, Doubleday, New York, NY, 1988

P. Carlson. "Donald Judd's Equivocal Objects", *Art in America*, Jan, 1984

M. P. Carroll. *The Cult of the Virgin Mary*, Princeton University Press, NJ 1986

G. Celant. "Introduction", *Arte Povera*, Praeger, New York, NY, 1969

—. "Tony Cragg and Industrial Platonism", *Artforum*, 20, 3, Nov, 1981

—. *Dennis Oppenheim*, Edizioni Charta Srl, 1997

W. Chadwick. *Women, Art, and Society*, Thames & Hudson, London, 1990

—. *Women Artists and the Surrealist Movement*, Thames & Hudson, London, 1991

A. Chave. "Minimalism and the Rhetoric of Power", *Arts*, Jan, 1990

G Chester & J. Dickey, eds. *Feminism and Censorship: The Current Debate*, Prism Press, Bridport, Dorset 1988

H.B. Chipp, ed. *Theories of Modern Art*, University Press of California, Los Angeles 1968

H. Cixous & C. Clément. *The Newly Born Woman*, tr. B. Wing, Manchester University Press 1986

K. Clark. *The Nude*, Pantheon Books, London, 1957

F. Colpitt: *Minimal Art: The Critical Perspective*, University of Washington Press, Seattle, 1990

J. Coplans. "Serial Imagery", *Artforum*, 7, 2, Oct, 1968

—. *Donald Judd*, Pasadena Art Museum, CA, 1971

M. Craig-Martin. *Minimalism*, Tate Gallery, Liverpool 1989

M. Crichton. *Jasper Johns*, Thames & Hudson, London, 1977

P. Crowther. "Barnett Newman and the Sublime", *Oxford Art Journal*, 7, 2, 1984

—. ed. *The Contemporary Sublime*, Art & Design, 40, 1995

M. Dabrowski. *Contrasts of Form: Geometric Abstract Art 1910-80*, MOMA, New York, NY, 1985

M. Daly. *Pure Lust: Elemental Feminist Philosophy*, Women's

Press, London, 1984

—. *Gyn/Ecology: The Metaethics of Radical Feminism*, Women's Press, London, 1979

—. *Beyond God the Father*, Women's Press, London, 1985

J.-L. Daval. *History of Abstract Painting*, Art Data 1989

H. Davies *et al. Blurring the Boundaries: Installation Art 1969-1996*, Museum of Contemporary Art, San Diego, CA, 1997

R. Davies & T. Knipe, eds. *A Sense of Place: Sculpture in Landscape*, London, 1984

A. Dempsey. *Styles, Schools Movements*, Thames & Hudson, London, 2002

J. De Mul. *Romantic Desire in (Post)Modern Art and Philosophy*, State University of New York Press, Albany, NY, 1999

N. de Oliveira *et al. Installation Art*, Thames & Hudson, London, 1994

—. *et al*, eds. *Installation Art in the New Millennium*, Thames & Hudson,London, 2003

E. Develing. *Carl Andre*, Gemeentenmeuseum, The Hague, 1969

—. & L. Lippard. *Minimal Art*, Stadtische Kunsthalle, Dusseldorf, 1969

W. Dube. *The Expressionists*, Thames & Hudson, London, 1972

S.C. Dubin. *Arresting Images: Impolitic Art and Uncivil Actions*, Routledge, London, 1992

G. Duby & M. Perrot. *Power and Beauty: Images of Women in Art*, Tauris Parke Books,

A. Dworkin. *Mercy*, Arrow 1990

—. *Intercourse*, Arrow, London, 1988

—. *Pornography: Men Possessing Women*, Women's Press, London, 1984

M. Eagleton, ed. *Feminist Literary Criticism*, Longman, London, 1991

—. ed. *Feminist Literary Theory: A Reader*, Blackwell, Oxford, 1986

H. Eisenstein. *Contemporary Feminist Thought*, Unwin Paperbacks, London, 1984

M. Eliade. *Shamanism: Archaic Techniques of Ecstasy*, Princeton University Press, 1972

—. *Myths. Dreams and Mysteries*, tr. Philip Mairet, Harper & Row, New York 1975

—. *A History of Religious Ideas*, I, Collins, London, 1979

—. *Ordeal by Labyrinth*, University of Chicago Press 1984

—. *Symbolism, the Sacred and the Arts*, Crossroad, New York, NY, 1985

A. Elsen. *Modern European Sculpture 1918-45*, New York, NY, 1979

J. Evans, ed. *The Flowering of the Middle Ages*, Thames & Hudson, London, 1966

J. Evola. *The Metaphysics of Sex*, East-West Publications 1985

Feminist Review, eds. *Sexuality: A Reader*, Virago, London, 1987

G. Ferguson. *Signs and Symbols in Christian Art*, Oxford University Press, London, 1961

J. Ferguson. *An Illustrated Encyclopædia of Mysticism*, Thames & Hudson, London, 1976

P. Fingesten. *The Eclipse of Symbolism*, University Press of California 1970

J. Fletcher & A. Benjamin, ed; *Abjection, Melancholia and Love: the Work of Julia*

Kristeva, Routledge, London, 1990

S. Foley. *Unitary Forms: Minimal Structures by Carl Andre, Donald Judd, John McCracken, Tony Smith*, Museum of Modern Art, San Francisco, CA, 1970

M. Foucault. *The History of Sexuality*, Penguin, London, 1981

—. *The Use of Pleasure: The History of Sexuality*, vol. 2, Penguin, London, 1987

C. Franklin, ed. *Erotic Art by Living Artists*, Directors Guild Publishers, Renaissance, California 1988

F. Frascina *et al*, eds. *Modern Art ad Modernism: A Critical Anthology*, Paul Chapman, London, 1988

J.G. Frazer. *The Golden Bough*, abridged edition, Macmillan, London, 1922/59

M. Fried. "New York Letter", *Art International*, 8, 3, Apl, 1964

—. *Three American Painters: Kenneth Noland, Jules Olitski, Frank Stella*, Fogg Art Museum, Harvard University, Cambridge, MA, 1965

—. "Art and Objecthood", *Artforum*, 5, Summer, 1967

M. Friedman. "Robert Morris: Polemics and Cubes", *Art International*, 10, 10, Dec, 1966

—. *14 Sculptors*, Walker Art Center, Minneapolis, MN, 1969

E. Fry. *Alice Aycock*, University of South Florida Art Galleries, Tampa, FL, 1981

—. "The Poetic Machines of Alice Aycock", *Portfolio*, Nov, 1981

—. *et al. Robert Morris*, Museum of Contemporary Art, Chicago, IL, 1986

R.H. Fuchs. *Richard Long*, Thames & Hudson, London, 1986

E. Gadon. *The Once and Future Goddess*, Aquarian Press, London, 1990

Sidney Geist. "The Birds", *Artforum*, 9, November 1970, 74-82

—. "The Centrality of the Gate", *Artforum*, 12, October 1973, 70-78

—. *Brancusi The Kiss*, Harper & Row, New York 1978

—. *Brancusi: A Study of the Sculpture*, Hacker, New York 1983

M. Ghyka. *The Geometry of Art and Life*, Sheed & Ward, New York, NY, 1946

P. Gibson & R. Gibson, ed. *Dirty Looks: Women, Pornography, Power*, British Film Institute, London, 1993

M. Gimbutas. *The Language of the Goddess*, Thames & Hudson, London, 1989

T. Godfrey. *Conceptual Art*, Phaidon, London, 1998

R. Goldwater & M. Treves, eds. *Artists on Art*, John Murray, London, 1975

—. *What is Modern Sculpture?*, MOMA, New York, NY, 1969

E.H. Gombrich. *Norm and Form: Studies in the Renaissance I*, Phaidon 1985

—. *Symbolic Images, Renaissance Studies II*, Phaidon, London, 1985

A. Goldsworthy. *Andy Goldsworthy*, Viking, London, 1990

—. *Hand to Earth: Andy Goldsworthy, Sculpture, 1976-1990*, Henry Moore Centre for Sculpture, Leeds, Yorkshire, 1990

—. *Stone*, Viking, London, 1994

—. *Wood*, Viking, London, 1996

—. *Sheepfolds*, Michael Hue-
Williams Gallery, London,
1996

—. *Andy Goldsworthy: A
Collaboration With Nature*,
Abrams, NY, 1996

—. *Hand to Earth: Andy
Goldsworthy Sculpture*, T.
Friedman, Thames and
Hudson, London, 1997

—. *Arch*, with D. Craig, Thames &
Hudson, London, 1999

—. *Wall*, intr. K. Baker, Thames &
Hudson, London, 2000

—. *Time*, Thames & Hudson,
London, 2000

—. *Midsummer Snowballs*, intr. J.
Collins, Abrams, New York,
NY, 2001

—. *Andy Goldsworthy – Refuges
D'Art*, Editions Artha, 2002

—. *Passage*, Thames & Hudson,
London, 2004

E. Goodheart. *Desire and Its
Discontents*, Columbia
University Press, New York,
NY, 1991

M. Gooding & W. Furlong. *Song of
the Earth*, Thames and
Hudson, 2002

E.C. Goossen. *The Art of the Real:
USA 1948-1968*, MOMA, New
York, NY, 1968

C. Greenberg. *Art and Culture*,
Beacon Press, Boston 1961

G. Greer. *The Obstacle Race: The
Fortunes of Women Painters
and Their Work*, Secker &
Warburg, London, 1979;
Picador, London, 1981

S. Griffin. *Pornography and Silence:
Culture's Revenge Against
Nature*, Women's Press,
London, 1981

J. Hall. *A Dictionary of Subjects
and Symbols in Art*, John
Murray, London, 1984

A.M. Hammacher. *The Evolution of
Modern Sculpture: Tradition
and innovation*, Abrams, New
York, NY, 1969

—. *The Sculpture of Barbara
Hepworth*, Abrams, New York
1968

M. Esther Harding. *Women's
Mysteries*, Rider, London,
1989

B. Haskell. *BLAM! The Explosion of
Pop, Minimalism, and
Performance, 1958-64*,
Whitney Museum of American
Art, New York, NY, 1984

—. *Donald Judd*, Whitney Museum
of American Art, New York,
1988

N.G. Heller. *Women Artists: An
Illustrated History*, Virago,
London, 1987

T. Hess. *Barnett Newman*, Walker,
New York, NY, 1969

M. Hester. *Lewd Women and
Wicked Witches: A Study of the
Dynamics of Male
Domination*, Routledge,
London, 1992

J. Hobhouse. *The Bride Stripped
Bare: The Artist and the Nude
in the Twentieth Century*,
Cape, London, 1988

R. Hobbs. *Robert Smithson:
Sculpture*, Cornell University
Press, Ithaca, New York, NY,
1981

M. Hoffman: *Sculpture Inside and
Out*, New York 1939

A. Hollander. *Seeing Through
Clothes*, Viking Press, New
York, NY, 1980

K. Honnef. *Contemporary Art*,
Benedikt Taschen, Cologne
1988

S. Hubbard, intr. *Sculpture At
Goodwood: A Vision For 21st
Century British Sculpture*,
Sculpture At Goodwood,
Sussex, 2002

M. Humm. *Feminisms: A Reader*,
Harvester Wheatsheaf, 1992

—. ed. *The Dictionary of Feminist Theory*, Harvester Wheatsheaf 1989

S. Hunter, ed. *An American Renaissance: Painting and Sculpture Since 1940*, Abbeville Press, New York, NY, 1986

—. *American Art of the 20th Century*, Thames & Hudson, London, 1973

L. Irigaray. *The Irigaray Reader*, ed. Margaret Whitford, Blackwell, Oxford 1991

—. *Je, tu, nous: Toward a Culture of Difference*, tr. A. Martin, Routledge 1993

W. Januszczak, ed. *Techniques of the World's Great Painters*, Phaidon 1980

E.H. Johnson. *American Artists on Art from 1940 to 1980*, Harper & Row, New York, NY, 1982

D. Judd. "Frank Stella", *Arts Magazine*, 36, Sept, 1962

—. "In the Galleries", *Arts Magazine*, 37, 10, Sept, 1963

—. "Local History", *Arts Yearbook* 7, 1964

—. "Black, White and Gray", *Arts Magazine*, 38, 6, Mch, 1964

—. "Specific Objects", *Arts Yearbook*, 8, Art Digest, New York, NY, 1965

—. "Barnett Newman", *Studio International*, 179, 919, Feb, 1970

—. *Complete Writings, 1959-1975*, Nova Scotia College of Art and Design, Halifax, Canada, 1975

—. *Complete Writings, 1975-1986*, Van Abbemuseum, Netherlands, 1987

P. Julian. *Dreamers of Decadence: Symbolist Painters of the 1890s*, tr. R. Baldick, Pall Mall Press 1971

C.G. Jung. *Memories, Dreams,*

Reflections, Collins 1967

S. Kappeler. *The Pornography of Representation*, Polity Press, Cambridge 1986

S. Kent & J. Morreau, eds: *Women's Images of Men*, Pandora Press, 1985

J.A. Kestner. *Mythology and Misogyny: The Social Discourse of Nineteenth-Century British Classical-Subject Painting*, University of Wisconsin Press, Madison 1989

—. ed. *Land and Environmental Art*, Phaidon, London, 1998

C. Knight. *Art of the Sixties and Seventies. The Panza Collection*, Rizzoli, New York, NY, 1987

N. Konstam. *Sculpture: The Art and the Practice*, Collins 1984

C. Kramarae & P.A. Treichler, eds. *A Feminist Dictionary*, Pandora Press, 1987

R.E. Krauss. "Richard Serra: Sculpture Redrawn", *Artforum*, May, 1972

—. "Sense and Sensibility: Reflections on Post 60's Sculpture", *Artforum*, vol. 12, no. 3, November 1973

—. *Passages in Modern Sculpture*, Thames & Hudson, London, 1977

—. & Eva Hesse: *Eva Hesse: Sculpture*, Whitechapel Art Gallery 1979

—. "Sculpture in the Expanded Field", *October*, 8, Spring 1978

—. et al. *Robert Morris*, Abrams, New York, NY, 1994

J. Kristeva. *Desire in Language: A Semiotic Approach to Literature and Art*, ed. L. Roudiez, tr. T. Gora et al, Blackwell, Oxford, 1982

—. *The Kristeva Reader*, ed. T. Moi, Blackwell, Oxford, 1986

D. Kuspit. "Sol LeWitt", *Art in*

America, 63, 5, 1975

—. "Authoritarian Abstraction", *Journal of Aesthetics and Art Criticism*, 36, 1, Autumn, 1977

—. "Donald Judd", *Artforum*, 23, 5, Feb, 1985

J. Kutner. "Brice Marden, David Novros, Mark Rothko: The Urge to Communicate through Non-Imagistic Painting", *Arts Magazine*, 50, 1, Sept, 1975

W. La Barre. *The Ghost Dance*, Allen & Unwin, London, 1972

J. Lacan and the *Ecole Freudienne: Feminine Sexuality*, ed. J. Mitchell and J. Rose, Macmillan, London, 1982

D.H. Lawrence. *Selected Essays*, Penguin, London, 1950

—. *Phoenix*, Heinemann, London, 1956

—. *Phoenix II*, Heinemann, London, 1968

—. *A Selection from Phoenix*, ed. A.A.H. Inglis, Penguin, London, 1971

P. Leider. "Literalism and Abstraction: Frank Stella's Retrospective at the Modern", *Artforum*, 8, April 1970

A. Le Normand-Romain *et al*. *Sculpture: The Adventure of Modern Sculpture in the Nineteenth and Twentieth Centuries*, Skira, Geneva, 1986

M. Levy. *Drawing and Sculpture*, Adams & Dart, Bath, Somerset 1970

David N. Lewis: *Constantin Brancusi*, St Martin's Press, New York 197

F. Licht. *Sculpture, 19th and 20th Centuries*, Michael Joseph, London, 1967

—. "Dan Flavin", *Artscanada*, Dec, 1968

L. Lippard. "New York Letter: April-June, 1965", *Art*

International, 9, 6, 1965

—. "New York Letter: Recent Sculpture as Escape", *Art International*, Feb, 1966

—. *Ad Reinhardt*, Jewish Museum, New York, NY, 1966

—. "An Impure Situation", *Art International*, 20 May, 1966

—. "The Silent Art", *Art in America*, 55, 1, Jan-Feb, 1967

—. "Sol LeWitt: Non-Visual Structures", *Artforum*, Apl, 1967

—. "Tony Smith", *Art International*, Summer, 1967

— "Rebelliously Romantic?", *New York Times*, 4 June, 1967

—. "Escalataion in Washington", *Art International*, 12, 1, Jan, 1968

—. ed. *Surrealists on Art*, Prentice-Hall, Englewood Cliffs, NJ, 1970

—. *Tony Smith*, Thames & Hudson, London, 1972

—. *Grids*, Philadelphia Institute of Contemporary Art, PA, 1972

—. *Six Years: The Dematerialization of the Art Object from 1966 to 1972*, Praeger, New York, NY, 1973

—. *From the Center: feminist essays on women's art*, Dutton, New York, NY, 1976

—. "Complexities: Architectural Sculpture in Nature", *Art in America*, Feb, 1979

—. "Dinner Party", *Art in America*, April 1980

—. *Ad Reinhardt*, Abrams, New York, NY, 1981

R. Long. *Richard Long: In Conversation*, Parts 1 & 2, MW Press, Noordwijk, Holland, 1985-86

—. *Richard Long*, text by R. Fuchs, Thames & Hudson, London, 1986

—. *Old World New World*, Anthony

d'Offay, London, 1988

—. *Richard Long: Walking in Circles*, Hayward Gallery/Thames & Hudson, London, 1992

—. *Richard Long*, Hatje Cantz, 1997

—. *A Walk Across England*, Thames & Hudson, London, 1997

—. *Mirage*, Phaidon, London, 1998

—. *Selected Walks, 1979-1996*, Morning Star Press, 1999

—. *Richard Long: a Moving World*, Tate Publishing, 2002

—. *Richard Long – Walking the Line*, Thames and Hudson, London, 2002

E. Lucie-Smith. *Sculpture Since 1945*, Phaidon, London, 1987

—. *Sexuality in Western Art*, Thames & Hudson, London, 1991

N. Lynton. *The Story of Modern Art*, Phaidon, London, 1989

—. *David Nash: Sculpture, 1971-90*, Serpentine Gallery, London, 1990

F. MacCarthy. *Eric Gill*, Faber, London, 1989

E. Male. *The Gothic Image*, Collins, London, 1961

J. van der Marck. *Wrapped Museum*, Museum of Contemporary Art, Chicago, IL, 1969

B. Marden. *Paintings, Drawings and Prints 1975-1980*, ed. Nicholas Serota, Whitechapel Art Gallery, London, 1987

E. Marks & I. de Courtivron, eds. *New French Feminisms: an Anthology*, Harvester Wheatsheaf, London, 1981

A. Martin. *Agnes Martin*, Institute of Contemporary Art, Philadelphia, PA, 1973

D. Mayhall. *The Minimal Tradition*, The Aldrich Museum of Contemporary Art,

Ridgefield, CT, 1979

D. McKinney. *Yves Klein, Brice Marden, Sigmar Polke*, Hirschl & Alder Modern, New York, NY, 1989

K. McShine. *Primary Structures*, Jewish Museum, New York, NY, 1966

G. Meaney. *(Un)Like Subjects: Women, Theory, Fiction*, Routledge, London, 1993

H.C. Merillat. *Modern Sculpture: The New Old Masters*, Dod, Mead & Co, New York, NY, 1974

J.C.J. Metford. *Dictionary of Christian Lore and Legend*, Thames & Hudson, London, 1983

F. Meyer. *Frank Stella*, Kunsthalle, Basel, 1976

J. Meyer, ed. *Minimalism*, Phaidon, London, 2000

U. Meyer. *Conceptual Art*, Dutton, New York, NY, 1972

D. C. Miller, ed. *Sixteen Americans*, MOMA, New York, NY, 1959

M. Miller. *The Garden as an Art*, State University of New York Press, Albany, 1993

C. Millett. "De Kooning, Newman, Rothko: des bâtards", *Art Press International*, 26, Mch, 1979

K. Millett. *Sexual Politics*, Doubleday, New York, NY, 1970

M. Miss. *Mary Miss: Interior Works*, Bell Gallery, University of Rhode Island, Autumn, 1981

T. Moi. *Sexual/ Textual Politics: Feminist Literary Theory*, Routledge, London, 1988

—. ed. *French Feminist Thought: A Reader*, Blackwell, Oxford 1987

R. Morgan. *The Word of a Woman: Selected Prose 1968-1992*, Virago 1993

H. Morphy & M. Boles, eds. *Art*

from the Land, University of
Washington Press, 2000

R. Morris. "Notes on Sculpture",
Artforum, Feb, 1966, Oct,
1966, June, 1967, Apl, 1969

—. "Aligned with Nazca",
Artforum, Oct, 1975

—. *Robert Morris: Mirror Works,
1961-1978*, Leo Castelli
Gallery, New York, NY, 1979

—. *Continuous Project Altered
Daily*, MIT Press, Cambridge,
MA, 1993

S. Morris. "A Rhetoric of Silence:
Redefinitions of Sculpture in
the 1960s and 1970s", in S.
Nairne, 1981

A. Moszynska. *Abstract Art*,
Thames & Hudson, London,
1990

E. Mullins. *The Painted Witch:
Female Body, Male Art*, Secker
& Warburg, London, 1985

L. Mulvey. *Visual and Other
Pleasures*, Macmillan, London,
1989

S. Munt, ed. *New Lesbian
Criticism: Literary and
Cultural Readings*, Harvester
Wheatsheaf, London, 1992

P. & L. Murray. *The Penguin
Dictionary of Art and Artists*,
Penguin, London, 1976

S. Nairne & N. Serota. *British
Sculpture in the Twentieth
Century*, White-chapel Art
Gallery, London, 1981

—. *State of the Art: Ideas & Images
in the 1980s*, Chatto, London,
1987

H. Nakamura. "Andy Goldsworthy
and Anthony Green", *Ikebana
Ryusei*, 38, April, 1988

L. Nead. *Female Nude: Art,
Obscenity and Sexuality*,
Routledge, London, 1992

T.A. Neff, ed. *A Quiet Revolution:
British Sculpture Since 1965*,

Thames & Hudson, London,
1987

C. Nemser. "An interview with Eva
Hesse", *Artforum*, May, 1970

—. "My Memories of Eva Hesse",
Feminist Art Journal, Winter,
1973

E. Neumann. *The Great Mother*,
Princeton University Press, NJ,
1972

S. Nicholson, ed. *The Goddess Re-
awakening: The Goddess
Principle Today*, Theosophical
Publishing House, New York,
NY, 1989

S. Nodelman. *Marden, Novros,
Rothko: Painting in the Age of
Actuality*, Institute for the
Arts, Rice University, Houston
1978

B. Oakes, ed. *Sculpting the
Environment*, Van Nostrand
Reinhold, New York, NY, 1995

—. *et al, Installation Art in the
New Millennium*, Thames &
Hudson,London, 2003

P. Osborne, ed. *Conceptual Art*,
Phaidon, London, 2002

E. Panofsky. *Studies in Iconology*,
Harper & Row, New York, NY,
1972

A.C. Papadakis, ed. *British and
American Art: The Uneasy
Dialectic*, Art & Design, 3, 9/1,
Academy Group, 1987

—. ed. *Abstract Art and the
Rediscovery of the Spiritual*,
Art & Design, 3, 5/6, Academy
Group, London, 1987

—. ed. *The New Romantics*, Art &
Design, 4, 11/12, Academy
Group, London, 1988

—. *et al*, eds. *New Art*, Academy
Group, London, 1991

R. Parker & G. Pollock. *Old
Mistresses: Women, Art an
Ideology*, Routledge & Kegan
Paul, London, 1981

M. Payne. *Reading Theory: An*

Introduction to Lacan, Derrida, and Kristeva, Blackwell, Oxford, 1993

J. Perreault. "A Minimal Future? Union-Made: Report on a Phenomenon", Arts Magazine, 41, March 1967

J. Perrone. "Seeing Through Boxes", Artforum, 15, Nov, 1976

K. Petersen & J.J. Wilson. Women Artists: Recognition and Reappraisal from the Early Middle Ages to the Twentieth Century Women's Press, London, 1978

M. Phillipson. Painting, Language and Modernity, Routledge, London, 1978

G. Picon. Surrealists and Surrealism 1919-1939, Skira/ Macmillan, London, 1983

R. Pincus-Witten. "Systematic Painting", Artforum, 5, 3, Nov, 1966

—. "Ryman, Marden, Manzoni: Theory, Sensibility, Mediation", Artforum, 10, 10, June, 1972

—. "Sol LeWitt", Artforum, 11, 6, Feb, 1973

—. Postminimalism, Out of London, New York, NY, 1977

M. Poirier & J. Necol. "The '60s in Abstract Painting: 13 Statements...Brice Marden", Art in America, Oct, 1983

—. "Color-coded Mysteries", ARTnews, Jan, 1985

G. Pollock. Vision and Difference: femininity, feminism and histories of art, Routledge, London, 1988

S. Prokopoff. A Romantic Minimalism, Institute of Contemporary Art, Philadelphia 1967

C. Ratcliff. "Once More With Feeling", ARTnews, 71, 4, Summer, 1972

—. "Abstract Painting, Specific Spaces: Novros and Marden in Houston", Art in America, 63, 5, Nov, 1975

—. In the Realm of the Monochrome, Renaissance Society, University of Chicago, Chicago, IL, 1979

—. "Mostly Monochrome", Art in America, 69, 4, Apl, 1981

—. "Robert Ryman Making Distinctions", Art in America, June, 1986

P. Rawson. The Art of Tantra, Thames & Hudson, London, 1973

—. The Erotic Art of the East, Weidenfeld & Nicolson, 1973

P. Redgrove & P. Shuttle. The Wise Wound: Menstruation and Everywoman, Paladin, London, 1986

—. The Black Goddess and the Sixth Sense, Bloomsbury, London, 1987

B. Redhead. The Inspiration of Landscape: Artists in National Parks, Phaidon 1989

W. Reh & C. Steenbergen. Architecture and Landscape, Prestel Publishing, 1996

K. J. Reiger, ed. The Spiritual Image in Modern Art, Theosophical Publishing House, Wheaton, Illinois 1987

A. Reinhardt. Art as Art: The Selected Writings of Ad Reinhardt, University of California Press, Berkeley, 1991

B. Reise. "'Untitled 1969': A Footnote on Art and Minimal Stylehood", Studio International, 177, April 1969

C. Riley II. Color Codes: Modern Theories in Color in Philosophy, Painting and Architecture, Literature, Music and Psychology, University

Press of New England, Hanover, NH, 1995

R.M. Rilke. *The Selected Poetry of Rainer Maria Rilke*, tr. S. Mitchell, Picador, London, 1987

A.C. Ritchie. *Sculpture in the Twentieth Century*, MOMA, New York, NY, 1952

C. Robins. "Object, Structure or Sculpture: Where Are We?", *Arts Magazine*, 40, 9, 1966

—. "Empty Paintings", *SoHo Weekly News*, 22 Apl, 1976

—. *The Pluralist Era: American Art, 1968-1981*, Harper & Row, New York, NY, 1984

F. Roh. *German Art in the Twentieth Century: Painting, Sculpture, Architecture*, Thames & Hudson, London, 1968

A. Rorimer. *New Art in the 60s and 70s*, Thames & Hudson, London, 2001

B. Rose. "ABC Art", *Art in America*, 53, 5, Nov, 1965

—. *A New Aesthetic*, Washington Gallery of Modern Art, Washington DC, 1967

—. *American Art Since 1900*, Thames & Hudson, London, 1967

—. *American Painting*, Skira/ Rizzoli International, New York, NY, 1986

H. Rosenberg. *The De-Definition of Art*, Horizon Press, New York, NY, 1972

—. *Barnett Newman*, Abrams, New York, NY, 1978/ 1994

—. *The Tradition of the New*, Da Capo Press, New York, NY, 1994

R. Rosenblum. "Frank Stella: Five Years of Variations on an Irreducible Theme", *Artforum*, 3, 6, Mch, 1965

—. *Frank Stella*, Penguin, London, 1971

—. "Notes on Sol LeWitt", in Legg, 1978

—. *Modern Painting and the Northern Romantic Tradition*, Thames & Hudson, London, 1978

—. "Picasso and the Anatomy of Eroticism", in *Studies in Erotic Art*, Basic Books, New York

—. *Jasper Johns' Paintings and Sculptures, 1954-1974*, Ann Arbor, Michigan, MI, 1985

—. "Romanticism and Retrospective: An Interview with Robert Rosenblum", in Papadakis, 1988

L. Rubin. *Frank Stella Paintings: 1958-1965*, New York, NY, 1986

W. S. Rubin. *Frank Stella*, New York Graphic Society, Greenwich, CT., 1970

—. *Frank Stella: 1970-1987*, Museum of Modern Art, New York, NY, 1987

M. Ryan, ed. *Gravity and Grace: The Changing Condition of Sculpture, 1965-1975*, Hayward Gallery, London, 1993

I. Sandler. "The New Cool-Art", *Art in America*, 53, 1, Feb, 1967

—. *The Triumph of American Painting*, Harper & Row, New York, NY, 1970

—. *American Art of the 1960s*, Harper & Row, New York, NY, 1988

—. *Art of the Postmodern Era: From the 1960s to the Early 1990s*, HarperCollins, London, 1997

G. Saunders. *The Nude: a new perspective*, Herbert Press, London, 1989

P. Schjeldahl. *Art in Our Time The Saatchi Collection*, Lund Humphries, London, 1984

P. Selz .*German Expressionist Painting*, University of California Press, Berkeley, CA, 1974

—. *Art in Our Times: A Pictorial History 1890-1980*, Thames & Hudson, London, 1982

E. Shanes. *Constantin Brancusi*, Abbeville, New York, NY, 1989

D. Shapiro & C. Shapiro, eds. *Abstraction Expressionism: A Critical Record*, Cambridge University Press 1990

L. Shearer. *Brice Marden*, Guggenheim Museum, New York, NY, 1975

R. Sherry. *Studying Women's Writings: An Introduction*, Edward Arnold, London, 1988

E. Showalter, ed. *The New Feminist Criticism*, Virago, London, 1986

—. ed. *Speaking of Gender*, Routledge, London, 1989

—. *Sexual Anarchy: Gender and Culture at the* Fin de Siècle, Virago, London, 1992

P. Sims. *From Minimalism to Expressionism*, New York, NY, 1963

H. Singerman, ed. *Individuals: A Selected History of Contemporary Art, 1945-1986*, Museum of Contemporary Art, Los Angeles, CA, 1986

M. Sjöo & B. Mor. *The Great Cosmic Mother*, Harper & Row, San Francisco 1987

H. J. Smagula. *Currents: Contemporary Directions in the Visual Arts*, Prentice-Hall, Englewood Cliffs, NJ, 1983

B. Smith. *Fluorescent Light, etc, from Dan Flavin*, National Gallery of Canada, Ottawa, 1969

—. *Donald Judd*, National Gallery of Canada, Ottawa, 1975

D. Smith. *Sculpture and Drawings*, ed. J. Merkert, Prestel-Verlag, Munich, 1986

R. Smith. "Sol LeWitt", *Artforum*, Jan, 1975

—. "Review", *Artforum*, Dec, 1975

—. "De Maria: Elements", *Art in America*, May, 1978

—. *Elizabeth Murray*, Dallas Museum of Art 1987

R. Smithson. "Entropy and the New Monuments", *Artforum*, 4, 10, June, 1966

—. "A Museum of Language in the Vicinity of Art", *Art International*, 12, 3, Mch, 1968

—. *The Writings of Robert Smithson*, ed. N. Holt, New York University Press, New York, NY, 1979

—. *Robert Smithson*, ed. J. Flam, University of California Press, Berkeley, CA, 1996

T. Sokolowski et al. *Robert Morris*, New York University Press, New York, NY, 1989

N. Spector. *Robert Ryman*, Whitechapel Art Gallery, London, 1977

D. Spender. *The Writing or the Sex? why you don't have to read women's writing to know it's no good*, Pergamon Press, New York, NY, 1989

W. Spies. *The Running Fence Project, Christo*, Abrams, New York, NY, 1977

N. Stangos, ed. *Concepts of Modern Art*, Thames & Hudson, London, 1981

F. Stella. *Working Space*, Harvard University Press, Cambridge, MA, 1986

—. *Frank Stella*, Madrid, 1995

K. Stiles & P. Selz, eds. *Theories & Documents of Contemporary Art: A Sourcebook of Artists' Writings*, University of

California Press, Berkeley, CA, 1996

W.J. Strachan. *Towards Sculpture: Maquettes and Sketches from Rodin to Oldenburg*, Thames & Hudson, London, 1976

E. Suderburg, ed. *Space, Site, Intervention*, University of Minnesota Press, Minneapolis, MN, 2000

S.R. Suleiman, ed. *The Female Body in Western Culture: Contemporary Perspectives*, Harvard University Press, Cambridge, Mass., 1986

J. Taylor et al. *Robert Rauschenberg*, Smithsonian Institute, Washington, 1976

G. Tiberghien. *Land Art*, Art Data, London, 1995

Lisa Tickner. "The Body Politic: Female Sexuality and Women Artists since 1970", *Art History*, 1:2, June 1978, 236-51

Andrew Tilly. *Erotic Drawings*, Phaidon, 1986

E. Tsai. *Robert Smithson Unearthed*, Columbia University Press, New York, NY, 1991

M. Tuchman. *American Sculpture of the Sixties*, Los Angeles County Museum of Art, 1967

—. *The New York School*, Thames & Hudson, London, 1971

—. *The Spiritual in Art: Abstract Painting 1880-1985*, Los Angeles County Museum of Art/ Abbeville Press, New York, NY, 1986

P. Tuchman. "Minimalism and Critical Response", *Artforum*, 15, 9, May, 1977

—. "Background of a Minimalist: Carl Andre", *Artforum*, Mch, 1978

—. "Minimalism", *Three Decades: The Oliver-Hoffmann*

Collection, Museum of Contemporary Art, Chicago 1988.

M. Tucker. *Robert Morris*, New York, NY, 1970

W. Tucker. *The Language of Sculpture*, Thames & Hudson, London, 1974

—. *Early Modern Sculpture: Rodin, Degas, Matisse, Brancusi, Picasso, Gonzalez*, Oxford University Press, New York 1974

G. de Vries, ed. *On Art: Artists' Writings on the Changed Notion of Art After, 1965*, Cologne, 1974

A.M. Wagner. *Three Artists (Three Women): Modernism and the Art of Hesse, Krasner and O'Keeffe*, University of California Press, Berkeley, 1996

D. Waldman. *Mark Rothko*, Thames & Hudson, London, 1978

B. Walker. *Tantrism: Its Secret Principles and Practices*, Aquarian Press, Wellingborough 1982

J. Walker. *Art and Artists on Screen*, Manchester University Press, Manchester, 1993

—. *Art & Outrage: Provocation, Controversy and the Visual Arts*, Pluto Press, London, 1999

—. *Art and Celebrity*, Pluto Press, London, 2003

M. Warner. *Alone Of All Her Sex: The Myth and Cult of the Virgin Mary*, Picador 1985

—. *Monuments and Maidens*, Weidenfeld & Nicholson, London, 1985

P. Webb. *The Erotic Arts*, Secker & Warburg, London, 1983

U. Weilacher et al. *Between Landscape Architecture and*

Land Art, Birkhauser Verlag AG, 1999

L. Weintraub. *The Maximal Implications of the Minimalist Line,* Edith C. Blum Art Institute, New York, NY, 1985

D. Wheeler. *Art Since Mid-Century: 1945 to the Present,* Thames & Hudson, London, 1991

R. Wittkower. *Sculpture: Process and Principles,* Harper & Row, New York, NY, 1977

H. Wolfflin. *Classic Art,* Phaidon 1952/ 80

G. Woods et al, eds. *Art Without Boundaries,* Thames & Hudson, London, 1972

M. Wudram. *Art of the Renaissance,* Weidenfeld & Nicolson, London, 1985

M. Yorke. *Eric Gill: Man of Flesh and Spirit,* Constable, London, 1981

CRESCENT MOON PUBLISHING

ARTS, PAINTING, SCULPTURE

The Art of Andy Goldsworthy
Andy Goldsworthy: Touching Nature
Andy Goldsworthy in Close-Up
Andy Goldsworthy: Pocket Guide
Andy Goldsworthy In America

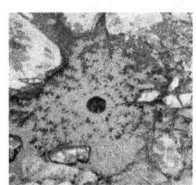

Land Art: A Complete Guide
The Art of Richard Long
Richard Long: Pocket Guide
Land Art In the UK
Land Art in Close-Up

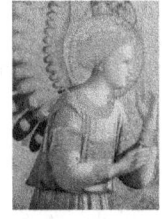

Land Art In the U.S.A.
Land Art: Pocket Guide
Installation Art in Close-Up
Minimal Art and Artists In the 1960s and After
Colourfield Painting
Land Art DVD, TV documentary
Andy Goldsworthy DVD, TV documentary
The Erotic Object: Sexuality in Sculpture From Prehistory to the Present Day

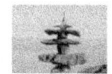

Sex in Art: Pornography and Pleasure in Painting and Sculpture
Postwar Art
Sacred Gardens: The Garden in Myth, Religion and Art
Glorification: Religious Abstraction in Renaissance and 20th Century Art
Early Netherlandish Painting
Leonardo da Vinci
Piero della Francesca
Giovanni Bellini
Fra Angelico: Art and Religion in the Renaissance
Mark Rothko: The Art of Transcendence

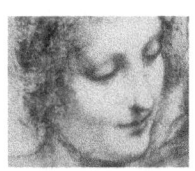
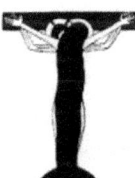

Frank Stella: American Abstract Artist
Jasper Johns
Brice Marden
Alison Wilding: The Embrace of Sculpture
Vincent van Gogh: Visionary Landscapes
Eric Gill: Nuptials of God
Constantin Brancusi: Sculpting the Essence of Things
Max Beckmann
Caravaggio
Gustave Moreau

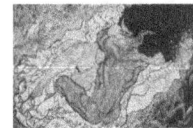

Egon Schiele: Sex and Death In Purple Stockings
Delizioso Fotografico Fervore: Works In Process 1
Sacro Cuore: Works In Process 2
The Light Eternal: J.M.W. Turner
The Madonna Glorified: Karen Arthurs

LITERATURE

J.R.R. Tolkien: The Books, The Films, The Whole Cultural Phenomenon
J.R.R. Tolkien: Pocket Guide
Tolkien's Heroic Quest
The *Earthsea* Books of Ursula Le Guin
Beauties, Beasts and Enchantment: Classic French Fairy Tales
German Popular Stories by the Brothers Grimm
Philip Pullman and *His Dark Materials*
Sexing Hardy: Thomas Hardy and Feminism
Thomas Hardy's *Tess of the d'Urbervilles*
Thomas Hardy's *Jude the Obscure*
Thomas Hardy: The Tragic Novels
Love and Tragedy: Thomas Hardy
The Poetry of Landscape in Hardy

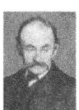
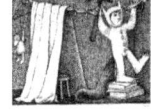

Wessex Revisited: Thomas Hardy and John Cowper Powys
Wolfgang Iser: Essays and Interviews
Petrarch, Dante and the Troubadours
Maurice Sendak and the Art of Children's Book Illustration
Andrea Dworkin

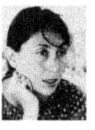
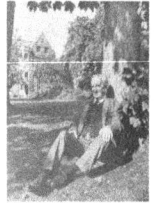

Cixous, Irigaray, Kristeva: The *Jouissance* of French Feminism
Julia Kristeva: Art, Love, Melancholy, Philosophy, Semiotics and Psychoanalysis
Hélène Cixous I Love You: The *Jouissance* of Writing
Luce Irigaray: Lips, Kissing, and the Politics of Sexual Difference
Peter Redgrove: Here Comes the Flood
Peter Redgrove: Sex-Magic-Poetry-Cornwall
Lawrence Durrell: Between Love and Death, East and West
Love, Culture & Poetry: Lawrence Durrell
Cavafy: Anatomy of a Soul

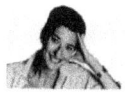

German Romantic Poetry: Goethe, Novalis, Heine, Hölderlin
Feminism and Shakespeare
Shakespeare: Love, Poetry & Magic
The Passion of D.H. Lawrence
D.H. Lawrence: Symbolic Landscapes
D.H. Lawrence: Infinite Sensual Violence
Rimbaud: Arthur Rimbaud and the Magic of Poetry

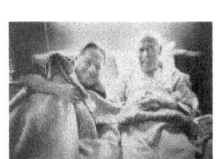
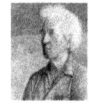

The Ecstasies of John Cowper Powys
Sensualism and Mythology: The Wessex Novels of John Cowper Powys
Amorous Life: John Cowper Powys and the Manifestation of Affectivity (H.W. Fawkner)
Postmodern Powys: New Essays on John Cowper Powys (Joe Boulter)
Rethinking Powys: Critical Essays on John Cowper Powys
Paul Bowles & Bernardo Bertolucci
Rainer Maria Rilke
Joseph Conrad: *Heart of Darkness*
In the Dim Void: Samuel Beckett
Samuel Beckett Goes into the Silence
André Gide: Fiction and Fervour
Jackie Collins and the Blockbuster Novel

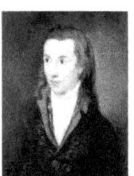

Blinded By Her Light: The Love-Poetry of Robert Graves
The Passion of Colours: Travels In Mediterranean Lands
Poetic Forms

POETRY

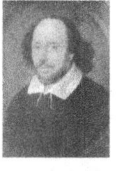
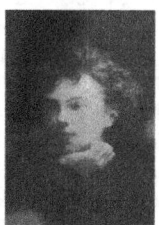

Ursula Le Guin: Walking In Cornwall
Peter Redgrove: Here Comes The Flood
Peter Redgrove: Sex-Magic-Poetry-Cornwall
Dante: Selections From the Vita Nuova
Petrarch, Dante and the Troubadours
William Shakespeare: Sonnets
William Shakespeare: Complete Poems
Blinded By Her Light: The Love-Poetry of Robert Graves
Emily Dickinson: Selected Poems
Emily Brontë: Poems

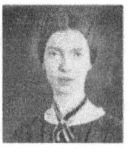
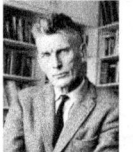
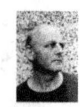

Thomas Hardy: Selected Poems
Percy Bysshe Shelley: Poems
John Keats: Selected Poems
Joh n Keats: Poems of 1820
D.H. Lawrence: Selected Poems
Edmund Spenser: Poems

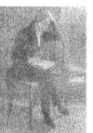
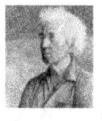
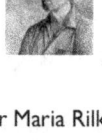

Edmund Spenser: Amoretti
John Donne: Poems
Henry Vaughan: Poems
Sir Thomas Wyatt: Poems
Robert Herrick: Selected Poems
Rilke: Space, Essence and Angels in the Poetry of Rainer Maria Rilke
Rainer Maria Rilke: Selected Poems
Friedrich Hölderlin: Selected Poems

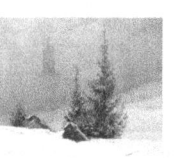
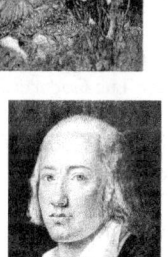

Arseny Tarkovsky: Selected Poems
Arthur Rimbaud: Selected Poems
Arthur Rimbaud: A Season in Hell
Arthur Rimbaud and the Magic of Poetry
Novalis: Hymns To the Night
German Romantic Poetry
Paul Verlaine: Selected Poems
Elizaethan Sonnet Cycles

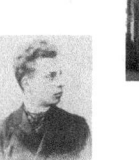
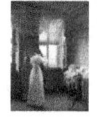

D.J. Enright: By-Blows
Jeremy Reed: Brigitte's Blue Heart
Jeremy Reed: Claudia Schiffer's Red Shoes
Gorgeous Little Orpheus
Radiance: New Poems
Crescent Moon Book of Nature Poetry
Crescent Moon Book of Love Poetry
Crescent Moon Book of Mystical Poetry

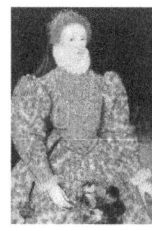

Crescent Moon Book of Elizabethan Love Poetry
Crescent Moon Book of Metaphysical Poetry
Crescent Moon Book of Romantic Poetry
Pagan America: New American Poetry

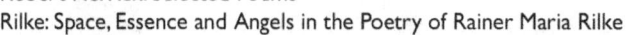

MEDIA, CINEMA, FEMINISM and CULTURAL STUDIES

J.R.R. Tolkien: The Books, The Films, The Whole Cultural Phenomenon
J.R.R. Tolkien: Pocket Guide
The *Lord of the Rings* Movies: Pocket Guide
The Cinema of Hayao Miyazaki
Hayao Miyazaki: *Princess Mononoke*: Pocket Movie Guide
Hayao Miyazaki: *Spirited Away*: Pocket Movie Guide
Tim Burton
Ken Russell
Ken Russell: *Tommy*: Pocket Movie Guide
The Ghost Dance: The Origins of Religion
The Peyote Cult
Cixous, Irigaray, Kristeva: The *Jouissance* of French Feminism
Julia Kristeva: Art, Love, Melancholy, Philosophy, Semiotics and Psychoanalysis
Luce Irigaray: Lips, Kissing, and the Politics of Sexual Difference
Hélene Cixous I Love You: The *Jouissance* of Writing
Andrea Dworkin
'Cosmo Woman': The World of Women's Magazines
Women in Pop Music
Discovering the Goddess (Geoffrey Ashe)
The Poetry of Cinema
The Sacred Cinema of Andrei Tarkovsky
Andrei Tarkovsky: Pocket Guide
Andrei Tarkovsky: *Mirror*: Pocket Movie Guide
Andrei Tarkovsky: *The Sacrifice*: Pocket Movie Guide
Walerian Borowczyk: Cinema of Erotic Dreams
Jean-Luc Godard: The Passion of Cinema
Jean-Luc Godard: *Hail Mary*: Pocket Movie Guide
Jean-Luc Godard: *Contempt*: Pocket Movie Guide
Jean-Luc Godard: *Pierrot le Fou*: Pocket Movie Guide
John Hughes and Eighties Cinema
Ferris Bueller's Day Off: Pocket Movie Guide
Jean-Luc Godard: Pocket Guide
The Cinema of Richard Linklater
Liv Tyler: Star In Ascendance
Blade Runner and the Films of Philip K. Dick
Paul Bowles and Bernardo Bertolucci
Media Hell: Radio, TV and the Press
An Open Letter to the BBC
Detonation Britain: Nuclear War in the UK
Feminism and Shakespeare
Wild Zones: Pornography, Art and Feminism
Sex in Art: Pornography and Pleasure in Painting and Sculpture
Sexing Hardy: Thomas Hardy and Feminism

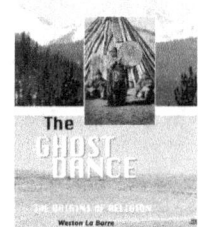
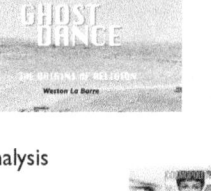
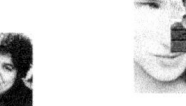

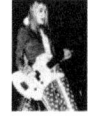
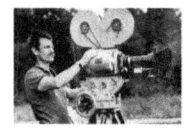
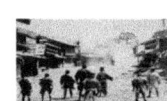
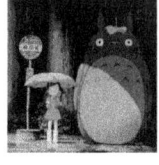
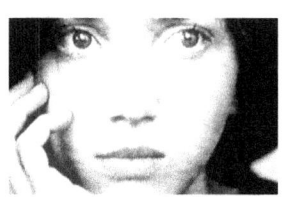

In my view *The Light Eternal* is among the very best of all the material I read on Turner. (Douglas Graham, director of the Turner Museum, Denver, Colorado)

The Light Eternal is a model monograph, an exemplary job. The subject matter of the book is beautifully organised and dead on beam. (Lawrence Durrell)

It is amazing for me to see my work treated with such passion and respect. (Andrea Dworkin)

CRESCENT MOON PUBLISHING
P.O. Box 1312, Maidstone, Kent, ME14 5XU, Great Britain. www.crmoon.com